The Good Grammar Book

A grammar practice book for
elementary to lower-intermediate
students of English

OXFORD
UNIVERSITY PRESS

Great Clarendon Street, Oxford OX2 6DP

Oxford University Press is a department of the University of Oxford.
It furthers the University's objective of excellence in research, scholarship,
and education by publishing worldwide in

Oxford New York

Athens Auckland Bangkok Bogotá Buenos Aires Cape Town
Chennai Dar es Salaam Delhi Florence Hong Kong Istanbul Karachi
Kolkata Kuala Lumpur Madrid Melbourne Mexico City Mumbai Nairobi
Paris São Paulo Shanghai Singapore Taipei Tokyo Toronto Warsaw

with associated companies in Berlin Ibadan

First published 2001

ISBN 0 19 431519 3 (with answers)
ISBN 0 19 431520 7 (without answers)

Typeset in ITC Stone by Pentacor plc, High Wycombe, Bucks.

Printed in China

Michael Swan & Catherine Walter

The Good Grammar Book

A grammar practice book for elementary to lower-intermediate students of English

WITH ANSWERS

OXFORD
UNIVERSITY PRESS

publisher's acknowledgements

The authors and the publisher wish to thank the following for their kind permission to reproduce cartoons:

Steven Appleby: p. 273 (from *The Truth About Love* by Steven Appleby, published by Bloomsbury); Cyrus Deboo: p. 71; The New Yorker Magazine Inc: pp. 4 (© 2001 Charles Barsotti from cartoonbank.com), 20 (© 2001 Charles Barsotti from cartoonbank.com), 53 (© 2001 Charles Barsotti from cartoonbank.com), 105 (© The New Yorker Collection 1990 Mick Stevens from cartoonbank.com. All rights reserved.), 117 (© The New Yorker Collection 2000 Christopher Weyant from cartoonbank.com. All rights reserved.), 187 (© The New Yorker Collection 1991 Peter Steiner from cartoonbank.com. All rights reserved.); Private Eye Magazine: p. 265 (Michael Heath); Punch Ltd: pp. 31 (H Martin), 47 (Fougasse), 52 (Nick Baker), 161 (W L Ridgewell), 187 (Martin Honeysett), 265 (Pete Dredge); The Sayle Agency: p. 183 (© Ronald Searle 1956); Robert Thompson: p. 117

The authors and the publisher wish to thank the following for their kind permission to use photographs, extracts and adaptations from copyright material:

The Ancient Art and Architecture Collection: p. 41 (Viking ship, cave painting); A P Watt Ltd on behalf of The National Trust for Places of Historical Interest or Natural Beauty: p. 109 (extracts from *The Elephant's Child* by Rudyard Kipling); Auto Express/Dennis Publishing Limited: p. 123 (motorbike); BlackStar.co.uk: p. 167; The Bridgeman Art Library: pp. 45 (rock painting of a horse, c. 15,000 BC), 111 (*Sunflowers* by Vincent van Gogh/National Gallery, London, UK); Charles Worthington, London: p. 179; the headmistress and children of Chilton School: p. 151; The Comedy Store Ltd: p. 135; Corel: p. 155 (Tower of London); Corbis Digital Stock: p. 111 (Eiffel Tower); Corbis UK Ltd: p. 123 (pleasure boat/Brad Miller, yacht/Patrick Ward); The Dian Fossey Gorilla Fund International, 800 Cherokee Avenue, SE Atlanta, Georgia 30315-1440 USA, 1-800-851-0203 (website: www.gorillafund.org): p. 103; Elizabeth Whiting and Associates: p. 7 (house); Faber and Faber: p. 245 (*Rondeau Redoublé* from *Making Cocoa for Kingsley Amis* by Wendy Cope); Flight International: p. 123 (aeroplane/Wagner); Greg Evans International: pp. 3 (young ethnic man), 155 (Taj Mahal, Edinburgh Castle); Holt Studios International Limited: p. 123 (tractor/Nigel Cattlin); Impact Photos: pp. 41 (Great Wall of China/Christophe Bluntzer), 45 (pyramids/Bruce Stephens, fireworks/Mike McQueen); International Music Publications Ltd: p. 45 (*Happy Birthday to You*. Words and music by Patty Hill and Mildred Hill. © 1935 Summy-Birchard Music, a division of Summy-Birchard Inc, USA. Keith Prowse Music Publishing Co. Ltd, London WC2H 0QY All rights reserved.); International Music Publications Ltd and Hal Leonard Music Corp: p. 213 (*Anything You Can Do* from the stage production *Annie Get Your Gun*. Words and Music by Irving Berlin. © 1946 by Irving Berlin Music Corp, USA, Warner/Chappell Music Ltd, London. Copyright Renewed. International Copyright Secured. All Rights Reserved.); Kenzo Parfums: p. 179; Mary Evans Picture Library: p. 45 (Sir Alexander Fleming); Photodisc: p. 41 (Stonehenge); The Professional Cookware Company: p. 135; Raleigh Industries Limited: p. 123 (bicycle); Robert Harding Picture Library: pp. 111 (Great Wall of China/Gavin Hellier), 155 (Globe Theatre/Fraser Hall); The Ronald Grant Archive: p. 45 (Alfred Hitchcock poster); The Royal Geographical Society: p. 111 (Peary at the North Pole); Tesco plc: p. 197; Thorntons plc: p. 197

Illustrations by:
Stefan Chabluk: pp. 19, 74, 85, 120, 142, 150, 153, 179, 181, 205, 254, 260, 268
Richard Coggan: pp. 11, 33, 78, 82, 99, 143, 192
Mark Duffin: pp. 15, 27, 58, 137, 146, 149, 160, 166, 172, 184, 189, 191, 210-11, 216, 225, 240, 267
Maureen and Gordon Gray: pp. 22, 23, 67, 102, 148, 153, 169, 183, 195, 201, 209, 211, 214
Jon Jackson: pp. 98, 261
Pete Lawrence of Oxford Designers and Illustrators, after Pantelis Palios: pp. 3, 26, 31-2, 38, 48, 55-6, 63, 89-91, 94, 96, 110, 112, 130-1, 138, 141, 151, 162, 171, 175, 185, 198, 206, 233, 246-7, 250-1, 258-9
Ed McLachlan: p. 200

Commissioned photography by:
Mark Mason: pp. 111, 197

Every effort has been made to trace the owners of copyright material used in this book, but we should be pleased to hear from any copyright holder whom we have been unable to contact.

contents

introduction	vi
words for talking about grammar	vii
list of units	ix
units	1
appendices	275
pre-test answers	283
answer key	285
index	318

authors' acknowledgements

Teachers in several countries were kind enough to try out sections of the draft material with their classes and send us their comments. These were extremely helpful, enabling us to make a large number of corrections and improvements. We are very grateful to the following individuals and institutions, and to their students:

- Renata Baranowska-Bogdan of Warsaw
- J A Cabo of the IES Villaviciosa, Spain
- Irena Dominiková of the Bell School, Prague
- Margarita Herrero of the IES Pedro Cerrada, Utebo, Spain
- Sumi Katsuura of Tokyo University of Technology
- Eimear Kelly-Włodarczyk of English Unlimited, Gdańsk, Poland
- Ewa Kubisz of the XIV L.O., Warsaw
- Takuro Mannen of Wako Kokusai High School, Saitama, Japan
- Maria-Jesús Martí of the IES Abat Oliba, Ripoll, Spain
- Daisy Rodrigues do Vale of the UNIT - Centro Universitário do Triângulo, Uberlândia-MG, Brazil
- Ruth Swan and the staff of The English Academy of Macerata, Italy
- Eszter Timár-Honyek of the Bell School, Budapest
- Christiane Wimmer of Munich, Germany

The book has benefited enormously from the hard work and professionalism of our editorial and design team at Oxford University Press. Our thanks to them, and to the many other OUP staff in Oxford and elsewhere who have provided help and advice. We owe a particular debt to our editor, Karl Clews, without whose meticulousness, patience, good humour and stamina this would not be nearly such a Good Grammar Book.

Finally, our thanks to Inge Bullock for keeping us organised and fed, and to our children for once again putting up with us while the writing was going on.

introduction

Who is this book for?

The Good Grammar Book is for all elementary and lower-intermediate level learners who want to improve their knowledge of English grammar.

What kind of English does the book teach?

The Good Grammar Book teaches the grammar of spoken and written British English. But it can also be used by students of American, Australian or other kinds of English – the grammatical differences are very small and unimportant.

How is the book organised?

There are 21 sections. A section covers one part of English grammar (for example: making questions and negatives; present tense verbs; problems with nouns). Each section contains a pre-test, several short units with explanations and exercises, and a 'test yourself' revision page.

Using the book: particular problems

If you have a particular problem with grammar (for example present tenses, the difference between *should* and *must*, or the position of adverbs), look in the index (pages 318-324) to find the right unit(s). Read the explanations and do the exercises. Check your answers in the answer key (pages 285-317).

Using the book: systematic study

If you are working without a teacher, we suggest:

1 DON'T go right through the book from beginning to end – some parts will be unnecessary for you.

2 Decide which sections you most need to study. Section 1, '*be* and *have*', for example? Section 8, 'questions and negatives'? Section 18, 'relative pronouns'? Or other sections?

3 Choose a section, and do the pre-test at the beginning. Then look at the pre-test answers on pages 283-284. These will tell you what your problems are, and which pages to study.

4 Go to the pages that you need. Read the grammar explanations, do the exercises, and check your answers in the answer key (pages 285-317).

5 In some units there are 'grammar and vocabulary' exercises for students who would like to learn more words. Try these as well if you want to.

6 Go to the 'test yourself' page at the end of the section, and try some or all of the questions.

7 Check your answers. If you still have problems, look at the explanations again.

If you know everything in the book, will you speak perfect English?

No, sorry!

1 Not many people learn foreign languages perfectly. (And not many people need to.) But this book will help you to speak and write much more correctly.

2 Books like this give short practical explanations. They cannot tell you the whole truth about English grammar. If you follow the rules in *The Good Grammar Book*, you will not make many mistakes. But if you want more complete information about difficult points, you need to get a higher-level book (perhaps later, when your English is more advanced).

3 Grammar is not the only important thing in a language. You also need a wide vocabulary, and – very important – you need a lot of practice in listening and speaking, reading and writing. Remember: this is a grammar practice book, not a complete English course.

We hope that you will enjoy using our book.

With our best wishes for your progress in English

Michael Swan. Catherine Walter

words for talking about grammar

active and passive: *I see, she heard* are **active** verbs; *I am seen, she was heard* are **passive** verbs.

adjectives: for example *big, old, yellow, unhappy.*

adverbs: for example *quickly, completely, now, there.*

affirmative sentences or statements are not questions or negatives – for example *I arrived.*

articles: *a/an* ('indefinite article'); *the* ('definite article').

auxiliary verbs are used before other verbs to make questions, tenses etc – for example *do you think*; *I have finished, she is working.* See also modal auxiliary verbs.

comparatives: for example *older, better, more beautiful, more slowly.*

conjunctions: for example *and, but, because, while.*

consonants: see vowels.

contractions: short forms like *I'm, you're, he'll, don't.*

conversational: see formal.

countable nouns: the names of things we can count – for example *one chair, three cars*; uncountable (or 'mass') nouns: the names of things we can't count, like *oil, rice.*

determiners: words like *the, some, many, my,* which go before (adjective +) noun.

double letters: *pp, tt, ee* etc.

formal, informal, conversational: We use formal language with strangers, in business letters etc: for example 'Good afternoon, Mr Parker. May I help you?' We use informal or conversational language with family and friends: for example 'Hi, John. Want some help?'

future verbs: for example *I **will go**, Ann **is going to write** to us.*

imperatives: forms like **Go home, Come** and **sit** down, **Don't worry**, which we use when we tell or ask people (not) to do things.

indirect speech: the grammar that we use to say what people say or think: for example *John said **that he was tired**.*

infinitives: *(to) go, (to) sleep* etc.

informal: see formal.

-ing forms: *going, sleeping* etc.

irregular: see regular.

leave out: If we say *Seen John?*, we are **leaving out** *Have you.*

modal verbs or modal auxiliary verbs: *must, can, could, may, might, shall, should, will* and *would.*

negative sentences are made with *not*: for example *I have **not** seen her.*

nouns: for example *chair, oil, idea, sentence.*

object: see subject.

opposite: *hot* is the **opposite** of *cold*; *up* is the **opposite** of *down.*

passive: see active.

past perfect tense: see perfect tenses.

past progressive tense: see past tenses.

past tenses: for example *went, saw, stopped* (**simple past**); *was going, were eating* (**past progressive**).

past participles: for example *gone, seen, stopped.*

perfect tenses: forms with *have/has/had* + past participle: for example *I have forgotten* (**present perfect**); *It has been raining* (**present perfect progressive**); *They had stopped* (**past perfect**).

plural: see singular.

possessives: for example *my, your; mine, yours; John's, my brothers'.*

prepositions: for example *at, in, on, between.*

present participles: for example *going, sleeping* etc (also called *-ing* forms).

present perfect tenses: see perfect tenses.

present tenses: for example *He goes* (**simple present**); *She is walking* (**present progressive**).

progressive (or 'continuous'): for example *I am thinking* (**present progressive**); *They were talking* (**past progressive**).

pronouns: for example *I, you, anybody, themselves*.

question tags: for example *isn't it?, doesn't she?*

reflexive pronouns: *myself, yourself* etc.

regular: plurals like *cats, buses*; past tenses like *started, stopped*; irregular: plurals like *teeth, men, children*; past tenses like *broke, went, saw.*

relative pronouns: *who, which* and *that* when they join sentences to nouns: for example *The man **who** bought my car.*

sentence: A sentence begins with a capital letter (A, B etc) and ends with a full stop (.), like this one.

simple past tense: see past tenses.

simple present tense: see present tenses.

singular: for example *chair, cat, man*; plural: for example *chairs, cats, men.*

spelling: writing words correctly: for example, we spell *necessary* with one *c* and double *s.*

subject and object: In *She took the money, everybody saw her*, the subjects are *she* and *everybody*; the objects are *the money* and *her.*

superlatives: for example *oldest, best, most beautiful, most easily.*

tense: *She goes, she is going, she went, she was going, she has gone* are different **tenses**.

third person: words for other people, not *I* or *you*: for example *she, them, himself, John, has, goes.*

uncountable nouns: see countable nouns.

verbs: for example *sit, give, hold, think, write.*

vowels: *a, e, i, o, u* and their usual sounds; consonants: *b, c, d, f, g* etc and their usual sounds.

other useful words

Here are some other words that are used in this book. Find them in your dictionary and write the translations here.

action ....

choose ....

common ....

complete (*verb*) ....

correct ....

description ....

difference ....

event ....

exclamation ....

explain ....

expression ....

form (*noun*) ....

go on, happen ....

in general ....

introduction ....

join ....

mean (*verb*) ....

meaning ....

necessary ....

news ....

normal ....

normally ....

particular ....

plan ....

polite ....

politely ....

possibility ....

possible ....

practise ....

predict ....

prefer ....

probable ....

pronounce ....

pronunciation ....

repeat ....

report ....

revision ....

rule ....

section ....

similar ....

situation ....

stressed (pronunciation) ....

structure ....

unnecessary ....

unusual ....

use (*noun*) ....

use (*verb*) ....

(word) order ....

list of units

SECTION 1   *be* and *have*   **pages 1–12**

grammar summary and pre-test   1
be   *I am happy today. Are we late?*   2–3
be: past   *Where were you?*
   I was in Glasgow.   4
be: future   *The bus will be full.*   5
there is   *There's a dog in the garden.*   6–7
have with *do*   *do you have? I don't have*   8–9
have without *do*: *have got*
   Have you got a cat?   10
have: actions   *He's having a shower.*   11
test yourself   *be* and *have*   12

SECTION 2   **present tenses**   **pages 13–30**

grammar summary and pre-test   13
simple present affirmative
   I work; you work; she works   14
simple present: use   *I work in a bank.*   15
simple present questions
   Do you remember me?   16–17
simple present negatives   *I don't know.*
   She doesn't ski.   18–19
simple present: revision   20
present progressive: forms   *I'm reading;*
   I'm not working.   21
present progressive: use
   I'm (not) working today.   22–23
present progressive questions
   Is it raining?   24
present progressive: revision   25
the two present tenses: the difference   26–27
non-progressive verbs   *I don't understand.*   28–29
test yourself   present tenses   30

SECTION 3   **talking about the future**
   pages 31–40

grammar summary and pre-test   31
going to   *Look – it's going to rain.*   32–33
present progressive
   What are you doing this evening?   34
the *will*-future: forms   *I will work.*
   They won't come.   35
will: predicting
   I think it will rain tomorrow.   36
will: deciding, refusing, promising
   I'll answer it.   37

which future?   *will, going to* or
   present progressive?   38
simple present for future
   Our train leaves at 8.10.   39
test yourself   future   40

SECTION 4   **past tenses**   **pages 41–50**

grammar summary and pre-test   41
simple past: forms
   I worked. I did not work.   42–43
simple past questions   *Did she pay?*
   What did she say?   44
questions without *did*   *Who phoned?*
   What happened?   45
simple past: use   *I left school in 1990.*   46
simple past: revision   47
past progressive
   What were you doing at 8.00?   48
simple past or past progressive?
   I walked / I was walking   49
test yourself   past tenses   50

SECTION 5   **perfect tenses**   **pages 51–70**

grammar summary and pre-test   51
present perfect: forms   *I have paid.*
   Has she forgotten?   52–53
finished actions: present perfect or
   simple past?   54–55
present perfect: news
   We've found oil in the garden!   56
present perfect and simple past:
   news and details   57
up to now (1)   *How much? How often?*   58–59
already, yet and *just*   60
up to now (2)
   I've been here since Tuesday.   61
up to now (3): present perfect progressive   62–63
present perfect or
   present perfect progressive?   64
simple past and present perfect: summary   65
present perfect and simple past:
   revision exercises   66–67
past perfect
   It had already begun when we arrived.   68–69
test yourself   perfect tenses   70

SECTION 6   modal verbs   pages 71–92

grammar summary and pre-test   71

modal verbs: introduction
  can, must, should etc   72

must   *You must be home by eleven.*
  Must you go?   73

mustn't and *needn't*
  We mustn't wake the baby.   74

have to
  Do you have to teach small children?   75

had to, will have to   *I didn't have to pay.*   76

should   *What should I tell John?*   77

can and *could*   *He can play the piano.*
  She couldn't write.   78–79

may and *might*   *It may snow.*
  I might have a cold.   80–81

must/can't: certainty   *She must be in.*
  He can't be hungry.   82

can and *could*: requests
  Can you lend me a stamp?   83

can, could and *may*: permission
  Can I use the phone?   84–85

shall in questions   *What shall we do?*   86

had better   *You'd better take your umbrella.*   87

would   *Would you like a drink?*
  I'd like to be taller.   88

used to   *I used to play the piano.*   89

perfect modal verbs
  I should have studied harder.   90–91

test yourself   modal verbs   92

SECTION 7   passives   pages 93–104

grammar summary and pre-test   93

passives: introduction
  English is spoken in Australia.   94

simple present passive
  We are woken by the birds.   95

future passive
  Tomorrow your bicycle will be stolen.   96

simple past passive
  I was stopped by a policeman.   97

present progressive passive
  It's being cleaned.   98

present perfect passive
  The house has been sold.   99

verbs with two objects
  We were given a week.   100

by with passives   *Who was it made by?*   101

passive or active? which tense?   102–103

test yourself   passives   104

SECTION 8   questions and negatives
  pages 105–116

grammar summary and pre-test   105

yes/no questions   *Is the taxi here?*
  Do I need a visa?   106–7

question words   *When will you see her?*   108–9

question-word subjects
  Who phoned? What happened?   110–111

negatives   *Dogs can't fly.*
  I don't know why.   112–113

negatives with *nobody, never* etc
  Nobody loves me.   114

negative questions   *Aren't you well?*   115

test yourself   questions and negatives   116

SECTION 9   infinitives and *-ing* forms
  pages 117–134

grammar summary and pre-test   117

infinitives: using *to*   *I want to go.*
  Must you go?   118

infinitives of purpose
  She went to Paris to study music.   119

verb + infinitive
  I hope to be an airline pilot.   120–121

verb + object + infinitive
  He wants me to cook.   122–123

adjective + infinitive
  glad to find you at home   124–125

adjectives with *enough/too* + infinitive
  too tired to sing   126

some letters to write; nothing to eat   127

it with infinitive subjects
  It's nice to be here with you.   128

-ing forms as subjects
  Smoking is bad for you.   129

verb + *...ing*
  I can't help feeling unhappy.   130–131

preposition + *...ing*
  Thank you for coming.   132–133

test yourself   infinitives and *-ing* forms   134

SECTION 10   special structures with verbs
  pages 135–144

grammar summary and pre-test   135

verbs with prepositions   *Wait for me.*   136

prepositions in questions
  Who did you go with?   137

phrasal verbs   *Come in, take off*
  your coat and sit down.   138–139

verbs with two objects

    Take the boss these letters. 140

have something done

    I have my hair cut every week. 141

imperatives *Come in. Don't worry.* 142

let's (suggestions) *Let's go.* 143

test yourself special structures with verbs 144

SECTION 11   articles: *a/an* and *the*
pages 145–158

grammar summary and pre-test 145

a/an; pronunciation of *the* 146

countable and uncountable *a car, cars; petrol* 147

the and *a/an* *Let's see a film.*

    I didn't like the film. 148–149

a/an *She's a doctor.* 150

a/an: describing people

    She's got a nice smile. 151

talking in general without *the*

    People are funny. 152–153

names *Mary, Africa, the USA* 154–155

special cases *in bed*; *after lunch*;

    a hundred; … 156–157

test yourself articles: *a/an* and *the* 158

SECTION 12   determiners   pages 159–178

grammar summary and pre-test 159

this, that, these and *those* 160–161

some and *any* *I need some sugar.*

    Have you got any? 162–163

any, not any, no and *none* 164

somebody, anything, nowhere, … 165

some/any or no article

    Have some toast. I don't like toast. 166

any = 'one or another – it's not

    important which' 167

much and *many* *How much milk?*

    How many languages? 168

a lot of and *lots of* 169

a little and *a few* *a little English;*

    a few words 170

enough money; fast enough 171

too, too much/many and *not enough* 172

all (of) my friends; all of them;

    they are all … 173

all children; every child 174

every and *each; every one* 175

both, either and *neither* 176

determiners and *of* *most people; most of us* 177

test yourself determiners 178

SECTION 13   personal pronouns; possessives
pages 179–186

grammar summary and pre-test 179

personal pronouns: *I* and *me* etc 180–181

possessives: *my, your* etc

    This is my coat. 182–183

possessives: *mine, yours* etc

    This is mine. 184

reflexive pronouns: *myself, yourself* etc 185

test yourself personal pronouns;

    possessives 186

SECTION 14   nouns   pages 187–198

grammar summary and pre-test 187

singular and plural nouns *cat, cats;*

    box, boxes 188

singular/plural *team, family;*

    jeans, scissors 189

more about countable and

    uncountable nouns 190–191

one and *ones* *a big one;*

    the ones on the chair 192

's and *s'* possessive: forms

    son's, sons', men's 193

's and *s'* possessive: use

    Ian's car; the boss's car 194–195

noun + noun

    Milk chocolate is a kind of chocolate 196–197

test yourself nouns 198

SECTION 15   adjectives and adverbs
pages 199–216

grammar summary and pre-test 199

adjectives *a beautiful little girl who was*

    not stupid 200–201

adverbs *He ate quickly.*

    It was badly cooked. 202–203

adverbs with the verb

    often, certainly, etc 204–205

interested and *interesting* etc 206

fast, hard, hardly, well, friendly, … 207

comparative and superlative

    adjectives: forms 208

comparative or superlative? 209

comparatives: use

    brighter than the moon 210–211

superlatives

    the highest mountain in the world 212

comparison of adverbs

    More slowly, please. 213

(not) as ... as
    Your hands are as cold as ice.   214–215
test yourself   adjectives and adverbs   216

SECTION 16   **conjunctions pages 217–226**
grammar summary and pre-test   217
conjunctions: introduction
    and, but, because ...   218
position of conjunctions
    If you need help, ask me.   219
before and *after*
    I talked to John before I phoned Peter.   220
tenses with time conjunctions
    I'll see you before you go.   221
because and *so; although* and *but*   222–223
and   *I speak Russian, English and Swahili.*   224
double conjunctions   *both ... and;*
    (n)either ... (n)or   225
test yourself   conjunctions   226

SECTION 17   ***if* pages 227–236**
grammar summary and pre-test   227
if: position; *unless*   228
if: future
    I'll phone you if I hear from Alice.   229
not real / not probable
    If dogs could talk, ...   230–231
If I go ..., I will ...; If I went ..., I would ...   232
If I were you ...   233
could = 'would be able to'
    We could go cycling if ...   234
unreal past   *If a had happened,*
    b would have happened.   235
test yourself   *if*   236

SECTION 18   **relative pronouns**
    pages 237–244
grammar summary and pre-test   237
relative *who* and *which*
    the keys which I lost   238–239
relative *that*   *a bird that can't fly*   240
leaving out relative pronouns
    the car (that) you bought   241
prepositions   *the man that she works for*   242
relative *what*   *It was just what I wanted.*   243
test yourself   relative pronouns   244

SECTION 19   **indirect speech pages 245–252**
grammar summary and pre-test   245
tenses and pronouns
    Bill said he was really happy.   246–247
indirect questions
    She asked him what his name was.   248
present reporting verbs
    She says she comes from London.   249
here and *now* → *there* and *then*   250
infinitives   *She told me to get out.*   251
test yourself   indirect speech   252

SECTION 20   **prepositions pages 253–264**
grammar summary and pre-test   253
at, in and *on* (time)   254–255
from ... to, until and *by*   256
for, during and *while*   257
in and *on* (place)   258
at (place)   259
other prepositions of place   260–261
prepositions of movement   262–263
test yourself   prepositions   264

SECTION 21   **spoken grammar**
    pages 265–274
grammar summary and pre-test   265
question tags
    This music isn't very good, is it?   266–267
short answers   *Yes, I have. No, they didn't.*   268
reply questions   *Oh, yes? Did they really?*   269
revision of spoken question and
    answer structures   270
leaving out words   *Don't know if she has.*   271
So am I. Nor can Pat.   272–273
test yourself   spoken grammar   274

APPENDICES   **pages 275–282**
appendix 1   common irregular verbs   275
appendix 2   active and passive
    verb forms   276
appendix 3   capital letters (A, B, C etc)   276
appendix 4   contractions   277
appendix 5   expressions with
    prepositions   278–279
appendix 6   word problems   280–282

SECTION 1 *be* and *have*

● grammar summary

be (*am/are/is/was/were*)

- We can use **adjectives, nouns** or expressions of **place** after *be*.
  She is late.   *I'm hungry.*   *Are you a doctor?*   *Is everybody here?*
- We use a special structure with *be* – *there is* – to introduce things: to say that they exist.
  There's a strange woman at the door.   *There are some letters for you.*
- *Be* can be an **auxiliary verb** in progressive tenses (see page 21) and passives (see page 93).
  She is working.   *It was made in Hong Kong.*

have (*have/has/had*)

- We can use *have* or *have got* to talk about **possession**, relationships and some other ideas.
  Do you have a car?   *I don't have any brothers or sisters.*   *Ann has got a headache.*
- And we can use *have* to talk about some kinds of **actions**.
  I'm going to have a shower.   *What time do you have breakfast?*
- *Have* can also be an **auxiliary verb** in perfect tenses (see Section 5).
  I haven't seen her all day.   *We knew that he had taken the money.*

● pre-test: which units do you need?

Try this small test. It will help you to decide which units you need. The answers are on page 283.

❶ Circle the correct answer.

▶ I *am* / *are* tired.
1 Mary *is* / *has* very happy today.
2 *Are* / *Have* / *Do* you hot?
3 *There is* / *It is* a new secretary in the office.
4 *Had you* / *Did you have* a good journey?

❷ Correct (✓) or not (✗)?

▶ I don't had lunch today. ✗
1 I'm not … I amn't … he's not … he isn't …
2 I not had lunch today. …
3 Do you got a car? …
4 My friends was late. …
5 I don't have many friends. …

❸ Make questions.

▶ The train was late. ...Was the train late?..........................
1 All the family will be at home. ....
2 There will be a meeting tomorrow. ....
3 Phil has got a headache. ....
4 Ann had a lesson yesterday. ....

To be or not to be,
that is the question.
(*Shakespeare*: Hamlet)

There's a thin man **inside every fat man.**
(*George Orwell*)

Is there life
before death?
(*Seamus Heaney*)

You can have it all,
but you can't do it all.
(*Michelle Pfeiffer*)

If you've got everything, you've got nothing.
(*Leni MacShaw*)

be   *I am happy today.   Are we late?*

+	*I am you are he/she/it is we are they are*
?	*am I? are you? is he/she/it? are we? are they?*
–	*I am not you are not he/she/it is not we are not they are not*

I am a doctor.   Are you American?   We are not ready.

❶ Put in *am, are* or *is*.

▶ You ...*are*........... late.

1 We .... very well.

2 My sister .... a doctor.

3 John and Ann .... in America.

4 I .... happy today.

5 I think you .... tired.

6 Our house .... very small.

In **conversation** and informal writing, we use **contractions**:

I'm   you're   he's   she's   it's   John's   the train's   we're   they're

I'm a doctor.   You're late.   John's in London.   The shop's open.   We're ready.

❷ Write these sentences with contractions.

▶ Ann is ill. ..*Ann's ill.*.......................................

1 We are all tired. ....

2 They are here. ....

3 I am sorry. ....

4 My name is Peter. ....

5 You are early. ....

6 The shop is closed. ....

To make questions (**?**) with *be*, we put the verb before the subject.

STATEMENT **+** :	*I am late.*	*The taxi is here.*	*We are late.*	*Your keys are in the car.*
QUESTION **?** :	*Am I late?*	*Is the taxi here?*	*Are we late?*	*Are my keys in the car?*

❸ Make questions.

▶ Bill / Scottish   ..*Is Bill Scottish?*..............

1 Marie / from Paris   ....

2 We / very late   ....

3 John / in bed   ....

4 The boss / in Japan   ....

5 His car / fast   ....

Do you know all these **question words**?

who   what   when   where   why   how

Contractions with *is*: **who's   what's   when's   where's   how's   why's**

Who's that?   **What's** this?   **When** is the party?   **Where's** the station?   **Why** are we here?

How are you?

❹ Put in question words with *are* or *'s*.

▶ '*Who's*........................ that?' 'It's my brother.'

▶ '*Where are*................ Joe and Ann?' 'In London.'

1 '................................. your name?' 'Maria.'

2 '................................. my glasses?' 'Here.'

3 '................................. your English teacher?' 'Mrs Allen.'

4 '................................. you late?' 'My watch is broken.'

5 '................................. the exam?' 'On Tuesday.'

6 '................................. your mother?' 'Very well, thanks.'

To make negative (−) sentences with *be*, we put *not* after *am/are/is* or *'m*, *'re*, *'s*.

I am not Scottish.   *We are not ready.*   *I'm not tired.*   *She's not here.*   *They're not my friends.*

We can also make contractions with *n't*: *you aren't*, *she isn't*, etc (BUT NOT ~~I amn't~~).

5 **Write negative (−) ends for the sentences.**

▶ It's winter, but (− cold) *it isn't cold.* ....

▶ I'm Greek, but (− from Athens) *I'm not from Athens.* ....

1 She's tired, but (− ill) ....

2 They are in England, but (− in London) ....

3 You're tall, but (− too tall) ....

4 We are late, but (− very late) ....

5 It's summer, but (− hot) ....

6 I'm a student, but (− at university) ....

We often use *be* with: *hungry, thirsty, cold, hot, right, wrong, afraid, interested, what colour?, what size?*
And we use *be* with **ages**.

Have you got anything to eat? I'm hungry.   *I'm cold.*   *It's very hot here in summer.*
'It's late.' 'You're right. Let's go.'   *Are you afraid of spiders?*   *What colour is her hair?*
What size are your shoes?   *'How old are you?' 'I'm 17.'*   *I'm interested in politics.*

6 **Complete the sentences under the pictures.**

▶ She is *hungry*.   1 He ....   2 She ....   3 ....   4 It ....

7 **Put in words from the box.**

afraid ✓   colour   interested   right   size

▶ He is a big man, but he is *afraid* of her.

1 You think I'm wrong, but I know I'm ....

2 What .... – small, medium or large?

3 What .... is your car?

4 Sorry, I'm not .... in her problems.

8 **Read the text, and then write about yourself.**

His name's Noureddin. He's from Rabat, in Morocco. He's a student. He's 21. He isn't married. He's interested in music and politics. He isn't interested in sport.

My name's ....
....
....
....
....
....

be: past *Where were you?   I was in Glasgow.*

+	I was you were he/she/it was we were they were
?	was I? were you? was he/she/it? were we? were they?
-	I was not you were not he/she/it was not we were not they were not
	Contractions: *wasn't, weren't*

Where were *you yesterday?   My mother* was *a singer.   I* wasn't *well last week.*

1 Put in *was* or *were*.

▶ In summer 1990 I ...was.......... in Brazil.

1 'We .... very happy to see you yesterday.' 'And I .... happy to see you.'
2 Lunch .... OK, but the vegetables .... not very good.
3 I can't find my keys. They .... here this morning.
4 It .... cold and dark, and we .... tired.
5 My grandmother .... a doctor, and her three children .... all doctors too.
6 '................ you in London yesterday?' 'No, I .... in Glasgow.'
7 'When .... your exam?' 'It .... yesterday.'

2 Put the words in the correct order to make questions.

▶ Ann at home yesterday was   *Was Ann at home yesterday?*...
1 good party was the   ....
2 people were the interesting   ....
3 teacher father your was a   ....
4 everybody was late   ....
5 John's brother school was with at you   ....

3 Put in *wasn't* or *weren't* and words from the box. Make sure you understand *actually*. Use a dictionary if necessary.

a teacher	in England	interesting ✓
late	well	with Anna

▶ The lesson ...wasn't interesting..............
   Actually, it was very boring.
1 You .... Actually,
   you arrived 10 minutes early.
2 My father ....
   Actually, he worked as a bus driver.
3 I .... yesterday.
   Actually, I was with Susan.
4 The children ....
   yesterday. The doctor came to see them.
5 We .... last week.
   We went to Scotland for a few days.

'And were you good while I was out?'

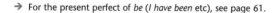

➔ For the present perfect of *be* (*I have been* etc), see page 61.

be: future   *The bus will be full.*

+	I/you/he/she/it/we/they **will be**
?	**will** I/you/she etc **be**?
-	I/you/he etc **will** not **be**

Contractions: *I'll, you'll* etc; *won't* (= will not)

It **will be** cold this evening.   **I'll be** at home all day tomorrow.
Where **will** we **be** ten years from now?   The exam **won't be** difficult.

1 **Look at the table and complete the text.**

Tomorrow *it will be* .... very hot in Cairo.
It .... hot in ....
.... warm in ....
.... cold in ....
.... very cold in ....

TOMORROW'S TEMPERATURES	
Cairo	35°
Rio	30°
Paris	23°
London	3°
Moscow	-18°

2 **Change these sentences to affirmative (+) or negative (-).**

▶ The bus will not be full.   *The bus will be full.* ....
▶ She'll be late.   *She won't be late.* ....
1 I'll be sorry.   ....
2 It will not be hot.   ....
3 We won't be at home.   ....
4 The shops will be closed.   ....
5 He'll be in Scotland.   ....
6 Ann will be at school.   ....

To make future questions with *be*, we put *will* before the **subject**.

STATEMENT **+** :   *We will be late.*   *Her brother will be here at 10.00.*   *The bus will be full.*

QUESTION **?** :   *Will we be late?*   *When will her brother be here?*   *Will the bus be full?*

3 **Make questions with *will ... be ...?***

▶ you / at home / this evening   *Will you be at home this evening?* ....
▶ when / lunch / ready   *When will lunch be ready?* ....
1 when / your father / in England   ....
2 Ann / at the party / with John   ....
3 everybody / here / at 8.00   ....
4 the train / late / again   ....
5 when / Joe and Mary / in the office   ....
6 the weather / good / tomorrow   ....
7 where / you / on Tuesday   ....

4 **Complete the sentences.**

1 (*your age*) This year I am ....   In 2000 I ....
Last year I ....   Next year I ....   In 20... I ....
2 (*a friend's age*) This year he/she ....   In 2000 ....
Last year ....   Next year ....   In 20... ....

there is   *There's a dog in the garden.*

	PRESENT	PAST
+	there is there are	there was there were
?	is there? are there?	was there? were there?
–	there is not there are not	there was not there were not
	Contractions: *there's; isn't, aren't, wasn't, weren't*	

We use ***there is, there are*** etc to say that something or somebody **exists**.
We often use ***there is, there are*** etc before ***a/an, some*** and ***any***.

There's a dog in the garden. (NOT ~~A dog is in the garden.~~)   **There are some** letters for you.
Is there any milk in the fridge? (NOT ~~Is any milk ...?~~)   **There isn't** much coffee.
Were there any phone calls? (NOT ~~Were any phone calls?~~)   **There was a** good film last night.

1 **Make some sentences with words from the three boxes, using *there is* etc.**

There is/are a lot of	water air grass dogs	in Africa in the USA
There isn't much	elephants trees cars	in Antarctica in London
There aren't many	people computers ...	on the moon in 1600 ...
There isn't/aren't any	(*you think of some more*	(*you think of some more places*
There wasn't/weren't any	*things*)	*or times*)

→ ... → ...

▶ *There are a lot of animals in Africa.* ....
▶ *There weren't any cars in 1600.* ....
1 ....
2 ....
3 ....
4 ....
5 ....
6 ....

To make questions with *there is* etc, we put *is* etc before *there*.

STATEMENT **+**:   *There is a letter for you.*   *There were some problems.*   *William says there are six eggs.*

QUESTION **?**:   *Is there a letter for me?*   *Were there any problems?*   *How many eggs are there?*

2 **Make present or past questions with *there is* etc.**

▶ any fruit juice in the fridge (*present*) ...*Is there any fruit juice in the fridge?*...................
▶ any letters for me (*past*) ...*Were there any letters for me?*...........
▶ how many people / in your family (*present*) ...*How many people are there in your family?*...
1 a doctor here (*present*) ....
2 any trains to London this evening (*present*) ....
3 much money in your bank account (*present*) ....
4 how many students / in your class (*present*) ....
5 a special price for students (*past*) ....
6 any mistakes in my letter (*past*) ....
7 many children at the swimming pool (*past*) ....
8 how many people / at the party (*past*) ....

FUTURE: ➕ there **will** be ❓ **will** there be? ➖ there **will** not be
Contractions: *there'll; won't* (= will not)

---

3 **Here is some information about an English town. Write sentences using *there is* etc.**

	1960	NOW	2050
people	300,000	500,000	800,000
cinemas	11	2	0
theatres	1	1	1
nightclubs	0	12	20
restaurants	50	76	120
hotels	35	130	180
supermarkets	0	23	200
universities	1	2	3

▶ *There were 300,000 people in 1960.*
▶ *There are two cinemas now.*
▶ *There will be 200 supermarkets in 2050.*
1 ....
2 ....
3 ....
4 ....
5 ....
6 ....
7 ....

4 **Write questions about life in the year 2100, with *Will there be ...?***

▶ (*cars*) *Will there be cars?* ....
1 (*trains*) ....
2 (*computers*) ....
3 (*good food*) ....

4 (*different countries*) ....
5 (*governments*) ....
6 (your question) ....

We don't use *it is* like *there is*. We usually use *it is* for something that we have already talked about, or that people already know about.

There's a car outside. It's a Ford. (NOT ~~It's a car outside.~~)

---

5 (Circle) **the correct form.**

1 *It's / There's* a new bookshop in East Street.
2 'Whose is that dog?' '*It's / There's* mine.'
3 Is *it / there* a bus stop in this street?

4 *There isn't / It isn't* a supermarket here.
5 'What's that?' '*It's / There's* my new calculator.'
6 'How's your new job?' '*It's / There's* interesting.'

6 GRAMMAR AND VOCABULARY: houses
Read the advertisement with a dictionary and complete the sentences.

▶ *There are two* .... floors.
▶ *There is a modern* .... kitchen.
1 .... living room.
2 .... study.
3 .... cloakroom.

4 .... two ....
5 .... four ....
6 .... gas ....
7 .... garage.
8 .... large ....

Price: £ 250000   ref.no.671749
Large new house situated in the village of Wickfield.

Modern kitchen, large living room, small study, downstairs cloakroom and shower room, 4 bedrooms, 2 bathrooms, gas central heating, double garage, large garden.

→ For the present perfect (*there has/have been*), see Section 5.

have with *do*   *do you have?*   *I don't have*

	PRESENT	PAST
+	I/you/we/they **have** he/she/it *has*	I/you/he/she/it/we/they **had**
?	**do** I/you/we/they **have**? *does* he/she/it **have**?	**did** I/you/he etc **have**?
−	I/you/we/they **do** not **have** he/she/it *does* not **have**	I/you/he etc **did** not **have**
	Contractions: *don't, doesn't, didn't*	

We can use *have* to talk about **possession, family** (and other) **relationships** and **illnesses**.

*I **have** a new car.   Ann **has** two sisters.   Pete **has** a nice girlfriend.   Joe **had** a cold last week.*

We also say that people **have** hair, eyes etc; and that things **have** parts.

*You **have** beautiful eyes.   Our old car only **had** two doors, but the new one **has** four.*

1 Circle the correct form.

▶ *John /* I have two brothers.
▶ *Mary has /* had a cold yesterday.
1 *My father / My parents* has two cars.
2 *We all / Sally* have blue eyes.
3 I *have / had* a headache yesterday evening.
4 I see that your brother *had / has* a new girlfriend.
5 *You / Paul* has very long hair.
6 These houses *have / has* big rooms.
7 I can't read this book – it *has / had* 800 pages.
8 Ann had a good job *last year / now*.

We can make **questions** (**?**) and **negatives** (**−**) with *do/does/did* + **infinitive** (without *to*).
(For questions and negatives without *do*, see page 10.)

STATEMENT **+**	QUESTION **?**	NEGATIVE **−**
I **have** *the keys.*	**Do** I **have** *the keys?*	I **do** not **have** *the keys.*
Joe *has a car.*	**Does** Joe **have** *a car?* (NOT ~~Does Joe has~~ ...)	Joe *doesn't* **have** *a car.*
Ann **had** *a cold.*	**Did** Ann **have** *a cold?* (NOT ~~Did Ann had~~ ...)	Ann **didn't have** *a cold.*

2 Make questions (**?**) or negatives (**−**) with *have*.

▶ you / a cat **?** *Do you have a cat?*
▶ Eric / many friends **−** *Eric doesn't have many friends.*
1 we / garden **−** We don't ....
2 they / any children **?** ....
3 Peter / a cold **?** ....
4 my aunt / a dog **−** ....
5 Mary / any brothers or sisters **?** ....
6 I / enough money **−** ....
7 Sally / a boyfriend **?** ....
8 Why / you / two cars **?** ....

3 Make sentences about Ann when she was six.

▶ a bicycle **?** *Did she have a bicycle?*   ▶ a dog **−** *She didn't have a dog.*
1 a computer **−** ....
2 very fair hair **+** ....
3 lots of friends **?** ....
4 many nice clothes **−** ....
5 her own room **?** ....

4 Write sentences about yourself with *I had* and *I didn't have*.

1 When I was a child, I had ....
2 When I was a child, I didn't have ....
3 ....
4 ....

	FUTURE
➕	*I/you/he/she/it/we/they* **will have**
❓	**will** *I/you/he* etc **have?**
➖	*I/you/he* etc **will** not **have**
	Contractions: *I'll, you'll* etc; *won't* (= *will not*)

We use **will (not) have** to talk about the future.

One day, everybody **will have** *enough food.*   *Mary says that she* **won't have** *children.*

To make **future questions** with **have**, we put *will* before the **subject**

STATEMENT ➕:   *John will have a car soon.*   *The baby will have blue eyes.*

QUESTION ❓:   *Will John have a car soon?*   *Will the baby have blue eyes?*

5 Read the text and complete the sentences about John's future.

This year, John doesn't have money, a job, a house, a girlfriend, a suit or a car.
He has a small room, a bicycle, old clothes, a guitar and a cat. But next year:

▶ more money ➕ .He will have more money...
▶ a small room ➖ .He won't have a small room..
▶ a cat ❓ .Will he have a cat?...
1 a job ➕ ....
2 a bicycle ➖ ....
3 a car ➕ ....
4 a house ❓ ....
5 a girlfriend ❓ ....
6 old clothes ➖ ....
7 a suit ➕ ....
8 a guitar ❓ ....

6 GRAMMAR AND VOCABULARY: relations
Put in words from the box. Use a dictionary if necessary.

uncle   aunt   cousin   niece   nephew

1 Bill's sister has three daughters and a son, and Bill's brother has three sons. So Bill has three
   nieces............ and four ....
2 Bill's father has two brothers, both married; and his mother has two sisters, one married. So Bill
   has three .... and four ....
3 Bill's uncles and aunts have eight children. So Bill has ....
4 And you? I have ....

➔ For auxiliary *have*, see page 52.
➔ For *have a bath* etc, see page 11.
➔ For *have got*, see page 10.

➔ For the present perfect (*I have had*), see page 52.
➔ For more about future tenses, see Section 3.

have without *do*: *have got*   *Have you got a cat?*

+	I/you/we/they **have got**	he/she/it *has* **got**
?	**have** I/you etc **got?**	*has* he/she/it **got?**
-	I/you etc **have** not **got**	he/she/it *has* not **got**
	Contractions: *I've, he's* etc; *haven't, hasn't*	

We often use *got* with *have*, especially in the **present**. This does not change the meaning: we use
have/has got like *have/has* to talk about **possession** etc.
I have got is the same as **I have.**
Have you got? is the same as **Do you have?** (We don't use *do/does* with *have got*.)
She hasn't got is the same as **She doesn't have.**

I've got a cat. (more natural than *I have a cat*)   **Has** she **got** a dog? (NOT ~~Does she have got~~ ...)
I haven't got a car.   **She's got** a sister.   **You've got** beautiful eyes.   **Have** you **got** a cold?

1 Write about John's possessions etc.

▶ a bicycle: ✓ ...John's got a bicycle..
▶ suits: 2 ...He's got two suits......................................
▶ a horse: ✗ ...He hasn't got a horse...............................
▶ any children: ✗ ...He hasn't got any children....................................
1 brothers: 2 ....
2 a car: ✗ ....
3 dogs: 3 ....
4 a dictionary: ✓ ....
5 long hair: ✗ ....
6 any sisters: ✗ ....

2 Write four sentences about your possessions etc. Use words from Exercise 1.

1 I've got ....   3 ....
2 ....   4 ....

To make questions (?) with *have got*, we put *have/has* before the **subject**.

STATEMENT +:   *I have got a cold.*   *Eric's got a fast car.*   *Sue and Joe have got tickets.*

QUESTION ?:   *Have you got a cold?*   *Has Eric got a fast car?*   *Have Sue and Joe got tickets?*

3 Ann and Bill have got a lot of money. Ask questions with *have got*.

▶ they / big house   Have they got a big house?............................
1 they / big garden   ....
2 Ann / good job   ....
3 Bill / big car   ....
4 they / plane   ....
5 they / any horses   ....

Past forms (*I had got*, etc) are **unusual**. We don't use *got* in the future.

*She **had** a fast car.* (more natural than *She had got a fast car*.)   *I **will have**.* (NOT ~~I will have got~~)

→ For auxiliary *have*, see page 52.   → For *have a bath* etc, see page 11.

have: actions   *He's having a shower.*

We use ***have*** in a lot of common expressions to talk about **actions**. (We don't use *have got* like this.)
*I usually **have breakfast** at seven o'clock.* (NOT ~~I have got breakfast~~ ...)   *I'm going to **have a shower**.*
*Would you like to **have something to eat**?*   *If Bill comes this weekend we'll **have a party**.*
*Mary **had a baby** in June.*   *Are you **having a good time**?*   *'**Have a good flight**.' 'Thanks.'*

1 **Complete the sentences. Use *have*, *has* or *had* with words from the box.**

| a baby | coffee | dinner | a game | a party ✓ | a shower | toast |

▶ The people next door .....*had a party*..................
  last night and I couldn't sleep.
1 I .... with John yesterday evening.
2 My boss usually .... at 11 o'clock.
3 Ann's going to .... in August.
4 I usually .... before breakfast.
5 We always .... for breakfast.
6 Would you like to .... of tennis?

2

3

4

5

6

We make simple present and past questions and negatives with ***do/does*** and ***did***.
*We **don't have** parties very often.*   ***Does** Bill **have** eggs for breakfast?*
***Did** you **have** a good journey?*   *We **didn't have** a holiday.*

2 **Make questions (❓) and negatives (➖).**

▶ (*good time* ❓) 'We went to Paris yesterday.' .*Did you have a good time?*'...........
▶ (*breakfast* ➖) I got up late this morning, so I .*didn't have breakfast.*.........
1 (*lunch* ❓) What time .... on Sundays?
2 (*good trip* ➖) Ann was in America last week. ....
3 (*shower* ➖) The hotel bathroom was very dirty, so I ....
4 (*good flight* ❓) Welcome to England, Mr García. ....
5 (*good game* ❓) 'Bill and I played tennis this morning.' ....
6 (*coffee* ➖) .... before I go to bed.

test yourself   *be* and *have*

1 **Write these sentences with contractions.**

▶ John is tired. ..*John's tired*...............................

1 They were not ready. ....

2 We are all here. ....

3 I am not a student. ....

4 Where is your house? ....

5 Ann is not English. (*two answers*)

....

OR ....

6 She will not be late. ....

2 **Circle the correct answers.**

▶ (Is)/ *Are* your brother at home?

1 *Where / Who / How* is the station?

2 *I / We* was in London yesterday.

3 *Are / Have* you thirsty?

4 Alice *is / has* three brothers.

5 My sister *is / has* 25 today.

6 'I *am / have* cold.' 'Put on a sweater.'

7 I *want / won't* be here next week.

3 **Change the sentences to questions or negatives.**

▶ It's Tuesday. **-** ...*It isn't Tuesday.* OR *It's not Tuesday*...

1 There's a taxi outside. **?** ....

2 Chris has got a headache. **?** ....

3 Joe has a car. **-** ....

4 Ann had a meeting yesterday. **?** ....

5 I had coffee for breakfast. **-** ....

6 There will be an English lesson tomorrow. **?** ....

7 I'm hungry. **-** ....

8 Ann's got a new car. **-** ....

9 She had a nice time at the party. **?** ....

10 The house has got a big garden. **?** ....

4 **Correct (✓) or not (✗)?**

▶ I don't had breakfast today. ✗

1 Do you got a bicycle? ...

2 Had you a good journey? ...

3 Jane is having a shower. ...

4 Is there any eggs in the fridge? ...

5 It is a new supermarket in High Street. ...

6 There won't be a lesson tomorrow. ...

7 Do you have a bicycle? ...

5 **Put in a suitable affirmative (⊞) or negative (⊟) form of *be* or *have*.**

Helen 1 .... fourteen. She 2 .... at a very nice school; she 3 ....
interested in the lessons – there 4 .... only two teachers that she doesn't like – and she
5 .... got lots of friends. (Two years ago she 6 .... at a different school;
the lessons 7 .... very good, and she 8 .... many friends, so she
9 .... very unhappy.) The school 10 .... twenty km from Helen's house,
so she gets up early. She 11 .... a quick wash, and then she 12 .... breakfast –
cereal and fruit juice if she 13 .... hungry. There 14 .... a school bus, but if
it 15 .... very cold her mother takes her by car. In the evenings she 16 ....
school work; she 17 .... much difficulty with this, so she usually finishes quickly.
Then she 18 .... supper. At ten o'clock she 19 .... a bath and goes to bed.
On Saturdays and Sundays she gets up at 12.00, 20 .... a quick lunch and goes straight
to her computer games.

◉ More difficult question

SECTION 2 present tenses

grammar summary

> SIMPLE PRESENT: *I work, she works, he doesn't work,* etc
> PRESENT PROGRESSIVE: *I am working, she is working, he isn't working,* etc

English has **two 'present' tenses**.

- We use the **simple present** mostly to talk about **things that are always true**, and **things that happen repeatedly**.
  > Dogs *eat* meat. My grandmother *lives* in Brighton. I *work* every Saturday.

- We use the **present progressive** (or 'present continuous') to talk about things that are happening just **around the time when we speak**.
  > Look! The dog's *eating* your shoe. I'm *working hard* these days.

- We can also use the **present progressive** to talk about the **future** (see page 34).
  > I'm *seeing* Lucy tomorrow.

pre-test: which units do you need?

Try this small test. It will help you to decide which units you need. The answers are on page 283.

❶ Correct (✓) or not (✗)?

▶ Look! It rains! ✗

1 I'm geting tired. ...
2 I'm watching TV every evening. ...
3 'What are you doing?' 'I'm reading.' ...
4 Andy always drive too fast. ...
5 John flys to New York every Monday. ...
6 I do not want to see that film. ...
7 Where do she works? ...
8 Where does she works? ...
9 Where does your sister live? ...
10 Where do the manager and his wife live? ...
11 What you are doing? ...
12 I'm not knowing her address. ...

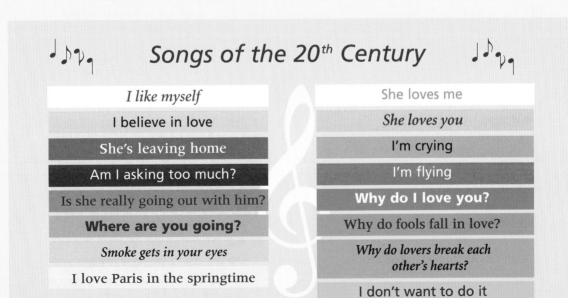

♩ ♪ ♩ ♩   *Songs of the 20th Century*   ♩ ♪ ♩ ♩

I like myself	She loves me
I believe in love	*She loves you*
She's leaving home	I'm crying
Am I asking too much?	I'm flying
Is she really going out with him?	**Why do I love you?**
Where are you going?	Why do fools fall in love?
Smoke gets in your eyes	*Why do lovers break each other's hearts?*
I love Paris in the springtime	I don't want to do it

simple present* affirmative   *I work; you work; she works*

I work	you work	he/she/it works	we work	they work
I live	you live	he/she/it lives	we live	they live
I stop	you stop	he/she/it stops	we stop	they stop

I **work** in a bank.
You **live** near my brother.
We **stop** the lessons at 5.00.

He **work**s in a restaurant.
She **live**s in Liverpool.
The train **stop**s at York.

HOW TO MAKE *HE/SHE/IT* FORMS

- **most verbs:**   + -*s*   work → works   know → knows   rain → rains
- **-s, -sh, -ch, -x:** + -*es*   pass → passes   wash → washes   teach → teaches   mix → mixes
- **exceptions:**   go → goes   do → does   have → has

1 **Write the *he/she/it* forms.**

| catch ✓ | come ✓ | cook | drink | fetch | fix | live | miss | push |
| read | run | smoke | stand | start | touch | watch | wish | write |

+ -*S*:   comes............   ....

....

+ -*ES*:   catches...........   ....

....

VERBS ENDING IN -*Y*

- **vowel + y**   -*ay*, -*ey*, -*oy*, -*uy*:   + -*s*   say → says
- **consonant + y**   -*dy*, -*ly*, -*py*, -*ry*, etc: -*y* → -*ies*   fly → flies

2 **Write the *he/she/it* forms.**

| buy ✓ | carry ✓ | copy | enjoy | fry | marry | play | stay | study | try |

+ -*S*:   buys........   ....

-*Y* → -*IES*: carries......   ....

3 **Put the words in the correct order.**

▶ eats dog too your much
   Your dog eats too much..........................

1 live I that house in
   ....

2 bank Ann in a works
   ....

3 badly violin plays the very Susan
   ....

4 Scotland those from children come
   ....

5 young very look you
   ....

4 **Circle the correct answers.**

▶ (We)/ My friend always wear old clothes.
▶ You /(John) always wears nice clothes.
1 We all / The boss thinks you're wonderful.
2 I / Catherine want a new job.
3 Bread / Books costs a lot.
4 Andy / Andy and Pete sings very well.
5 Mary / Mary and Ian like parties.
6 You / She drive too fast.
7 Our cat / Our cats never catches mice.
8 That child / Children makes a lot of noise.
9 That bus / All those buses go to the station.
10 My father / My mother and father teaches
   English.

---

* Also called 'present simple'

simple present: use *I work in a bank.*

We use the simple present to talk about:
- things that are always true.

  The sun rises in the east. My parents live near Dover.

- habits and things that happen repeatedly.

  Joe plays golf on Saturdays.

PAST	NOW	FUTURE

PAST	NOW	FUTURE

We **often use** the simple present with words that tell you how often: for example *always, never, often, sometimes, usually, once a day, twice a week, every year, all the time.*

She always forgets my birthday. *I often get headaches.* *You never listen to me.*
We play basketball twice a week. *It rains all the time here.*

1 **Complete the sentences with the correct forms of verbs from the boxes.**

ask	get up ✓	go	make	play	speak

▶ Peter always ...*gets up*............. late on Sundays.
1 Ann and John sometimes .... tennis at weekends.
2 My mother often .... French at home.
3 Small children .... questions all the time.
4 Sarah .... to Oxford to see her mother twice a week.
5 I .... more mistakes in English when I'm tired.

say	sit	try	wash	watch

6 Andy always .... his clothes on Saturdays.
7 That child never .... 'Thank you.'
8 He .... in the same chair every evening.
9 She .... to go skiing every year.
10 My father .... TV most evenings.

2 **GRAMMAR AND VOCABULARY: seven useful things**
Use a dictionary if necessary. Put the beginnings and ends together. Put -(e)s on the verb if necessary.

1 A dishwasher wash.*es*	A clothes. ...
2 A cooker make...	B food cool. ...
3 Freezers keep...	C food hot. ...
4 A fridge keep...	D food very cold. ...
5 Washing machines wash...	E copies of papers. ...
6 Photocopiers make...	F plates, cups, etc. *1*
7 A camera take...	G photographs. ...

photocopier
camera
fridge
freezer
cooker
washing machine
dishwasher

We **do not** use a present tense to talk about **how long** something has lasted (see page 61).

*I **have known** her since 1990.* (NOT ~~I know her since 1990.~~)

→ For word order with words like *always, often, sometimes,* see page 204.

simple present questions   *Do you remember me?*

?	**do** I work? **do** you work? **does** he/she/it work? **do** we work? **do** they work?

We make simple present **questions** (**?**) with *do/does* + **subject** + **infinitive** (without *to*).

STATEMENT ➕	QUESTION ?
I know	**Do** I know?
You think	**Do** you think? (NOT ~~Think you?~~)
He likes	**Does** he like? (NOT ~~Does he likes?~~)
She remembers	**Does** she remember?
It helps	**Does** it help?
We want	**Do** we want?
They understand	**Do** they understand?

① Put in *do* or *does*.

▶ *Do*............. you know my friend Andy?

▶ *Does*.......... this bus go to Cambridge?

1 .... Ann want to come with us?

2 .... your parents live near here?

3 .... you speak Chinese?

4 .... Sarah go to school on Saturdays?

5 .... this shop sell stamps?

6 .... Bill and Harry play golf?

② Make questions.

▶ They smoke. *Do they smoke?*..

▶ Ann teaches French. *Does Ann teach French?*..............................

1 The Oxford bus stops here. ....

2 The teachers know her. ....

3 You play the piano. ....

4 John works in a restaurant. ....

5 This train stops at York. ....

6 We need more eggs. ....

7 Mary likes parties. ....

8 Peter speaks Spanish well. ....

Do you know all these **question words**?
what   when   where   who   why   how   how much   how many   what time

What do you **think?** (NOT ~~What think you?~~)   **Where does** Lucy **live?** (NOT ~~Where lives Lucy?~~)
How much does this **cost?** (NOT ~~How much this costs?~~)
What time does the train **leave?** (NOT ~~What time the train leaves?~~)

③ Choose the correct subject.

▶ How much does ..*the ticket*................ cost? (*the ticket / the tickets*)

1 Where do .... live? (*your daughter / your children*)

2 What time does .... start? (*the lesson / the lessons*)

3 What do .... want? (*you / the girl*)

4 When does .... finish? (*the holidays / the holiday*)

5 Why do .... talk so fast? (*that woman / those women*)

6 What do .... think of the new boss? (*you / she*)

→ For questions without *do*, like *Who lives here?*, see pages 110–111.

4 **Choose the correct question word and put in *do* or *does*.**

how ✓	how many	how much ✓	what	when	where	why

▶ *How much does* .... the ticket cost?
▶ *How do* .... you pronounce this word?
1 .... your children live?
2 .... she want?
3 .... the holidays start?
4 .... the teacher talk so fast?
5 .... languages .... he speak?

5 **Make questions.**

▶ Where / she live? ...*Where does she live?*......................
1 What / you want? ....
2 What / this word mean? ....
3 What time / the film start? ....
4 How much / those shoes cost? ....
5 Why / she need money? ....
6 How / this camera work? ....
7 Where / you buy your meat? ....
8 Who / you want to see? ....

Be careful when questions have **long subjects** – the word order does not change.
Where does Ann   *live?*
Where does your other sister   *live?*
Where does your sister's old English teacher live?
(NOT ~~*Where lives your sister's old English teacher?*~~ OR ~~*Where does live your ...*~~)

6 **Make questions.**

▶ The President and his wife live in Madrid.
  Where ...*do the President and his wife live?*...........................
1 Peter and Ann's children play football on Saturdays.
  When ....
2 The film about skiing in New Zealand starts at 8.00.
  What time ....
3 The second word in the first sentence means 'kind'.
  What ....
4 The man in the flat downstairs wants to change his job.
  Why ....
5 A ticket for Saturday's concert costs €15.
  How much ....

GRAMMAR AND VOCABULARY: common simple present questions

How do you pronounce this word?   *How do you spell that?*   *What does this word mean?*
How much does it cost / do they cost?   *Do you know Ann?*   *Where do you live/work?*
What do you do? (= 'What is your job?')   *How do you do?* (= 'I'm pleased to meet you.')
What time does the train/bus/plane leave/arrive?   *What time does the film/concert/class start?*

➔ For more information about questions, see pages 106–111.
➔ For short answers like *Yes, I do / No, I don't*, see page 268.

simple present negatives   *I don't know.   She doesn't ski.*

▬	I **do not** work You **do not** work? he/she/it **does** not work we/they **do not** work
	Contractions: *don't, doesn't*

We make simple present **negatives** (▬) with *do/does not* + **infinitive** (without *to*).

STATEMENT ➕	NEGATIVE ▬
I know	*I **do not** know* (NOT ~~I know not~~)
You think	*You **do not** think*
He likes	*He **does** not like*
She remembers	*She **does** not remember*
It helps	*It **does** not help*
We want	*We **do not** want*
They understand	*They **do not** understand*

1 Make negative sentences. Use *do not* or *does not*.

▶ I play chess. (*cards*) ...I do not play cards. ....

1 You speak Arabic. (*Chinese*) ....

2 Bill plays the piano very well. (*guitar*) ....

3 We agree about most things. (*holidays*) ....

4 Alan and John live near me. (*George and Andrew*) ....

5 My father writes novels. (*poetry*) ....

6 Barbara works in London. (*live*) ....

7 Henry likes old books. (*parties*) ....

2 Make negative sentences. Use *don't* or *doesn't*.

1 I like jazz. (*pop music*) ....

2 The train stops at Bristol. (*Cardiff*) ....

3 Peter remembers names very well. (*faces*) ....

4 We know our Member of Parliament. (*his wife*) ....

5 Alice teaches engineering. (*mathematics*) ....

6 The children play football on Mondays. (*hockey*) ....

7 The shops open on Sunday mornings. (*afternoons*) ....

3 Complete the negative sentences, using words from the box.
You can use *do not / does not* or *don't / doesn't*, as you like.

fish   in Britain   much petrol ✓   much tennis
on Sundays   Russian   your phone number

▶ My car / use ...My car doesn't use much petrol. ....

1 Our cat / like ....

2 Ann / speak ....

3 I / remember ....

4 Oranges / grow ....

5 The postman / come ....

6 We / play ....

4 Choose one verb to make each sentence negative.

▶ It *doesn't snow* very often in San Francisco. (*snow, sing, play*)

1 I like football, but I .... cricket at all. (*think, like, remember*)
2 She lives in Japan, but she .... a word of Japanese. (*sing, work, speak*)
3 I'm sorry – I .... your name. (*eat, remember, work*)
4 He works in New York, but I .... what he does. (*know, use, come*)
5 Mary's really tired, but she .... to go to bed. (*help, want, walk*)
6 We .... a big flat – just one bedroom. (*work, play, want*)
7 Phil .... very hard, but he makes a lot of money. (*work, stand, stop*)
8 Ann's parents .... I'm the right man for their daughter. (*write, read, think*)

5 GRAMMAR AND VOCABULARY: games
Look at the table, and write five or more sentences like this:

Ann plays tennis, but she doesn't play cards.
....
....
....
....
....
....
....
....
....
....
....

	tennis	football	rugby	basketball	baseball	chess	cards	hockey	badminton
Ann	✔	✗	✗	✔	✔	✗	✗	✗	✔
Pete	✗	✔	✗	✗	✗	✔	✔	✗	✗
Joe	✔	✗	✔	✔	✗	✗	✔	✔	✔
Sarah	✗	✔	✗	✗	✔	✔	✗	✗	✗

6 What games do you play? And what games do you not play?
....
....

NOTE: one negative word is enough (see page 114).

Nobody understands me. (NOT ~~Nobody doesn't understand me.~~)
She **never** phones me. (NOT ~~She doesn't never phone me.~~)

→ For more information about negative structures, see pages 112–115.

simple present: revision

⊞	*I/you/we/they work he/she/it works*
?	*do I/you/we/they work? does he/she/it work?*
⊟	*I/you/we/they do not work he/she/it does not work*
	Contractions: *don't, doesn't*

1 **Look at the picture, and complete the sentence correctly.**

A what he does?
B what does he does?
C what does he do?
D what does he to do?

2 (Circle) **the correct answers.**

1 Where *do / does* your sister live?
2 *My cat / My cats* don't like fish.
3 This car *don't / doesn't* go very fast.
4 This train *stop / stops* at every station.
5 Why *do English people / English people do* drink so much tea?

6 The post office doesn't *open / opens* on Sundays.
7 When does *your holiday start / start your holiday*?
8 My parents both *play / plays* golf.
9 *That café / Those cafés* stays open all night.
10 Her letters don't *say / to say* very much.

3 **Make sentences.**

▶ Ann (*live*) in Birmingham ⊞ ......*Ann lives in Birmingham.*....................
▶ you (*speak*) Chinese ? ......*Do you speak Chinese?*....................
▶ Sarah (*like*) classical music ⊟ ......*Sarah doesn't like classical music.*....................
1 I (*like*) getting up early ⊟ ....
2 you (*want*) something to drink ? ....
3 Joe (*play*) football on Saturdays ⊞ ....
4 you (*remember*) her phone number ? ....
5 that clock (*work*) ⊟ ....
6 she often (*fly*) to Paris on business ⊞ ....
7 it (*rain*) much here in summer ⊟ ....
8 elephants (*eat*) meat ? ....
9 he (*think*) he can sing ? ....
10 we (*need*) a new car ⊞ ....

Why computers are like women:
Nobody understands the language that they use when they talk to other computers.
They never tell you what is wrong; and if you don't know, you're in trouble.
They remember your smallest mistakes for ever.
Why computers are like men:
They know a lot of things but they are very stupid.
After you get one for yourself, you soon see a better one.
They like to go fast but they always crash.

---

present progressive*: forms   *I'm reading; I'm not working.*

+	I **am** working	you **are** working	he/she/it **is** working	we/they **are** working
-	I **am not** working	you **are not** working	he/she/it **is not** working etc	

Contractions: *I'm, you're, he's* etc (*not*) *...ing; you aren't, he isn't* etc *...ing*
What's he ...ing?, Where's she ...ing?, When's it ...ing? etc

---

We make **present progressive** verbs with *be* (*I am, you are* etc – see page 2) + *...ing*.
John is studying Russian.   I'm not working today.
We use **contractions** (*I'm, John's, isn't* etc) in **conversation** and **informal writing**.

1 Make present progressive affirmative (+) and negative (-) sentences.

▶ The lesson <u>is starting</u> now. (*start* +)
▶ Joan <u>is not working</u> today. (*work* -)
1 You .... too fast. (*talk* +)
2 The cat .... a bird. (*eat* +)
3 Bill .... dinner now. (*cook* +)
4 I .... this party. (*enjoy* -)
5 I .... a good book. (*read* +)
6 It .... now. (*rain* -)
7 You .... to me. (*listen* -)
8 I .... very happy today. (*feel* +)
9 Peter .... to school this week. (*go* -)
10 We .... a bit of English. (*learn* +)

HOW TO MAKE *-ING* FORMS

- **most verbs:** + *-ing*   work → work**ing**   sleep → sleep**ing**
- **verbs ending in -*e*:** (-e̸) + *-ing*   make → mak**ing**   hope → hop**ing**
- **-*ie* changes to** *y* + *-ing*   lie → l**ying**

2 Write the *-ing* forms of these verbs.

break <u>breaking</u>   clean ....   come ....   die ....   enjoy ....
go ....   live ....   make ....   play ....   sing ....
start ....   wash ....   write ....

DOUBLING (*stopping, running*, etc)

- **one vowel + one consonant**
  → **double consonant +** *-ing*   stop → stop**ping** (NOT ~~stoping~~)   run → run**ning**
- **two vowels:** don't double   sleep → sleep**ing**   wait → wait**ing** (NOT ~~waitting~~)
- **two consonants:** don't double   want → want**ing** (NOT ~~wantting~~)   help → help**ing**
- **Only double in STRESSED syllables**   beGIN → begin**ning** BUT HAPpen → happen**ing**

3 Write the *-ing* forms of these verbs.

get ....   feel ....   put ....   hit ....
jump ....   rain ....   rob ....   shop ....
shout ....   sit ....   slim ....   dream ....
stand ....   talk ....   turn ....
ANswer ....   OPen ....   VIsit ....
forGET ....

---

* Also called 'present continuous'

present progressive: use   *I'm (not) working today.*

We use the **present progressive** to say that things are (not) happening **now** or **around now**.

I'm working just now.   *It's raining again.*   *Jane's taking driving lessons.*

PAST   NOW   FUTURE

I'm sorry, I can't come out. I'm working just now. (Compare: *I **work** every day. – see page 15)*
Look – it's raining again. (Compare: *It rains every day here.*)
Jane's taking driving lessons. (Compare: *A lot of people **take** lessons with that driving school.*)
I'm not enjoying this party. (Compare: *I usually **enjoy** parties.*)

1 **Make present progressive sentences.**

▶ Ann / read / the newspaper. ...*Ann's reading the newspaper.*...................................
1 The baby / cry / again. ....
2 It / snow / again. ....
3 You / look / very beautiful today. ....
4 Your coffee / get / cold. ....
5 I / play / a lot of football this year. ....
6 We / wait / for a phone call. ....
7 Chris and Helen / spend / a week in France. ....

2 **Look at the pictures and use the verbs in the box to say what Helen is doing.**

brush	brush	drink	get up ✓	go	listen to	open	read	read	wash

▶ ...*She's getting up.*...............
1 .... her face.
2 .... her teeth.
3 .... the radio.
4 .... coffee.
5 .... the newspaper.
6 .... her hair.
7 .... letters.
8 .... the door.
9 .... to work.

3 Make negative (–) present progressive sentences.

▶ I / not ask for / a lot of money. ...I'm not asking for a lot of money...........................

1 He / not listen / to me. ....

2 I / not work / today. ....

3 It / not rain / now. ....

4 She / not wear / a coat. ....

5 They / not learn / very much. ....

6 We / not enjoy / this film. ....

7 You / not eat / much these days. ....

4 GRAMMAR AND VOCABULARY: clothes
Use the words in the box to say what the people are (not) wearing. Use a dictionary if necessary.

John   Ann   Sandra   David

belt	blouse	boots	cardigan	coat	dress	glasses	hat	jacket
raincoat	shoes	shirt	skirt	socks	suit	sweater	trousers	

John is wearing a white shirt, a blue sweater, a blue jacket, grey trousers with a blue belt, blue socks and black shoes. He is not wearing glasses.

Ann is wearing ....

....

....

Sandra ....

....

....

David ....

....

....

NOTE: We **do not** use a present tense to say **how long** something has lasted (see page 61).
I've been waiting since 9.00. (NOT ~~I'm waiting since 9.00.~~)

→ We often use the **present progressive** to talk about the **future**. See page 34.

present progressive questions   *Is it raining?*

We make present progressive questions with *am/are/is* + **subject** + *...ing*

STATEMENT ➕ :   *It is raining.*   *You are working.*   *The children are making something.*

QUESTION ? :   *Is it raining?*   *Are you working?*   *What are the children making?*

❶ Make questions.

▶ everybody / listen / to me ? ...*Is everybody listening to me?*...................................

1 you / wait / for somebody ? ....

2 your boyfriend / enjoy / the concert ? ....

3 those men / take / our car ? ....

4 you / talk / to me ? ....

5 it / snow ? ....

6 we / go / too fast ? ....

❷ Complete the questions.

▶ 'Those people aren't speaking English.' 'What language ...*are they speaking?*........................ '

1 'Bill's writing something on the wall.' 'I can't see – what .... '

2 'The train's stopping!' 'Why .... '

3 'They're eating now.' 'What .... '

4 'They're playing a game.' 'What game .... '

5 'I'm going now. Goodbye.' 'Wait! Where .... '

Be careful when questions have **long subjects** – the word order does not change.

Is   Ann   working today?
Are Ann and her mother   working today?
Are Ann and her mother and father and the others working today?
(NOT ~~*Are working today Ann and her mother and father and the others?*~~)

❸ Put the words in the correct order.

▶ the President and his wife / are / staying / where / ?
  Where are the President and his wife staying?..

▶ those people over there / French / are / speaking / ?
  Are those people over there speaking French?..

1 laughing / why / all those people / are / ?
  ....

2 is / eating / that big black dog / what / ?
  ....

3 going / everybody in your family / to Scotland / for Christmas / is / ?
  ....

4 what game / those children / playing / are / ?
  ....

5 Ann and her friends / studying / are / where / ?
  ....

➔ For more information about questions, see pages 106–111.

present progressive: revision

+	*I am working*	*you are working*	*he/she/it/is working*	*we/they are working*
?	*am I working?*	*are you working?*	*is/he/she/it working?*	*are we/they working?*
-	*I am not working*	*you are not working*	*he/she/it/is not working* etc	

Contractions: *I'm, you're, he's* etc (not) *...ing; you aren't, he isn't* etc *...ing*
What's he ...ing? Where's she ...ing? When's it ...ing? etc

1 Put the words in the correct order.

▶ me you talking are to ? ..Are you talking to me?...
1 getting are you up ? ....
2 you what drinking are ? ....
3 not you are listening . ...
4 going where you are ? ....
5 talking fast too I am ? ....
6 I film enjoying not this am . ...
7 looking all those people at are what ? ....
8 am for you I cooking this not . ...

2 Make present progressive sentences.

▶ I / look for / the station **+** ..I'm looking for the station.................................
▶ you / work / tonight **?** ..Are you working tonight?.................................
▶ it / rain **-** .It isn't raining.................................
1 Peter / try / to save money **+** ....
2 why / those children / cry **?** ....
3 all your friends / play football / this afternoon **?** ....
4 she / look / very well today **-** ....
5 I think she / make / a big mistake **+** ....
6 you / wear / your usual glasses **-** ....
7 I / hope / to get a new job **+** ....
8 the 10.15 train from London to Edinburgh / run / today **?** ....
....

3 Complete the text with verbs from the boxes.

1–5: come ✓ look not wear snow walk wear

And Mrs Alexander ▶ ..is coming........ down the steps of the plane now. It is very cold and it
1 .... heavily, but she 2 .... very happy. She 3 .... a dark blue
dress with a black coat and boots, but she 4 .... a hat. She really is a very beautiful
woman. Her husband 5 .... down the steps with her.

6–11: kiss look return say stop try

Now Mrs Alexander and her husband 6 .... at the crowd and smiling. The photographers
7 .... to get nearer, but the police are 8 .... them. What a day! At last,
after twenty years, this wonderful woman 9 .... to her own country. Now the President
10 .... her hand. What 11 .... he .... to her, do you think?

the two present tenses: the difference

SIMPLE PRESENT: *I work* etc	PRESENT PROGRESSIVE: *I'm working* etc
• things that are **always true** • things that happen **all the time,** **repeatedly, often, sometimes, never, etc**	• things that are happening **now** • things that are happening **around now**
The sun rises in the east. *She often wears red.* *I play tennis.*	*The sun is not shining today.* *She's wearing a blue dress.* *I'm playing a lot of tennis these days.*

1 **Put the expressions in the correct places.**

every day ✓   just now   nearly always   now ✓   on Fridays   these days
this afternoon   today   very often   when I'm tired

SIMPLE PRESENT: *I work* etc

every day ....

....

....

PRESENT PROGRESSIVE: *I'm working* etc

now ....

....

....

2 **Use the verbs in the box to complete the sentences.**

chase ✓   chase   drive   eat   fly   play
play   rain   sell   speak   work   write

Cats *chase* .... mice.

▶

But *this cat is*
not chasing mice.

Cows .... grass.

1

But this cow ....
....

Planes ....

2

But this ....
....

It often ....

3

But ....
.... now.

John .... hard.

4

But ....
.... today.

Ann .... tennis.

5

But ....
.... now.

John .... English.

6 你好

But ....
....

Bill .... a bus.

7

But ....
....

This shop ....
books.

8

But ....
....

Carol ....
the piano.

9

But she ....
....

Simon ....
poetry.

10

But ....
....

Dogs ....
cats.

11

But this ....
....

3 Verb forms and use: complete the sentences with the correct verb forms.

▶ '*Do you smoke?*' .... 'No, never.' (*you / smoke*)

▶ 'What *are you eating?* .... ' 'A cheese sandwich.' (*you / eat*)

1 'Where .... these days?' 'In a garage.' (*she / work*)

2 '..................................... here in summer?' 'Not very often.' (*it / rain*)

3 'Bonjour.' 'Sorry, I .... French.' (*not speak*)

4 'Your English .... better.' 'Oh, thank you.' (*get*)

5 '..................................... golf?' 'Yes, but not very well.' (*you / play*)

6 'Who .... to?' 'My boyfriend.' (*you / write*)

7 'Where's Susan?' '..................................... now.' (*she / come*)

8 Well, goodnight. .... to bed. (*I / go*)

9 Water .... at 100°C. (*boil*)

10 '.....................................?' 'Not yet.' (*that water / boil*)

4 GRAMMAR AND VOCABULARY: things to read
Look at the pictures and numbers, and write sentences with *often* and *now*.
Use a dictionary if necessary.

▶ (2, 1) *She often reads newspapers, but now she's reading a short story.*

▶ (3,4) *She often reads magazines, but now she's reading a biography.*

1 (5,9) He ....

2 (8,10) She ....

3 (1,7) He ....

4 (4,2) I ....

5 (2,6) They ....

6 (3,5) He ....

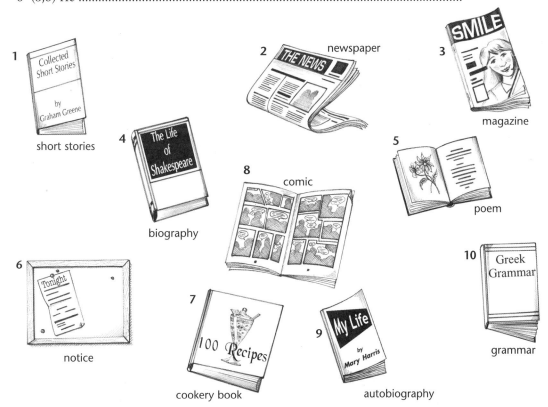

1 short stories
2 newspaper
3 magazine
4 biography
5 poem
6 notice
7 cookery book
8 comic
9 autobiography
10 grammar

➔ For the position of adverbs like *often*, *these days* etc, see page 204.

non-progressive verbs   *I don't understand.*

Some verbs are normally used in **simple tenses**, not progressive, even if we mean '*just now*'.
*I **like** this weather.* (NOT ~~I'm liking this weather.~~)   *What **does** he **want**?* (NOT ~~What is he wanting?~~)

hate, know, like, love, mean, need, prefer, seem, understand, want

*I **hate** this music.*   '*We're late.*' '*I **know**.*'   *I **love** that colour.*   ***Do** you **understand**?*
*What **does** this **mean**?*   *I **need** some help.*   '*Tea?*' '*I **prefer** juice.*'   *Ann **seems** unhappy.*

1 Complete the sentences with verbs from the box.

want ✓   like   need   not understand   prefer   seem

▶ What ..*does*.... Paul ..*want*... for his birthday?
1 'Przepraszam!' 'Sorry, I ....'
2 'Would you like some coffee?' 'I .... tea, if that's OK.'
3 'What do you think of this music?' 'I .... it.'
4 This room .... very cold. Is the heating on?
5 I'm going to the shops. .... we .... anything?

2 Make sentences.

▶ Ann / seem / unhappy today ➕ ...*Ann seems unhappy today.*..............................
▶ you / need / help ❓ ..*Do you need help?*..............................
▶ I / know / her name ➖ .*I don't know her name.*..............................
1 what / this word / mean ❓ ....
2 Rob / want / to see the doctor ➖ ....
3 I think / she / love / me ➕ ....
4 Peter / seem / tired ➕ ....
5 we / need / a new car ➖ ....
6 you / know / that man ❓ ....
7 I / hate / cold weather ➕ ....

agree, believe, depend, matter, mind, recognise, remember

'*This is a terrible film.*' '*I **don't agree**.*'   '*Sorry I'm late.*' '*It **doesn't matter**.*'
*I **recognise** her, but I **don't remember** her name.*   '*Can I borrow the car?*' '*It **depends**. Until when?*'
'*There's no more orange juice.*' '*I **don't mind**. I'll have water.*'

3 Make negative (➖) sentences with the verbs in the box.

agree ✓   believe   matter   mind   recognise   remember

▶ Ann thinks you're right, but the boss ..*doesn't agree*..............................
1 'I'm sorry – I've broken a glass.' 'It ....'
2 'What's Bill's phone number?' 'I ....'
3 Perhaps I've seen her before, but I .... her.
4 Peter says he's a student, but I .... him.
5 'Supper will be very late.' 'I .... – I'm not hungry now.'

Think, see, look and *feel* can be **progressive** with one meaning but **not** with another.

NON-PROGRESSIVE (*I think* etc)	CAN BE PROGRESSIVE (*I'm thinking* etc)

think (**that** …) = 'have an opinion'
  I *think* you're wrong.
see = 'understand'
  I *see* what you mean.
look like = 'seem like'
  That *looks like* our train.
feel = 'have an opinion'
  I *feel* you're making a mistake.
	think (**about** …) = 'plan, look at ideas'
	  I'm *thinking* about the holidays.
	see = 'meet'
	  I'm *seeing* the doctor today.
	look = 'turn eyes towards'
	  What *are* you *looking* at?
	feel ill/tired etc (can be progressive or simple)
	  I'm *feeling* ill. OR I *feel* ill.

4 **Put in the correct verb forms.**

  1 We .... the bank manager this afternoon. (*see*)
  2 'I .... you're crazy.' 'I ....' (*think; see*)
  3 'What .... about?' 'Life.' (*you / think*)
  4 Why .... at me? (*that woman / look*)
  5 She .... your sister. (*look like*)
  6 I .... that she doesn't like me. (*feel*)

5 GRAMMAR AND VOCABULARY: some useful answers with non-progressive verbs
Make sure you know all the expressions in the box. Use a dictionary if necessary.
Then circle the best answers.

> I hope so.   I hope not.   I don't remember.   I don't understand.
> It doesn't matter.   I think so.   I don't think so.   I know.
> I don't know.   I see.   I don't mind.   It depends.

  ▶ 'Is Ann enjoying her holiday?' ⟨*I hope so.*⟩ / '*I don't mind.*'
  1 'Agresti, min ruggide flochsch?' '*I don't think so.*' / '*I don't understand.*'
  2 'We're not happy with your work.' '*I hope so.*' / '*I see.*'
  3 'Is Joe coming to dinner?' '*I see.*' / '*I hope not.*'
  4 'Do you like this music?' '*I think so.*' / '*I don't remember.*'
  5 'Is that Mary getting into the taxi?' '*I know.*' / '*I don't think so.*'
  6 'Who wrote 'War and Peace'?' '*It depends.*' / '*I don't know.*'
  7 'It's Tuesday'. '*I think so.*' / '*I know.*'
  8 'Can you lend me some money?' '*It depends.*' / '*It doesn't matter.*'
  9 'We're too early.' '*I don't know.*' / '*It doesn't matter.*'
  10 'What's Phil's address? '*I don't remember.*' / '*It depends.*'
  11 'Sorry, this coffee isn't very good.' '*I don't mind.*' / '*I hope so.*'

6 **Write personal answers.**

  ▶ Will everybody in the world speak English one day? *I think so. / I don't think so. / I hope so. /
     I hope not. / I don't mind. / I don't know.*
  1 Is your English getting better? ....
  2 Will you be rich and famous one day? ....
  3 What were you doing at 8.00 in the morning on February 16th last year?
     ....
  4 How many stars are there in the sky? ....

test yourself present tenses

1 **Write the simple present _he/she/it_ forms.**

go .goes.. live .... pass .... play .... stand .... teach .... try .... wash ....

2 **Write the _-ing_ forms.**

call _calling_.. fly .... hold .... make .... play .... sit .... stop ....

3 **Make simple present sentences.**

▶ Ann (_speak Chinese_ ➕) .Ann speaks Chinese....
▶ you (_live here_ ❓) .Do you live here?....
▶ this clock (_work_ ➖) .This clock doesn't work...
1 you (_drive_ ❓) to school ....
2 Granny (_drink_ ➖) coffee ....
3 I (_travel_ ➕) a lot in Europe ....
4 Alex (_want_ ➕) to be a doctor ....
5 The fast train (_stop_ ➖) at this station ....
6 you (_speak English_ ❓) to your children ....

4 **Make present progressive sentences with expressions from the box.**

cook	not listen	sell	snow	not work ✓

▶ 'Why aren't you at the office?' 'I'.m not working................. today.'
1 I'm sorry – John can't come to the phone for the moment. He .... lunch.
2 'It's raining.' 'No, it's not. It ....'
3 You .... to me.
4 There's a man at the door. He .... vegetables.

5 **Circle the correct answers.**

▶ 'Your English _gets_ /(_is getting_)better.' 'Oh, thank you.'
1 'Where's Susan?' '_She comes_ / _She's coming_ now.'
2 '_Do you smoke?_' / '_Are you smoking?_' 'No, never.'
3 John cooks dinner _now_ / _every Sunday_.
4 I'm reading a lot of magazines _these days_ / _when I go on holiday_.
5 I work late _all this week_ / _most Tuesdays_.

6 **Make questions.**

1 why / all those people / look at me / ? ....
2 the 7.15 train to London / run / on Saturdays / ? ....
3 where / you and Ann / have lunch / today / ? ....
4 that man in the dark coat at the bus-stop / work / in your office / ? ....
....

7 **Correct (✓) or not (✗)?**

1 You're driving too fast. ...
2 What is this word meaning? ...
3 I'm not wanting a drink just now. ...
4 Where are you living now? ...
5 I'm thinking you're wrong. ...
6 Sorry, I'm not understanding. ...

SECTION 3 talking about the future

● grammar summary

There are **three** common ways to talk about the **future** in English:

- with the *going to* structure.
    *I'm really **going to stop** smoking.*
- with the **present progressive**.
    ***I'm seeing** John this evening.*
- with *will*.
    *Ann **will be** in the office from 10.00 till 2.00.*

We use *going to* or the **present progressive** especially when the future has some **present** reality: for example to talk about plans that we have already made.
In some cases we can use the **simple present** to talk about the future.
    *Her train **arrives** at 15.37.   I'll phone you when I **get** home.* (See page 221.)

● pre-test: which units do you need?

Try this small test. It will help you to decide which units you need. The answers are on page 283.

1 Correct (✓) or not (✗)?

▶ You eat with us this evening? .✗.
1 'There's somebody at the door.' 'I go.' ...
2 Will Ann and Johnny be here tomorrow? ...
3 I promise I write again soon. ...
4 Look at those clouds – it will snow. ...
5 The car won't start. ...

6 I'm working in London next week. ...
7 The concert starts at 8.00 this evening. ...
8 Mary's going to have a baby. ...
9 Do you play tennis with Peter this weekend? ...
10 Do you think it's raining tomorrow? ...
11 I think it won't rain. ...

'It's going to be wet again today.'

going to   *Look – it's going to rain.*

+	I **am going to** drive you **are going to** drive he/she **is going to** drive etc
?	**am** I **going to** drive? **are** you **going to** drive? **is** he/she **going to** drive? etc
–	I **am not going to** drive you **are not going to** drive etc
	For contractions (*I'm, aren't* etc), see pages 2 and 277.

We often use *going to* when we can **see the future in the present** – when a future situation is **starting**, or clearly **on the way**.

 Look – it's **going to rain**.

 Rebecca's **going to have a baby** next month.

1 Look at the pictures. What is going to happen? Use the words in the box.

▶ She is ..... *going to post a letter.* ....

1 The woman ....

2 He ....

3 She ....

4 The cars ....

5 He ....

6 The ball ....

break the window
crash
drink coffee
have breakfast
play the piano
post a letter ✓
read a letter

We often use *going to* to talk about **intentions** – things that people **have decided** (not) to do. This structure is common in conversation.

I'm going to take a holiday next week.   *Peter's not going to study* chemistry.
What are you going to wear this evening?   *Lucy is going to go to* France next year.

2 Make questions with *going to*.

▶ you / cook supper   *Are you going to cook supper?* ....

▶ when / your brothers / be here   *When are your brothers going to be here?* ....

1 Ann / change her school   ....

2 where / you / put that picture   ....

3 what / you / buy for Bill's birthday   ....

4 Eric / play football / tomorrow   ....

5 when / you / stop smoking   ....

6 Alice / go to university   ....

③ Ann is talking about her holiday next week. Look at the pictures and complete the sentences.

do any work   drive to Italy ✓   fly ✓   learn some Italian   read English newspapers
stay in a nice hotel   swim a lot   take photos   visit museums   write postcards

▶ No, I'm not going to fly. ....   4 ....
▶ I'm going to drive to Italy. ....   5 ....
1 ....   6 ....
2 ....   7 ....
3 ....   8 ....

④ GRAMMAR AND VOCABULARY: two-word verbs
Make sure you know the verbs in the box. Use a dictionary if necessary. Then look at the pictures and complete the sentences.

plug in   unplug   switch on/off   turn on/off   turn up/down

▶ She ...is going to.......................... switch on the radio.
1 She .... off the radio.
2 .... turn up ....
3 .... down ....
4 .... on ....
5 .... off ....
6 .... turn on the tap.
7 .... the tap.
8 .... plug in the iron.
9 .... unplug the ....
10 .... the hair-dryer.
11 ....

→ For more about two-word verbs ('phrasal verbs'), see pages 138–139.

NOTE: In **informal** speech (and songs), we often say *gonna* for *going to*.

present progressive   *What are you doing this evening?*

+	I **am** working you **are** working he/she/it **is** working we/they **are** working
?	**am** I working? **are** you working? **is** he/she/it working? **are** we/they working?
–	I **am not** working you **are not** working he/she/it **is not** working
	For contractions (*I'm, aren't*, etc), see pages 2 and 277.

We can use the **present progressive** with a **future meaning**, especially when we talk about **plans for a fixed time and/or place.**

'What are you doing this evening?' 'I'm staying in.'   *Where are you going on holiday?*
Joe's coming round this evening.   *I'm starting a new job next week.*

1 **Look at Bill's diary and correct the sentences.**

▶ He's staying in Berlin on Friday night.
No, he's coming back to England on Friday night.

1 He's seeing John Parker on Sunday afternoon.
....

2 He's going to the Birmingham office by car.
....

3 He's having dinner with Stewart on Tuesday.
....

4 He's going to the theatre on Thursday evening.
....

5 His new secretary is starting on Friday.
....

6 Phil and Monica are going to his wedding on Saturday.
....

Sunday
John Parker morning

Monday
to Birmingham (1.15 train)

Tuesday
lunch Stewart 1.00

Wednesday
theatre with Ann and Joe

Thursday
new secretary starting

Friday
to Berlin LH 014   8.00;
back LH 135   16.40

Saturday
Phil and Monica's wedding

2 **A friend of yours is going on holiday soon. Write questions.**

▶ when / leave   *When are you leaving?*   3 how / travel ....
▶ take / sister   *Are you taking your sister?*   4 take / dog ....
1 where / stay ....   5 who / go with you ....
2 how long / stay ....   6 when / come back ....

3 GRAMMAR AND VOCABULARY: **five professions**
(Use a dictionary if necessary.) Jane is seeing five people next week, one each day: her bank manager, her solicitor, her accountant, her dentist and her doctor. Who is she seeing when? Fill in the table and complete the sentences.

> She's seeing her bank manager before her doctor. She's seeing her doctor on Tuesday. She's seeing her dentist two days after her bank manager. She's seeing her accountant two days after her doctor.

1 She's seeing .... on Monday.
2 .... on Tuesday.
3 .... on Wednesday.
4 .... on Thursday.
5 .... on Friday.

Monday	
Tuesday	*doctor*
Wednesday	
Thursday	
Friday	

the *will*-future: forms   *I will work.   They won't come.*

+	I/you/he/she/it/we/they **will** work
?	**will** I/you/he etc work?
−	I/you/he etc **will not** work
	Contractions: *I'll, you'll,* etc; *won't* (= *will not*)

1 Put the words in the correct order.

▶ here George be will   ...George will be here.. tomorrow.

▶ drive station to you the I'll   ...I'll drive you to the station....................... now.

1 begin class will the   .... at 9.30.

2 be they'll home   .... soon.

3 examination will the difficult be I think   ....

4 walk we'll party the to   ....

5 her not speak will I to   ....

2 Make negatives (−) and questions (?).

▶ 'I ...won't finish............ this work today.' 'When ...will you finish........ it?' (*finish*)

▶ 'John ......won't be.............. here tomorrow.' '...Will he be here........ on Tuesday?' (*be*)

1 'Annie .... here at ten.' 'When .... here?' (*be*)

2 'I .... time for lunch.' '............................. time for a sandwich?' (*have*)

3 'You .... any pens in there.' 'Where .... one?' (*find*)

4 'The children .... to school in Ely.' 'Where ....?' (*go*)

5 'Bob .... much money if he sells that car.' 'How much ....?' (*get*)

Be careful when questions have **long subjects** – the word order does not change.

What time will **you**	leave?	
What time will **the bus**	leave?	(NOT ~~*What time will leave the bus?*~~)
What time will **the bus for the dinner and dance** leave?		(NOT ~~*What time the bus ... will leave?*~~)

3 Make questions with *will*.

1 what time / tomorrow evening's concert / start? ....

2 when / you and the family / get back from Paris? ....

3 you / be / here tomorrow? ....

4 you and your mother / be / here tomorrow? ....

5 where / you / be / this evening? ....

6 the children / have enough money / for the journey? ....

7 how soon / you know / the answer? ....

8 John and Susan / want / to play golf tomorrow? ....

NOTE: After *I* and *we*, some people say *shall* instead of *will*. The meaning is the same; *will* is more common in modern English.

Contractions: *I shall* → *I'll*   *we shall* → *we'll* etc   *shall not* → *shan't*

➜ For *shall* in offers, see page 86.

will: predicting   *I think it will rain tomorrow.*

We use *will* + **infinitive** to **predict** – to say things that we **think, guess** or **know** about the **future**, or to ask questions about the future.

*I think it **will snow** tomorrow.*   *Be quick, or you**'ll miss** your train.*
*Ann **won't be** here this evening.*   *When **will** you **know** your exam results?*

1 These are sentences from real conversations. Put in forms of *will* with expressions from the box. (C: the speaker used a contraction: *'ll* or *won't*.)

change   not snow   start   tell   go to sleep soon

1 You make me so unhappy: I .... crying in a moment. (C)
2 Do you think that all this money .... your life?
3 It .... tonight, will it, John? (C)
4 And they said 'Benjamin's tired, he ....' (C)
5 She .... you how to do it.

We usually say *I don't think ... will*, NOT *I think ... won't*.

*I **don't think** she**'ll** be late.* (NOT USUALLY *I think she won't be late.*)

2 What do you think will happen? Make your own predictions, with *I think* or *I don't think*.

▶ *I think* .... it *will rain* .... tomorrow. (*rain*)
▶ *I don't think* .... *I'll get* .... money in the post tomorrow. (*get*)
1 .... it .... tomorrow. (*snow*)
2 .... I .... a letter from America tomorrow. (*get*)
3 .... I .... rich in ten years. (*be*)
4 .... I .... famous in ten years. (*be*)
5 .... people .... English everywhere in the year 2100. (*speak*)

3 GRAMMAR AND VOCABULARY: giving directions
Complete the letter. Put *'ll* with the verbs and put in the words from the box.
Use a dictionary if necessary.

apple trees   bridge   door   house   key   old house   the road ✓   great time

Dear Pamela and Simon
To find the house: when you get to Llanbrig, drive through the town and take
▶ *the road* .... for Caernarvon. After about 6 km, you (*pass*) ▶ *'ll pass* .... an
1 .... on the left. Immediately after that, you (*come to*) 2 .... a
bridge. Turn left after the 3 ....; very soon you (*come to*) 4 ....
a crossroads. Go left again, and you (*see*) 5 .... our 6 .... on the
right in about 300m. You (*recognise*) 7 .... it because it's got a green
8 .... and four 9 .... You (*find*) 10 .... the
11 .... under a mat outside the back door.
Enjoy your holiday. I'm sure you (*have*) 12 .... a 13 ....
Love
Susan

→ For present tenses after *if*, *when* etc (*I'll phone you **if/when I have** time*), see pages 221 and 229.

will: deciding, refusing, promising *I'll answer it.*

We can use *will* when we **decide or agree** to do things, and when we talk about **refusing** (saying 'no') and **promising**. We **don't** use the **simple present** in these cases.

OK, I really will stop smoking.　　*She won't speak to me.*　　*I'll phone you.* (NOT ~~I phone you.~~)

Things can 'refuse'.

The car won't start.　　*This pen won't write.*

We often use *will* at the moment when we decide something.

'There's someone at the door.' 'I'll go.' (NOT ~~I go.~~)　　*'That's the phone.' 'I'll answer it.'*

❶ Put in words from the box with *'ll* or *won't*.

do	go shopping	go to bed ✓	help	start	stop	tell ✓	wash

▶ I'm tired. I think I *'ll go to bed.*
▶ I don't know what he wants.
　He *won't tell* us.
1 I .... the cups; can you dry them?
2 'Can somebody post my letters?'
　'I .... it.'

3 'My motorbike ....' 'No petrol?'
4 The baby .... crying. Can you sing to her?
5 'There's no food in the house.'
　'I ....'
6 'I can't move this table.' 'I .... you.'

❷ It's time to change your life. Look at the ideas in the box and write six promises with *will* or *won't* – the most important first.

always think before I speak　　be nice to everybody　　drive too fast
fall in love every week　　go for a walk every day　　go to bed early
learn another language / a musical instrument　　read more　　relax
smile at everybody　　smoke　　study English every day　　talk more slowly
talk to strangers　　think about myself too much　　work harder　　(*your own promise*)

▶ *I'll talk more slowly.* ....
▶ *I won't drive too fast.* ....
1 ....
2 ....

3 ....
4 ....
5 ....
6 ....

❸ GRAMMAR AND VOCABULARY: useful expressions with *I'll*
Look at the expressions in the box. Use a dictionary if necessary.
Then circle the best answers.

I'll think about it.　　I'll see. (= 'I'll think about it.')　　(I'll) see you tomorrow/later.
(I'll) see you.　　I'll give you a ring/call. (= 'I'll phone you.')　　I'll tell you tomorrow/later.

1 'Can I use your car?'　　A 'I'll see.'　B 'I'll see you.'
2 'When do you want to play tennis?'　　A 'I'll see you tomorrow.'　B 'I'll tell you tomorrow.'
3 'I've got to go now.'　　A 'I'll see you.'　B 'I'll think about it.'
4 'Would you like to come dancing with me?'　　A 'I'll think about it.'　B 'I'll see you later.'
5 'Can we talk about it some more?'　　A 'I'll give you a ring.'　B 'I'll see you.'
6 'Goodbye now.'　　A 'See you tomorrow.'　B 'I'll see.'

which future? *will, going to* or present progressive?

There are some differences between these three ways of talking about the future. The differences are not always important; often we can use two or three different forms to talk about the same thing.

PREDICTIONS

Going to: we can see the future in the present: we see things coming or starting.
Will: we think or believe things about the future.

Look out! You're going to break that glass!
(I can see it now.)

Don't give him a watch – he'll break it.
(I think so, because I know him.)

1 **Circle the best form.**

▶ Mary (*is going to*) / *will* have a baby.
1 Perhaps we *are going to* / *will* meet again one day.
2 Be careful, or you *are going to* / *will* fall.
3 Look – Andy *is going to* / *will* fall off his bike!
4 I think you *are going to* / *will* love Scotland.
5 Look at those clouds: it*'s going to* / *will* rain.

DECISIONS

Will: we are making decisions.   *Going to*: decisions are already made

'We've got a letter from Jan.' 'OK, I'll answer it.'
'There are a lot of letters to answer.' 'I know. I'm going to do them all on Tuesday.'

2 **Put in *I'll* or *I'm going to*.**

▶ I've decided. ...*I'm going to*...... stop smoking.
1 'I don't want to cook tonight.' 'All right, then. .... cook.'
2 'I haven't got any money.' 'No? OK. .... pay.'
3 'Do you want to go out tonight?' 'No, ... wash my hair.'
4 'Those trousers are dirty.' 'Really? Oh, yes, they are. .... wash them.'
5 'Is Ann eating with us?' 'Wait a minute. .... ask her.'

PLANS

Going to and the **present progressive** are often both possible when we talk about plans.
We use the **present progressive** mostly for **fixed plans** with a definite time and/or place.

I'm going to see Ann some time soon.   *I'm meeting Pat at the theatre at 8.00.*
I think John's going to study biology.   *Sarah's starting university on September 17th.*

3 **In three of these sentences, the present progressive is possible. Which three?
Rewrite them with the present progressive.**

> Jack is going to arrive at 4.00.   I'm going to learn Spanish one of these days.
> I'm going to fly to Glasgow tomorrow.   Al's going to tell me about his problems.
> We're going to spend next week in Ireland.   Are you going to answer those letters?

1 ....
2 ....
3 ....

simple present for future   *Our train leaves at 8.10.*

We can use the **simple present** to talk about **timetables**, cinema/theatre **programmes** and **dates**.
*Our train **leaves** at 8.10.*   *What time **does** your flight **arrive**?*   *The film **starts** at 7.30.*
*My birthday **is** on a Tuesday this year.*

1 **Make sentences.**

▶ The flight / leave / at 9.30 ➕ *...The flight leaves at 9.30......*
▶ What time / the film / start ❓ *...What time does the film start?......*
▶ This bus / stop / at Mill Road ➖ *...This bus doesn't stop at Mill Road......*
1 The next lesson / start / at 2.00 ➕ ....
2 This term / end / on March 12th ➕ ....
3 When / the concert / finish ❓ ....
4 We / have / a lesson / next Thursday ➖ ....
5 This train / stop / at Reading ❓ ....
6 The play / start / at 8.00 ➕ ....
7 What time / you / arrive / in Rome ❓ ....
8 The banks / close / at 3.00 tomorrow ➕ ....
9 The 7.15 train / stop / at every station ➕ ....

2 **Complete the sentences under the pictures.**

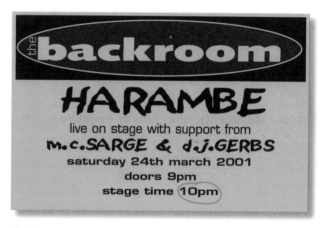

1 The flight ....
  at ....

2 The concert .... at ....

Operator	WT	TE
STRATFORD-upon-AVON	...	1145
Warwick	...	1212
Leamington Spa	...	1217
Banbury	...	1236
Kings Sutton	...	...
Heyford	...	...
Tackley	...	1245
Oxford . . . . *arr*	...	1258

3 The train .... at Oxford
  at ....

→ For simple present after *if*, *when* etc, see pages 229 and 221.

test yourself   future

1 Write the contracted forms.

▶ I am going to   ..*I'm going to*......

1 I will   ....

2 She will   ....

3 It will not   ....

2 Make statements (+), questions (?) or negative sentences (–) with *going to*.

▶ John / start work / tomorrow + ..*John is going to start work tomorrow.*......................

1 Mary / phone / this evening ? ....

2 I / stop / smoking + ...

3 Peter / marry / his boss + ...

4 It / rain – ....

5 I / cook steak / this evening + ...

6 When / you / have a haircut ? ....

7 When / you and your wife / come and see us ? ....

....

3 Make statements, questions or negative sentences with *will*.

1 I / be / here next week + ...

2 We / have / enough money for a holiday – ....

3 Where / I find / the key ? ....

4 John / pass / his exams – ....

5 I think / the train / late + ...

6 all this money / change your life ? ....

4 Make statements, questions or negative sentences with the present progressive.

▶ When / you / leave ? ..*When are you leaving?*...

1 I / see / Andrew tonight + ...

2 How / you / travel to Ireland ? ....

3 I / use / the car tomorrow – ....

4 John and Sylvia / stay / with us tomorrow + ...

5 What time / the people from London / arrive ? ....

5 Circle the best form.

1 Ann *is going to* / *will* have a baby.

2 Perhaps I *will see* / *am seeing* you again one day.

3 'There's someone at the door.' '*I go.*' / '*I'll go.*'

4 I promise I *tell* / *I'll tell* you tomorrow.

5 I *will see* / *am seeing* the doctor tomorrow at 10.30.

6 Look – Joe *is going to* / *will* show us something interesting.

7 'I don't want to drive.' 'OK. *I'm going to* / *I'll* drive.'

8 'Shall we go out?' 'No, *I'll* / *I'm going to* wash my clothes.'

9 I think *I'm taking* / *I'll take* guitar lessons one day.

SECTION 4 past tenses

grammar summary

> SIMPLE PAST: *I worked, she worked, he didn't work*, etc
> PAST PROGRESSIVE (OR 'PAST CONTINUOUS'): *I was working, she was working, he wasn't working*, etc

English has **two 'past' tenses**.

- We use the **simple past** for **complete finished actions**. We often use it in **stories**.
  *I **wrote ten letters** yesterday.*   *A man **walked** into a police station and **asked** ...*
- We use the **past progressive** to talk about actions which were **unfinished** at a past time.
  *'What **were** you **doing** at 10.00 last night?' 'I **was writing** letters.'*

pre-test: which units do you need?

Try this small test. It will help you to decide which units you need. The answers are on page 283.

1 Which is correct – A, B or both?

- ▶ A I losed your address. Ⓑ I lost your address.
- ▶ Ⓐ I broke a window. Ⓑ John broke a window.
- 1 A The rain stoped. **B** The rain stopped.
- 2 A You never visitted me in hospital. **B** You never visited me in hospital.
- 3 A I didn't know the answer. **B** I didn't knew the answer.
- 4 A Where did everybody go? **B** Where everybody went?
- 5 A When John and his family did arrive? **B** When did John and his family arrive?
- 6 A Who said that? **B** Who did say that?
- 7 A At ten o'clock last night I read. **B** At ten o'clock last night I was reading.
- 8 A When I saw John, he was playing tennis. **B** When I saw John, he played tennis.
- 9 A When Ann came home, John was cooking supper. **B** When Ann came home, John cooked supper.

◀ About 6,000 years ago, somebody painted this picture on a cave wall in Namibia, south-west Africa.

About 2,200 years ago, Shi Huangdi completed the Great Wall of China. ▼

▲ Stonehenge, in southern England, is about 4,800 years old. Who built it? Nobody knows.

◀ About 1,200 years ago, Vikings from Scandinavia made this beautiful ship.

simple past: forms   *I worked.*   *I did not work.*

	REGULAR VERBS	AN IRREGULAR VERB
+	I/you/he/she/it/we/they **work**ed	I/you/he/she/it/we/they **went**
−	I/you/he/she/it/we/they **did not work**	I/you/he/she/it/we/they **did not go**
	Contraction: *didn't*	

HOW TO MAKE REGULAR SIMPLE PAST FORMS

- **most verbs:** + *-ed*   work → worked   help → helped   rain → rained
- **after** *-e*: + *-d*   hope → hoped   like → liked

❶ Write the simple past.

walk *walked*   arrive ....   change ....   cook ....

hate ....   live ....   pass ....   shave ....   watch ....

VERBS ENDING IN *-Y*

- **vowel** *(a, e, o)* + y → *-yed*   play → played   enjoy → enjoyed
- **consonant** *(d, l, r etc)* + y → *-ied*   try → tried   reply → replied

❷ Write the simple past.

stay ....   study ....   cry ....   annoy ....   carry ....

hurry ....   pray ....

DOUBLING *(stopped, planned, etc)*

- **one vowel + one consonant**
  → double consonant + *-ed*   stop → stopped (NOT ~~stoped~~)   plan → planned
- **two vowels:** don't double   seem → seemed   wait → waited (NOT ~~waitted~~)
- **two consonants:** don't double   want → wanted (NOT ~~wantted~~)   help → helped
- **only double in** STRESSED **syllables**   preFER → preferred   BUT WONder → wondered

❸ Write the simple past.

shop ....   rain ....   start ....   rob ....   slim ....

jump ....   shout ....   slip ....   fit ....   turn ....

VIsit ....   reGRET ....   deVElop ....   GALlop ....

OPen ....   ANswer ....   reFER ....

With **irregular** verbs, you have to learn the simple past forms one by one (see page 275).

go → **went**   see → **saw**   buy → **bought**   pay → **paid**

❹ Write as many of the simple past forms as you can. Check them on page 275, and learn the ones that you don't know.

become ....   begin ....   break ....   bring ....   catch ....   come ....

drink ....   eat ....   fall ....   feel ....   forget ....   get ....   give ....

hear ....   hold ....   keep ....   know ....   learn ....   leave ....   let ....

make ....   pay ....   put ....   read ....   say ....   shut ....   sit ....

speak ....   stand ....   take ....   tell ....   think ....   write ....

We make simple past negatives (−) with *did not/didn't* + infinitive (without *to*).

STATEMENT +	NEGATIVE −
He **cleaned** the car.	He *did not clean* the car. (NOT ~~He did not cleaned the car.~~)
He **started** early.	He *did not start* early. (NOT ~~He did not starts early.~~)
She **saw** you.	She *didn't see* you. (NOT ~~She didn't saw you.~~)
John **went** to Rome.	John *didn't go* to Rome.

5 Circle the correct form.

▶ I *break* / (broke) a cup yesterday.

▶ Ann did not (play) / *played* tennis this morning.

1 Harry *work* / *worked* last Sunday.

2 I didn't *know* / *knew* where I was.

3 I didn't *feel* / *felt* well last night.

4 Ann *come* / *came* to see us at the weekend.

5 I didn't *see* / *saw* Bill at the party.

6 Peter didn't *write* / *wrote* to me for a long time.

7 The train did not *arrive* / *arrives* on time.

8 Mary didn't *like* / *likes* / *liked* her teacher.

6 Make simple past negative sentences.

▶ I played hockey. (*football*) ...I didn't play football.....................................

1 We spoke Spanish together. (*Arabic*) ....

2 My uncle taught mathematics. (*science*) ....

3 Bill cooked the potatoes. (*the fish*) ....

4 I took my mother to the mountains. (*my father*) ....

5 We told our parents everything. (*the police*) ....

6 I wrote to my sister. (*my brother*) ....

7 I liked the party. (*the music*) ....

8 We knew her address. (*phone number*) ....

7 Complete the sentences with affirmative (+) or negative (−) verbs.

▶ I didn't break this window, but (*the other one* +) ...I broke the other one..........................

▶ I worked last week, but (*the week before* −) ...I didn't work the week before..................

1 He didn't change his trousers, but (*his shirt* +) ....

2 She answered the first question, but (*the others* −) ....

3 He phoned her, but (*go to her house* −) ....

4 I didn't bring any flowers, but (*some chocolates* +) ....

5 She didn't buy a coat, but (*a very nice dress* +) ....

6 I ate the vegetables, but (*the meat* −) ....

7 We kept the photos, but (*the letters* −) ....

8 They didn't speak English, but (*German* +) ....

9 My grandfather shaved on weekdays, but (*at weekends* −) ....

8 Write five things that you didn't do yesterday.

1 I didn't ....

2 ....

3 ....

4 ....

5 ....

simple past questions   *Did you pay?   What did she say?*

?	**did** I work? **did** you work? **did** he/she/it work? **did** we work? **did** they work?

We make simple past questions (?) with *did* + subject + infinitive (without *to*).

STATEMENT ➕	QUESTION ?
He cleaned the car.	*Did he clean the car?* (NOT ~~Did he cleaned the car?~~)
The class went to Rome.	*Where did the class go?* (NOT ~~Where did the class went?~~)

1 Circle the correct form.

▶ I *take /* (*took*) my father to Spain last week.

▶ Did you (*hear*) */ heard* me?

1 Did John *bring / brought* his wife with him?

2 When did Ann *start / starts* school?

3 I *see / saw* Eric in the supermarket yesterday.

4 Why did you *leave / left* your job?

5 Did Fred *speak / spoke* to you about Andy?

6 Where did that woman *keep / kept* all her money?

7 Derek *learn / learnt* English when he was young.

8 Sorry – I *forget / forgot* to buy milk.

2 Make simple past questions.

▶ John enjoyed the food, but (*the music* ?) *did he enjoy the music?* ....

1 She listened to everything, but (*remember it* ?) ....

2 You didn't pay Andy, but (*the others* ?) ....

3 You liked the book, but (*the film* ?) ....

4 He played football, but (*well* ?) ....

5 You gave them some help, but (*any money* ?) ....

3 Make simple past questions with *what*, *who* and *where*.

▶ Pete saw somebody. *Who did he see?* ....

1 John went somewhere. ....

2 Bill bought something. ....

3 Alice married somebody. ....

4 Mary broke something. ....

5 Mike stayed somewhere. ....

Be careful when questions have **long subjects** – the word order does not change.

Where did Ann	*stay?*
Where did Ann and her mother	*stay?*
Where did Ann and her mother and the children stay? (NOT ~~Where stayed Ann ...?~~ OR ~~Where did stay ...?~~)	

4 Make simple past questions.

▶ Jake and his wife went to Moscow. *Where did Jake and his wife go?* ....

1 Mrs Potter's two boys played football yesterday.
  When ....

2 All the people in the class felt tired.
  Why ....

3 The big man with the grey beard said something.
  What ....

4 The people who were sitting at the back of the bus started to sing.
  Why ....

questions without *did* *Who phoned? What happened?*

> When *who* and *what* are **subjects**, we make questions without *do/does/did*. Compare:
> '*Who*SUBJ phoned?' '*Sue*SUBJ phoned.' (NOT '*Who did phone?*')
> '*Who*OBJ **did** you see?' '*I saw Sue*OBJ.'
> '*What*SUBJ happened?' '*Something*SUBJ nice happened.' (NOT '*What did happen?*')
> '*What*OBJ **did** he say?' '*He said something*OBJ nice.'

1 Circle the correct form.

▶ Who (gave) / *did give* you that ring?
▶ What *wanted John?* / (*did John want?*)
1 Who *said* / *did say* that?
2 What *made* / *did make* that noise?

3 Who *asked she* / *did she* ask?
4 Who *told* / *did tell* you?
5 What *fell* / *did fall* out of your bag?
6 What *put you* / *did you put* in the soup?

2 Complete the questions.

▶ 'Somebody heard me.' 'Who heard you? .... '
▶ 'I heard somebody.' 'Who did you hear? .... '
1 'I phoned somebody.' 'Who .... '
2 'Somebody wrote to me.' 'Who .... '
3 'Something broke the window.' 'What .... '
4 'I broke something.' 'What .... '
5 'Mary played something.' 'What .... '
6 'Something fell off the table.' 'What .... '

3 GRAMMAR AND VOCABULARY: beginnings
Make sure you know all the words in the first box. Use a dictionary if necessary.
Then complete the questions, and see if you can put in the answers.

build   compose   direct   discover ✓   invent   paint

A Patty and Mildred Hill, in 1893.	**D** Alexander Fleming, in 1928. ✓
B Stone Age people, about 15,000 years ago.	**E** Probably the Chinese, about 1,000 years ago.
C Alfred Hitchcock, in 1963.	**F** King Khufu of Egypt, about 4,600 years ago.

▶ Who discovered ....
penicillin? D.

1 Who ....
the Great Pyramid? ...

2 Who ....
gunpowder? ...

3 Who ....
this picture? ...

4 Who ....
the film 'The Birds'? ...

Hap–py Birth–day to you,

5 Who ....
'Happy Birthday To You'? ...

→ For more about questions like these, see page 110.

simple past: use   *I left school in 1990.*

We often use the simple past to talk about when things happened.

I left school in 1990.   *I didn't see Ann yesterday.*   ***What time** did you arrive?*

PAST	1990		YESTERDAY		9?	10?	11?	NOW

We use the simple past, not the present perfect (*have seen*, etc) with finished time-expressions.

I saw that film last week. (NOT ~~I have seen that film last week.~~)
Did you pay William on Sunday? (NOT ~~Have you paid William on Sunday?~~)

1 **Put the beginnings and ends together, using the verbs in the box.**

die ✓   forget   learn   like   read   speak   stop

1 Shakespeare ....*died*............	A birthday on Monday. ...
2 I .... my girlfriend's	B in 1616. *1*
3 That's a really good book.	C so I .... my lessons last week. ...
4 When we were children	D I .... it last year. ...
5 I didn't .... my piano teacher	E we always .... French at home. ...
6 When did you	F to speak Spanish so well? ...

Note the **word order** with *ago*.

*I started this job **three years ago**.* (NOT ...~~ago three years.~~)   *It happened **a long time ago**.*

2 **How long ago was your last birthday? Ten days ago? Five weeks ago? Eight months ago?**
Write the answer, and answer the other questions.

1 my last birthday	3 last January ....
2 last Tuesday	4 my third birthday ....

We often use the **simple past** for things that happened **one after another**, for example in **stories**.

*He **parked** his car, **went** into the station and **bought** a ticket. Then he **had** a cup of coffee and ...*

3 **Put simple past verbs into the story.**

1–6:   come   hear   open   say   not see   stand
7–10:   give   hold   not read   take
11–15:   run   say   not speak   turn   write

He 1 .... outside her door for a long time. Then he 2 .... her
footsteps inside the house. She 3 .... the door and 4 .... out.
At first she 5 .... him, but then she 6 .... 'Oh, hello, Harold.'
He 7 .... a paper out of his pocket and 8 .... it to her.
She 9 .... it in one hand, but 10 .... it. 'Listen,'
he 11 .... She 12 .... 'I 13 .... you this letter
because –' She 14 .... back into the house. He 15 .... and walked
slowly down the street.

simple past: revision

	REGULAR VERBS	AN IRREGULAR VERB
➕	I/you/he/she/it/we/they **work**ed	I/you/he etc **went**
❓	**did** I/you/he etc **work**?	**did** I/you/he etc **go**?
➖	I/you/he/ etc **did not work**	I/you/he etc **did not go**
	Contraction: *didn't*	

❶ Complete the sentences with affirmative (➕) verbs, questions (❓) or negatives (➖).

▶ She didn't feel well last night, but (*OK this morning* ➕) .*she felt OK this morning.*......................

▶ 'I bought a new coat yesterday.' ('*shoes* ❓') .*'Did you buy shoes?'*......................

▶ We saw the Eiffel Tower, but (*see Notre Dame* ➖) ..*we didn't see Notre Dame.*..............

1 I didn't learn much French at school, but (*a lot of Latin* ➕) ....

2 I remembered to buy the bread, but (*the milk* ➖) ....

3 I spoke to Ann's father, but (*her mother* ➖) ....

4 'Peter didn't phone yesterday.' ('*this morning* ❓') ....

5 I didn't take the bus to London; (*the train* ➕) ....

6 I know you went to Singapore, but (*Malaysia* ❓) ....

7 The train stopped at Edinburgh, but (*Glasgow* ➖) ....

8 'Did the children see a film?' ('*two films* ➕') ....

9 'I ate your cake.' ('*my chocolates* ❓') ....

❷ Make simple past questions.

▶ Ann and her brother went to Beijing.   Where .*did Ann and her brother go?*..............................

1 Sarah and her baby came out of hospital this morning.   When ....
....

2 Peter's friends from the office gave him a bicycle.   Why ....
....

3 The small woman with long hair said something.   What ....
....

4 The children bought something.   What ....

5 Somebody left a bicycle in the garden.   Who ....

6 Something fell off the table.   What ....

7 Bill found a cat in his office.   Who ....

❸ Look at the picture, and complete the sentence correctly.

A did you remember
B did you remembered
C do you remembered
D did you to remember

'That reminds me, dear - .... the sandwiches?'

past progressive*   *What were you doing at 8.00?*

➕	*I **was** working you **were** working he/she/it **was** working we/they **were** working*
❓	***was** I working? **were** you working? **was** he/she/it working? **were** we/they working?*
➖	*I **was not** working you **were not** working he/she/it **was not** working etc*
	Contractions: *wasn't, weren't*

We make the **past progressive** with *was/were + ...ing*. (For spelling rules, see page 21.)
*At 8 o'clock **I was waiting** for a train. What **were** you **doing**?*

We use the **past progressive** to say what was (not) happening **around** (before, at and perhaps after) **a past time**.
*'What **were** you **doing** at 8.00? **Were** you **watching** TV?'* (NOT *What did you do ...?*)
*'At 8.00? No, I **wasn't watching** TV. I **was playing** cards.'* (NOT *I played ...*)

PAST	8.00	NOW

1 **What were the people doing yesterday evening?
Look at the pictures and complete the sentences
with words from the box.
Use past progressive verbs.**

cook supper dance drive home	
not watch TV play cards ✓	

▶ At 9.15 Sarah ....*was playing cards.*..............
1 At 10.30 Fred and Alice ....
2 At 8.20 Keith ....
3 At 7.50 Mary ....
4 At 11.00 Oliver ....

We make past progressive questions with *was/were + subject + ...ing*.

STATEMENT ➕:	*It was raining.*	*You were working.*	*All the children were singing.*
QUESTION ❓:	*Was it raining?*	*Were you working?*	*What were all the children singing?*

2 **Write questions.**

▶ 'At 10.00 I was reading.' (*a newsaper*) ...*'Were you reading a newspaper?'*.............................
▶ 'When I saw Peter he was eating.' (*what*) *'What was he eating?'*...................................
1 'When I went into Pat's office, she was writing.' (*letters*) ....
2 'At lunchtime Joe was shopping.' (*where*) ....
3 'At 8.30 Ann was cooking.' (*what*) ....
4 'When I arrived, all the children were crying.' (*why*) ....
5 'At midnight, Mary and Jack were driving.' (*to Scotland*) ....

3 **What were you doing at 10 o'clock last night?**

....

* Also called 'past continuous'

simple past or past progressive? *I walked / I was walking*

We use the simple past to talk about a complete action (long or short).
We use the past progressive for actions which were not complete at a past time.

Joe got up at 7.00 and worked from 9.00 to 4.00.

At 8.00, when Joe came home, I was reading.

| w o r k |
| PAST   7.00   9.00   4.00   **NOW** |

| PAST   8.00   **NOW** |

1 Simple past or past progressive?

- ▶ I (lived) / *was living* in France for eight years.
- ▶ Sue *lived* / (*was living*) in France when her uncle died.
- 1 At 6.15, when you phoned, I *had / was having* a shower.
- 2 We *watched / were watching* TV all evening.
- 3 Bill *watched / was watching* TV when Ann came in.
- 4 My father *worked / was working* hard all his life.
- 5 They got married while they *studied / were studying* at London University.
- 6 Yesterday we *drove / were driving* from Oxford to Edinburgh and back.
- 7 It was a nice evening, so she *walked / was walking* home from work.

We often use the past progressive and the simple past together, for example with *while*.
Past progressive: longer action or situation.
Simple past: complete shorter action that happened during the longer action.

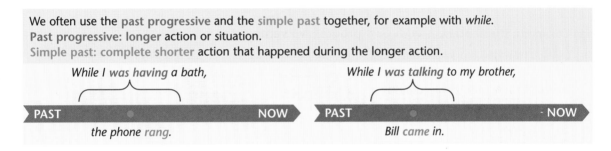

While I was having a bath,

| PAST   ●   **NOW** |

the phone rang.

While I was talking to my brother,

| PAST   ●   · **NOW** |

Bill came in.

2 Put in the simple past or the past progressive.

- ▶ While I ...was walking.... down the road, I ..saw................. Bill. (*walk; see*)
- 1 While I .... the newspaper, the cat .... on to the table. (*read; jump*)
- 2 Alan .... Helen while he .... in Morocco. (*meet; travel*)
- 3 Sally .... her leg while she .... (*break; ski*)
- 4 While I ...., somebody .... my car. (*shop; steal*)

We can use **when** in **different ways** with past tenses.

When Ann came home, John **was cooking** supper. (Ann came home **during** the cooking.)
When Ann came home, John **cooked** supper. (**First** Ann came home; **then** John cooked supper.)

3 Put in the correct tense (simple past or past progressive).

- ▶ When I went out, it ..was raining......... (*rain*)
- ▶ When Mary got home, she ..made.. tea. (*make*)
- 1 When I saw John, he .... (*shop*)
- 2 When John saw me, he .... (*stop*)
- 3 When we asked, they .... 'No'. (*say*)
- 4 When I walked in, they .... (*talk*)
- 5 When I dropped the glass, it .... (*break*)
- 6 When I phoned him, he .... (*work*)

test yourself   past tenses

❶ Write the simple past forms.

like ..*liked*....   bring ....   cry ....   feel ....   stay ....   stop ....

❷ Make simple past sentences.

▶ the train / stop / at every station ➕ ...*The train stopped at every station.*..........................

▶ when / my letter / arrive ❓ ...*When did my letter arrive?*...

▶ the doctor / remember / my name ➖ ...*The doctor didn't remember my name.*.................

1 what / all those people / want ❓ ....

2 all your brothers / send / birthday cards ❓ ....

3 the baby / eat / some toothpaste this morning ➕ ....

4 the teacher / answer / my question ➖ ....

❸ Make questions.

▶ John did something. (*what*) ...*What did John do?*...

1 Peter telephoned. (*why*) ....

2 Mary expected something. (*what*) ....

3 Something happened. (*what*) ....

4 Somebody took the car. (*who*) ....

❹ Complete the sentences with past progressive verbs.

▶ When I walked in (*children fight* ➕) ...*the children were fighting*...................

1 At 9.00 on Sunday (*we watch TV* ➕) ....

2 When I saw him he was holding a paper, but (*read* ➖) ....

3 When you heard them, (*they speak English* ❓) ....

❺ Put in simple past or past progressive verbs.

▶ They ...*told*.................... the police that they ...*were playing*............ cards at 10.00. (*tell; play*)

1 When I .... out of the house I took my umbrella because

   it .... (*go; rain*)

2 This morning I .... the newspaper before I went out. (*read*)

3 .... you .... the football match last night? (*watch*)

4 When I .... into the room they ....

   about clothes. (*walk; talk*)

5 At 8 o'clock yesterday morning I .... in the sea. (*swim*)

❻ Put verbs from the box (simple past or past progressive) into the text.

drive	open	pass	pull	run	shine ✓	sing	start	turn	wait

It was a beautiful morning. The sun ▶ ...*was shining*.......... and birds 1 ....
About five thousand people 2 .... in front of the Palace. At 10.00, the guards
3 .... the Palace gates, and the President's car 4 .... out and
5 .... left into Democracy Street. The crowds 6 .... to sing the
National Anthem. Then suddenly, just as the President's car 7 .... the Ritz Hotel,
a man 8 .... out in front of it and 9 .... a gun from his pocket.

◉ More difficult question

SECTION 5 perfect tenses

grammar summary

> (SIMPLE) PRESENT PERFECT: *I have worked, she has worked, he hasn't worked*, etc
> PRESENT PERFECT PROGRESSIVE: *I have been working, he has been working*, etc
> PAST PERFECT: *I had worked, she had worked*, etc

We use the **present perfect** to talk about **past** actions with some **importance now**.
I've written to John, so he knows what's happening.

We use the **present perfect progressive** mostly to say **how long** things have been going on **up to now**.
I have been writing letters since breakfast time.

When we are already talking about the past, we use the **past perfect** to talk about an **earlier time**.
Yesterday I found some old letters that Kate had written to me from Germany.

pre-test: which units do you need?

Try this small test. It will help you to decide which units you need. The answers are on page 283.

1 **Which is correct – A, B or both?**

▶ (A) Yesterday I broke a cup.   **B** Yesterday I broken a cup.
▶ (A) The postman has already come.   (B) The postman has just come.
1 **A** You haven't drank your tea.   **B** You haven't drunk your tea.
2 **A** Have Mary and her children arrived?   **B** Have arrived Mary and her children?
3 'What's the problem?'   **A** 'I lost my keys.'   **B** 'I have lost my keys.'
4 **A** When have you lost your keys?   **B** When did you lose your keys?
5 **A** I bought a mountain bike last week.   **B** I have bought a mountain bike last week.
6 **A** I went to London twice this week.   **B** I've been to London twice this week.
7 **A** Did you ever visit Dublin?   **B** Have you ever visited Dublin?
8 **A** Angela has gone to Ireland.   **B** Angela has been to Ireland.
9 **A** We know Julia since 1996.   **B** We have known Julia since 1996.
10 **A** I've had this sweater for years.   **B** I've had this sweater since years.
11 **A** I knew that I have seen her before.   **B** I knew that I had seen her before.
12 **A** Has Bill phoned yet?   **B** Has Bill phoned today?
13 **A** It's rained for hours.   **B** It's been raining for hours.

He's not here. He's gone to Paris.

Look what I've found!

Who's taken my coat?

I've made a cake. Would you like some?

Have you ever been to Canada?

Bill hasn't come in yet.

I've already read it.

She's been here since Monday.

I've been studying English for three years.

Nobody was there. They had all gone home.

present perfect: forms   *I have paid.   Has she forgotten?*

	REGULAR VERBS	AN IRREGULAR VERB
+	*I **have** worked you **have** worked he/she/it **has** worked* etc	*I **have** seen* etc
?	***have** I worked? **have** you worked? **has** he/she/it worked?* etc	***have** I seen?* etc
−	*I **have not** worked you **have not** worked* etc	*I **have not** seen* etc
	For contractions (*I've, he's, haven't*), see page 277.	

To make the **present perfect**, put *have/has* with the **past participle** (*worked, seen,* etc).
Regular past participles end in *-ed*, like simple past tenses (for spelling rules, see page 42).

*work → **work**ed   hope → **hop**ed   stop → **stopp**ed   try → **tri**ed*

With **irregular** verbs, the **past participle** is often **different** from the simple past tense.
You have to learn the forms one by one (see page 275).

*see → **seen**   speak → **spoken**   go → **gone**   buy → **bought***

1 Write as many of the irregular past participles as you can. Check them on page 275,
and learn the ones that you don't know.

become ...*become*...   begin ...*begun*...   break ....   bring ....
come ....   drink ....   eat ....   fall ....   forget ....
give ....   hear ....   hold ....   keep ....   know ....
learn ....   leave ....   let ....   make ....   pay ....
put ....   read ....   say ....   shut ....   sit ....
stand ....   take ....   tell ....   think ....   write ....

2 Write affirmative (+) or negative (−) present perfect sentences.

▶ I (*speak* +) to the boss   ...*I have spoken to the boss.*...
▶ they (*eat* −) anything   ...*They have not eaten anything.*...
1 she (*forget* +) my address   ....
2 I (*make* +) a mistake   ....
3 you (*shut* −) the door   ....
4 Alan (*work* +) very hard   ....
5 I (*hear* −) from Mary   ....
6 John (*learn* −) anything   ....
7 I (*break* +) a cup   ....
8 we (*remember* +) Ann's birthday   ....
9 The rain (*stop* +)   ....
10 I (*see* −) a newspaper today   ....

'Somewhere with no irregular verbs.'

We make present perfect questions with *have/has* + subject + past participle.

STATEMENT ➕ : *You have paid.* *The rain has stopped.* *The children have gone to Dublin.*

QUESTION ❓ : *Have you paid?* *Has the rain stopped?* *Where have the children gone?*

3 Make present perfect questions.

▶ John / leave ? ..Has John left?..........................
▶ why / Mary / go home ? ..Why has Mary gone home?.............
▶ where / you / put the keys ? ..Where have you put the keys?.............
1 we / pay ? ....
2 Bill / phone ? ....
3 you / hear the news ? ....
4 the dogs / come back ? ....
5 what / Barbara tell the police ? ....
6 why / Andy and Sarah / bring the children ? ....
7 what / you / say to Mike ? ....

Be careful when questions have **long subjects** – the word order does not change.

Has   Ann   *arrived?*
Have Ann and her mother   *arrived?*
Have Ann and her mother and father and the others arrived?
(NOT *Have arrived Ann and her mother and father and the others?*)

4 Make present perfect questions.

1 the Sunday newspapers / arrive ?
   ....
2 all those people / go home ?
   ....
3 the secretary from your father's office / telephone ?
   ....
4 where / the family in the flat upstairs / go ?
   ....
5 why / all the students in Mr Carter's class / give him presents ?
   ....

5 Look at the picture and put the words in the correct order.

seen	I	ball	sorry	your	haven't	no ✓

'No, ...,'

C Barsotti

finished actions: present perfect or simple past?

PRESENT PERFECT: WE THINK ABOUT THE PAST AND THE PRESENT TOGETHER
When we think about the **past and present together,** we normally use the present perfect.

I've written to John, so he knows what's happening now.
I've made a cake. Would you like some?
Look – I've bought a new dress.

FINISHED ACTION	PRESENT PERFECT	PRESENT
letter (yesterday) ——→	*I've written to John.* ←————	*John knows now.*
cake (this morning) ——→	*I've made a cake. Would you like some?* ←—	*I'm offering you some now.*
new dress (last Tuesday) —→	*Look – I've bought a new dress.* ←————	*I'm showing you now.*

SIMPLE PAST: WE THINK ONLY ABOUT THE PAST, NOT THE PRESENT
When we think **only about the past,** we most often use the simple past.

My grandfather wrote me a lot of letters.
  (He's dead now; I'm not thinking about the present.)
I made a cake for the children, but they didn't like it.
  (I'm not talking about the present.)
I bought a new dress for the party last Tuesday.
  (I'm thinking only about last Tuesday.)

1 **Read the sentences and the questions, and circle the correct answers.**

  ▶ Ann has bought a new coat. *Has she got the coat now?* (YES) / PERHAPS
  ▶ Grandma came to stay with us. *Is Grandma with us now?* YES / (PROBABLY NOT)
  1 I made a cup of tea. *Is there tea now?* YES / PROBABLY (NOT)
  2 Eric has made a cake. *Is there a cake now?* YES / PROBABLY NOT
  3 Jane went to France. *Is she there now?* YES / DON'T KNOW
  4 Alan has gone to Scotland. *Is he there now?* (YES) / DON'T KNOW
  5 Pat and Al started a business. *Is the business still running?* YES / DON'T KNOW
  6 Sue has started guitar lessons. *Is she taking lessons now?* YES / DON'T KNOW
  7 The cat has run away. *Is the cat at home now?* NO / DON'T KNOW
  8 The doctor sent Bill into hospital. *Is he there now?* YES / DON'T KNOW
  9 Pete lost his glasses. *Has he got his glasses now?* NO / DON'T KNOW
  10 Ann has cut all her hair off. *Has she got any hair now?* (NO) / DON'T KNOW

We don't normally use the present perfect with words for a finished time.
I've seen Ann. OR *I saw Ann yesterday.* BUT NOT ~~I've seen Ann yesterday.~~

2 What are the people saying? Look at the pictures and complete the sentences with verbs from the box. Use the present perfect.

break ✓	buy	cut	send	stop

▶ 'Somebody .has broken.......... the window.'
1 'John .... us a postcard.'
2 'I .... a hat.'
3 'I .... my finger.'
4 'The rain ....'

3 Put the beginnings and ends together, and put in the present perfect verbs.

break ✓	forget	leave	lose	see

1 Joe ..has broken........ his leg,	A 'Sorry. I know him, but I .... his name.' ...
2 Ann can't get into her house	B 'Yes, his girlfriend .... him.' ...
3 'He's looking unhappy.'	C because she .... her keys. ...
4 'Who's that?'	D 'No, I .... it.' ...
5 'That's a good film. Shall we go?'	E so he can't go skiing. 1

Note the difference between *gone* (*to*) and *been* (*to*) in present perfect sentences.

'*Where's John?*' '*He's* **gone to** *Paris.*' (He's there now.)   *Mary's* **gone** *swimming. She'll be back at 6.00.*
I've **been to** *Italy lots of times* (and come back) *but I've never* **been to** *Spain.*

4 Put in *been* or *gone*.

1 'Where's Ann?' 'She's .... shopping.'
2 Peter's .... shopping: the fridge is full.
3 Have you ever .... to China?
4 They're not here. They've all .... out.
5 I haven't .... to the cinema for weeks.
6 Joe's .... to live in Greece.

We use the **simple past**, not the present perfect, in stories (see page 46).

5 GRAMMAR AND VOCABULARY: housework
Put simple past verbs into the story. Use a dictionary if necessary.

Once upon a time there was a beautiful girl called Cinderella. Her two sisters made her do all the housework. Every day she (*get*) ▶ .got............ up early, she (*sweep*) ▶ ....swept........ the floors, she (*make*) 1 .... the beds, she (*polish*) 2 .... the furniture, she (*wash*) 3 .... and (*iron*) 4 .... the clothes, she (*wash up*) 5 .... all the dishes and (*put*) 6 .... them away. She (*tidy*) 7 .... all the rooms, and she (*do*) 8 .... hundreds of other jobs.

6 Now put present perfect verbs into the conversation.

SISTERS: Well, Cinderella, ▶ .have you done............ everything? 1 ....
              the floors? 2 .... the beds? 3 .... the furniture?
              4 .... the clothes? 5 .... them?
              6 .... the dishes? And 7 .... them away?
              8 .... all the rooms?
CINDERELLA: No, I 9 .... anything. I'm going to marry the Prince. Goodbye!

present perfect: news *We've found oil in the garden!*

We often use the **present perfect** to give **news**: to tell people about **new things** that have happened.

*The Prime Minister **has arrived** in Washington for talks with the President.*   *Ann **has bought** a new car.*
*A plane **has crashed** at Heathrow Airport.*   *Some new people **have moved** into the house next door.*

1 When John Wells arrived home from work, his family gave him a lot of news. Complete
the sentences.

| come   die   eat   find ✓   go   steal   win |

3 Dad! You .... a
lot of money in the lottery!

▶ Hello, dear. We ...'ve found.........
   oil in the garden!

4 Hi! Somebody ....
   the car!

1 Dad! The cat ....
   your supper!

5 Surprise! Grandma ....
   to stay for a month!

6 Daddy! The goldfish ....!

2 Hi, John. Mary ....
   to Australia with a soldier!

2 Here are some sentences from radio news broadcasts. Put in the correct verbs.

| arrive ✓   close   die   leave   marry   stop |

▶ England footballers ...have arrived..................... back in Britain after their match in Rome.
1 Singer Alex Haverty .... his long-time girlfriend Katy Bowen.
2 Charles Blackstock, Member of Parliament for East Chilbury, ...
   at the age of 57.
3 Once again, bad weather .... the tennis final at Wimbledon.
4 The Foreign Minister .... London for a two-day visit to Berlin.
5 Heavy snow .... hundreds of roads in Scotland.

We don't normally use the present perfect with words for a finished time.

We've found oil in the garden. BUT NOT ~~We've found oil in the garden yesterday.~~
A plane has crashed at Heathrow Airport. BUT NOT ~~A plane has crashed at 3.15 this afternoon.~~

3 Circle the words for a finished time.

(a few days ago)   always   this week   last week   never   now   then   today   yesterday   in 1990

4 Correct (✓) or not (✗)?

▶ My father has changed his job. ✓.
▶ Andy has gone to Scotland last week. ✗.
1 Look what Peter has given me yesterday! ...
2 I've seen a great programme last night. ...
3 I think everybody has arrived now. ...

4 Mary has written to me three weeks ago. ...
5 Sorry – I've forgotten your name. ...
6 I've forgotten Mike's birthday last Tuesday. ...
7 Everybody has gone home at 10 o'clock. ...
8 There's nobody here! What has happened ? ...

present perfect and simple past: news and details

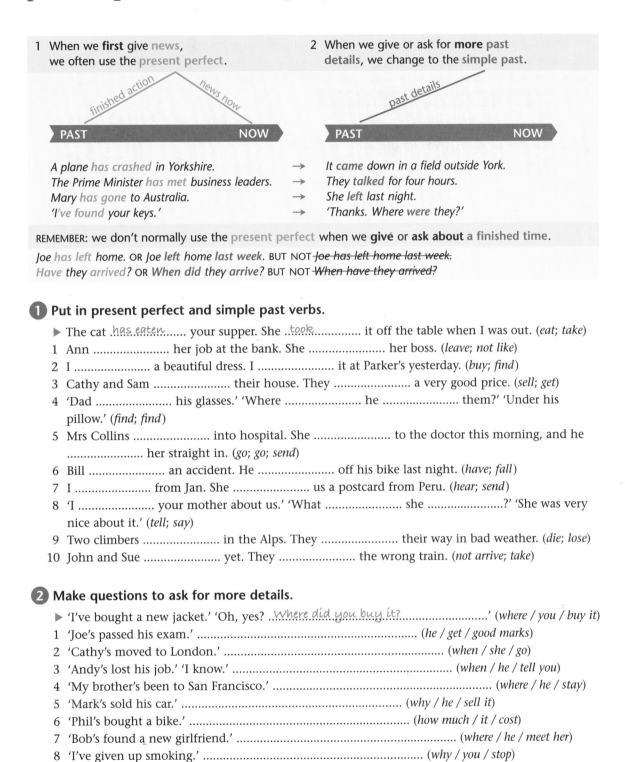

1 When we **first** give news, we often use the present perfect.

finished action | news now

PAST ▸ NOW ▸

A plane has crashed in Yorkshire.
The Prime Minister has met business leaders.
Mary has gone to Australia.
'I've found your keys.'

2 When we give or ask for **more** past details, we change to the simple past.

past details

PAST ▸ NOW ▸

→ It came down in a field outside York.
→ They talked for four hours.
→ She left last night.
→ 'Thanks. Where were they?'

REMEMBER: we don't normally use the present perfect when we **give** or **ask about** a finished time.

Joe has left home. OR Joe left home last week. BUT NOT ~~Joe has left home last week~~.
Have they arrived? OR When did they arrive? BUT NOT ~~When have they arrived?~~

1 Put in present perfect and simple past verbs.

▶ The cat .....has eaten...... your supper. She ....took.......... it off the table when I was out. (*eat; take*)

1 Ann .... her job at the bank. She .... her boss. (*leave; not like*)

2 I .... a beautiful dress. I .... it at Parker's yesterday. (*buy; find*)

3 Cathy and Sam .... their house. They .... a very good price. (*sell; get*)

4 'Dad .... his glasses.' 'Where .... he .... them?' 'Under his pillow.' (*find; find*)

5 Mrs Collins .... into hospital. She .... to the doctor this morning, and he .... her straight in. (*go; go; send*)

6 Bill .... an accident. He .... off his bike last night. (*have; fall*)

7 I .... from Jan. She .... us a postcard from Peru. (*hear; send*)

8 'I .... your mother about us.' 'What .... she ....?' 'She was very nice about it.' (*tell; say*)

9 Two climbers .... in the Alps. They .... their way in bad weather. (*die; lose*)

10 John and Sue .... yet. They .... the wrong train. (*not arrive; take*)

2 Make questions to ask for more details.

▶ 'I've bought a new jacket.' 'Oh, yes? .....Where did you buy it?....................' (*where / you / buy it*)

1 'Joe's passed his exam.' .... (*he / get / good marks*)

2 'Cathy's moved to London.' .... (*when / she / go*)

3 'Andy's lost his job.' 'I know.' .... (*when / he / tell you*)

4 'My brother's been to San Francisco.' .... (*where / he / stay*)

5 'Mark's sold his car.' .... (*why / he / sell it*)

6 'Phil's bought a bike.' .... (*how much / it / cost*)

7 'Bob's found a new girlfriend.' .... (*where / he / meet her*)

8 'I've given up smoking.' .... (*why / you / stop*)

up to now (1) *How much? How often?*

We often use the **present perfect** to say **how much** we have done **up to now.**

I've done six different jobs *since Christmas.*   *I've done* no work at all *so far* (= 'up to now') *today.*
Joe is saving €20 a week. He started 8 weeks ago. Up to now he's saved €160.

PAST ▶ €20 +€20 +€20 +€20 +€20 +€20 +€20 +€20 = €160 ▶ NOW

1 Look at the pictures and complete the sentences.

▶ I .have washed up thirty............. glasses this morning. (*wash up*)
1 I .... cups of coffee today. (*drink*)
2 I .... letters since breakfast. (*write*)
3 I .... books this week. (*read*)
4 Joe .... kilometres so far this year. (*drive*)
5 I .... in .... different houses in my life. (*live*)
6 That child .... chocolates already today. (*eat*)

We can use the **present perfect** to say **how often** things have happened **up to now.**

That's a wonderful film. I've seen it three times.   *Sally has only been to Ireland once.*
We've often wanted to come and see you.

We can use the **present perfect** to **ask** if things have happened **up to now**, or to say that they **haven't** happened **up to now.** We often use *ever* and *never* in these sentences.

*She's **never written** to me.*   *Has the boss phoned?*
*We **haven't been** to Scotland this year.*

*Have you **ever seen** a ghost?*

PAST ?EVER •• EVER •• EVER •• EVER? ▶ NOW

*I've **never seen** one.*

PAST NEVER ⊗ NEVER ⊗ NEVER ⊗ NEVER ▶ NOW

2 Make present perfect sentences.

▶ I / never/ read / Shakespeare   .I've never read Shakespeare...............
▶ I / break / my arm / three times   .I've broken my arm three times...........
▶ Peter / pay / for his lessons ?   .Has Peter paid for his lessons?.........
1 Joe / change / his job / twice this year   ....
2 you / ever / write / a poem ?   ....
3 I / never / climb / a mountain   ....
4 how often / she / ask / you for money ?   ....
5 I / often / try / to stop smoking   ....
6 Alex / phone / me / six times this week   ....
7 Charles / speak / to you / today ?   ....
8 Mary / not / tell / me / her new address   ....
9 you / ever / break / your leg ?   ....
10 We / not / play / football / this year   ....

➔ For word order with *often, never* etc, see page 204.

When we are talking about a **finished period of time**, we use the **simple past** to say how much **happened** or how often things **happened**. Compare:

*I **haven't done** any work **this afternoon**.* (Said in the afternoon.)
*I **didn't do** any work **this afternoon**.* (Said in the evening.)

3 **Read the sentences and circle the correct answers.**

▶ *'A lot of people came to see me in hospital.'* Was the speaker in hospital when he/she said this?
A Yes (**B**) No

1 *'I didn't enjoy school.'* Was the speaker at school when he/she said this?
A Yes **B** No

2 *'I've been to sleep three times during the lesson.'* When did the speaker say this?
A During the lesson **B** After the lesson

3 *'I didn't travel much in December.'* When did the speaker say this?
A In December **B** Later

4 *'My computer has crashed three times this morning.'* When did the speaker say this?
A In the morning **B** Later

5 *'Joseph Adams made many friends during his life.'* Was Joseph Adams alive when the speaker said this?
A Yes **B** No

4 **Circle the correct answers.**

▶ Our team *won* / (*has won*) two matches this year.
▶ Our team (*won*) / *has won* two matches last year.
1 *Did you ever go* / *Have you ever been* to Wales?
2 I *never read* / *have never read* any of his books.
3 Carol *stayed* / *has stayed* with us last week.
4 All my life I *wanted* / *have wanted* to fly a plane.
5 I haven't bought any clothes *this year* / *last year*.
6 I worked very hard *this week* / *last week*.

5 **Write three things that you didn't do yesterday, and three things that you have never done.**

1 I didn't .... yesterday.
2 ....
3 ....
4 I have never ....
5 ....
6 ....

6 GRAMMAR AND VOCABULARY: entertainments
Make sure you know all the words in the box. Use a dictionary if necessary.

| the cinema the circus the opera the theatre |
| a rock / jazz / classical music concert a rock / jazz festival |

How often have you been to the different kinds of entertainment? Write sentences. Example:

▶ *I've been to the circus once in my life. I've been to a rock concert twice this year.* ....
  I've never been to the opera. ....
  ....
  ....
  ....
  ....

already, yet and *just*

We often use the present perfect with *already* (= '*earlier than somebody expected*').
Note the word order: *already* comes after *have*.

'Newspaper?' 'No, thanks. I've *already* read it.'   You're late. We've *already* started.

1 **Complete the sentences with *already* and verbs from the box (present perfect).**

| cook   finish   get up   go ✓   leave   pay |

▶ 'Where's Pete?' 'He's *already gone* .... home.'   3 'Can you wake Helen?' 'She ....'
1 'Shall I pay?' 'No, I ....'   4 'Let's have fish.' 'I .... chicken.'
2 'What time's the train?' 'It ....'   5 'When's the film?' 'It ....'

We also often use the present perfect with *yet* (= '*up to now*') in questions and negatives.
Note the word order: *yet* usually comes at the end of a sentence.

'Have you spoken to John *yet*?' 'No, not *yet*. He hasn't come in *yet*.'

2 **Make questions (?) and negatives (−) with *yet*.**

▶ my sister / phone **?** *Has my sister phoned yet?* ....
▶ the postman / come **−** *The postman hasn't come yet.* ....
1 Bill / find a job **−** ....
2 you / finish that book **?** ....
3 I / start work **−** ....
4 you / have supper **?** ....

And we often use the present perfect with *just* (= '*a short time ago*'). *Just* comes after *have*.

I've *just* come back from Spain.   The rain has *just* stopped.

3 **Do these things, and then write sentences to say what you have just done.**

▶ (*touch your ear*) ...*I have just touched my ear.*...................................
1 (*look at the floor*) ....
2 (*think about your home*) ....
3 (*move your feet*) ....
4 (*put your hand on your head*) ....

4 **It is eight o'clock in the morning. Look at the table and say what Ann has (not) done. Use present perfect verbs with *already*, *yet* and *just*.**

▶ She *has just had a cup of coffee.*...........................
▶ She *hasn't got dressed yet.*...............................
▶ She *has already done a lot of work.*.......................
1 She .... letters.
2 She .... mother.
3 She .... kitchen.
4 She .... newspaper ....
5 She .... some toast.
6 She .... radio ....

have a cup of coffee	7.55	✓
get dressed	−	✓
do a lot of work	+	✓
write letters	three	
telephone mother	7.57	
clean kitchen	+	
read newspaper	−	
make toast	7.59	
listen to the radio	−	

up to now (2) *I've been here since Tuesday.*

We use the **present perfect**, not the present, to say **how long** something has continued **up to now**.

I've been here since Tuesday. (NOT ~~I am here since Tuesday.~~)
I've known John for ten years. (NOT ~~I know John for ten years.~~)

We can say how long with *since* or *for*.
We use *since* when we give the beginning of the time (for example *since Tuesday*).
We use *for* when we give the length of the time (for example *for three days*).

I've been here *since Tuesday.*	*I've been* here *for three days.* (NOT ... ~~since three days.~~)
I've known Mary *since 1980.*	*I've known* Mary *for a very long time.*
I've had this car *since April.*	*I've had* this car *for six months.*

1 Put in *since* or *for*.

1 .... six weeks
2 .... Sunday
3 1996
4 .... ten years
5 .... yesterday
6 .... breakfast time
7 .... a long time
8 .... five minutes
9 .... July
10 .... last week
11 .... a day
12 .... this morning

2 How long have you known people? Write sentences.

▶ *I've known my English teacher since September.* ....
1 I've known .... for ....
2 I've ....
3 ....
4 ....

3 How long have you had things? Write sentences.

1 *I've had these shoes for six months.* ....
2 I've had my .... since ....
3 ....
4 ....
5 ....

4 Make present perfect questions with *How long ...?*

▶ you / be / in this country   *How long have you been in this country?* ....
▶ Mary / have / her job   *How long has Mary had her job?* ....
1 you / know / Mike   ....
2 you / be / a student   ....
3 your brother / be / a doctor   ....
4 Andrew / have / that dog   ....
5 David and Elizabeth / be / together   ....

Be, know and *have* are **non-progressive** verbs (see page 28). With most other verbs, we use the **present perfect progressive** (see page 62) to say how long things have continued up to now.

How long **have** *you* **been waiting?**

up to now (3): present perfect progressive*

+	I have **been** working you **have been** working he/she/it **has been** working etc
?	**have** I **been** working? **have** you **been** working? **has** he/she/it **been** working? etc
−	I **have not been** working you **have not been** working etc
	For contractions (*I've, he's, haven't* etc), see page 277.

We make the **present perfect progressive** with *have/has been* + ...*ing*.

*We **have been living** here since April.   John's **been working** in the bank for three months.*

We use the **present perfect progressive** (with most verbs) to say **how long** things have been continuing **up to now**. (For *be, have* and *know*, see page 61.)

*I've **been learning** English for four years.   It's **been raining** all day.*
*Have you **been waiting** long?*

> *We've **been travelling** for six hours.*

PAST ▨▨ ▨▨ ▨▨ ▨▨ ▨▨ ▨▨   NOW ▨▨ ▨▨

❶ Make present perfect progressive sentences. Use *for* or *since* (see page 61).

▶ John started learning Chinese in February. Now it's July. (*for*)
  John has been learning Chinese for five months.

▶ It started raining on Sunday. It's still raining. (*since*)
  It's been raining since Sunday.

1 Mary started painting the house on Monday. Now it's Friday. (*for*)
  ....

2 We started driving at six o'clock. Now it's ten o'clock. (*for*)
  ....

3 Ann started working at Smiths in January. (*since*)
  ....

4 Joe started building boats when he was 20. Now he's 40. (*for*)
  ....

5 We started waiting for the bus at 8.30. (*since*)
  ....

6 Prices started going up last year. (*since*)
  ....

❷ Make questions beginning *How long ...?*

▶ you / study / maths   *How long have you been studying maths?*
1 Jane / talk / on the phone   ....
2 your brother / work / in Glasgow   ....
3 Eric / drive / buses   ....
4 that man / stand / outside   ....
5 you / play / the piano   ....

❸ How long have you been learning English?

  ....

* Also called 'present perfect continuous'

We **don't** use **present tenses** to say **how long** things have been going on.

They've been living here since 1998. (NOT They are living here since 1998.)
I've been learning English for three years. (NOT I'm learning English for 3 years.)

4 Correct (✓) or not (✗)?

▶ I'm waiting for her since this morning. ✗

▶ I'm still waiting for her now. ✓

▶ I've been waiting for her for four hours. ✓

1 We have been driving for about six hours. ...

2 How long are Ann and Peter working here? ...

3 Sue has been talking on the phone all day. ...

4 I have been sitting in this office since 9.00. ...

5 She's working here since 1998. ...

6 Are you studying hard these days? ...

We often use the **present perfect progressive** when we say **how** we have **been filling our time (up to now).**

We've been playing a lot of tennis in the last few weeks.
Sorry I haven't written to you – I've been travelling.
'You look tired.' 'Yes, I've been working in the garden.'

5 Look at the pictures and say what the people have been doing. Use the verbs in the box (present perfect progressive).

play	play	swim	teach	travel ✓	write

▶ She has been travelling. ....

1 .... the piano.

2 .... football.

3 ....

4 .... letters.

5 ....

present perfect or present perfect progressive?

We use the present perfect mostly for finished actions.
We use the **present perfect progressive** mostly for **unfinished** actions continuing up to now (often when we say how long).

PRESENT PERFECT: *I have written* etc | PRESENT PERFECT PROGRESSIVE: *I have been writing* etc

finished actions

Mike has learnt how to cook spaghetti.
I've written to John, so he knows everything.

PAST ✉ ☺ NOW

unfinished actions → now

Jane has been learning Greek since August.
The children have been writing letters all day.

PAST ✉ ✉ ✉ ✉ ✉ ✉ ✉ ✉ NOW

We use the present perfect to say **how much** or **how often**. Compare:
We've travelled to nine countries this year.   *We've been travelling all this year.*

❶ Circle the correct form.

▶ How long have you *learnt /* *been learning* the piano?
▶ Look! I have *bought /* *been buying* a coat.
1 It has *rained / been raining* since Tuesday.
2 John has *broken / been breaking* his leg.
3 He hasn't *told / been telling* me his address.

4 How long have we *driven / been driving* now?
5 Have you ever *read / been reading* this book?
6 Hello! I've *waited / been waiting* for you for hours!
7 How long have you *played / been playing* tennis?
8 How many games have you *played? / been playing?*

We don't use the **progressive** with *be, have* (meaning 'possess'), *know* and other non-progressive verbs (see page 28).

I've been here since Tuesday. (NOT ~~I've been being~~ ...)
How long have you had your car? (NOT ~~How long have you been having~~ ...?)
We've only known each other for two weeks. (NOT ~~We've only been knowing~~ ...)

❷ Put in the present perfect or present perfect progressive.

▶ I ..*have had*..... these shoes for a year. (*have*)
▶ How long *have*.. you ..*been waiting*...? (*wait*)
1 It .... all day. (*snow*)
2 We .... this dog for years. (*have*)

3 Ann .... all day. (*work*)
4 John .... ill this week. (*be*)
5 How long .... you ....
Andrew? (*know*)

We prefer the present perfect for very long, unchanging situations. Compare:
He's been standing there for hours.   *The castle has stood on this hill for 900 years.*

❸ Circle the best answer. (Both are correct, but one is more usual.)

1 We've *lived / been living* in London since January.
2 They've *lived / been living* in London all their lives.
3 My father has *worked / been working* here for 47 years.
4 I've *worked / been working* here for two weeks.

simple past and present perfect: summary

SIMPLE PAST: *I worked/wrote/drove etc*

finished actions

- **finished actions, no connection with present**
  My grandfather worked for a newspaper.   I drove back from York last night.
- **with words for a finished time, like *yesterday, in 1990, ago, then, when***
  I saw Ann yesterday. (NOT ~~I have seen Ann yesterday.~~)   *Bill phoned three days ago.*
  When did you stop smoking? (NOT ~~When have you stopped smoking?~~)
- **stories**
  A man walked into a café and sat down at a table. The waiter asked ...
- **details (time, place etc) of news**
  The cat has eaten your supper. She took it off the table.
  Bill has had an accident. He fell off his bicycle when he was going to work.

(SIMPLE) PRESENT PERFECT: *I have worked/written/driven etc*

A finished actions

- **thinking about past and present together**
  I've written to John, so he knows what's happening now.   Jane has found my glasses, so I can see again.
- **news**
  A plane has crashed at Heathrow airport.   The Prime Minister has left for Paris.
- **up to now: how much/many; how often**
  I've drunk six cups of coffee today.   My father has often tried to stop smoking.
- **up to now: things that haven't happened; questions; *ever* and *never***
  John hasn't phoned.   Has Peter said anything to you?   Have you ever seen a ghost? I've never seen one.
- ***already, yet* and *just***
  'Where's Peter?' 'He's already gone home.'   Has the postman come yet?   'Coffee?' 'I've just had some.'
- **NOT with words for a finished time**
  I saw Penny yesterday. She's getting married. (NOT ~~I have seen Penny yesterday.~~)

B unfinished actions continuing up to now
(only with *be, have, know* and other non-progressive verbs)

- **to say how long (often with *since* and *for*)**
  How long have you been in this country?   We've had our car for seven years.
  I've known Jake since 1996. (NOT ~~I know Jake since 1996.~~)

PRESENT PERFECT PROGRESSIVE: *I have been working/writing/driving etc*

unfinished actions continuing up to now (most verbs)

- **to say how long (often with *since* and *for*)**
  Have you been waiting long?   I've been learning English since last summer.
  We've been driving for three hours – it's time for a rest.
  DON'T use a present tense to say how long.
  I've been living here since January. (NOT ~~I'm living here since January.~~)
- **to say how we have been filling our time up to now**
  Sorry I haven't written. I've been travelling.   'You look tired.' 'Yes, I've been working in the garden.'
- **NOT USUALLY to talk about long, unchanging situations**
  The castle has stood on this hill for 900 years.

present perfect and simple past: revision exercises

1 **Put in the correct form (one word).**

▶ I <u>wrote</u>........ to my brother yesterday. (*write*)

▶ I have just <u>written</u>..... to my sister. (*write*)

1 The lessons .... last week. (*begin*)

2 You've .... three cups today. (*break*)

3 Why have you .... home early? (*come*)

4 Who has .... my coffee? (*drink*)

5 We .... too much last night. (*eat*)

6 John .... off his bicycle yesterday. (*fall*)

7 I'm sorry, I've .... your name. (*forget*)

8 I've .... my address to the police. (*give*)

9 We .... what they wanted. (*know*)

10 Somebody has .... my umbrella. (*take*)

2 **Make questions (?) or negatives (−).**

▶ She finished the book. − <u>She didn't finish the book.</u>

▶ The rain has stopped. ? <u>Has the rain stopped?</u>

1 All those people went home. ? ....

2 Peter has told us everything. − ....

3 The postman has been. ? ....

4 Pat has been working all day. ? ....

5 Eric and Angela bought a new house. − ....

6 Mary's boyfriend forgot her birthday. ? ....

3 **Make questions.**

▶ The letter arrived. (*when*) <u>When did the letter arrive?</u>

▶ Somebody told her. (*who*) <u>Who told her?</u>

1 Everybody has gone home. (*why*) ....

2 Ann's been learning Chinese. (*how long*) ....

3 George closed the door. (*why*) ....

4 The people in the big house have gone on holiday. (*where*)

....

5 The President and his family visited Russia. (*when*)

....

6 Jan's father and mother have been travelling in Scotland. (*how long*)

....

7 Something has happened. (*what*) ....

4 **Somebody has just said these sentences. Read the questions and circle the correct answers.**

▶ 'Joe has found a new girlfriend.' *Has he got the girlfriend now?* (YES) / PERHAPS

▶ 'Then a cat came into the house.' *Is the cat in the house now?* YES / (PROBABLY NOT)

1 'I've made coffee.' *Is there coffee now?* YES / PROBABLY NOT

2 'So Eric made soup.' *Is there soup now?* YES / DON'T KNOW

3 'And Bill has started Japanese lessons.' *Is he taking lessons now?* YES / DON'T KNOW

4 'Jill and Bob opened a driving school.' *Is the school still running?* YES / DON'T KNOW

5 '... because Pete lost his glasses.' *Has he got his glasses now?* NO / DON'T KNOW

6 'Alan has gone to America.' *Is he there now?* YES / DON'T KNOW

7 'We had a good time in Italy.' *Are they there now?* YES / NO

8 'July has been a good month for business.' *Is it still July?* YES / NO

5 Put in the verbs from the boxes (simple past or present perfect).

not be ✓	happen	have	lose	not pass	spend

Last year ▶ _was not_ a good year for Pete and Sonia. Pete 1 .... a car accident and 2 .... a month in hospital, Sonia 3 .... her job, the children 4 .... their school exams, and a lot of other bad things 5 ....

be	buy	change	have	open	pass

This year 6 .... much better. Pete 7 .... his job, and is making much more money. They 8 .... a new house. Sonia 9 .... a small restaurant, and it's going very well. They 10 .... a baby. And the other children 11 .... all their exams this time.

6 Put in the simple past, present perfect or present perfect progressive.

▶ 'Where's the car?' 'Bill _has taken_ it. He _needed_ it to go shopping.' (*take; need*)

▶ I _have bought_ tickets for the match. Do you want to come with me? (*buy*)

▶ My grandfather _went_ to school in Ireland. (*go*)

▶ How long _have_ you _been standing_ there? (*stand*)

1 'I .... my job.' 'Why?' 'I .... the hours.' (*change; not like*)

2 'Look – I .... some money.' 'Where .... you .... it?' (*find; find*)

3 Mike .... his new watch. (*already lose*)

4 The company .... a lot of money last year. (*lose*)

5 .... Andrew .... to the boss yet? (*speak*)

6 It .... since Sunday. (*snow*)

7 You can have the newspaper. I .... it. (*finish*)

8 I .... mathematics from 1996 to 1998. (*study*)

9 'You're looking happy.' 'Yes, I .... my exam.' (*pass*)

10 How long .... you .... Mary? (*know*)

11 .... you ever .... a poem? (*write*)

12 We .... for the electrician all day yesterday. (*wait*)

13 'Where's Robert?' 'He .... out.' (*just go*)

14 'Do you like skiing?' 'I .... it.' (*not try*)

15 That child .... chocolate all day. (*eat*)

7 Circle the correct answers.

I ▶ know / (have known) Adrian for a very long time – we 1 *are / have been* friends since our first day at school, thirty years 2 *ago / before / since*. He 3 *came / has come* round to see me last night to ask for my advice. His company 4 *did / has been doing* very well for the last few years, and they 5 *opened / have opened* several new offices. They 6 *just asked / have just asked* Adrian to move to Scotland, to run an office there. He 7 *didn't decide / hasn't decided* what to do yet. He doesn't really want to move: he 8 *never lived / has never lived* outside Manchester, and he 9 *bought / has bought* a new house there last year. But the new job would be interesting, and very well paid. We 10 *talked / have talked / have been talking* about it for a long time last night, but of course I couldn't tell him what to do.

past perfect   *It had already begun when we arrived.*

+	I **had** seen you **had** seen he/she/it **had** seen etc
?	**had** I seen? **had** you seen? **had** he/she/it seen? etc
-	I **had not** seen you **had not** seen he/she/it **had not** seen etc
	Contractions: I'd, you'd etc; hadn't

To make the **past perfect**, put **had** with the **past participle** (*seen, lost* etc).
(For irregular past participles, see page 275.)

She didn't phone Alan because she'd lost his number.   *It was a film that I hadn't seen before.*

1 Make past perfect sentences.

▶ I couldn't get in because I ..*had forgotten*.......... my keys. (*forget* +)

▶ Ann wasn't at home. Where .....*had*.................. she ....*gone*..............? (*go* ?)

▶ The telephone wasn't working because we ..*hadn't paid*........... the bill. (*pay* -)

1 The woman told me that she .... in China a few years before. (*work* +)

2 Everything in the garden was brown because it .... (*rain* -)

3 The bathroom was full of water. What ....? (*happen* ?)

4 I knew I .... that man somewhere before. (*see* +)

5 We were surprised to see Mark, because we .... his letter. (*get* -)

6 After three days the dogs came back home. Where ....? (*be* ?)

7 They gave me some money back because I .... too much. (*pay* +)

8 There was nothing in the fridge. I could see that Peter .... the shopping. (*do* -)

We use the past perfect when we are already talking about the past, and want to talk about an earlier past time.

Our train was late, and we ran to the cinema. But the film had already begun.

EARLIER PAST   PAST   NOW

I got out of the car and went into the school. It was empty. Everybody had gone home.
I was glad that I had caught the early bus.   Anna wondered if anyone had told Jim.
We couldn't understand why Sue hadn't locked the door.

2 Circle the correct answers.

▶ I (*didn't recognise*) / *hadn't recognised* Helen, because she *cut* / (*had cut*) her hair very short.

1 No one *understood* / *had understood* how the cat *got* / *had got* into the car.

2 Joe *didn't play* / *hadn't played* in the game on Saturday because he *hurt* / *had hurt* his arm.

3 When I *looked* / *had looked* in all my pockets for my keys, I *started* / *had started* to get very worried.

4 Liz *never travelled* / *had never travelled* by train before she *went* / *had gone* to Europe.

5 I *arrived* / *had arrived* at the shop at 5.30, but it *already closed* / *had already closed*.

6 I *didn't have* / *hadn't had* much money after I *paid* / *had paid* all my bills last week.

3 Put in the simple past or the past perfect.

▶ Bill ...*didn't tell*... anybody how he ...*had got*...... into the house. (*not tell; get*)

▶ Emma ..*went*.. to France last week. Before that, she ...*had*.. never ..*been*... outside Ireland. (*go; be*)

1 When their mother .... home, the children .... all the sweets. (*get; eat*)

2 Yesterday I .... a man who .... at school with my grandmother. (*meet; be*)

3 It .... to rain, and I .... that I .... my window. (*start; remember; not close*)

4 I .... a letter on my desk that I .... never .... (*find; open*)

5 I .... Bob I couldn't go to the theatre, but he .... already .... the tickets. (*tell; buy*)

We use the **past perfect after** *when* to show that something is **completely finished**.

*When I **had watered** all the flowers, I sat down and had a cool drink.*
*When Susan **had done** her shopping, she went to visit her sister.*

---

4 Make sentences using the past perfect after *when*.

▶ Jan finished her dinner. Then she sat down to watch TV.
When Jan had finished her dinner, she sat down to watch TV.

▶ David phoned his girlfriend. Before that he did his piano practice.
David phoned his girlfriend when he had done his piano practice.

1 George ate all the chocolate biscuits. Then he started eating the lemon ones.
....

2 I turned off the lights in the office. Then I locked the door and left.
....

3 I borrowed Karen's newspaper. Before that she read it.
....

4 Mark had a long hot shower. Before that he did his exercises.
....

5 Barry phoned his mother with the good news. Then he went to bed.
....

NOTHING HAD CHANGED

When I went back to my old school
nothing had changed.

Well, OK,
the place had closed down.

Doors stood wide,
windows had lost their glass,
ceilings had fallen.
Travellers had camped in the dining-room,
and left their names on the walls.

Wind blew
through the rooms where I had sat for so long
and learnt so little.
Rubbish piled up in the corners.

But nothing important had changed.

Evan Stabetsi

→ For the past perfect in reported speech, see page 247.

test yourself   perfect tenses

1 **Put in the past participles.**

go .*gone*....... break .... bring .... come .... drink .... eat ....
forget .... give .... leave .... make .... stand .... stay ....
stop .... take .... think .... try ....

2 **Make affirmative (⊞) sentences, questions (❓) or negatives (⊟).**

▶ She has not studied French. (*Russian* ⊞) .*She has studied Russian.*....................................
▶ It hasn't snowed today. (*rained* ❓) .*Has it rained?*...
▶ They've been to Greece. (*Turkey* ⊟) .*They haven't been to Turkey.*..................................
1 We've been swimming. (*walking* ⊟) ....
2 They haven't written. (*phoned* ⊞) ....
3 I had seen her before. (*spoken to* ⊟) ....
4 She hasn't been to New York. (*Chicago* ❓) ....
5 He hasn't bought a motorbike. (*car* ⊞) ....
6 She's been studying German. (*Italian* ❓) ....

3 **Circle the correct answers.**

▶ Have you *saw* / *seen* this film before?
1 Our football team *lost* / *has lost* all its games this year. It *lost* / *has lost* all its games last year too.
2 *Did you ever drive* / *Have you ever driven* a bus?
3 My brother speaks good English, but he *has never had* / *never had* lessons.
4 *Did you see* / *Have you seen* Paul yesterday?' 'No, but he *just phoned* / *has just phoned*.'
5 Have you done the shopping *yet* / *yesterday* ?
6 I started this job *for eight weeks* / *eight weeks ago* / *ago eight weeks*.
7 *I'm* / *I've been* in this school *for* / *since* five years.
8 'What time does the lesson start?' '*It's already started*.' / '*It already started*.'

4 **Circle the correct answers.**

1 *We know* / *We've known* / *We've been knowing* John and Andy *for* / *since* years.
2 *I work* / *I'm working* / *I've been working* here since last summer.
3 'Good news! John *passed* / *has passed* his exam.' '*Has he got* / *Did he get* good marks?'
4 'Mary *went* / *has gone* to London.' 'When *did she leave?* / *has she left?*'
5 This house has *stood* / *been standing* here for 500 years.

5 **Put in the simple past or past perfect.**

1 When I .... him, I .... that
  I .... him before. (*see; know; meet*)
2 He .... enough money for food because he ....
  so many clothes. (*not have; buy*)
3 The meeting .... when I .... (*already start; arrive*)
4 The car .... down because I ....
  to put oil in. (*break; forget*)
5 I .... Mary for the first time thirty years ago. (*meet*)

◉ More difficult questions

SECTION 6 modal verbs

grammar summary

MODAL VERBS: *can   could   may   might   shall   should   will   would   must   (ought to)*
PAST AND FUTURE OF MODALS: *be able to   have to*
VERBS THAT ARE LIKE MODALS: *used to   had better   needn't*

The **modal verbs** are a special group of **auxiliary verbs**. We use them **before other verbs** to express certain meanings – for example **permission, ability, possibility, certainty.**

Modals have **different grammar** from other verbs. For example, they have **no -s** on the third person singular: we say *he can*, NOT ~~he cans~~.

Used to, had better and *needn't* are similar to modals in some ways, and they are included in this section. A less common verb – *ought to* – is not practised here. For *will*, see pages 35–37.

pre-test: which units do you need?

Try this small test. It will help you to decide which units you need. The answers are on page 283.

1 Correct (✓) or not (✗)?

▶ She cans play the piano. ✗

1 Can you to sing? ... ✓
2 I may not be here this evening. ...
3 You don't must open that door. ...
4 Must you go? ...
5 Last year I must work on Saturdays. ...
6 When do you have to leave? ...
7 You will have to get the 10.15 train. ...
8 You have better go home now. ...
9 We mustn't pay now, but we can if we want to. ...
10 Where did you use to live? ...
11 I use to play a lot of tennis. ...
12 Would you like coming out with us? ...
13 Shall I make coffee? ...
14 I should have told you everything. ...

2 Complete the sentences. (More than one answer may be possible.)

1 .... I use your phone?
2 .... you lend me a pen?
3 She has very good clothes. She .... have a lot of money.
4 She doesn't answer the phone. She .... be at home.
5 People .... smile more often.
6 One day, people .... to go to the moon on holiday.

Are TV chefs creating a nation that **can't cook?**

BBC Good Food

modal verbs: introduction *can, must, should* etc

can, could	may, might	shall, should	will, would	must

The **modal verbs** are a special group of **auxiliary verbs**.
They are **different** from most other verbs **in four ways**.

+ INFINITIVES WITHOUT *TO*

After **modals**, we use infinitives without *to*. (After **other** verbs, we use infinitives with *to*.)

Can *I use your phone?* (NOT ~~Can I to use~~ ...)   *Joe **can't** swim.*   *I **may** be out tonight.*
BUT *I **want** to use her phone.*   *I'd **like** to go home.*   *Joe **seems** to have a cold.*

1 Circle the correct answers.

▶ Can you *play* / *to play* the guitar?   3 Could you *pass* / *to pass* the orange juice?
▶ I don't want *play* / *to play* football today.   4 We hope *get* / *to get* a bigger flat soon.
1 Ann seems *be* / *to be* very tired.   5 Chris may *be* / *to be* here at the weekend.
2 Peter hasn't phoned. He must *be* / *to be* away.   6 I want *speak* / *to speak* to the manager.

NO -*S*

Modal verbs have no -*s* on the third person singular (*he/she/it* form). (**Other** verbs have -*s*.)

*John **can** speak Korean.* (NOT ~~John cans~~ ...)   *Barbara **may** be late.*   *This **must** be your coat.*
BUT *John **knows** my father.*   *Ann **seems** to be ill.*   *The cat **wants** to go out.*

2 Add -*s* or nothing (-).

▶ Ann play.*s* tennis.   ▶ Bill can.-. swim.   1 Our cat like... fish.   2 It may... rain.
3 She must... pay now.   4 Harry work... in London.   5 Sue should... phone her mother.
6 The train seem... to be late.   7 Bill might... come and see us.   8 Joe want... to go home.

NO *DO*

We make **modal questions** (❓) and **negatives** (➖) without *do*. (Other verbs have *do*.)

Can you help me? (NOT ~~Do you can help me?~~)   *You **must** not tell Philip.*
Do you know my friend Jeremy?   *Sally **doesn't** cook very well.*

3 Make questions (❓) or negatives (➖).
(Negatives in this exercise: *cannot/can't; must not/mustn't; may not*)

▶ Ann can't speak Russian. (*Chinese* ❓) ...*Can she speak Chinese?*.......
▶ Mary must wash her clothes. (*do it now* ➖) ...*She mustn't do it now*.......
1 Mike can't swim. (*ski* ❓) ....
2 John can play football. (*poker* ➖) ....
3 Maria must play the piano. (*sing* ➖) ....
4 Robert may go to Italy. (*go this week* ➖) ....
5 Ann must work on Saturday. (*Sunday* ❓) ....

NO INFINITIVES OR PARTICIPLES

Modal verbs have no infinitives or participles: ~~to can, maying, musted~~.
Instead, we use **other verbs**: *can* → ***be able to*** (see page 79); *must* → ***have to*** (see page 76).

must *You must be home by eleven.* *Must you go?*

➕	I **must** go	you **must** go	he/she/it **must** go etc	(NOT ~~I must to go~~, NOT ~~he/she/it musts go~~)
❓	**must** I go?	**must** you go?	**must** he/she/it go? etc	(NOT ~~do I must go?~~)

In **affirmative** (➕) sentences, we use *must* when we mean: '**This is necessary.**'
*I **must get up** early tomorrow.   You **must fill in** this form.* (NOT ~~You must to fill~~ ...)

❶ Complete the sentences with *must* and verbs from the box.

be ✓	go	hurry	pay	speak	stop	study	write

▶ FATHER: You ...*must be*... home by eleven.
1 TEACHER: You .... in ink.
2 FRIEND: We .... – we're late.
3 DOCTOR: You .... smoking.

4 TAX OFFICE: You .... the tax now.
5 TEACHER: Your daughter .... harder.
6 BOSS: You .... politely on the phone.
7 MOTHER: That child .... to bed now.

In **affirmative** (➕) sentences, we also use *must* when we mean: '**This is a very good idea.**'
*You **must visit** us while we're in Paris.   Pat and Jan are so nice – we **must see** them again.*

❷ Put the beginnings and ends together. Add *must* and verbs from the box.

go	have	phone	read ✓	see

1 Smith's latest book is her best, I think.	A I .... her tonight. ...
2 I haven't heard from Annie for ages.	B You ...*must read*... it. Shall I lend it to you? *1*
3 The woods are full of flowers.	C My mother made it; you .... a piece. ...
4 This cake is delicious.	D You .... it. It's a cinema classic. ...
5 'Velocity' is a wonderful film.	E We .... for a walk this weekend. ...

In **questions** (❓), we use *must* when we mean: '**Is this really necessary?**'
To make **questions** with *must*, we put *must* before the **subject**
*Must we **tell** the police when we change addresses?   Must you **talk** so loud?   Must you **go**?*

❸ A new student is asking some questions about next week's exam. Complete the questions. Use *Must I ...?* and verbs from the box.

answer	bring ✓	come	pay	sit	stay

▶ ...*Must I bring*... any paper?
1 .... any money?
2 .... to this room?

3 .... in my usual place?
4 .... every question?
5 .... if I finish early?

Have to (see pages 75–76) means the same as **must**.
Must has no past (~~musted~~) or infinitive (~~to must~~). Instead, we use **had to** and (to) **have to** (see page 76).

→ For another use of *must*, see page 82.

mustn't and *needn't*   *We mustn't wake the baby.*

▬	I *must not* go	you *must not* go	he/she/it *must not* go etc
▬	I *need not* go	you *need not* go	he/she it *need not* go etc
	Contractions: *mustn't; needn't*		

Must has **two negatives** (▬): we use *mustn't* when we mean '*Don't do this.*'
we use *needn't* when we mean '*This isn't necessary.*'

You *mustn't* **smoke** here.   You *mustn't* **take** pictures here.   We *mustn't* **wake** the baby.
You *needn't* **pay** now; you can pay when the work is finished.   We *needn't* **hurry** – we're early.

❶ **Complete the sentences with *mustn't* and the verbs in the box.**

light ✓   make   smoke   use   wash

At a campsite: ▶ .You mustn't light....... fires.
1 .... dishes in the showers.
2 .... noise after 10 pm.
On a plane: 3 .... a mobile phone.
4 .... in the toilets.

❷ **Put the beginnings and ends together. Add *needn't* and verbs from the box.**

drive   give   make   make   wake ✓

1 You ..needn't wake......................... me up;	A I can walk. ...
2 You .... breakfast for me;	B I'll buy *The Times* at the station. ...
3 You .... lunch for me;	C I'll have lunch in the canteen. ...
4 You .... me to the station;	D I'll just have coffee. ...
5 You .... me your newspaper;	E I've got an alarm clock. 1.

❸ ***Mustn't* or *needn't*?**

▶ We ...mustn't............. hurry – we'll get too tired.
▶ We ...needn't............. hurry – we're early.
1 You .... stay up late – you've got school tomorrow morning.
2 You .... stay up late to wash the dishes – I'll wash them in the morning.
3 We .... leave the door open – the rain will come in.
4 We .... leave the door open – Peter has got a key.
5 You .... write to John about this – I've already written to him.
6 You .... write to John about this – if you do, he'll tell everybody.
7 You .... drive so fast – the police will stop you.
8 You .... drive so fast – we've got a lot of time.
9 I .... look in the cupboard again – I've looked in there twice.
10 I .... look in the cupboard – Ann has put my birthday present in there.

Affirmative (➕) *need* is not a modal verb.

He **needs to** go now. (NOT ~~He need go now.~~)

Don't/doesn't have to (see page 75) means the same as *needn't*.

have to   *Do you have to teach small children?*

Have to is not a modal verb, but we use *have to* like *must* (see page 73), and we use *don't have to* like *needn't* (see page 74).

+	I/you/we/they **have to** go he/she/it *has* **to** go
?	**do** I/you/we/they **have to** go? *does* he/she/it **have to** go?
-	I/you/we/they **do not have to** go he/she/it *does* **not have to** go
Contractions: *don't; doesn't*	

We use **have to** when we want to say '**This is necessary**' / '**Is this necessary?**' (like *must*).

You **have to drive** on the left in Britain.   I **have to go** to New York for a meeting every month.
My sister **has to work** on Saturdays.   **Do** your children **have to take** lunches to school?

❶ Complete the sentences with *has to* and expressions from the box.

be ✓   be   be   carry   have   wear

▶ An accountant .has.to.be. good with numbers.   3 A politician .... good at speaking.
1 A cook .... very clean hands.   4 A builder .... heavy things.
2 An army officer .... a uniform.   5 A secretary .... good at spelling.

❷ Put the beginnings and ends together. Add *Do/Does ... have to*.

1 'I'm a swimming teacher.'	A '................................. finish it today?' ...
2 'Here is some work for you and Ian.'	B '................................. speak Spanish?' ...
3 'I want you to go to your aunt's party.'	C '................................. tell you now?' ...
4 'Jo and Alec work for a Mexican firm.'	D '............................ stay until the end?' ...
5 'When would you like your holiday?'	E '.Do.you.have.to............. teach small children?' 1

We use **don't/doesn't have to** when we want to say '**this is not necessary**' (like *needn't*).

You **don't have to phone** Jean; she knows already. (NOT ~~You mustn't phone~~ ...: see page 74)

❸ Complete the sentences with *don't/doesn't have to* and verbs from the box.

arrive   close   give ✓   go   post   speak   water

▶ You .don't.have.to.give..................... any food to the fish; they only eat in the morning.
1 You .... the windows; I'll close them later.
2 Emma .... the flowers; I watered them earlier.
3 Alice .... those letters; Cathy's going to the post office.
4 You .... by train; Marianne will drive you.
5 You .... French; everyone here understands English.
6 Oliver .... early; he can come at 10.

NOTE: We normally use **have to**, not **must**, when we talk about **rules** and **laws**.
You **have to drive** on the left in England. (NOT USUALLY ~~You must drive on the left~~ ...)

had to, will have to   *I didn't have to pay.*

	PAST: *HAD TO*	FUTURE: *WILL HAVE TO*
✚	*I/you/he etc **had to** go*	*I/you/he etc **will have to** go*
❓	*did I/you/he etc **have to** go?*	*will I/you/he etc **have to** go?*
➖	*I/you/he etc **did not have to** go*	*I/you/he etc **will not have to** go*
	Contractions: *I'll, you'll etc; didn't; won't*	

We use **had to** for the **past** and **will have to** for the future of **must** and **have to** (see pages 73–75).
(**Had to** and **will have to** are not modals.)

*My mum **had to leave** school at sixteen.*   ***Did** you **have to** tell Jo?*   *I **didn't have to** pay.*
*Alice **will have to start** school next September.*   *Al **won't have to** come.*

❶ Write about the things that John had to do (✚), and didn't have to do (➖), at school.

▶ (*learn French* ✚) .He had to learn French.
▶ (*play tennis* ➖) .He didn't have to play tennis.
1 (*learn Russian* ➖) ....
2 (*learn maths* ✚) ....
3 (*learn music* ➖) ....
4 (*play football* ✚) ....
5 (*write poems* ➖) ....
6 (*write stories* ✚) ....

❷ Make questions with *Did ... have to ...?*

▶ you / learn French at school Did you have to learn French at school?
▶ Annie / work last Saturday Did Annie have to work last Saturday?
1 John / pay for his lessons ....
2 Mary / take an exam last year ....
3 Joe and Sue / wait a long time for a train ....
4 you / show your passport at the airport ....
5 the children / walk home ....
6 Peter / cook supper ....

❸ Complete the sentences. Use *'ll have to, will ... have to ...?* or *won't have to* with the verbs in the box.

ask   get   get   go   learn   play   study ✓   work

▶ Cara wants to be a doctor. She .'ll have to study... hard.
1 Ann needs a new passport. She .... a form from the post office.
2 Bob's got a new car, so he .... to work by bus.
3 'I've got a job with a Spanish company.' '........................ you .... Spanish?'
4 'John wants to be a pianist.' 'He .... for hours every day.'
5 'Can I go home early?' 'I don't know. You .... the boss.'
6 I'm working next Sunday, but I .... on Saturday.
7 'Liz wants to go to the US.' '........................ she .... a visa?'

should   *What should I tell John?*

➕	I **should** go you **should** go he/she/it **should** go etc (NOT ~~I should to go~~)
❓	**should** I go? **should** you go? **should** he/she/it go? etc (NOT ~~do I should go?~~)
➖	I **should not** go you **should not** go he/she/it **should not** go etc
	Contractions: *shouldn't*

We use *should* to talk about a **good thing to do**.

*You **should be** more careful.   **Should** I **wear** a tie?   People **shouldn't drive** fast in the rain.*

1 Complete the sentences with *should* and *shouldn't* and the verbs *in italics*.

▶ If someone doesn't speak your language very well, you ..*shouldn't speak*............... fast; you
..*should speak*.................... slowly and carefully. (*speak; speak*)

1 If you need a pen, you ...., 'Give me that pen'; you
...., 'Could I borrow your pen, please?' (*say; say*)

2 If people want to live until they're very old, they .... a lot of fruit and
vegetables; they .... a lot of cakes and chocolate. (*eat; eat*)

3 In a big city, you .... careful with your money; you
.... your bag on a chair in a restaurant. (*be; leave*)

4 When you're driving, you .... for hours and hours without stopping; you
.... and walk round every two hours. (*drive; stop*)

5 When people are travelling by plane, they .... lots of water; they
.... uncomfortable shoes. (*drink; wear*)

2 Make questions with *should I* and the question words and verbs from the box.

QUESTION WORDS:	What ✓	What	What time	Where	Where	Who
VERBS:	arrive	put	phone	sit	tell ✓	wear

▶ '..*What should I tell*............................... John?' 'Tell him I left early.'

1 .... 'At about 7.00.'

2 '... first?' 'Mr Andrews.'

3 .... 'Your blue dress.'

4 .... 'At the end of the table.'

5 '... this box?' 'On the shelf.'

We use *must* to talk about what's **necessary**, and we use *should* to talk about what's **good**

*I **must** get a new passport: I'm travelling next month.   I **should** eat more fruit, but I don't like fruit.*

3 Put in *should* or *must*.

▶ 'Do I look all right?' 'You ..*should*......... get a haircut.'

1 I can't leave; I .... finish this work today.

2 I .... take more exercise, but I'm too busy.

3 You .... n't smoke near babies.

4 The sign says we .... n't smoke here.

5 What .... I do to get a visa?

6 You .... be over 16 to buy cigarettes here.

7 'What music .... I play?' 'I'd like Mozart.'

> **Letters to a magazine**
>
> Should I give up smoking?
> Should I marry Bob?
> Should I move to Woking?
> Should I change my job?
> Should I dye my hair green?
> Should I tell his wife?
> Should I ask a magazine
> How to live my life?
>
> *Lewis Mancha*

can and *could* *He can play the piano. She couldn't write.*

+	*I* **can** go *you* **can** go *he/she/it* **can** go etc	(NOT ~~I can to go,~~ NOT ~~he cans go~~)
?	**can** *I* go? **can** *you* go? **can** *he'/she/ it* go? etc	(NOT ~~do I can go?~~)
–	*I* **cannot** go *you* **cannot** go *he/she/it* **cannot** go etc	(NOT ~~I can not go~~)
	Contraction: *can't*	

I **can** speak Italian.   *I* **can** read Spanish, but I **can't** speak it.   **Can** *you* sing?

1 Write sentences with *but* about what David can and can't do.

▶ (*speak*) He can speak German, but he can't speak Hindi. **4**
1 (*play*) .... baseball.
2 (*play*) .... violin.
3 (*remember*) ....
4 (*eat*) .... cherries.

To make questions (**?**) with *can*, we put *can* before the **subject**.

Can Bill swim?   **Can Alice** speak Chinese?   When *can* I pay?

2 Make questions with *can*.

▶ 'Little Mary is ten months old now.' (*walk*) ...'Can she walk?'................................
▶ 'John is starting the violin.' (*what / play*) ......'What can he play?'..............................
1 'My brother wants to work in a restaurant.' (*cook*) ....
2 'My daughter's going to Spain.' (*speak Spanish*) ....
3 'Bill and Lisa want to buy a house.' (*how much / pay*) ....
4 'Can I help in any way?' (*drive a bus*) ....
5 'Some colours look bad on me.' (*wear red*) ....
6 'Ann and I have got a lovely hotel room.' (*see the sea*) ....
7 'I want to learn the piano.' (*read music*) ....
8 'My brother is looking for a job.' (*what / do*) ....

3 Write three things that you can do, and three things that you can't do.

1 I can ....
2 I can't ....

> *Dance while you can.*
> (W H Auden)

> You can do what you want, if you don't think you can't.
> So don't think you can't; think you can.
> *(Charles Inge on the philosophy of Coué)*

+	I **could** go	you **could** go	he/she/it **could** go etc	(NOT ~~I could to go~~)
?	**could** I go?	**could** you go?	**could** he/she/it go? etc	(NOT ~~did I could go?~~)
–	I **could not** go	you **could not** go	he/she/it **could not** go etc	

Contraction: *couldn't*

To talk about the **past**, we use *could*.

I **could** talk when I was thirteen months old.	I **could** walk when I was ten months old.
I **couldn't** understand the teacher yesterday.	How **could** you say that to me?

4 **What could you do at six years old? Look at the words in the box. Use a dictionary if necessary. Then make some sentences with I could or I couldn't.**

climb trees	dance	fight	play chess	play the piano	read	run fast	sing	write

....
....
....

5 **Use *could* with the verbs *in italics* to complete the story.**

My brother's baby was unusual. When she was three months old she (*say*) ▶ .*could say*......... 15 words. When she was a year old she (*name*) 1 .... all the colours, and she (*count*) 2 .... to 100. When she was three she (*read*) 3 .... easy books. She (*not write*) 4 ...., but she (*tell*) 5 .... wonderful stories, and she (*remember*) 6 .... every story that she heard. She (*not walk*) 7 .... until she was nearly two, though.

Can does **not** have an **infinitive** (~~to can~~) or a **past participle** (~~I have could~~).
Instead, we use (**to**) *be able* and *been able* + infinitive with *to*. (These are not modals.)

I want **to be able to** speak German. (NOT ...~~to can speak German.~~)
I'll **be able to** drive soon.   I have never **been able to** play ball games.

6 **Put in *to be able to* or *been able to*.**

1 I hope .... give you an answer soon.
2 I've never .... understand your mother.
3 Sue has always .... do work that she liked.
4 Our cat would like .... open the fridge door.

7 **Complete the sentences with *will be able to* and verbs from the box.**

LIFE IN THE FUTURE

do	eat	play	remember	travel

1 People .... a lot of food and not get fat.
2 Eighty-year-olds .... tennis and football.
3 People .... very fast.
4 People won't forget. Everybody .... things clearly.
5 All of this will cost money. .... everybody
.... all these wonderful things? Or only rich people?

→ For other uses of *can* and *can't*, see pages 82–85.

may and *might*   *It may snow.   I might have a cold.*

+	I **may** go you **may** go he/she/it **may** go etc
−	I **may not** go you **may not** go he/she/it **may not** go etc
	No contractions: ~~mayn't~~

We use *may* to say that things are **possible** – **perhaps** they are (not) true, or perhaps they will (not) happen.

*'What's that animal?' 'I'm not sure. It **may** be a rabbit.'*   *I **may** go to Wales at the weekend.*
*We **may not** be here tomorrow.*

We do **not use** *may* in this way in **questions**.

*It **may** snow.* BUT NOT ~~May it snow?~~

❶ Rewrite the sentences with *may*.

▶ Perhaps Sarah's ill. .....*Sarah may be ill.*...
▶ Perhaps we'll go out. ....*We may go out.*..
1 Perhaps it won't rain. ....
2 Perhaps we'll buy a car. ....
3 Perhaps Joe is not at home. ....
4 Perhaps Ann needs help. ....
5 Perhaps the baby's hungry. ....
6 Perhaps I won't change my job. ....
7 Perhaps she's married. ....
8 Perhaps he doesn't want to talk to you. ....

❷ Put the beginnings and ends together; put in *may* with words from the box.

not be   give   go ✓   not have   snow   stay

1 'What are your plans for next year?'	A 'I'm not sure. I ...*may go*............... to America.' *1.*
2 'Are you going to buy that coat?'	B 'Not sure. We .... at home.' ...
3 'Where are you all going on holiday?'	C 'It's early; he .... out of bed yet.' ...
4 'Shall we phone Pete now?'	D 'Yes. I think it ....' ...
5 'It's getting very cold.'	E 'Perhaps; I .... enough money.' ...
6 'What are you giving Oliver for his birthday?'	F 'I don't know. I .... him a sweater.' ...

Note the difference between *may not be* (= 'perhaps is not') and *can't be* (= 'is certainly not').

*She **may not be** at home – I'll phone and find out.*   *She **can't be** at home: she went to Spain this morning.*

→ For the use of *may* to ask for and give **permission** (for example *May I talk to you for a minute?*), see page 85.

+	I **might** go	you **might** go	he/she/it **might** go etc
?	**might** I go?	**might** you go?	**might** he/she/it go? etc
-	I **might not** go	you **might not** go	he/she/it **might not** go etc
	Contraction: *mightn't*		

We can use *might* in the same way as *may* – especially if we are **not so sure** about things.

'Are you ill?' 'Not sure. I **might** have a cold. Or perhaps not.'   I **might not** be here tomorrow.

Might is unusual in questions.

3 John has no money. He is thinking about things that might happen. Put in verbs from the box with *might*.

buy	fall	find	make	send	win ✓

I ▶ ..*might win*.. a lot of money in the lottery. Or I 1 .... some money in the street.
Or Uncle Max 2 .... me $1,000. Or a rich woman 3 .... in love with me.
Or the bank 4 .... a mistake. Or somebody 5 .... my old car.

4 *Might* or *might not*? Circle the correct answers.

▶ Kate had a big lunch, so she *might want /* (*might not want*) to eat this evening.
1 It's getting late. I *might finish / might not finish* this work on time.
2 If the traffic gets very bad we *might miss / might not miss* the train.
3 If he's had a good day, your dad *might give / might not give* you money for the cinema.
4 Andrew's story is so good that his teacher *might believe / might not believe* he wrote it.
5 Helen's not feeling well today – I'm afraid she *might pass / might not pass* her exam.
6 Alan wasn't at the last meeting. He *might know / might not know* the new members.

5 GRAMMAR AND VOCABULARY: jobs
Complete the sentences with *might be* and words from the box. Use a dictionary if necessary.

a businessman	a chef	a farmer ✓	a gardener	a lawyer
an opera singer	a pilot	a politician	a vet ✓	

▶ Little Henry likes animals. When he grows up he ..*might be a farmer or a vet*...............................
1 Angela loves aeroplanes. She might ....
2 George is interested in money. ....
3 Ann likes singing and she has a very loud voice. ....
4 Peter likes talking. ....
5 Alice likes arguing. ....
6 John likes cooking. ....
7 Mary likes flowers. ....

We may live without poetry, music and art;
  We may live without conscience, and live without heart;
We may live without friends, we may live without books;
  But civilised man cannot live without cooks.
(Owen Meredith)

Science fiction is the
literature of *might be*.
(J Cherryh)

must/can't: certainty *She must be in. He can't be hungry.*

We can use *must* to say that something **seems sure/certain**.

*Ann's gone to bed. She **must** be tired. (= 'I am certain that she is tired.')*
*Look at her clothes. She **must** have plenty of money. (= 'I feel sure that she has plenty of money.')*

1 **Rewrite the sentences *in italics* with *must*.**

▶ Her light's on. *She's certainly in.* ....She must be in. ....

1 John's coming to see me. *I'm sure he wants something.* He ....

2 Listen to her accent. *I feel sure she's French.* ....

3 Look at all those books. *He certainly reads a lot.* ....

4 So you're studying politics. *I'm sure that's interesting.* ....

5 Are those his shoes? *He certainly has very big feet.* ....

6 Do you live in Barton? *You certainly know Paul Baker.* ....

2 **Read the text, look at the picture and complete the sentences with *must*.**

A woman left her hotel room three days ago. Nobody has seen her since. The picture shows
some things that the police have found in her room. What do they know about her?

▶ .She must like chocolate. ....   3 .... golf.

▶ .She must have small feet. ....   4 .... money.

1 .... speak .... or ....   5 .... interested in ....

2 .... hair.   6 .... dog.

The **negative** of *must* (to talk about **certainty**) is *can't*.

*It **can't** be true. (= 'It's certainly not true.') (NOT ~~It mustn't be true.~~)*
*She always wears old clothes. She **can't** have much money.*

3 **Rewrite the sentences *in italics* with *can't*.**

▶ Her light's out. *I'm sure she's not at home.* ......She can't be at home. ....

1 Listen to his accent. *He is certainly not American.* ....

2 He has a very expensive car. *I'm sure he's not a teacher.* ....

3 She's very bad-tempered. *I feel sure she doesn't have many friends.* ....

....

4 I filled up the car yesterday. *I'm sure we don't need petrol.* ....

5 He had lunch an hour ago. *He's not hungry: it's impossible.* ....

6 The cinema's half empty. *I'm sure the film isn't very good.* ....

→ For more about *must*, see pages 73–74.   → For more about *can*, see pages 78–79 and 83–85.

can and *could*: requests   *Can you lend me a stamp?*

We can **ask people to do things** (make requests) with *can you ...?* This is informal; we often use it when we are talking to **friends**; and also, for example, in **shops and restaurants**.

Joe, can you lend me a stamp?   *Can you bring me some more butter?*

Could you ...? is more **formal** and **polite**; we often use it, for example, when we are talking to **strangers, older people, teachers or bosses**. *Could you possibly ...?* is **very** polite.

Excuse me, Mr Andrews, could you lend me a stamp?
I'm sorry to trouble you, but could you possibly watch my luggage while I get a coffee?

1 Complete the sentences with the words from the box.

clean	drive	give ✓	hold	lend	pass	tell ✓

▶ Can you ....*give*............ me a receipt?
▶ Could you ...*tell*.............. me your name?
1 Could you .... me the rice?
2 Can you .... my suit?

3 Can you .... this bag?
4 Could you .... me to the station?
5 Could you possibly .... me a pen?

2 Find better ways of asking people to do these things. (I = informal, P = polite, PP = very polite).

▶ Open the window. (I) ...*Can you open the window?*...................
▶ Lend me a pen. (P) ...*Could you lend me a pen?*...................
▶ Help me. (PP) ...*Could you possibly help me?*...................
1 Open the door. (I) ....
2 Give me an envelope. (P) ....
3 Pass me the sugar. (I) ....
4 Watch my children for a minute. (P) ....
5 Tell me the time. (P) ....
6 Change some dollars for me. (PP) ....

3 GRAMMAR AND VOCABULARY: buying and paying
Make sure you know the words in the box, and then use them in requests beginning *Can you ...?*

bill	catalogue ✓	estimate	menu	price list	receipt

▶ (*You are telephoning a clothing company.*) ...*Can you send me your catalogue?*......
1 (*You have just paid a taxi driver.*) .... give me a ....
2 (*You have just sat down in a restaurant.*) .... bring me the ....
3 (*You are talking to a builder.*) .... give me an ....
4 (*You are in a car showroom and you want to know how much the cars cost.*)
   .... give me your ....
5 (*You have finished a meal in a restaurant.*) .... bring me the ....

➔ For other uses of *can*, see pages 78–79 and 84–85.

can, could and *may*: permission *Can I use the phone?*

> We use *can I ...?* or *can we ...?* to **ask** if it is **OK** to do things (to ask permission).
>
> *Can I use the phone, please?*   *Mum, can I leave the table now?*   *Can we wait here?*
>
> We often use *Can I have ...?* and *Can we have ...?* to ask for things.
>
> *Can I have your address, please?*   *Can we have some water?*

❶ Make questions with *Can I ...?* or *Could I ...?*

DON'T SAY THIS!	SAY THIS (to your sister, a friend, a waiter, your secretary)
▶ Lend me your pen.	(*borrow*) *Can I borrow your pen (, please)?* ....
1 I want a glass of water.	(*have*) ....
2 I'm going to use your pencil.	(*use*) ....
3 I want some more coffee.	(*have*) ....
4 I'll put my coat here.	(*put*) ....

> *Could ...?* is **more formal and polite** than *can ...?*, so we use it, for example, with **strangers, older people, teachers and bosses.** *Could I possibly ...?* is **very** polite.
>
> *Could we leave our luggage here until this afternoon?*   *Could I possibly borrow your paper for a moment?*

❷ Make polite questions with *Could I ...?*

DON'T SAY THIS!	SAY THIS (to a stranger, a teacher, a boss, an older person)
▶ Lend me your pen.	(*borrow*) *Could I borrow your pen, please?* ....
1 I need to use your calculator.	(*use*) ....
2 I'm leaving early today.	(*leave*) ....
3 I want to take your photo.	(*take*) ....
4 Lend me your newspaper.	(*borrow*) ....
5 I'm going to turn on the TV.	(*turn on*) ....

> We use *can* (➕)/*can't* (➖), but not *could/couldn't*, to say that it **is** or **isn't OK** to do things.
> (*You can't* is like *you mustn't* – see page 74.)
>
> *You can leave your books here if you want. (NOT ~~You could leave your books~~ ...)*
> *You can't use the gym between 1.00 and 2.00.*

❸ Put the beginnings and ends together. Add *can* and verbs from the box.

borrow ✓   eat   park   play   turn on   watch

1 If you don't have a torch,	A .... in this car park. ...
2 The children	B they .... the cake in the kitchen. ...
3 Tell the boys that	C you *can borrow* .... mine. 1
4 If you're cold,	D you .... the heating. ...
5 If you're bored,	E .... in the garden. ...
6 Only teachers	F you .... television. ...

4 What do the signs tell you? Use _You can't ... here_ with words and expressions from the box.

cycle	park ✓	smoke	take photos	use mobile phones

▶ .....*You can't park here.*.................

1 ....

2 ....
....

3 ....

4 ....
....

We use **_Can I/we ...?_** to **offer help**.

Can I help you?   **_Can we_** book the tickets for you?   **_Can I_** carry those for you?

---

5 Use _Can I ...?_ to offer help in these situations.

▶ Your friend has just come home from hospital. Offer to do some shopping for her.
.....*Can I do some shopping for you?*.................

1 You're going to make a cup of tea for yourself. Offer to make one for your sister.
....

2 You work in a shop. A customer walks in. Offer to help her.
....

3 Offer to drive your brother to the station.
....

4 Your friend has got a headache. Offer to get some aspirins for her.
....

In **very formal** situations, and in **schools**, we often use **_May I ...?_** to **ask** if something is **OK**, or _You may_ (_not_) to **say** that something **is/isn't OK**.

May I have your name, please, sir?   **_May I_** use the toilet please, Mrs Roberts?
You may open your books now.   **_You may_** ask questions after the Prince has finished speaking.
This is a tourist visa: **_you may not_** take a paid job.   **_You may not_** leave until the bell rings.

---

6 A teacher is telling her class what to do. Complete the text with _may_ and verbs from the box.

Please work in groups. You ▶ ....*may talk*...... in your group, but please talk quietly.
You 1 .... to another group, and you 2 ....
the room. You 3 .... your dictionaries. If you want to use other
books, you 4 .... them from the shelf; but only one person
5 .... the group at a time. Each group 6 ....
the computer for twenty minutes; I will tell you when it is your turn. If you
finish before the time is up, you 7 .... other work, but please
work quietly.

do
leave
not leave
take
talk ✓
not talk
use
use

→ For other uses of _can_ and _could_, see pages 78–79 and 83.   → For the use of _may_ to talk about possibility, see page 80.
→ For offers with _shall_, see page 86.

shall in questions   *What shall we do?*

We often use *shall I ...?* or *shall we ...?* when we are asking or suggesting **what to do**.

Shall I put the lights on?   *Where **shall we** meet tomorrow?*   ***Shall we** go and see Bill?*

1 **Make sentences with *Shall I ...?***

▶ put / the meat / in the fridge ? ..*Shall I put the meat in the fridge?*......................

▶ what / tell / the police ? ...*What shall I tell the police?*...............................

1 what / buy / for Sandra's birthday ? ....

2 when / phone you ? ....

3 pay / now ? ....

4 clean / the bathroom ? ....

5 how many tickets / buy ? ....

6 where / leave the car ? ....

7 what time / come this evening ? ....

8 shut / the windows ? ....

2 **Make sentences with *Shall we ...?***

▶ what time / leave ? ..*What time shall we leave?*................................

▶ watch / a video tonight ? ..*Shall we watch a video tonight?*.....................

1 go out / this evening ? ....

2 have / a game of cards ? ....

3 how / travel to London ? ....

4 what / do at the weekend ? ....

5 where / go on holiday ....

6 look for / a hotel ? ....

7 what time / meet Peter ? ....

8 how much bread / buy ? ....

We can use *Shall I ...?* to **offer** politely to **do things for people**.

Shall I take your coat?   *Shall I make you some coffee?*

3 **Make sentences offering to:**

▶ carry somebody's bag ..*Shall I carry your bag?*.............................

1 post somebody's letters ....

2 do somebody's shopping ....

3 make somebody's bed ....

4 read to somebody ....

5 drive somebody to the station ....

6 make somebody a cup of tea ....

→ For offers with *can*, see page 85.

→ For *I shall* (meaning the same as *I will*), see page 35.

had better   *You'd better take your umbrella.*

➕	I **had better** go you **had better** go he/she/it **had better** go etc
➖	I **had better not** go you **had better not** go he/she/it **had better not** go etc
	Contractions: *I'd better, you'd better,* etc

I/you/etc **had better** do this means *'This is **a good thing** to do now.'*
*You'd **better** take your umbrella.*   *I'd **better not** stay any longer; I've got work to do.*
We use **had better** to talk about the **present**, not the past.
*You'd **better** stop that, young lady.* (NOT ~~You've better~~ ...)

1 **Put the beginnings and ends together. Use *'d better* with the verbs in the box.**

not drink   go   phone ✓   phone   not sit   stop

1	My husband worries if I'm late;	A	I .... it. ...
2	This milk smells bad;	B	I .*'d better phone*................... him. *1*
3	That chair looks very dirty;	C	we .... the doctor. ...
4	The baby's temperature is 40°;	D	we .... and get some. ...
5	You have to get up early tomorrow;	E	you .... to bed. ...
6	There's almost no petrol in the car;	F	you .... on it. ...

We use both *had better* and *should* to say *'This is a good thing to do now.'*
We use *should*, BUT NOT *had better*, to say *'This is a good thing to do in general.'*
*We're late (now). We'd **better** phone Mum.* OR *We **should** phone Mum.*
*You **should** always drive very carefully near schools.* (NOT ~~You had better always drive~~ ...)

2 **Write *'d better* where it's possible; in other places write *should*.**

▶ 'I can't move the fingers of my left hand.' 'You .*'d better*........... go to hospital.'
▶ Everyone in the world ..*should*........... get enough food to eat.
1 If you don't like cats, you .... not come with us to Ann's house.
2 If you see an accident, you .... remember the time.
3 Oh, no, look – my car window's broken. I .... call the police.
4 Teachers .... mark homework and give it back as soon as possible.
5 The swimming pool closes in ten minutes; we .... swim now.
6 People .... drive more slowly when it's raining.

NOTE: we don't use *You'd better* ... to **ask** people politely to do things.
Could you open the door for me? (NOT ~~You'd better open the door for me.~~)
Would you like to wait here for a minute? (NOT ~~You'd better wait here~~ ...)

And note that we don't usually say *You had better* ... to customers, teachers or bosses.
*You **might want** to try a larger size.* (NOT ~~You'd better try~~ ...)

would   *Would you like a drink?   I'd like to be taller.*

We often use *would* in the expression *I'd like* (= '*I would like*'), to **ask** for things. It is more polite than *I want*.

I'd like a return ticket, please.   *I'd like a seat by the window.*

We can offer things with *would you like ...?*

Would you like a drink?   *How many eggs would you like?*

1 Make sentences with *I'd like ..., please* or *Would you like ...?*

▶ two tickets ➕ ..I'd like two tickets, please......................................

▶ coffee ❓ .Would you like coffee?..

1 a black T-shirt ➕ ....

2 an aspirin ❓ ....

3 the newspaper ❓ ....

4 an ice cream ➕ ....

5 some more toast ❓ ....

6 a receipt ➕ ....

We can use *would like to* to talk about things that people **want to do**.

I'd like to learn Chinese.   *What would you like to do on Sunday?*
Would you like to have lots of brothers and sisters?   *I wouldn't like to be an astronaut.*

2 Which of these things would you like to be or do? Write sentences beginning *I'd like to ...* or *I wouldn't like to ...*

▶ be shorter ...I'd like to be shorter. OR I wouldn't like to be shorter.....................

1 be taller ....

2 be younger ....

3 be older ....

4 go to the moon ....

5 live in a different country ....

6 have a lot of dogs ....

7 write a book ....

8 (*your sentence*) ....

We often use *Would you like to ...?* in invitations.

Would you like to come to Scotland with us?

Don't confuse *would like* (= 'want') and *like* (= 'enjoy'). Compare:

I'd like some coffee, please. (NOT *I like some coffee, please.*)   *I like coffee but I don't like tea.*
Would you like to go skating today? (NOT *Do you like to go ...?*)   *Do you like skating?*

3 Circle the correct forms.

1 *Do / Would* you like to come to dinner with us?

2 *I like / would like* mountains.

3 *Do / Would* you like to go out now?

4 Do you like dancing? *Yes, I do. / Yes, please.*

5 *I like / would like* to get up late tomorrow.

6 *I don't / wouldn't* like old music.

7 *I don't / wouldn't* like to be an animal.

→ For sentences like *I'd like you to come early tomorrow*, see page 122.
→ For *would* in sentences with *if*, see page 230.

used to   *I used to play the piano.*

+	I **used to** play you **used to** play he/she/it **used to** play etc
?	**did** I **use to** play? **did** you **use to** play? **did** he/she/it **use to** play? etc
−	I **did** not **use to** play you **did** not **use to** play he/she/it **did** not **use to** play etc

I used to play the piano. I don't play now.

PAST ♪ ♪ ♪ ♪ ♪ ✗ ✗ ✗ ✗ ✗ NOW

We use **used to** + infinitive for **finished habits and situations**: things that were true, but are not now.
(*Used to* is not really a modal: we make **questions** and **negatives** with *did*.)

I **used to play** the piano, but I stopped.   Pat **used to have** long fair hair.
Where **did** you **use** to live before you came here?   I **didn't use** to like fish, but now I do.

1 Make sentences about people hundreds of years ago. Begin *(Most) people used to ...* or
(Most) people didn't use to ... or *A lot of people used to ...*

▶ be farmers .Most.people.used.to.be.farmers..............................
▶ have cars ..People.didn't.use.to.have.cars..............................
1 travel on foot or on horses ....
2 go to school ....
3 learn to read ....
4 cook on wood fires ....
5 live very long ....
6 work very long hours ....

WE USED TO
BE A TREE.

To talk about **present** habits and situations, we use the **simple present**, NOT ~~use to~~.

I **play** a lot of tennis. (NOT ~~I use to play a lot of tennis.~~)

2 Make sentences about past and present habits and situations.

▶ John / rugby / tennis ..John.used.to.play.rugby..Now.he.plays.tennis..........................
1 Ann / study German / French ....
2 Bill / live London / Glasgow ....
3 Mary / read a lot / TV ....
4 Joe / driver / hairdresser ....
5 Alice / coffee / tea ....
6 Peter / lots of girlfriends / married ....

3 Make questions about a very old person's past.

▶ where / go to school .Where.did.you.use.to.go.to.school?.........................
1 have dark hair   Did ....
2 play football ....
3 where / work ....
4 enjoy your work ....
5 go to a lot of parties ....

4 Write a sentence about your past.

I used to ....

perfect modal verbs   *I should have studied harder.*

+ **?** **-**	***I should have* gone** ***you should have* gone** ***he/she/it should have* gone** etc ***should I have* gone?** ***should you have* gone?** ***should he/she/it have* gone?** etc ***I should not have* gone** ***you should not have* gone** etc
	Contraction: *shouldn't*

If somebody **didn't do** something that was important, we can say *he/she* **should have done** it.

*Ann **should have gone** to the doctor yesterday, but she forgot.*
*I **should have studied** harder when I was at school.*

① **Look at the pictures and complete the sentences with *should have*, using the verbs in the box.**

arrived   been   brought   brought   locked   put   told ✓

1   2   3

4   5   6

▶ You ..*should have told*... me that you were coming.
1   He .... his car.
2   You .... here at 2 o'clock.
3   She .... more sugar in.
4   We .... a map.
5   They .... at the station earlier.
6   I .... my umbrella.

If somebody did something wrong, we can say *he/she* **shouldn't have done** it.

*You **shouldn't have told** the policeman that he was stupid.*

→ For *would have* with *if*, see page 235.

2 Look at the pictures and complete the sentences with *shouldn't have*, using the words in the box.

eaten	gone	played	spent

1 I ....
so much.
2 He ....
all his money on clothes.
3 I ....
to bed so late last night.
4 We ....
poker with that nice man.

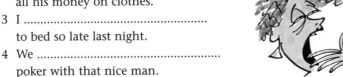

If somebody didn't do something that was possible, we can say *he/she* **could have done it**.
*I **could have gone** to university, but I didn't want to.*

---

3 Complete the sentences with *could have*, using words from the box.

been	gone	lent	married	studied	won

1 Ann .... John or Peter, but she didn't love either of them.
2 Why didn't you ask me for money? I .... you some.
3 I .... mathematics, but I decided to do languages instead.
4 Our team .... the match, but they didn't try hard enough.
5 The holiday was OK, but it .... better.
6 We .... to Paris last weekend, but we thought this weekend would be better.

If we say something *may have happened*, we mean that **perhaps** it (has) happened.
*Pat isn't answering the phone. She **may have gone** out.* (= 'Perhaps she's gone out.')

---

4 Rewrite these sentences with *may have*.

▶ Perhaps Shakespeare went to Italy. *Shakespeare may have gone to Italy.*
1 Perhaps she's broken her leg. ....
2 Perhaps I've lost my keys. ....
3 Perhaps Alice has gone back home. ....
4 Perhaps my great-grandfather was a soldier. ....
5 Perhaps I've found a new job. ....
6 Perhaps this house was a school once. ....

If we say that something *must have happened*, we mean that we **feel sure** that it (has) happened.

---

5 Rewrite the sentences *in italics* with *must have*.

▶ The exam was easy. *I'm sure I've passed.* *I must have passed.*
1 Her office is locked. *I'm sure she's gone home.* ....
2 I can't find my umbrella. *I feel sure I left it on the bus.* ....
3 Ann hasn't come. *I'm sure she's forgotten.* ....
4 The car isn't here. *I'm sure John has taken it.* ....

test yourself modal verbs

1 Correct (✓) or not (✗)?

▶ John cans swim. ✗
▶ I must go now. ✓
1 I don't must see Andrew today. ...
2 Anna can't to speak English. ...

3 Last year I must sell my car. ...
4 Would you like to have some coffee? ...
5 It may rain tomorrow. ...
6 I mustn't work on Saturdays, but I can if I like. ...

2 Circle the correct answers.

▶ (Can) / Should / Mustn't I help you?
1 If you travel to Morania you *can / should / must* have a visa.
2 You *shouldn't / don't have to / couldn't* laugh at old people.
3 Passengers *must / must not / should not* smoke in the toilets.
4 I think you *should / must / may* eat less and take more exercise.
5 You *mustn't / may not / needn't* tell me if you don't want to.
6 You *may / have to* drive on the left in Britain.

3 Change the times of these sentences.

▶ Helen can ski.   ..Helen could ski................................... when she was 3 years old.
1 I can speak French now.   .... soon.
2 Everybody must fill in a big form.   .... last year.
3 Everybody must fill in a big form.   .... next year.

4 Choose the correct verbs to rewrite the sentences with the same meaning.

▶ I know how to swim. (*can / may*) ..I can swim..
1 It is necessary for you to phone Martin. (*must / might*) ....
2 It is possible that Ann will be here this evening. (*can / might*) ....
3 It is not necessary for you to wait. (*mustn't / needn't*) ....
4 It's not good for people to watch TV all the time. (*mustn't / shouldn't*) ....
5 Do you want me to open a window? (*shall / will*) ....

5 Correct (✓) or not (✗)?

1 Where did you use to go to school? ...
2 I often use to go skiing. ...

3 You should had told me before. ...
4 You have better to stop smoking. ...

6 Circle the correct answers.

1 She has new clothes every week. She *can / could / must* have plenty of money.
2 She doesn't answer the phone. She *mustn't / can't / shouldn't* be in her office.
3 Bill isn't here. He *may has gone / may have gone / may have go* home.

7 Make these sentences more polite. (Different answers are possible.)

▶ Give me some water. ..Can I have some water?.................................
1 I want a cup of coffee. ....
2 Can I take a photograph of you? ....
3 Close the door, John. ....

◉ More difficult questions

SECTION 7 passives

grammar summary

When **A** does something to **B**, there are often two ways to talk about it: 'active' and 'passive'.

- We use **active** verbs if we want **A** to be the **subject**.
  *Mrs Harris **cooks** our meals.*   *Andrew **broke** the window.*
- We use **passive** verbs if we want **B** to be the **subject**.
  *Our meals **are cooked** by Mrs Harris.*   *The window **was broken** by Andrew.*

We make **passive verbs** with *be* (*am, are, is* etc) + **past participle** (*cooked, broken* etc).
Passive verbs have the **same tenses** (simple present, present progressive, present perfect etc) as **active** verbs.
For a list of active and passive tenses, see page 276.

pre-test: which units do you need?

Try this small test. It will help you to decide which units you need. The answers are on page 283.

1 **Correct (✓) or not (✗)?**

▶ English is spoken in New Zealand. ✓
▶ I born in Manchester. ✗
1 I was studied German for three years. ...
2 Ann invited to a party by her boss. ...
3 How is written your name? ...
4 'Where's your coat?' 'It's being cleaned.' ...

5 Our car has been stolen. ...
6 When is that window broken? ...
7 This book was written from my father. ...
8 I was given your name by a friend of mine. ...
9 The new road will finished in July. ...

2 **Circle the best way to continue.**

1 She lives in an old house. **A** Somebody built it in 1730.   **B** It was built in 1730.
2 My friend Andrew takes photographs of animals and birds.
  A He sells them for a lot of money.   **B** They are sold by him for a lot of money.

DO YOU KNOW? (Answers at the bottom of the page)

1 **Which of these is used to boil water?**
  A a fridge   B a sink   C a kettle   D a hot water bottle

2 **Which US President was killed in a theatre?**
  A Lincoln   B Kennedy   C Eisenhower   D Nixon

3 **Which game is played with a racket?**
  A golf   B cricket   C football   D tennis

4 **If you are being served, where are you?**
  A in a shop   B in a church   C in the sea   D in hospital

5 **The Olympic Games have never been held in:**
  A Melbourne   B Tokyo   C London   D Chicago

6 **Which of these metals was discovered by Marie Curie?**
  A uranium   B radium   C gold   D platinum

7 **Which of these was not written by Shakespeare?**
  A Hamlet   B The Sound of Music C Othello   D Julius Caesar

8 **Which country was governed by the Pharaohs?**
  A Sweden   B China   C Egypt   D Japan

Answers: 1C, 2A, 3D, 4A, 5D, 6B, 7B, 8C

---

passives: introduction *English is spoken in Australia.*

When **A** does something to **B**, there are often two ways
  to talk about it: 'active' and 'passive'.
We use active verbs if we want **A** to be the **subject**.
We use passive verbs if we want **B** to be the **subject**.
We make **passive** verbs with *be* (*am, are, is* etc) + **past participle** (*cooked, seen* etc).

ACTIVE			PASSIVE		
A		**B**	**B**		**(A)**
Mrs Harris	*cooks*	*our meals.*	*Our meals*	*are cooked*	*by Mrs Harris.*
Somebody	*saw*	*her in Belfast.*	*She*	*was seen*	*in Belfast.*
The government	*will close*	*the hospital next year.*	*The hospital*	*will be closed*	*next year.*

Passive verbs have the **same tenses** (simple present, present progressive, present perfect etc) as active
verbs. For a list of active and passive tenses, see page 276.

1 Which picture goes with which sentence?

▶ The policeman helped the old lady. A
1 The policeman was helped by the
  old lady. ...
2 The car hit a tree. ...
3 The car was hit by a tree. ...

4 Annie loves all dogs. ...
5 Annie is loved by all dogs. ...
6 The Queen photographed the tourists. ...
7 The Queen was photographed by the
  tourists. ...

A  B   C    D

E  F  G  H

2 Circle the correct answer.

1 English *speaks / spoken / is spoken* in Australia.
2 I *studied / was studied* French for three years at school.
3 We *spent / was spent* too much money on holiday.
4 This window *broke / was broken* by your little boy.
5 Her clothes *made / are made* in Paris.
6 This book *written / was written* by my brother.
7 The new university *will open / will opened / will be opened* by the Prime Minister.
8 Ann *was driving / was driven* much too fast, and she *stopped / was stopped* by the police.

Sometimes we make passives with *get* instead of *be*, especially in spoken English.

*I **get paid** on Fridays.*   *My window **got broken** by the wind.*

simple present passive   *We are woken by the birds.*

+	I **am** woken you **are** woken he/she/it **is** woken etc
?	**am** I woken? **are** you woken? **is** he/she/it woken? etc
-	I **am not** woken you **are not** woken he/she/it **is not** woken etc
	For contractions (*I'm, isn't* etc), see pages 2, 277.

We use the **simple present passive** like the simple present active, for things that are **always true**, and things that happen **all the time, repeatedly, often, sometimes, never** etc (see page 15).

*I **am paid** every two weeks.   **Is** Jeremy **liked** by the other children?   Stamps **aren't** sold here.*

→ For spelling rules for adding *-ed* to verbs, see page 42; for irregular past participles, see page 275.

1 **Complete the sentences with *am/are/is*.**

▶ A lot of paper ..*is*... made from wood.

1 What .... this called in English?

2 I .... paid on the first of every month.

3 Jane .... often sent to the Singapore office.

4 .... any classes taught on Wednesdays?

5 More chocolate .... eaten in the US than in any other country.

6 Not very much .... known about Shakespeare's childhood.

7 We .... woken by the birds every morning.

8 .... you seen by the same doctor every week?

2 **Put simple present passive verbs into these sentences.**

▶ A lot of olive oil ..*is used*..... in Greek cooking. (*use*)

1 Arabic .... from right to left. (*write*)

2 Those programmes .... by millions of people every week. (*watch*)

3 Stamps .... in most newsagents in Britain. (*sell*)

4 The police say that nothing .... about the child's family. (*know*)

5 In English, 'ough' .... in a lot of different ways. (*pronounce*)

6 Spanish .... in Peru. (*speak*)

7 Cricket .... by two teams of eleven players. (*play*)

8 Our windows .... once a month. (*clean*)

3 **Make simple present negatives and questions.**

▶ 'Jaguar cars ..*are not made*............................ in America.' (*not make*)

'Where ..*are they made?*............................' 'In the UK.'

1 'My name .... with a Y.' (*not spell*)

'How ....' 'L, E, S, L, I, E.'

2 'That kind of bird .... around here.' (*not usually see*)

'Where ....' 'In warmer countries.'

3 '*Where* .... like *were*.' (*not pronounce*)

'How ....' 'Like *wear*.'

4 'Diamonds .... in Scotland.' (*not find*)

'Where ....' 'In South Africa, for example.'

5 'My sister .... very well.' (*not pay*)

'How much ....' 'I don't remember.'

future passive   *Tomorrow your bicycle will be stolen.*

+	I **will be** woken	you **will be** woken	he/she/it **will be** woken etc
?	**will** I **be** woken?	**will** you **be** woken?	**will** he/she/it **be** woken? etc
−	I **will not be** woken	you **will not be** woken	he/she/it **will not be** woken etc
	For contractions: (*I'll, won't* etc), see page 277.		

We use the **future passive** like the future active (see page 35), to say things that we **think, guess** or **know** about the **future,** or to ask questions about the future.

*One day all the work **will be done** by machines.   Where **will** the match **be played?***

1 Make future passive sentences with the verbs from the box.

| clean   close ✓   finish   open   send   speak |

▶ The motorway .....will be closed... for three days.
1 The museum .... by the Queen.
2 One day English .... everywhere.
3 This job .... in a few days.
4 Your room .... while you're out.
5 Your tickets .... to you next week.

2 Make future passive negatives and questions.

▶ 'The football match .....won't be played................. on Saturday.' (*play*)
  'When ...will it be played?............' 'On Sunday.'
1 'The visitors .... to the hotel by bus.' (*take*)
  'How ....' 'By taxi.'
2 'The new library .... in the Central Square.' (*build*)
  'Where ....' 'Behind the Police Station.'
3 'English .... at the conference.' (*speak*)
  'What language ....' 'Chinese.'

3 Make five future passive sentences from the table.

Next year Tomorrow Next week Tonight One day In 20 years	your bed / bicycle / breakfast / food / clothes / dinner / glasses / house / room / work	clean / cook / do / eat / make / send to Canada / steal / wash / take away	by	a small man in a raincoat / a black cat / two old ladies / a beautiful woman / people from another world / the President / a big dog / your old friend Peter / a machine

.....Tomorrow your bicycle will be stolen by your old friend Peter.....
....
....
....
....
....

TOMORROW...

simple past passive   *I was stopped by a policeman.*

➕	*I **was** woken you **were** woken he/she/it **was** woken etc*
❓	***was** I woken? **were** you woken? **was** he/she/it woken? etc*
➖	*I **was not** woken you **were not** woken he/she/it **was not** woken etc*

For contractions: (*wasn't* etc), see page 277.

We use the **simple past passive like the simple past** active, for **complete finished actions and events** (see page 46).

*This table **was made** by my grandfather.   **Was** the letter **signed**?   We **weren't met** at the door.*

❶ Complete the sentences with *was/were*.

1 The fire .... seen in Renton, a kilometre away.
2 Most of the matches .... won by Indian teams.
3 These keys .... found in the changing room – are they yours?
4 We couldn't find the station, but we .... helped by a very kind woman.
5 I .... stopped by a policeman in Green Road this morning.
6 Yesterday a man .... caught trying to burn down the Town Hall.

❷ Put simple past passive verbs into these sentences.

1 Our passports .... by a tall woman in a uniform. (*take*)
2 These books .... in the classroom yesterday. (*leave*)
3 I don't think this room .... yesterday. (*clean*)
4 We .... at the airport by a driver from the university. (*meet*)
5 Nobody .... what was happening. (*tell*)
6 He .... away to school when he was twelve. (*send*)

❸ Make simple past passive negatives and questions.

▶ 'We ..*weren't paid*............................... when we finished the work.' (*not pay*)
   'When ...*were you paid?*...............................' 'Two months later.'
1 'My father .... in England.' (*not educate*)
   'Where ....' 'In Germany.'
2 'The letters .... on Tuesday.' (*not post*)
   'When ....' 'On Thursday.'
3 'This .... in butter.' (*not cook*)
   'How ....' 'In margarine.'
4 'My suit .... in England.' (*not make*)
   'Where ....' 'In Hong Kong.'
5 'The restaurant bill .... in cash.' (*not pay*)
   'How ....' 'With a credit card.'

We use a passive structure – ***to be born*** – to give somebody's date or place of birth.

*I **was born** in 1964.* (NOT ~~I born in 1964.~~)   *My sister **was born** in Egypt.*

❹ Write a sentence about your date and place of birth.

I ....

present progressive passive   *It's being cleaned.*

+	I am **being** watched you **are being** watched he/she/it **is being** watched etc
?	am I **being** watched? **are** you **being** watched? **is** he/she/it **being** watched? etc
−	I am **not being** watched you **are not being** watched he/she/it **is not being** watched etc
	For contractions (*I'm*, *isn't* etc), see pages 2 and 277.

We use the **present progressive passive** like the present progressive active, for things that are happening **now** (see page 22), or for things that are **planned for the future** (see page 34).

'Where's the carpet?' 'It's being cleaned.'   *When **are** you **being seen** by the doctor?*

1 Questions and answers. Use the words in the box to complete answers to the questions.
Use the present progressive passive.

grass / cut ✓	I / send	it / clean	my hair / cut	she / interview	watch / repair

▶ 'Can we play on the football pitch?' 'No, <u>the grass is being cut.</u> ....'
1 'Can't you wear your blue suit tonight?' 'No, ...,'
2 'Did Alice get that new job?' 'Not yet – .... today.'
3 'What time is it?' 'Sorry, I don't know: ....,'
4 'Why the big smile?' ' .... to Hawaii for a week.'
5 I usually read a magazine while ....

2 GRAMMAR AND VOCABULARY: travelling by air
Make sure you know the words in the box. Use a dictionary if necessary. Then make six or more sentences about what is being done in this airport.

SUBJECTS: baggage	boarding passes	business people	cars	departures		
passengers ✓	passports	reservations	tickets			
VERBS: announce	check	check in ✓	make	meet	park	print sell x-ray

<u>Passengers are being checked in.</u> ....
....
....
....

present perfect passive   *The house has been sold.*

+	*I **have been** seen* *you **have been** seen* *he/she/it **has been** seen etc*
?	***have** I **been** seen?* ***have** you **been** seen?* ***has** he/she/it **been** seen? etc*
–	*I **have not been** seen* *you **have not been** seen* *he/she/it **has not been** seen etc*
	For contractions (*I've* etc), see page 277.

We use the **present perfect passive** like the present perfect active (see pages 54–61), to talk about past actions and events which are **important now** – for example, when we give people news.

*The house on the corner **has been sold**.*   *We **haven't been invited** to Ann's party.*

① **News: put the verbs into the present perfect passive.**

▶ A new university ...*has been opened*............................ in Kew today by the Prince of Wales. (*open*)

1 Lord Retlaw .... for drunk driving. (*arrest*)

2 An old painting from a school in Wales .... for $250,000 by an American museum. (*buy*)

3 An 18-year-old soldier .... in an accident in Devon. (*kill*)

4 The two lost children .... alive and well in a London park. (*find*)

5 An unknown actor .... to star in the new film of 'Macbeth'. (*choose*)

② **'It's never been done.' Make a sentence for each picture.**

cut

▶ It's never been cut.............................

ride

1 ....

wear

2 ....

open

3 ....

use

4 ....

play

5 ....

verbs with two objects *We were given a week.*

Some verbs (for example *give, lend, promise, send* and *show*) can have two objects: a **person** and a **thing** (see page 140). If the **person** is last, we use *to*.

They gave Susan a prize. OR *They gave a prize to Susan.*
We sent Andy a birthday card. OR *We sent a birthday card to Andy.*

These verbs have two possible passive structures.

Susan was given a prize. OR *A prize was given to Susan.*
Andy was sent a birthday card. OR *A birthday card was sent to Andy.*

The structure with the person first (*Susan was given* ...) is very common.

1 **Put the beginnings and ends together.**

1 Jack has been promised a trip to Mexico	A to finish our English homework. ...
2 Ann has been shown several houses,	B while mine is being repaired. ...
3 We've been given three days	C but she hasn't seen one she likes. ...
4 I was sent an invitation to Alex's party,	D if he passes his exams. 1
5 I'm being lent a new car	E but I don't think I'll go. ...

2 **Make two sentences with each set of words. Use the simple past passive.**

▶ lend / everyone / skis / for the day *Everyone was lent skis for the day. Skis were lent to everyone for the day.*

1 give / the younger children / picture books ....

2 lend / Anna and Joe / a car / by the Watsons ....

3 promise / Nathan / a new computer ....

4 send / some people / two invitations / by mistake ....

5 show / most of us / a film about Wales ....

3 **Make simple past passive negatives and questions.**

▶ My class / not give / a test *My class wasn't given a test.* ....
Who *was given a test?* .... / *Was* anybody *given a test?*

1 Cathy / not promise / a place ....
Who .... / .... anybody ....

2 We / not give / enough time ....
Who .... / .... anybody ....

3 Jon / not show / the hall ....
Who ....
/ .... any of the musicians ....

4 I / not give / an explanation ....
Who .... / .... anybody ....

by with passives   *Who was it made by?*

With **passives**, we are mostly interested in **the action** – in **what happens**.

The missing child has been found.   The ear-rings were made in the first century BC.
German is spoken in Austria.   Thousands of fish were killed, but no one knows how.

If we want to say **who** or **what** does the action, we use **by**.

*The missing child was found **by** a French family.   The ear-rings were made **by** a Roman goldsmith.*
*Urdu is spoken **by** a lot of people in London.   Thousands of fish were killed **by** the chemicals.*

1 Complete each sentence with *by ...* and the best expression from the box.

| a farmer   a tree   loud music   my granddaughter   a committee ✓   the government |

▶ The name of the new school is being decided ...by a committee... of parents
and governors.
1 Most of the cost of university education is paid ....
2 All the neighbours were woken up .... coming from the flat.
3 I'm being taught how to use a computer ....
4 A big box of Roman jewellery has been found in a field ....
in Kent.
5 The window was broken .... that fell over in the storm.

In passive questions, we usually prefer **Who ... by?**, especially in spoken English.

*I really like the statue in the square. **Who** was it made **by**?   **Who** were you invited **by**?*

By whom ...? is also possible, especially in writing.

2 Ask past questions with *Who ... by?*

▶ 'Look at this beautiful photo.' (*take*) ...'Who was it taken by?'.......................
1 '*Dune* is my favourite science fiction book.' (*write*) ....
2 'Do you remember that song *Over the Rainbow*?' (*sing*) ....
3 That's a wonderful picture. (*paint*) ....
4 '*Casablanca* is the greatest film of all time.' (*direct*) ....
5 'Our village school is a beautiful building.' (*build*) ....
6 'I really like the name of the new school.' (*choose*) ....

We **only** use *by ...* if it is **really necessary**. (80% of passive sentences are made without *by ...*)

3 Cross out the expression *in italics* if you feel it gives no useful information.

▶ A 54-year-old accountant was arrested for drunk driving last night ~~by the police.~~
1 'Romeo and Juliet' was written *by Shakespeare.*
2 All of these birds have been seen in Britain *by people who watch birds.*
3 Everest was first climbed in 1953 *by mountain climbers.*
4 This house was built *by Frank Lloyd Wright.*
5 My sister's books have been translated into thirty languages *by translators.*
6 Sugar is made from sugar cane and sugar beet *by sugar companies.*
7 This letter wasn't written *by an English person.*

passive or active? which tense?

We choose passive or active so that we can **start the sentence** with the **thing or person** that we are **talking about.**

PASSIVE: *St Paul's Cathedral was built between 1675 and 1710.* (talking about the Cathedral)
PASSIVE: *St Paul's Cathedral was built by Christopher Wren.* (talking about the Cathedral)
ACTIVE: *Christopher Wren built St Paul's Cathedral.* (talking about Christopher Wren)

1 Make active and passive sentences.

▶ Shakespeare / 'Hamlet' / 1601 / write
Write about Shakespeare. ...Shakespeare wrote 'Hamlet' in 1601.............
Write about 'Hamlet'. 'Hamlet' was written by Shakespeare in 1601...........

1 this sweater / Ann's mother / make
Write about Ann's mother. ....
Write about this sweater. ....

2 Janet / the electricity bill / last week / pay
Write about Janet. ....
Write about the electricity bill. ....

3 the first television / J. L. Baird / 1924 / build
Write about the first television. ....
Write about J. L. Baird. ....

We choose **passive or active** to **continue** talking about the **same thing or person.**

Spanish is a useful language for travelling. It is spoken in most of Central and South America.
   (Better than *People speak it in most ...*)
We've got two cats. They catch a lot of mice. (Better than *A lot of mice are caught by them.*)

2 Circle the best way to continue.

1 This ice cream has a very unusual taste.   **A** I think someone makes it with coconut milk.
   B I think it's made with coconut milk.
2 Rice is important in Cajun cooking.   **A** People serve it with every meal.
   B It's served with every meal.
3 Barry is very good to his parents.   **A** He visits them two or three times a week.
   B They are visited by him two or three times a week.
4 Carlo Vane is very popular at the moment.   **A** They play his songs on the radio every day.
   B His songs are played on the radio every day.
5 Alice is a very good poet.   **A** She won a national poetry prize last year.
   B A national poetry prize was won by her last year.

3 Put each verb into the simple present passive or active.

Gorillas (*find*) ▶ ...*are found*.... in several countries in central Africa. They are about 1.6 metres tall, and they (*cover*) 1 .... with black or brown hair.

Gorillas' lives (*spend*) 2 .... in groups. Each group (*have*) 3 .... five to ten gorillas in it. The gorillas in a group (*walk*) 4 .... about 0.5 to 1.0 km per day, looking for food. They (*not eat*) 5 .... all the leaves in one part of the forest before moving on; some leaves (*leave*) 6 .... on the trees and plants. At night gorillas (*sleep*) 7 .... in nests; these nests (*make*) 8 .... of branches and leaves. The number of gorillas living in Africa today (*not know*) 9 ...., but it is certain that this number is getting smaller. Why? Because in the countries where the gorillas (*live*) 10 ...., more and more trees (*cut down*) 11 .... every year.

© The Dian Fossey Gorilla Fund International 2001

4 Revision of passives: circle the correct tense in each sentence.

▶ Baseball is *being played* / (*is played*) by two teams of nine players.
1 How many languages *are spoken* / *will be spoken* in 2100?
2 Yesterday, letters *are sent* / *was sent* / *were sent* to all the members of the club.
3 What kind of oil *is used* / *has been used* in Mexican cooking?
4 'Where's your car?' *'It's repaired.'* / *'It's being repaired.'* / *'It's been repaired.'*
5 Oh, dear, I'm late – *is my name* / *has my name been* called yet?

5 Revision of passives: write the passive verbs in the correct tenses.

▶ Potatoes ....*were brought*................ to Europe from South America in the 1500s. (*bring*)
1 Your class .... by Mrs Nash on Monday next week. (*teach*)
2 Five hundred years ago, Latin .... by people all over Europe. (*speak*)
3 I'm working at home today because my office .... (*paint*)
4 Someone's been using my desk – all my papers .... (*move*)
5 'Two' and 'too' .... the same. (*pronounce*)

test yourself   passives

1 (Circle) **a passive or active verb form.**

1 Derek *posted / was posted* his letter to the university today.
2 We did a lot of work for the school, but we *didn't pay / weren't paid*.
3 My friend Douglas *speaks / is spoken* seven languages.
4 The letter H *doesn't pronounce / isn't pronounced* in French.
5 A new hospital *will build / will be built* in the town centre.
6 You can't come in here – the room *is cleaning / is being cleaned*.
7 We *have invited / have been invited* to John's party tonight.

2 **Put simple present, simple past or future passive verbs into these sentences.**

▶ 'Frankenstein' ...*was written*............... by Mary Shelley. (*write*)
1 Butter .... from milk. (*make*)
2 Last night two men .... in a fight in a nightclub. (*kill*)
3 One day all our work .... by machines. (*do*)
4 English .... as a second language by millions of people. (*speak*)

3 (Circle) **the best way to continue.**

1 I was really hungry.   **A** I ate six eggs.   **B** Six eggs were eaten by me.
2 George Yeo's new book is very good.   **A** People bought 10,000 copies in the first week.
   B 10,000 copies were bought in the first week.
3 This milk tastes funny.   **A** I think someone has left it out of the fridge for too long.
   B I think it's been left out of the fridge for too long.
4 Zoë takes good care of her car.   **A** She checks the oil and tyres every week.
   B The oil and tyres are checked by her every week.

4 **Put present perfect or present progressive passive verbs into these sentences.**

▶ 'Is the Army Museum still in Green Street?' 'No, it *has been closed*...........................' (*close*)
1 Don't look now, but I think we .... (*follow*)
2 Hello, police? I'd like to report a theft. My handbag .... (*steal*)
3 'Why did you take the bus?' 'My car ....' (*repair*)
4 I think someone's been in my room – some books .... (*move*)
5 'There's nobody here.' 'No, all the students .... home.' (*send*)
6 'When .... you ....' 'Tomorrow morning.' (*interview*)

5 **Use the words *in italics* as the subjects and verbs of passive sentences.**

▶ *Nedjma* is sure she's going to get a pay rise. (*promise*)
   Nedjma has been promised a pay rise............................
1 All the passengers received *meal tickets*. (*give*)
   ....
2 *Ellen* has seen the plans for the new building. (*show*)
   ....
3 Someone has promised all the office workers *a week's holiday*. (*promise*)
   ....
4 Someone sent a bill for the repairs to *Laura*. (*send*)
   ....

◉ More difficult questions

SECTION 8 questions and negatives

● grammar summary

To make **questions**, we normally put an **auxiliary verb before the subject**.
John has gone. → ***Has John** gone?*   *She's leaving.* → *When **is she** leaving?*

To make **negatives**, we put *not* or *n't* after an auxiliary verb (*be, have, can* etc).
John is working. → *John **is not** working.*   *I **could** swim* → *I **couldn't** swim.*

If there is **no other auxiliary** verb, we use *do*.
*I **live** in Manchester.* → *Where **do** you live?*   *He said 'Hello'.* → *What **did** he say?*
She likes cold weather. → *She **doesn't** like cold weather.*

We do **not** use *do* when a **question word** is the **subject**.
***What** happened?* (NOT ~~What did happen?~~)

● pre-test: which units do you need?

Try this small test. It will help you to decide which units you need. The answers are on page 283.

❶ Correct (✓) or not (✗)?

▶ I not speak English. ✗
1 Does she works in London? ...
2 Will Ann and her family arrive by train? ...
3 Did you knew John at school? ...
4 Play you tennis? ...
5 Why you are tired? ...
6 How well do you know him? ...

7 What time does the film start? ...
8 What is your new boyfriend like? ...
9 Who did tell you that? ...
10 I won't be here tomorrow. ...
11 I couldn't find my glasses nowhere. ...
12 Isn't she beautiful! ...
13 'Aren't you coming?' 'Yes, I am.' ...

'I married you for your money, Leonard. Where is it?'

'It's an honest piece.'

yes/no questions   *Is the taxi here?   Do I need a visa?*

AM I?   HAVE YOU?   CAN SHE?   DO YOU?   DOES HE?

All *yes/no* questions begin with a verb.
To make questions: put an auxiliary verb before the subject.
(Auxiliary verbs are *be* (*am, are* etc), *have/has/had, will, would, can, could, shall, should, may, might* and *must*.)

STATEMENT ➕ :   *The taxi is here.   Ann has arrived.   The train will be late.   You can pay.*

QUESTION ❓ :   *Is the taxi here?   Has Ann arrived?   Will the train be late?   Can you pay?*

① Put the words in the right order to make questions.

▶ you ready are   ..Are you ready?...

▶ telephoned she has Mary   ..Has she telephoned Mary?.............................

▶ swim your brother can   ..Can your brother swim?...............................

1 tired are you   ....

2 he at is home   ....

3 go must now you   ....

4 Spanish they speak can   ....

5 tomorrow you be here will   ....

6 she will arrive by train   ....

7 forgotten her keys she has   ....

8 your sister is playing tennis   ....

If there is no auxiliary verb: put *do/does/did* before the subject and use the infinitive (without *to*).

STATEMENT ➕ :   *I need a visa.*
QUESTION ❓ :   *Do I need a visa?* (NOT ~~Need I a visa?~~, NOT ~~Do I to need a visa?~~)

STATEMENT ➕ :   *John wants to go home.*
QUESTION ❓ :   *Does John want to go home?* (NOT ~~Does John wants to go home?~~)

STATEMENT ➕ :   *She knew Mary.*
QUESTION ❓ :   *Did she know Mary?* (NOT ~~Did she knew Mary?~~)

② Make questions with *you.*

You want to know if somebody:

▶ understands   ..Do you understand?..............   3 knew Andrew   ....

▶ called you   ..Did you call me?..................   4 went skiing last winter   ....

1 drinks coffee   ....

2 likes jazz   ....   5 works in London   ....

③ Make questions with *he.*

You want to know if somebody:

▶ plays football   ..Does he play football?..

1 speaks Arabic   ....

2 knows Mr Peters   ....

3 works at home   ....

4 lived in Birmingham   ....

5 went home last week   ....

We **don't** put *do* with **other auxiliary verbs.**

Can you swim? (NOT ~~Do you can swim?~~)

4 **Circle the correct question.**

▶ (A) Will you be ready soon?   **B** Do you will be ready soon?

▶ **A** Live you in London?   (B) Do you live in London?   **C** Are you live in London?

1 **A** Do you are tired?   **B** Do you tired?   **C** Are you tired?

2 **A** Do you must go now?   **B** Must you go now?

3 **A** Do you speak Japanese?   **B** Speak you Japanese?   **C** Are you speak Japanese?

4 **A** Do you have been to China?   **B** Have you been to China?

5 **A** Were you go to work by car?   **B** Did you go to work by car?   **C** Went you to work by car?

6 **A** Can she sing?   **B** Does she can sing?

7 **A** Is Ann looking for a job?   **B** Does Ann looking for a job?   **C** Is Ann look for a job?

Only put **one verb** before the **subject**

Is her father working today? (NOT ~~Is working her father today?~~)
Has your brother got children? (NOT ~~Has got your brother children.~~)
Did those people telephone again? (NOT ~~Did telephone those people again?~~)

Be careful when questions have **long subjects.** The word order does not change.

Is Ann	*coming tomorrow?*
Are Ann and her mother	*coming tomorrow?*
Are Ann and her mother and father and Uncle George coming tomorrow?	

(NOT ~~Are coming tomorrow Ann and her mother and father and Uncle George?~~)

5 **Make *yes/no* questions.**

▶ The boss's secretary travels a lot.
Does the boss's secretary travel a lot?

▶ The President and her husband have arrived.
Have the President and her husband arrived?

1 Your sister Caroline is talking to the police.
....

2 All the people here understand Spanish.
....

3 Most of the football team played well.
....

4 Everybody in the office is working late today.
....

5 The man at the table in the corner is asleep.
....

6 The 7.30 train for London leaves from Platform 2.
....

→ For more about questions with *have*, see pages 8–11.
→ For more practice with present questions, past questions etc, see Sections 2–5.
→ For question tags like *It's late, **isn't it**?*, see pages 266–267.

question words *When will you see her?*

WHERE IS . . . ?   WHEN CAN . . . ?   WHY DOES . . . ?

Questions with *where, when, why* etc normally have the same word order as *yes/no* questions (pages 106–107).
We put *am/are/is/was/were* or another auxiliary verb (*have, will, can* etc) before the subject

STATEMENT ➕ :	*Anna is in Russia.*	*I will see her on Tuesday.*
QUESTION ❓ :	*Where is Anna?*	*When will you see her?* (NOT ~~When you will see her?~~)

If there is no other auxiliary verb, we use *do/does/did* + infinitive (without *to*).

STATEMENT ➕ :	*He likes his job.*	*I came here to learn English.*
QUESTION ❓ :	*How does he like his job?*	*Why did you come here?* (NOT ~~Why you came here?~~)

1 **Make questions with the words in the boxes.**

how	when ✓	when	where ✓	where	why

▶ (*you staying?*) ..'Where are you staying?'.. 'At the Park Hotel.'
▶ (*you arrive?*) ....'When did you arrive?'.. 'Last night.'
1 (*you here?*) .... 'To see Scotland.'
2 (*you been today?*) .... 'To Edinburgh.'
3 (*you going to Glasgow?*) .... 'Next weekend.'
4 (*you like Scotland?*) 'How .... 'It's great!'

how	when	when	where	why

5 (*you come here?*) .... 'By car.'
6 (*you come by car?*) .... 'I like driving.'
7 (*you live?*) .... 'In Germany.'
8 (*you leaving?*) .... 'Next Tuesday.'
9 (*we see you again?*) ....
   'I'll be back next summer.'

We often ask questions with *how* + adjective/adverb.

How old *is your sister?*   **How tall** *are you?*   **How fast** *can you run?*

2 **Here are some common expressions with *how*. Use them to complete the questions.**

How old ...? ✓	How far ...?	How long ...?	How tall ...?
How big ...?	How fast ...?	How often ...?	How well ...?

▶ 'How old are .... you?' '37 next birthday.'
1 '.. your house from here?' 'About 5 km.'
2 '.. John?' 'Very tall – nearly two metres.'
3 '.. she driving?' 'The police say she was doing 160 km/h.'
4 '.. see your parents?' 'Every week.'
5 '.. Ann's flat?' 'Very small – just one room and a bathroom.'
6 '.. stay in China?' 'I was there for six months.'
7 '.. speak Spanish?' 'Not very well.'

Some questions begin with **what + noun.**

What time is the film? **What time** does the train leave? (NOT USUALLY At what time ...?)
What colour are her eyes? (NOT ~~What colour have~~ ...?) **What colour** is your car?
What size are you? (buying clothes) **What size** would you like?
What sort of books do you read? **What sort of** films do you like? (OR **What kind of** ...?)

3 Put the beginnings and ends together, and put in an expression with *What ...*

1 '..What time............ does her plane arrive?'	A 'Eight o'clock, if it's not late.' 1
2 '............................ is the baby's hair?'	B '................................, small or large?' ...
3 '............................ music do you play?'	C 'She hasn't got any.' ...
4 'I'd like a packet of rice, please.'	D 'Pop, mostly.' ...
5 'Can I borrow one of your sweaters?'	E 'I don't remember – it was very late.' ...
6 '............................ holidays do you prefer?'	F 'Sure. .... would you like?
7 '............................ did you get home?'	Blue? Green?' ...
8 'I need a sweater.' '......................... are you?'	G 'Extra large.' ...
	H 'We usually go to the mountains.' ...

To ask for **descriptions**, we often use *What is/are/was/were ... like?*

'Where have you been?' 'In Ireland.' '**What was** the weather **like**?' 'OK.'
'**What's** your new boyfriend **like**?' 'He's very nice.'
'My brother writes detective stories.' 'Yes? **What are** they **like**?' 'Not very good, really.'

4 Make questions with *What ... like?*, using expressions from the box.

your new girlfriend	your new house	your new car	your new job
your new boss ✓	your new school	your new neighbours	

▶ 'What's your new boss like?'....................................... 'He's not very good at his job.'
1 .... 'She's beautiful.'
2 .... 'Very noisy. They have parties all night.'
3 .... 'OK – it's a bit slow.'
4 .... 'Great – we've got much more room.'
5 .... 'It's interesting. I travel a lot.'
6 .... 'The teachers aren't much good.'

GRAMMAR AND VOCABULARY: some more useful questions

Where are you from? *Where do you come from?* (NOT ~~From where~~ ...? – see page 137)
How long have you been here? *How long are you here for?* (= 'Until when ...?')
How long does it take to get to London? *How long does it take to learn English?*
How do you spell that word? *How do you pronounce this word?*

→ For questions with *who*, *what* and *which*, see page 110.

> *I keep six honest serving-men*
> *(They taught me all I knew):*
> *Their names are What and Why and When*
> *And How and Where and Who.*
> (Rudyard Kipling)

question-word subjects *Who phoned? What happened?*

We use **who** for **people** and **what** for **things**.

*'**Who** did you see?' 'John.' '**What** did he say?' 'Nothing much.'*

When *who* and *what* are **subjects**, we make questions without *do/does/did*. Compare:

*'**Who**^{SUBJ} phoned?' '**Mike**^{SUBJ} phoned.'* (NOT ~~'Who did phone?'~~)
*'**Who**^{OBJ} **did** you see?' 'I saw Mike^{OBJ}.'*
*'**What**^{SUBJ} happened?' 'Something^{SUBJ} terrible happened.'* (NOT ~~'What did happen?'~~)
*'**What**^{OBJ} **did** he say?' 'He said something^{OBJ} terrible.'*

The same thing happens when subjects begin with **which, what,** or **how much/many**.

Which team won? (NOT ~~Which team did win?~~)   *What country won the World Cup in 1966?*
How many people work here? (COMPARE *How many people^{OBJ} did you^{SUBJ} see?*)

1 Circle the correct form.

▶ Who (lives) / *does live* in that house?
▶ What (happened) / *did happen* to Joe?
1 Who *plays / does play* the piano?
2 What *made / did make* that noise?
3 Who *married she? / did she marry?*
5 What *means this word? / does this word mean?*
4 What *said you? / did you say?*
6 Who *told / did tell* you?

2 Complete the questions.

▶ 'I saw some dogs.' 'How many .dogs did you see?...................'
▶ 'One of those cars belongs to Mary.' 'Which car .belongs to Mary?.........................'
1 'A lot of people came to her party.' 'How many people ....'
2 'Peter caught a train.' 'Which train ....'
3 'One of those buses goes to the station.' 'Which bus ....'
4 'Douglas speaks a lot of languages.' 'How many languages ....'
5 'Alice likes music.' 'What sort of music ....'

3 Look at the picture and complete the sentences.

▶ Who loves Fred? .Alice and Mary.......
1 Who does Fred love? ....
2 .... Ann? ....
3 .... love? Joe.
4 .... Alice? ....
5 .... love? Mary.
6 .... love? Ann.
7 .... Nobody.

4 Can you write four more questions and answers about the picture?

1 ....
2 ....
3 ....
4 ....

5 Make questions. Ask about the words *in italics*.

▶ (a) John broke *the window*. (b) *John* broke the window.
(a) What did John break? (b) Who broke the window?

1 (a) Mary bought *a coat*. (b) *Mary* bought a coat.
....

2 (a) The bus hit *that tree*. (b) *The bus* hit that tree.
....

3 (a) *Ann* lost the office keys. (b) Ann lost *the office keys*.
....

4 (a) Fred is studying *Arabic*. (b) *Fred* is studying Arabic.
....

5 (a) *Mike* hates computers. (b) Mike hates *computers*.
....

6 Write questions about the pictures, using the words in the box. Do you know
the answers? (They are at the bottom of the page.)

| build ✓   build   paint   first reach   write |

▶ The Eiffel Tower

▶ Who built the Eiffel Tower? ....
1 ....
2 ....
3 ....
4 ....

1 The North Pole

2 *War and Peace*

3 The Great Wall of China

4 *Sunflowers*

7 Write questions about books, plays or songs. Ask some people.

Who wrote ....

....

→ For the difference between *which* and *what*, see page 281.

→ For *whom*, see page 282.

4 Van Gogh

▶ Gustave Eiffel   1 Robert Peary in 1909   2 Leo Tolstoy   3 The Emperor Shi Huangdì (and a lot of other people)

negatives *Dogs can't fly. I don't know why.*

AM **NOT**   HAVE **NOT**   WILL **NOT**   **CANNOT**   **DO NOT**

To make negative sentences: put *not* after an auxiliary verb
(Auxiliary verbs are: *be* (am etc), *have/has/had, will, would, can, could, shall, should, may, might, must.*)

It *is* **not** *raining.*   I *have* **not** *seen Bill.*   *She* **cannot** *understand me.*

In **conversation** we usually use **contractions** (see page 277):

aren't   isn't   wasn't   weren't   haven't   hasn't   hadn't   won't (= 'will not')   wouldn't
can't   couldn't   shan't   shouldn't   mightn't   mustn't
We say *I'm not,* NOT ~~I amn't~~. We can also say *you're not* (= *you aren't*), *he's not, she's not,* etc.

It *isn't* / *It's* **not** *raining.*   *We* **weren't** *at home.*   *I* **haven't** *seen Bill.*
She **can't** *understand me.*   *You* **mustn't** *tell anybody.*   *I'm* **not** *ready.*

1 **Make negative sentences. Use contractions.**

▶ Dogs can swim. (*fly*) ...*Dogs can't fly.*...

1 Milk is white. (*red*) ....

2 The children are at school. (*at home*) ....

3 Joe has been to Japan. (*Egypt*) ....

4 You must give this letter to Ann. (*her mother*) ....

5 I'll be here tomorrow. (*in the office*) ....

6 I could talk when I was two years old. (*swim*) ....

7 We were in London yesterday. (*Birmingham*) ....

8 I'm Scottish. (*English*) ....

2 **Write five things that you can't do. Here are some suggestions.**

dance   draw   drive   play chess/bridge etc   play the piano/guitar etc
remember faces   remember names   ride a horse   sing
speak French/Chinese etc   understand maths

▶ *I can't speak German.*...

1 ....

2 ....

3 ....

4 ....

5 ....

'There are three things that
I can't remember: names, faces,
and I've forgotten the other.'

3 **Write five things that you probably won't do next week. Here are some suggestions.**

go to New York   get married   get rich   play football   become President
write a poem   buy a car   make a cake   read Shakespeare   climb Mount Everest

▶ *I probably won't go to Paris next week.*...

1 ....

2 ....

3 ....

4 ....

5 ....

If there is no auxiliary verb, we use *do/does/did* + *not/n't* + infinitive (without *to*).

I like → *I don't like*   *She knows* → *She doesn't know* (NOT ~~She doesn't knows~~)
He arrived → *He did not arrive* (NOT ~~He did not arrived~~)   *It rained* → *It didn't rain*

4 Make negative sentences.

▶ Cats eat meat. (*potatoes*) .Cats don't eat potatoes.
▶ Cervantes wrote 'Don Quixote'. (*Mozart*) ..Mozart didn't write 'Don Quixote'.
1 Shakespeare lived in London. (*New York*) ....
2 Dictionaries tell you about words. (*phone books*) ....
3 The earth goes round the sun. (*round the moon*) ....
4 Most Algerians speak Arabic. (*Russian*) ....
5 Fridges keep food cold. (*cookers*) ....
6 The Second World War ended in 1945. (*1955*) ....
7 John knows my parents. (*my sister*) ....

5 Use expressions from the two boxes, and write five things that you don't do.

| buy socks   dance   go to sleep   play football   play the violin   ride a bicycle |
| sing   speak English   study mathematics   write poetry |

| after breakfast   at Christmas   at school   in London   in the bath   in the middle of the night |
| in the middle of the road   in the sea   on the bus   on the telephone   on Tuesdays |

▶ I don't buy socks in London.
1 ....
2 ....
3 ....
4 ....
5 ....

6 Complete these negative sentences. Use *aren't, haven't, doesn't* etc.

1 'What's the time?' 'I .... know.'
2 'What was the film like?' 'It .... very good.'
3 'Would Ann like some coffee?' 'No, she .... drink coffee.'
4 I .... seen Joe for weeks. Is he OK?
5 Pat and Jim .... very happy with their new car.
6 'Can I see you tomorrow?' 'I .... be here. How about Tuesday?'
7 'Was the lesson any good?' 'I .... understand a word.'
8 She .... buy the coat; it was too expensive.
9 The baby .... got much hair.
10 'Can we go?' 'In a minute. I .... ready.'

7 GRAMMAR AND VOCABULARY: four words for people who can't do things
Put the beginnings and ends together. Use a dictionary if necessary.

1 Some **handicapped** people	A can't see. ...
2 A **blind** person	B can't hear. ...
3 A **deaf** person	C can't read or write. ...
4 An **illiterate** person	D can't move or work normally. 1

→ For more practice with present negatives, past negatives etc, see Section 2–5.   → For more about negatives with *have*, see page 8–11.

negatives with *nobody, never* etc   *Nobody loves me.*

We can make negative sentences with **nobody, nothing, nowhere, never, no, hardly** (= 'almost not') and similar words. With these words, we **do not** use **not** or **do/does/did**.

Nobody loves me. (NOT ~~Nobody doesn't love me.~~)
He said *nothing*. (NOT ~~He didn't say nothing.~~)
She *never* writes to me. (NOT ~~She doesn't never write to me.~~)
I've got *no* money. (NOT ~~I haven't got no money.~~)
I can *hardly* understand him. (NOT ~~I can't hardly understand him.~~)

1 Put the sentences in order.

▶ up father early my gets never   ...My father never gets up early...................

1 lives house nobody that in   ....

2 my understand I'll dog never   ....

3 children me the nothing told   ....

4 money I no have   ....

5 the could road I see hardly   ....

2 Change the sentences.

▶ She didn't say anything. (*nothing*) ...She said nothing...

1 I didn't see anybody. (*nobody*)   ....

2 We didn't have any trouble. (*no*)   ....

3 My parents don't go out. (*never*)   ....

4 I looked for the dog, but it wasn't anywhere in the house. (*nowhere*)

....

5 I didn't eat anything yesterday. (*nothing*)   ....

6 It didn't rain for three months. (*hardly*)   ....

7 John didn't speak, Mary didn't speak, Bill didn't speak. (*nobody*)

....

3 Make the sentences negative.

▶ I drink coffee. (*not*) ...I don't drink coffee..

▶ I drink coffee. (*never*) ...I never drink coffee..

▶ Somebody telephoned. (*nobody*) ...Nobody telephoned..

1 My grandmother drives fast. (*never*)   ....

2 Andrew plays the guitar. (*not*)   ....

3 When she talked, I understood. (*nothing*)   ....

4 I like Ann's new shoes. (*not*)   ....

5 Something happened this morning. (*nothing*)   ....

6 There's somewhere to sit down in the station. (*nowhere*)   ....

7 I watch TV. (*hardly*)   ....

8 Somebody wants to play tennis. (*nobody*)   ....

| I never hated a man enough to give him diamonds back.
 (Zsa Zsa Gabor) | I have nothing to say, and I am saying it, and that is poetry.
 (John Cage) | Sometime they'll give a war and nobody will come.
 (Carl Sandburg) |

negative questions *Aren't you well?*

CONTRACTED (CONVERSATIONAL)	UNCONTRACTED (FORMAL, UNUSUAL)
n't after auxiliary verb	*not* after subject
Why isn't it ready yet? *Doesn't she know?*	*Why is it not ready yet?* *Does she not know?*
We say *aren't I?*, NOT ~~amn't I?~~	
'**Aren't I** next?' 'No, I am.' (BUT NOT ~~I aren't next.~~)	

1 Make these questions more conversational.

▶ Are you not well? ..*Aren't you well?*...

1 Can you not swim? ....

2 Do you not speak Spanish? ....

3 Were the shops not open? ....

4 Has Ann not arrived? ....

5 Did she not know him? ....

6 Why are you not working? ....

We often use negative questions to **make sure that something is true.**

***Didn't you go** and see Peter yesterday? How is he?* (= 'I believe you went and saw Peter ...')

2 Make negative questions to make sure that these things are true.

▶ I think you went to Scotland last week. ..*Didn't you go to Scotland last week?*............

1 I think you speak Arabic. ....

2 I think that's Bill over there. ....

3 I believe you studied at Oxford. ....

4 Perhaps this is your coat. ....

5 I think her mother is a doctor. ....

6 I thought Joe was at the party. ....

We can use negative questions as **exclamations.**

***Isn't it** cold!*   ***Doesn't your hair** look nice!*   ***Weren't those children** noisy!*

3 Make exclamations.

▶ It's surprising. *Isn't it surprising!*....................   3 That child is dirty. ....

1 They're late. ....   4 It's hot. ....

2 She looks tired. ....   5 John works hard. ....

Notice how we use *yes* and *no* in answers to **negative questions.**

'Don't you like it?' '**Yes** (I like it).'   *'Aren't you ready?'* '**No** (I'm not ready).'

4 Add *Yes* or *No* to the answers.

▶ 'Aren't you ready?' '.*Yes*......................, I am.'   4 'Hasn't she paid?' '............................, she has.'

1 'Don't you like her?' '........................, I don't.'   5 'Wasn't he at home?' '......................., he was.'

2 'Can't you help me?' '......................., I can't.'   6 'Didn't she phone?' '....................., she didn't.'

3 'Isn't this nice?' '....................................., it is.'

test yourself   questions and negatives

❶ Make questions with *she*.

▶ live in England? _Does she live in England?_ ....

1 been to America? ....

2 like dancing? ....

3 can swim? ....

4 be here tomorrow? ....

5 watch TV yesterday? ....

❷ Make negative sentences.

▶ I can speak French. (*Spanish*) ..._I can't speak Spanish._ ....

1 Ann is at home. (*at work*) ....

2 I've forgotten your name. (*your face*) ....

3 Peter drives buses. (*taxis*) ....

4 We went to Spain. (*Portugal*) ....

5 You must use this phone. (*that one*) ....

❸ Put in suitable question words.

▶ '_What time_.......... is the film?' 'Eight o'clock.'

1 '................................ is her hair?' 'Black.'

2 '................................ are you?' '1 metre 84.'

3 '................................ music do you like?' 'Pop.'

❹ Correct (✓) or not (✗)?

▶ I did not understand. ✓

1 Does your brother living with you? ...

2 Are coming to the party all your friends? ...

3 Did you see Bill yesterday? ...

4 Play you football? ...

5 Why you are tired? ...

6 What time does the lesson start? ...

7 What is your boss like? ...

❺ Ask about the words *in italics*.

▶ *She* said something. _Who said something?_ ....

▶ She said *something*. _What did she say?_ ....

1 *Julia* cooked dinner. ....

2 Julia cooked *eggs*. ....

3 *The ball* hit Joe. ....

4 The ball hit *Joe*. ....

5 Ann plays *the guitar*. ....

6 *Ann* plays the guitar. ....

❻ Put in *Yes* or *No*.

1 'Isn't she coming?' '..........., she isn't.'

2 'Aren't you tired?' '..........., I am.'

3 'Didn't Bill phone you?' '..........., he did.'

4 'Can't you find your keys?' '..........., I can't.'

❼ Correct (✓) or not (✗)?

1 Who did tell you that? ...

2 Isn't the weather nice! ...

3 Nobody didn't help me. ...

4 I had no money. ...

5 Will be there tomorrow both your parents? ...

◉ More difficult questions

SECTION 9 infinitives and -ing forms

● grammar summary

> INFINITIVES: (to) go, (to) break, (to) see etc
> -ING FORMS (ALSO CALLED 'GERUNDS'): going, breaking, seeing etc

We can use both -ing forms and infinitives as subjects (but -ing forms are more common).
Smoking is bad for you. (More natural than *To smoke is bad for you.*)

We can use **infinitives** to say **why** we do things.
I got up early to catch the 7.15 train.

After some verbs we use **infinitives**; after **others** we use **-ing** forms.
I expect to pass my exams. (NOT ~~I expect passing~~ ...)   *I'll finish studying in June.* (NOT ~~I'll finish to study~~ ...)

We can use **infinitives after some adjectives** and **nouns**.
She's ready to leave.   *I'm glad to see you.*   *I've got work to do.*

After **prepositions** we use **-ing** forms, not infinitives.
You can't live without eating. (NOT ...~~without to eat.~~)
I usually watch TV before going to bed. (NOT ... ~~before to go to bed.~~)

Infinitives often have *to* before them; but not always.
I want to go home, but I can't go now.

● pre-test: which units do you need?

Try this small test. It will help you to decide which units you need. The answers are on page 283.

❶ Correct (✓) or not (✗)?

▶ I want see you. ✗
▶ Can I help you? ✓
1 It's necessary to get a visa. ...
2 I hope to not have problems at university. ...
3 I went to Mexico for learning Spanish. ...
4 His parents wanted him to be a doctor. ...
5 You can get there faster by take the train. ...
6 I'm too tired for working now. ...

7 I stopped to smoke last year. ...
8 She keeps telephoning me. ...
9 We decided going by bus. ...
10 I'm glad seeing you. ...
11 The lesson was easy to understand. ...
12 We had nowhere to sleep. ...
13 Learning languages is difficult. ...

'This one's for not asking, and this one's for not telling.'

infinitives: using *to*   *I want to go.   Must you go?*

We usually put *to* with infinitives

I want to go home. (NOT *I want go home.*)   *It's important to get enough sleep.*
I telephoned my sister to say sorry.

But we use infinitives without *to* after *do/does/did* in questions and negatives (see pages 106 and 113).

Does John speak Russian? (NOT *Does John to speak ...*)   *I didn't understand.*

We also use infinitives without *to* after the modal verbs *can, could, may, might, will, would, shall, should, must* and *had better* (see Section 6).

I can't swim. (NOT *I can't to swim.*)   *Must you go now?*   *We had better find a hotel.*

---

1 **Put in *to* or nothing (–).**

▶ I don't want ..*to*.. stay at school.
▶ What time does the train ..*–*.. leave?
1 Do you ...... play golf?
2 It's nice ...... be at home again.

3 It may ...... snow this weekend.
4 I must ...... remember ...... phone Andy.
5 Do we ...... need ...... buy petrol?
6 Jane seems ...... be tired today.

2 **Put in words from the box, with or without *to*.**

ask ✓   buy   go   hear   help   learn   lend ✓   see

▶ I'm writing ......*to ask*............... for your help.
▶ Can you ..*lend*.................... me some money?
1 Maria went to America .... English.
2 Can you .... me with the cooking?

3 I'd like .... you for a minute.
4 Where did you .... those boots?
5 I expect .... from my family soon.
6 I don't want .... by bus.

We make negative infinitives with *not (to)* + verb.

*Try **not to forget** your keys.* (NOT *... to not forget ...*)   *Be careful **not to wake** Peter up.*
*I told you **not to telephone** me here.*   *I'm sorry **not to stay** longer.*
*The company did **not make** any money last year.*   *You must **not park** in front of the school.*

---

3 **Put in *not to* with infinitives from the box.**

break   go to sleep   have   have   laugh ✓   make   talk

▶ Please try ..*not to laugh*................................ when Bill sings.
1 It's nice .... a headache any more.
2 Be careful .... those glasses.
3 Please try .... in the lessons.
4 Tell the children .... so much noise.
5 I'd like .... so much work.
6 Bill must learn .... about himself all the time.

→ For infinitives without *to* after *let, make, see* and *hear*, see pages 280-281.
→ For sentences like *No, I don't want to,* see page 271.

infinitives of purpose *She went to Paris to study music.*

We use an **infinitive with** *to* to say **why** we do something.
*I turned on the TV **to watch** the news.*   *Joanna went to Paris **to study** music.*

① Complete the sentences with the infinitives of the verbs in the box.

ask for	buy	catch	drive	finish	meet	learn	turn on ✓	wait for

▶ Use this button .to turn on........................... the computer.
1 Oliver got up early .... Mark to the station.
2 I was late, so I ran .... my bus.
3 Ann wrote to me .... Joe's address.
4 I sat in the waiting room .... the doctor.
5 Bob's gone to the airport .... his uncle.
6 I went to town on Saturday .... a present for my cousin's birthday.
7 I stayed up late last night .... my English homework.
8 Alice went to Beijing .... Chinese.

② Write sentences with infinitives.

▶ We wanted to go to the cinema, so Mum gave us some money.
  Mum gave us some money to go to the cinema....
1 I wanted to clean the top of the fridge, so I stood on a chair.
  ....
2 Roger wants to buy a book, so he's gone to town.
  ....
3 We wanted to get warm, so we moved closer to the fire.
  ....
4 If you want to open the front door, use this key.
  ....
5 I wanted to tell George about the meeting, so I left a note.
  ....
6 Jane wanted to earn some pocket money, so she got a part-time job.
  ....

③ GRAMMAR AND VOCABULARY: cooking
Make sure you know the words in the box. Use a dictionary if necessary. Then complete the sentences.

VERBS: bake	boil	cut	fry	measure ✓	mix	weigh	
NOUNS: bowl	frying pan	jug	knife	oven	saucepan	scales	

▶ You use a measuring jug ...to measure........... water, milk etc.
1 You use scales .... things.
2 You use an oven .... things.
3 You use a frying pan .... things.
4 You use a saucepan .... things.
5 You use a bowl .... things.
6 You use a knife .... things.

verb + infinitive   *I hope to be an airline pilot.*

After some verbs we use **an infinitive with** *to*.

*I **hope to go** to Ireland later this year.*   ***Did** Jeremy **agree to help** you with your work?*

1 **Read the texts, and write down the verbs that are followed by an infinitive with *to*.**

I'm eighteen, and I <u>hope to</u> be an airline pilot. My parents have <u>agreed to</u> pay for lessons if I do well in my exams. My brother says girls shouldn't be pilots, but I refuse to listen to him.

▶ ...hope to.......
▶ ...agreed to...
1 ....

When I started to work here, my boss promised to give me interesting work, travelling to Europe and Asia. I expected to enjoy my job. But all my work is boring, and I don't do any travelling. I've tried to talk to my boss, but she doesn't listen. Now I've decided to look for another job.

2 ....
3 ....
4 ....
5 ....
6 ....

I've always been afraid of water. Then one day last year I thought, 'I don't want to live like this'. So I found some special lessons for people like me. I'm learning to swim, and next summer I plan to take water-skiing lessons.

7 ....
8 ....
9 ....

I needed to be at work early this morning. But I forgot to set my alarm clock, and I woke up at 7.30 instead of 6.30. Then everything seemed to go wrong. I had no clean shirts, the bus was late, ...

10 ....
11 ....
12 ....

I began to learn karate four years ago, and I've continued to go to lessons twice a week since then. I love it. I've visited some other karate clubs, but I prefer to learn at my own club, because the teaching is so good.

13 ....
14 ....
15 ....

After ***begin, start, continue*** and ***prefer*** we can also use ***-ing*** forms with the same meaning.

When did you begin to learn / begin learning karate?
I started to have / started having these headaches about a month ago.
The President continued to speak / continued speaking for an hour and a half.
I prefer to live / prefer living in the country – the city is too noisy.

→ For *-ing* forms after *try* and *forget*, see pages 281–282.

> Love... Everyone feels it,
>   has felt it, or expects to feel it.
>   *(Anthony Trollope, 1883)*

> War will stop when men refuse to fight.
>   *(Pacifist slogan, 1936)*

> We must learn to live together as brothers ...
> *(Martin Luther King, 1964)*

> Gentlemen always seem
>   to remember blondes.
>   *(Anita Loos, 1925)*

> He preferred to be good
> rather than to seem good.
>   *(Sallust, of Cato, 54 B.C.)*

> Stop the world, I want to get off!
>   *(Anthony Newley, 1961)*

❷ Complete the sentences with verbs from the boxes and *to*.

1–4:	agree	decide	expect ✓	need	plan ✓	try

▶ ALICE: 'The exam seemed easy. I was surprised when I got a low mark.'
Alice *expected to* .... pass the exam; she was surprised when she got a low mark.

▶ David and Cathy have got plane tickets and hotel reservations for Corsica.
David and Cathy are *planning to* .... go to Corsica.

1 Annie is going to Singapore. A visa is necessary, and she hasn't got one.
Annie .... get a visa.

2 JANE: 'Could you possibly lend me £5?' ANDY: 'Sure.'
Andy has .... lend £5 to Jane.

3 JOE: 'Shall I go to the cinema or stay at home? Cinema, perhaps? No, I'll stay at home.'
Joe has .... stay at home.

4 Lizzie was expecting a call from Sarah. Sarah rang the number, but it was engaged.
Sarah .... phone Lizzie, but the number was engaged.

5–10:	forget	learn	promise	refuse	start	want

5 Oliver lives in the US, but he took all his driving lessons in France.
Oliver .... drive in France.

6 PATRICK: 'I will write to you every day, Barbara.'
Patrick has .... write to Barbara every day.

7 BOB: 'I was going to post a birthday card to my mother, but I didn't remember.'
Bob .... post his mother's birthday card.

8 PHILIP: 'Please, please lend me your car.' AGNES: 'No, no, no and no.'
Agnes has .... lend her car to Philip.

9 Helen's parents are sending her to England for two weeks. Helen is not happy.
Helen doesn't .... go to England.

10 Susan said her first word when she was seven months old.
Susan .... talk when she was seven months old.

11–15:	begin	continue	hope	prefer	seem

11 Mark plays the piano and the trumpet. The trumpet is his favourite.
Mark can play the piano, but he .... play the trumpet.

12 Annie usually stops work at 5.00, but yesterday she didn't stop until 7.00.
Annie .... work until 7.00 yesterday.

13 John swims every day; he's going to try for the national team next year.
John .... be in the national swimming team next year.

14 'I'm not sure, but I think Rebecca was worried yesterday evening.'
Rebecca .... be worried yesterday evening.

15 Lee sat down to write a letter to her brother yesterday, but she didn't finish it.
Lee .... write a letter to her brother yesterday.

➔ For infinitives in indirect speech (after *tell*, *ask* etc), see pages 123 and 251.
➔ For sentences like *I don't want to*, see page 271.

verb + object + infinitive   *He wants me to cook.*

We often say that we **want somebody to do** something.

*My boyfriend **wants me to do** all the cooking.* (NOT *... ~~wants that I do all the cooking~~.*)

We can use **would like** in the same way.

*I'd **like you to listen** to this song.* (NOT *~~I'd like that you listen~~ ...*)

1 Make sentences with *want* or *would like*.

▶ MRS LEWIS: Ann, can you post my letters, please? (*want*)
Mrs Lewis wants Ann to post her letters..

1 SARAH: John, could you cook tonight? (*would like*)
....

2 POLICEMAN: Please move your car, sir. (*want*)
.... the man ....

3 MOTHER: Helen, please wash your face. (*want*)
Helen's mother .... her ....

4 BILL: Andy, can you help me? (*would like*)
.... him.

5 ROGER: Karen, could you lend me some money? (*would like*)
.... lend him ....

6 JAKE: Be quiet for a minute, Peter. (*want*)
....

7 DAVID: Alice, can you have dinner with me? (*would like*)
....

8 MIKE: The government should put more money into schools. (*would like*)
....

2 Different people want Alice to do different things. Complete the sentences.

buy a better guitar	buy him	do something ✓	go to America with him
go to Russia with her	lend her	spend every weekend	take him for	work

▶ Everybody .wants her to do something..
1 Her boss .... harder.
2 Her little brother .... a bicycle.
3 Her dog .... a walk.
4 Her boyfriend ....
5 Her friend Martha .... a blue dress.
6 Her guitar teacher ....
7 Her mother .... at home.
8 Her sister ....

We can use some other verbs like this. For example: *ask, expect, help, need, tell*.

I asked Peter to work with me.   The doctor *told me to take* a holiday.

3 **Change the sentences.**

▶ They thought that we would be late. (*expect*)   They expected us to be late.

1 I didn't say to Alan 'Go home.' (*tell*)   ....

2 I said to Fred 'Please be quiet.' (*ask*)   ....

3 Do you think she'll phone? (*expect*)   ....

4 I carried the books with Joe. (*help*)   I helped ....

5 The policewoman said to me 'Show me your driving licence.' (*tell*)

  .... me .... her ....

6 Ann finished the work with me. (*help*)   Ann ....

7 I said to the shop assistant 'Can you help me?' (*ask*)   ....

8 You must stay with me. (*need*)   I need ....

4 **What do/did your parents want you to do/be in life?**

▶ My parents want me to be a doctor.

▶ My parents wanted me to study engineering.

  ....

5 GRAMMAR AND VOCABULARY: vehicles
Make sure you know the words in the box. Use a dictionary if necessary. Then look at the advertisements and say what the advertisers want you to buy.

| bike   motorbike   motorboat   plane   tractor ✓   yacht |

▶ They want me to buy a tractor.

1 ....

2 ....

3 ....

4 ....

5 ....

products, contact Trakta for the address of your nearest dealer.

TRAKTA TRACTORS
Quality & Performance
Trakta Tractors (UK) Ltd.,
Belmarsh Court, Belmarsh Park, Cheltham Y0

BARRIES
NEW SPEC MACHINES ARRIVING
NOW
CALL US FOR THE BEST DEALS

MACHINES TO CLEAR
DVR300............£5590
ALPHA.............£5450

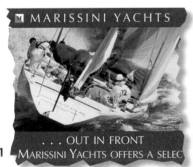

MARISSINI YACHTS

. . . OUT IN FRONT
1 MARISSINI YACHTS OFFERS A SELEC

Sorensen.... Setting a new standa
in design and performance.'

3   S O R E N S E N

HEATHFIELD H300 HYBRID

• 4130 Molloy frame • 24-speed Hitalo gears
2

CELGA 113A

1000 hours AF/E. CofA to
4 November. New leather seats

→ For *let, make, hear,* and *see* + object + infinitive, see page 281.

adjective + infinitive   *glad to find you at home*

We can use **adjective + infinitive** (with *to*) to say **what we think** of things that people do. We do this with adjectives like *clever, crazy, right, silly, stupid* and *wrong*.

*You're **crazy to think** you can get there in an hour.*   *You were **clever to bring** an umbrella.*

1 **Write sentences with infinitives.**

▶ Angela carries all her money in one bag. She's wrong.
   Angela's wrong to carry all her money in one bag.

▶ Annie got to the airport early. She was clever.
   Annie was clever to get to the airport early.

1 Eleanor listens to Mark. She's silly.

....

2 Elizabeth took the train without a ticket. She was wrong.

....

3 I sat on my glasses. I was stupid.

....

4 I washed a white shirt with a red one. I was wrong.

....

5 You believe Luke. You're silly.

....

6 You eat a good breakfast. You're right.

....

7 You lent money to Chris. You were crazy.

....

We can also use **infinitives** (with *to*) **after adjectives** for **feelings**, like *afraid, glad, happy, pleased, sad, surprised, unhappy*.

*Mum will be **glad to find** you at home.*   *I'm **pleased to meet** you.*

2 **Complete the text with expressions from the boxes.**

> 1–4: glad to leave ✓   happy not to have   pleased to find
> sorry to say   unhappy to think

Five years ago, I went to Australia to start a new job. I was ▶ ...*glad to leave*............... London,
but I was very 1 .... goodbye to my friends and family, and my mother was
2 .... that I would be so far away.

   I was a bit afraid of my new life, so I was 3 .... any problems when I
arrived. Sydney was beautiful, and I was 4 .... friendly people in the office,
an interesting job and a lovely apartment.

> 5–7: happy to be   pleased to see   surprised to find

Everything went well in Australia, but I never felt really at home there, and in the end I decided to
come back. Today I arrived in London, for the first time in five years. I was
5 .... so many changes, but I am really 6 .... here
again. On the way from the airport I started to cry – I was so 7 .... a big red
London bus.

Some adjectives describe the **following infinitive**, not the subject. This happens with *difficult, easy, hard, impossible, good, nice* and *interesting.*

He is often **difficult to understand.** (= 'It is often **difficult to understand him.**')
They are very **interesting to watch.** (= 'It is very **interesting to watch them.**')
Languages are **hard to learn** perfectly.   Tickets for the match are **impossible to buy.**
Do you think the meat is still **good to eat?**

3 Join the beginnings and ends, and put in verbs from the box.

dislike ✓   eat   find   open   read

1 Everybody likes my uncle; he's	A impossible to dislike........................ 1.
2 'Are these apples	B difficult ...., isn't it? ...
3 Good restaurants aren't	C good ....?' 'No, don't eat them.' ...
4 Thank you for that book – it was	D very interesting ....
5 This door is	E easy .... in this town. ...

4 Make sentences with the infinitives of verbs from the box.

clean   climb   pronounce   remember ✓   see you   understand   wear

▶ My phone number / easy   *My phone number is easy to remember.*........................

1 It / good   ....
2 Grammar / sometimes difficult   ....
3 That mountain / impossible   ....
4 This shirt / nice   ....
5 The word 'sixth' / hard   ....
6 This furniture / easy   ....

5 GRAMMAR AND VOCABULARY: school subjects
Make sure you know the words in the box. Use a dictionary if necessary. Then write five or more sentences to say what you think about some of the subjects.

| biology   chemistry   English   geography   history   literature
mathematics / maths (*singular*)   philosophy |
|---|

1 .... is easy to learn.
2 .... is hard to learn.
3 .... is easy to understand.
4 .... is difficult to understand.
5 .... is interesting to study.
6 ....
7 ....
8 ....

adjectives with *enough/too* + infinitive *too tired to sing*

After adjective + *enough*, we can use an infinitive (with *to*). Note the word order – see page 171.

Julie's old enough to drive now. (NOT *Julie's enough old* ...)   *John isn't strong enough to carry that.*

1 Make sentences with *is/isn't old enough to* ...

IN BRITAIN – AT WHAT AGE CAN YOU ...?	
When you are	**you can**
13	work part-time
16	leave home
16	leave school
17	drive a car
18	vote
18	change your name
21	drive a bus

Alice is 13.   Mark is 16.   Cathy is 17.
John is 18.   Liz is 21.

▶ John *is old enough to drive* .... a car.
▶ Alice *isn't old enough to drive* .... a car.
1 Alice .... part-time.
2 Alice .... home.
3 Mark .... school.
4 Cathy .... home.
5 Cathy .... vote.
6 John .... his name.
7 Liz .... a bus.

After *too* + *adjective*, we can use an infinitive (with *to*).

I'm too tired to sing.   *Alice was very afraid – too afraid to speak.*

2 Change two sentences into one. Use *too ... to* ...

▶ I'm very sleepy. I can't drive. *I'm too sleepy to drive.* ....
1 Helen is very ill. She can't work. ....
2 My grandfather is very old. He can't travel. ....
3 I'm very bored. I can't listen any longer. ....
4 Cara's very hot. She can't play tennis. ....
5 I'm very hungry. I can't work. ....

We can use *too* + *adjective* + infinitive in a different way.

They're too big to carry. (= 'Nobody can carry them, because they're too big.')
It's too cold to drink. (= 'Nobody can drink it, because it's too cold.')

3 Make sentences with *too ... to* ...

▶ This homework / difficult / do *This homework is too difficult to do.* ....
1 This box / heavy / lift ....
2 This soup / salty / eat ....
3 This book / boring / finish ....
4 That plate / hot / touch ....
5 Some animals / small / see ....
6 That sign / dirty / read ....

> Middle age: the age when you're too old to
> play tennis and too young to play golf.
> (*Ansel Adams*)

some letters to write; nothing to eat

We can often use **infinitives with** *to* after **nouns**.

*I've got **some letters to write**.   Sorry – I haven't got **any money to lend** you.*

1 Complete the sentences with the expressions from the box.

dress to wear	friend to see	homework to do	letters to post
shopping to do	stories to tell ✓	video to watch	

▶ My uncle always has very interesting ...*stories to tell*................... about his year in Nepal.
1 Please can I go out tonight, Dad? I've got no ....
2 I'm going to the post office – have you got any ....
3 I think I'll stay at home tonight. I'm a bit tired, and I've got a good ....
4 Have you got a .... to the party, or will you have to buy one?
5 If you've got any .... we can go to the supermarket later.
6 I'll be home a bit late tonight – I've got a .... after work.

We can use **infinitives with** *to* after words like ***somebody, anything*** and ***nowhere*** (see page 165).

*Would you like **something to drink**?   I haven't got **anything to read**; can I borrow this book?*
*There's **nothing to eat** in the fridge.   Those poor people have **nowhere to live**.*

2 Complete the sentences with *somebody* etc and the verbs *in italics*.

▶ POLICEMAN: Move on, please. There's (*see*) ..*nothing to see*...........................
1 I can't go to the party: I don't have (*wear*) ....
2 Could I possibly use this table? I need (*work*) ....
3 When I arrived, there was (*do*) .... – all the work was finished.
4 Everyone in our class was ill today, so our teacher had (*teach*) ....
5 I'll be with you in a few minutes – I have (*finish*) ....
6 All my friends are out of town tonight, and I've got (*go*) ....
7 Everybody needs (*love*) ....
8 My brother couldn't find (*stay*) .... in Bristol.
9 Have you found (*help*) .... you with the disco on Saturday?
10 Your arms are full – give me (*carry*) ....

NOTHING TO EAT

She had nothing to eat.
They made a film about her
because she had nothing to eat.

Her husband
was killed in the war.
They wrote a book about
how he was killed in the war.

Her mother and brother
were executed by the revolutionaries.
There was an opera about it.

Both her children died
(there was no hospital).
You can see the photographs
at an exhibition in London.

Then somebody wrote a poem.

Still
she had nothing to eat.

Lewis Mancha

it with infinitive subjects   *It's nice to be here with you.*

We don't often begin sentences with infinitive subjects (like *To be here with you is nice*).
More often, we begin with *it* and put the infinitive later.
The structure *It is/was/etc + adjective + infinitive* (with *to*) is very common.

It's nice to be here with you.   *It was good to see you again.*   *It's important to remember people's names.*

1 Complete these sentences about a summer holiday. Use *It was* and words from the box.

> a bit hard to understand   dangerous to swim   expensive to eat   impossible to be
> interesting to see   nice to have   really good to get away ✓   very easy to make

▶ *It was really good to get away* .... from home and work.
1 .... sunshine every day.
2 .... how other people live.
3 Sometimes .... the language if people talked fast.
4 .... friends.
5 .... in restaurants, but the food was wonderful.
6 The sea was beautiful, but ....
7 There were so many things to do that .... bored.

2 GRAMMAR AND VOCABULARY: learning and using a language: what is important?
Make sure you know the words in the box. Use a dictionary if necessary.
Then make sentences with *It's important to ...*, *It's not necessary to ...* or *It's important not to ...* .
Different answers are possible: for ours, see the answer key.

> bilingual   comprehension   correctness   immediate   mistake   practise
> pronunciation   regularly   results   rules   translate   vocabulary

LEARNING
▶ study regularly *It's important to study regularly.* ....
▶ study six hours a day *It's not necessary to study six hours a day.* ....
▶ expect immediate results. *It's important not to expect immediate results.* ....
1 practise grammar ....
2 translate everything ....
3 read a lot ....
4 read things that interest you ....

PRONUNCIATION
5 have perfect pronunciation ....
6 have good enough pronunciation ....

GRAMMATICAL CORRECTNESS
7 make too many mistakes ....
8 speak without mistakes ....

COMPREHENSION
9 practise listening to English ....

VOCABULARY
10 know 3,000–5,000 words ....
11 know 50,000 words ....
12 have a good English-English dictionary ....
13 have a good bilingual dictionary ....

-ing forms as subjects *Smoking is bad for you.*

We often use *-ing* forms (also called 'gerunds') **as subjects** – more often than infinitives.
Smoking *is bad for you.* (More natural than *To smoke is bad for you.*)
Swimming *is good exercise.*   ***Driving*** *makes me tired.*   ***Travelling*** *takes a lot of my time.*

❶ Complete the sentences.

▶ ..S̲w̲i̲m̲m̲i̲n̲g̲............ is slower than ...r̲u̲n̲n̲i̲n̲g̲................. (*running; swimming*)

1 .... is more dangerous than .... (*reading; skiing*)
2 .... is faster than .... (*flying; going by train*)
3 .... costs more than .... (*washing; eating*)
4 .... is easier than .... (*speaking; writing*)
5 .... is harder than .... (*listening; understanding*)
6 .... is more interesting than .... (*shaving; shopping*)

❷ Make three more sentences like the ones in Exercise 1. Use some of the words in the box.

cycling	learning	running	shopping	sleeping	teaching	thinking	writing

1 ....
2 ....
3 ....

We can put **objects** after *-ing* forms.
Learning languages *is difficult and takes time.* (NOT *... ~~are difficult~~ ... – learning is singular.*)
Eating chocolate *does not make you slim.*

❸ Complete this list of activities with verbs from the box (use *-ing* forms). Then number them in order of interest: 1 = most interesting (for you); 8 = least interesting.

buy	cook	learn	listen to	look after	meet	play	read

.... cards ...   . poetry ...   . music ...
.... meals ...   . languages ...   . friends ...
.... children ...   . clothes ...

In notices, you often see NO before *-ing* forms.
NO SMOKING   NO WAITING

❹ GRAMMAR AND VOCABULARY: public notices
Which words go with which notice?
Use a dictionary if necessary.

NO PARKING 1̲.   NO SMOKING ...
NO FISHING ...   NO CYCLING ...
NO CAMPING ...

→ For comparatives (*more dangerous, faster* etc), see page 208.

verb + ...ing *I can't help feeling unhappy.*

After some verbs we use *-ing* forms.
Some of these verbs are: *keep (on)* (= 'continue', 'not stop'), *finish*, *stop*, *give up* (= 'stop', for habits), *go*, *can't help* (= 'can't stop myself'), *suggest*, *practise*, *enjoy*, *love*, *like*, *(not) mind* (= '(not) dislike'), *dislike*, *hate*.

I can't help feeling unhappy.   *Do* you *mind* sharing a room?   Alex *has gone* swimming.

---

1 **Do you remember how to spell *-ing* forms of verbs? Look at the rules on page 21 if you are not sure. Then complete the sentences with *-ing* forms.**

▶ We enjoy ..*playing*................ tennis in the morning. (*play*)
1 Has Ann finished .... her photos? (*take*)
2 John's given up .... sweets. (*eat*)
3 'Where's Helen?' 'She's gone ....' (*shop*)
4 I have to practise .... so I can pass my test. (*drive*)
5 Alec suggested .... at the supermarket. (*stop*)

2 **Write sentences using the expressions in the box with *-ing* forms.**

| He can't help   She enjoys ✓   They've just finished   He's given up   They're going
All that week, it kept   She's practising   She's suggesting ✓   It's just stopped |

▶ *She enjoys skiing.*............

▶ *She's suggesting*...........
   going to Rome................

1 ....
....

2 ....
....

3 ....
....

4 ....
....

5 ....
....

6 ....
....

7 ....
....

| X | X | X | X | X | X | | 0 | | ♥ | | ♥ | | ♥ | ♥ | ♥ | ♥ |
| hate | | | dislike | | | don't mind | | | | like | | | | | love | |

3 Put in *-ing* forms of the verbs in the box.

get up ✓   play   study   wash   watch   wear   work

▶ I hate .....getting up........................ in the winter before the sun is up.

1 George dislikes .... dishes, so he often eats out.

2 I don't like playing baseball, but I like .... it.

3 I don't mind .... late if my boss asks me.

4 Joe's two-year-old sister loves .... with her toys in the bath.

5 Jan and her sister like .... each other's clothes.

6 When I was at school, I hated .... history.

4 Write about six things you love/hate etc doing. Use expressions from the box or write about other things.

cooking dinner for friends	dancing until 1 a.m.	eating out with friends	getting up early
listening to loud music	lying on a sunny beach	reading novels	swimming in the ocean
travelling to new places	walking in the mountains	walking in the rain	watching old films

▶ .....I love walking in the mountains.......................

1 ....

2 ....

3 ....

4 ....

5 ....

6 ....

'I love walking in the rain.'

After *love, like* and *hate* we can also use **infinitives with** *to* with the same meaning.

*I **love** singing.* = *I **love** to sing.*   *Ann **likes** to go out / going out with friends.*

*Mum **hates** to cook / cooking on an electric cooker.*

(BUT NOT ~~I dislike to listen to opera.~~ AND NOT ~~Do you mind to wait for a few minutes?~~)

preposition + ...ing *Thank you for coming.*

When we have **preposition + verb**, we must use an **-ing** form.

The children are tired of going to the same place every summer. (NOT ... ~~are tired of to go to~~ ...)
She spoke for an hour without using notes. (NOT ... ~~without to use~~ ...)
Thank you for coming.   *I worry about spending too much money.*

→ For spelling of *-ing* forms, see page 21.

1 **Put the beginnings and ends together.**

1 Every morning, my dad worries about	A working all my life. ...
2 Please don't leave without	B watering my garden while I'm on holiday. ...
3 I don't like the idea of	C telling me that you're going. ...
4 Are you interested in	D going to Vienna with us next weekend? ...
5 I'll pay you for	E being late for his train. *1*

2 **Add -ing forms of the verbs in the box.**

be ✓   go   hear   smoke   wash   watch

▶ Alice dreams of ..*being*.................... an opera singer, but she can't sing very well.

1 I'm tired of .... the same old stories; doesn't John realise he's boring us?

2 Which British Prime Minister was famous for .... big cigars?

3 I'm thinking of .... to Greece next summer – have you ever been there?

4 Eric's interested in .... football on television, but not in playing it.

5 Don't worry about .... the dishes – I'll wash them in the morning.

3 **Make sentences with *very / quite / not very good at ...ing* or *bad at ...ing*.**

	RUN	SWIM	CYCLE	DRAW	SING
JANE	★	●	☆	○	☆
BOB	☆	●	○	★	☆
SUE	★	★	☆	○	☆
MARK	★	☆	★	☆	○

KEY	
★	VERY GOOD
☆	QUITE GOOD
○	NOT VERY GOOD
●	BAD

▶ (*Jane / run, swim*) ...*Jane is very good at running, but bad at swimming.*...............

▶ (*Sue / run, cycle*) .....*Sue is very good at running, and quite good at cycling.*...............

1 (*Bob / run, cycle*) ....

2 (*Sue / draw, sing*) ....

3 (*Mark / swim, run*) ....

4 (*Bob / swim, sing*) ....

5 (*Jane / run, cycle*) ....

6 (*Mark / sing, draw*) ....

4 **What are you good or bad at? Write two or more sentences about yourself.**

....

....

....

We use **by ...ing** and **without ...ing** to say **how** people do something.

*I earn my pocket money **by working** in a petrol station.*   *She passed her exams **without studying**.*

5 Make sentences with *by ...ing* or *without ...ing*.

▶ When I left the house this morning, I didn't close the windows.
I left the house this morning without closing the windows.

▶ Al got a wonderful job. He was in the right place at the right time.
Al got a wonderful job by being in the right place at the right time.

1 Ellie stayed awake. She drank lots of coffee.
....

2 Eric drank three glasses of water. He didn't stop.
....

3 Charles woke us up. He turned the TV on.
....

4 You can find out the meaning of a word. Use a dictionary.
....

5 Mike paid for his new house. He didn't borrow any money.
....

6 Sue lost her driving licence. She drove too fast, too often.
....

7 Carl did all his homework. He didn't ask for any help.
....

8 Teresa cooks all her food. She doesn't use any salt.
....

After **before, after** and **since**, we can use an **-ing** form or **subject + verb**.

*I usually read the paper **before going** to work.* OR *... **before I go** to work.*
*Ann always felt better **after talking** to Pete.* OR *... **after she had talked** to Pete.*
*Bill has changed a lot **since getting** married.* OR *... **since he got** married.*

6 Rewrite the expressions *in italics*, using *-ing* forms.

▶ Jack usually has a cup of hot milk *before he goes to bed.* *before going to bed* ....
1 I always wash my hair *after I swim.* ....
2 *Since she passed her exam*, Cynthia has seemed much happier. ....
3 We always phone Aunt Jane *before we visit her.* ....
4 My grandmother was never really well *after she broke her leg.* ....
5 *Before he crashed his car*, Luke always drove too fast. ....
6 Jane's bought a lot of new clothes *since she got her new job.* ....

Sometimes *to* is a preposition (for example *I look forward to your answer*).
In this case we must use *-ing* forms of verbs after *to*.

*I look forward **to hearing** from you.* (NOT ~~I look forward to hear from you.~~)

test yourself   infinitives and *-ing* forms

❶ Circle the correct answer.

1 I would like *see / to see* you again.
2 Can you *help / to help* me?
3 Is it necessary *buy / to buy* a ticket now?

4 I hope *go / to go* to America in July.
5 Try *not to / to not* forget your keys.

❷ Put in the correct form of the verb.

▶ I promise ..*to phone*.... you every day. (*phone*)
▶ She suggested ...*seeing*...... a doctor. (*see*)
1 We agreed .... together. (*work*)
2 I didn't expect .... John there. (*see*)
3 I'm really going to stop .... (*smoke*)
4 I can't keep .... – I'm too tired. (*drive*)
5 Ann has decided .... a car. (*buy*)

6 The boss refused .... to me. (*talk*)
7 I thought of .... you a birthday card, but I forgot. (*send*)
8 They still haven't finished .... (*talk*)
9 Bill doesn't want .... with us. (*come*)
10 Your English is good, but you must practise .... (*speak*)

❸ Circle the correct answer.

▶ We need ... tickets.
  Ⓐ to get   B getting
1 It is important ... 'No' sometimes.
   A to say   B say   C saying
2 ... to work takes a lot of time.
   A To drive   B Drive   C Driving

3 You can't live without ...
   A to eat.   B eat.   C eating.
4 I came here ... my sister.
   A to see   B for see   C for seeing
5 After ... work, I went home.
   A finish   B to finish   C finished   D finishing

❹ Rewrite the sentences with infinitives.

▶ I saw Mary. I was happy. *I was happy to see Mary.*.....................................
1 I found a cat in my bed. I was surprised. ....
2 I didn't have time to phone you. I was sorry. ....
3 You can easily remember my phone number. My phone number is ....

❺ Circle the correct answer.

1 Can you lend me something ...
   A to read?   B for read?   C for reading?

2 I can't come out – I've got a lot of letters ...
   A to write.   B writing.   C for writing.

❻ Rewrite the sentences with *too* or *enough*.

1 It's very heavy. Nobody can lift it. (*too*) It's too ....
2 He's 18, so he can vote. (*enough*) He's ....
3 I'm very tired. I can't drive. (*too*) ....

❼ Write sentences with *want* or *would like*.

1 BOSS: Mary, can you answer the phone? (*want*) The boss ....
   ....
2 ANN: Pat, could you look after the children? (*would like*) ....
   ....

◉ More difficult questions

SECTION 10 special structures with verbs

grammar summary

Several different structures are practised in this section:

- **verbs followed by prepositions**
  Look at this.

- **prepositions in *wh*-questions**
  Who are you writing to?

- **phrasal verbs**
  Hurry up – we're late.

- **verbs with two objects**
  Can you lend me some money?

- ***to have something done***
  I have my hair cut every week.

- **imperatives**
  Come in and have some coffee.

- ***let's***
  Let's go and see a film tonight.

pre-test: which units do you need?

Try this small test. It will help you to decide which units you need. The answers are on page 283.

1 **Put in the correct preposition.**

▶ Listen .to............ this.   1 I don't agree .... you.   2 What happened .... your car?
3 What time do we arrive .... the station?

2 **Write the question for this answer.**

1 '.....................................?' 'I'm from Germany.'

3 **Which is/are correct? Circle the letter(s) of the correct sentence(s).**

▶ (A)She's looking for a hotel.   (B)She's looking at a hotel.   C She's looking a hotel.
1 A She put on her coat.   B She put her coat on.   C She put on it.   D She put it on.
2 A Peter gave Mary a rose.   B Peter gave a rose to Mary.
3 A Did you have my coat cleaned?   B Did you have cleaned my coat?
   C Did you let clean my coat?
4 A Park not here.   B Do park not here.   C Do not park here.   D Not park here.
5 A Let's not go.   B Let's don't go.   C Let's go not.

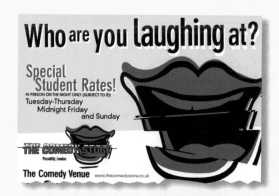

verbs with prepositions *Wait for me.*

With some verbs, we put a **preposition** (*for, to, at* etc) **before an object**.

Wait for me! (NOT ~~Wait me!~~)   *I* **listen to** *a lot of music.* (NOT ~~I listen a lot of music.~~)

1 Put the beginnings and ends together, and put in verbs from the box.

```
1–5: ask      believe ✓    belong      laugh      wait
6–10: happened   listen    look    talks    think
```

1 Do you believe..............	A at my pronunciation. ...
2 I know my English is bad, but please don't	B for it and I'll give it to you. ...
3 If you're late, I'll	C for you. ...
4 If you want anything, just	D in life after death? *1*
5 Does this coat	E to you? ...
6 I've got something important to say: please	F about himself. ...
7 Their garden is wonderful.	G about the future. ...
8 Jan lives from day to day. She doesn't	H at those roses! ...
9 He's very boring: he always	I to her? ...
10 Paula's an hour late. What's	J to me. ...

2 Look again at Exercise 1, and write the preposition after each verb.

▶ ask *for*......   1 believe ....   2 belong ....   3 happen ....   4 laugh ....

5 listen ....   6 look ....   7 talk ....   8 think ....   9 wait ....

You **arrive at/in** a place (NOT ~~to~~).

The train **arrives at** *Oxford Station at 17.15.*   *When did you* **arrive in** *Britain?*

You **get into / out of** a car; you **get on/off** a bus, train, plane or ship.

I **got out of** *the taxi at Piccadilly Circus.*   *We* **got off** *the bus at Trafalgar Square.*

look after = 'watch and take care of'; **look for** = 'try to find'

Could you **look after** *the children this evening?*   *I'm* **looking for** *my glasses.*

You **pay** a person or a bill; you **pay for** something that you buy.

'Have you **paid Joe**?' *'Yes, I* **paid his bill** *last week.'*   *Can you* **pay for** *the drinks?*

3 Put in the prepositions.

1 Don't wait .... me if I'm late.

2 What time did you arrive .... the airport?

3 Please listen .... me – this is important.

4 I'm looking .... John's house while he's away.

5 We're looking .... a bigger house.

6 Did you ask .... coffee?

7 We need to talk .... money.

8 'Whose is that car?' 'It belongs .... Carola.'

9 I forgot to pay ...... the tickets.

10 I don't want to think .... the future.

11 She got .... her car and drove away.

12 I couldn't get .... the bus because it was full.

13 'What's happened .... your hand?' 'I cut it on some glass.'

→ For more about *at, in* and *to*, see pages 258–262.

→ For more about prepositions, see pages 253–264.

→ For phrasal verbs like *come in, sit down*, see page 138.

prepositions in questions   *Who did you go with?*

1 **Put in prepositions from the box.**

about	for ✓	for	from	to	to	with

▶ What are you looking .*for*.........?

1 Who did Ann send the money ....?

2 Where is your wife ....?

3 What's your book ....?

4 Who are you in love .... now?

5 What are you all waiting ....?

6 Who are you writing ....?

2 **Write questions beginning *Who/What* and ending with prepositions.**

▶ *'Who did you buy your car from?'* .... 'I bought my car from Henry.'

1 .... 'I'm thinking about life.'

2 .... 'She works for my aunt.'

3 .... 'We were talking about you.'

4 .... 'I'm interested in most things.'

5 .... 'We're looking at that aeroplane.'

6 .... 'I stayed with Eric.'

3 **Complete the questions.**

1 'I'm thinking.' '............... about?'

2 'I've got a letter.' '............... from?'

3 'She hit him.' '............... with?'

4 'I'm writing postcards.' 'Who ....?'

5 'I've bought a present.' 'Who ....?'

6 'Jane has arrived.' '............... from?'

4 GRAMMAR AND VOCABULARY: **sharp tools**
Make the questions and write the answers.

▶ cut bread ..*What do you cut bread with? A breadknife*...............

1 cut wood ....?

   .... or ....

2 shave ....?

   ....

3 make holes ....?

   ....

4 cut hair ....?

   ....

axe

pair of scissors

drill

saw

razor

breadknife

→ For more about prepositions, see pages 253–264.

phrasal verbs   *Come in, take off your coat and sit down.*

Some verbs have **two parts**. The second part is a small **adverb** (*back, away, out* etc).
These verbs are called 'phrasal verbs'.
The small adverbs are not the same as prepositions (but some of them look the same).

SOME COMMON PHRASAL VERBS

be in/out/away/back   get out   get up   go away   go/come back   go on (= 'continue')   *go in/out*
hurry up   lie down   look out   look round   sit down   stand up   turn round   wake up

---

'Can I speak to Ann?' 'She's not **in**.'   **Come back** soon.   This headache won't **go away**.
Look out!   **Come in** and **sit down**.   It's time to **get up**.

---

① **Complete the sentences.**

▶ The door opened and I went ...*in*..............

▶ *Come*............ back and see us soon.

1 I usually .... up at seven o'clock in the morning.

2 Shall we .... out this evening?

3 I heard a noise behind me and turned ....

4 I can't go .... Can we stop for a minute?

5 I'm going home for a bit. I'll be .... after lunch.

6 Hurry ....! We're late.

7 I'm not feeling well. I'm going to .... down for an hour.

8 'I love you.' '..................... away!'

② **Look at the pictures and complete the captions.**

1 Wake .... !   2 Please sit ....   3 Come .... !

Some **phrasal verbs** can have **objects**.

SOME COMMON PHRASAL VERBS THAT CAN HAVE OBJECTS

bring back   fill in (a form)   *fill up   give back   give up* (= 'stop doing')   *let in*
look up (something in a dictionary etc)   *pick up   put down   put on* (clothes)
switch/turn on/off (lights, electrical appliances)   *take away   take off* (clothes)
throw away   turn up/down (radio, TV, heater)   *wash up* (cups, plates etc)

---

*Please **fill in** this form and post it.   I'm trying to **give up** smoking.*
*I **put on** my best clothes for the interview.   Shall I **switch on** the lights?*
*Could you **turn down** the radio?   Don't **throw away** the newspaper.*

In phrasal verbs, *up* often means '**completely**'.

---

*I'll **cut up** the wood.   Let's **clean up** the house.   **Fill up** your glass.   I **tore up** her letter.*

---

3 Here are some sentences from books and conversations. Complete the phrasal verbs with words from the boxes.

back	down	down	off	on	on	up

1 It was a good feeling to put .... dry clothes and eat a large cooked breakfast.
2 Switch .... the kettle and sit on that chair while I make tea.
3 Put .... your paper and listen to me.
4 Switch .... the lights when you are not using them.
5 It's hot in here. Do you mind if I turn .... the heater a bit?
6 If you find a café, could you bring .... a couple of sandwiches?
7 I think I'll wash .... the plates and cups now.

break	fill	give	let	look	pick	take

8 If you want to know what grammar is, ... up the word in the dictionary.
9 You can't .... up a newspaper these days without reading about terrible things.
10 She got ill and had to .... up her job.
11 He .... in six goals in four games.
12 Why did you have to .... in the form?
13 I .... off my shoes whenever I can.
14 .... up the firewood into little pieces, can you?

The **small adverb** can usually go before or after the **object**.

Switch on the kettle. OR *Switch the kettle on.*   *He let in six goals.* OR *He let six goals in.*

When the **object** is a pronoun (*him, her, it* etc), the **small adverb** must go after it.

Switch it on. (NOT ~~Switch on it.~~)   *He let them in.*   *Take it away.*

4 Change the sentences twice.

▶ She put on her coat. ..She put her coat on.   She put it on...
▶ I washed up the plates. .I washed the plates up.   I washed them up.......................................
1 Could you turn down the TV? ....
2 You can throw away the potatoes. ....
   ....
3 Why don't you take off your glasses? ....
   ....
4 Please put down that knife. ....
5 Shall I fill up your glass? ....
6 I'll switch on the heating. ....

→ For verbs with prepositions (for example *look at, listen to*), see page 136.

verbs with two objects   *Take the boss these letters.*

bring	buy	cook	fetch	find	get	give	lend	make	offer	pass
pay	promise	read	send	show	teach	take	tell	write		

Some **verbs** can have **two objects**. Two different structures are possible:

1 VERB + PERSON + THING	2 VERB + THING + TO/FOR + PERSON
I gave Peter lunch yesterday.	*I gave lunch to Peter yesterday.*
Could you take the boss these letters?	*Could you take these letters to the boss?*
I've made everybody tea.	*I've made tea for everybody.*

Most often, we use **verb** + person + thing, especially with personal pronouns (*me, you* etc).

Can I show you my photos?   *I wrote her a long letter, but she never answered.*
I'm going to put John to bed and tell him a story.   *I've bought you a present.*

1 Change the structure.

▶ Send Mary the bill. .....Send the bill to Mary...
▶ I'll make some tea for you. ...I'll make you some tea................................
1 I lent Joe my bicycle yesterday. ....
2 I often read stories to Lucy. ....
3 Carol teaches small children mathematics. ....
4 Ruth showed the photo to the others. ....
5 Sue often gives her mother flowers. ....
6 Could you buy a newspaper for me? ....
7 I tried to find a hotel room for my parents. ....
8 Could you pass this paper to Mr Andrews? ....
9 Bob has written a ten-page letter to Ann. ....
10 I want to get a good watch for Peter for Christmas. ....

2 Who gave who what? Write sentences. Put the person before the thing.

JOE: chocolates → SALLY: a book → FRED: flowers → ANNIE: a picture → LUKE: a sweater
→ MARY: a camera → JOE

▶ ...Joe gave Sally chocolates..................... 3 ....
1 Sally .... 4 ....
2 .... 5 ....

3 Can you complete these quotations with words from the box?

buy	find	give	give	lend ✓

▶ Friends, Romans, countrymen, *lend*............... me your ears. (Shakespeare: 'Julius Caesar')
1 A four-year-old child could understand this. Run out and .... me a four-year-old child.
   (Groucho Marx: 'Duck Soup')
2 .... me liberty or .... me death. (Patrick Henry)
3 Money can't .... you love. (traditional)

We don't use *describe, explain, say, suggest* or *borrow* in the **verb** + **person** + **thing** structure.
(NOT *Explain me this, She said me 'hello'*, NOT *Can I borrow you a stamp?*)

have something done   *I have my hair cut every week.*

If you *have something done*, you **don't do it yourself**; somebody does it for you.
*I **have my hair cut** every week.*   *I **have my car serviced** at the garage every 10,000 km.*

Fred cuts his hair himself.

Eric has his hair cut at Franco's.

1 **Ann is very practical: she likes doing things herself. Bill is not so practical: he has things done by other people. Complete the sentences.**

▶ Ann checks her oil herself.   Bill ...*has his oil checked*.......................... at the garage.
1 Ann checks her tyres herself.   Bill .... at the garage.
2 Ann changes her oil herself.   Bill .... at the garage.
3 Ann repairs her car herself.   Bill .... at the garage.
4 Ann cleans her shoes herself.   Bill .... on the way to work.
5 Ann does the gardening herself.   Bill .... for him.

2 Make sentences with *should have* ...

▶ John's car is running badly. (*check*) ...*He should have it checked*..................
1 Mary's watch isn't going. (*repair*) ....
2 Mike's trousers are dirty. (*clean*) ....
3 John and Helen's kitchen window is broken. (*repair*) ....
4 Pete's hair is getting very long. (*cut*) ....
5 Tom and Janet's new car has done 10,000 km. (*service*) ....

➔ For *should*, see page 77.

imperatives *Come in.   Don't worry.*

Imperatives are like **infinitives without** *to*. We use them, for example, to **tell people what to do**, to give them **advice**, or to give them **friendly invitations**.

Turn left at the next crossroads.   Always *hold* the tennis racket like this. (NOT ~~Hold always~~ ...)
Pay here.   *Try* again.   *Come* and have dinner with us.   *Have* some more meat.

Negative imperatives begin *do not*, *don't* or *never*.

Please *do not* park here.   *Don't* listen to him.   *Never* tell her that she's wrong. (NOT ~~Tell her never~~ ...)

---

1 **Which words go with which picture?**

  ▶ DRIVE SLOWLY A
  1 TURN LEFT ...
  2 DON'T TOUCH ...
  3 DO NOT PICK FLOWERS ...

  A   B   C   D

---

2 **How do you get from the station to Church Street?**
Complete the directions.

go ✓	go	take	turn	turn	turn

  ▶ ..Go........... out of the station, 1 .... right, and
  2 .... down Station Road. 3 .... left into
  Platt Street, then 4 .... the first on the right.
  After the car park, 5 .... left, and Church
  Street is the second on the right.

station
Platt Street
car park
Station Road
Church Street

---

3 GRAMMAR AND VOCABULARY: some common imperative expressions
Make sure you know the expressions in the box. Use a dictionary if necessary.
Then complete the sentences.

| 1–5: Be careful!   Have a good journey/holiday.   Help!   Hurry up!   Look out! ✓   Sleep well. |
| 6–11: Come in.   Don't forget ...   Don't worry.   Follow me.   Have some (more) ... |
| Make yourself at home.   Sit down.   Wait for me! |

  ▶ *Look out!*... There's a child crossing the road in front of you!
  1 .... We're going to be late.
  2 .... There's ice on the steps.
  3 .... I can't swim!
  4 '...' 'Thanks. I'll send you a postcard.'
  5 'I'm going to bed.' 'Goodnight. ....'
  6 'I'll be home late tonight.' 'OK. .... your keys.'
  7 .... I can't walk as fast as you!
  8 '... coffee.' 'No thanks. If I drink any more I won't be able to sleep.'
  9 'I'd like to speak to the manager, please.' 'Of course, sir. ...., please.'
  10 'Jill's gone into hospital.' '... She'll be all right.'
  11 Hello. .... in and .... down. Please
  ....

We don't use imperatives, even with *please*, to ask for things politely (see page 83).

Could you tell me the time? (NOT ~~Tell me the time, please.~~)

let's (suggestions)   *Let's go.*

We can make **suggestions** with *let's* (or *let us* – very formal) + **infinitive without *to*.**

*I'm tired. **Let's go** home.*   ***Let's eat** out this evening.*   ***Let's see** what's on TV.*

The negative is ***Let's not ...*** or ***Don't let's ...*** (informal).

***Let's not go** camping this summer.*   ***Let's not tell** John about Mary and Pete.*
***Don't let's** invite that fool Raymond.*

1 Look at the pictures and complete the suggestions, using *Let's (not)* ...

▶ Let's go for a walk.

1 Let's not ....

2 .... play ....

3 .... cards.

4 .... go ....ing.

5 ....

6 ....

7 .... watch ....

8 .... go ....

2 GRAMMAR AND VOCABULARY: cities and countries

Do you know the English names for cities and countries round the world? Complete the conversations using names in the box. Use a dictionary if necessary.

Athens	Bangkok	Beijing	Copenhagen	Istanbul	Lisbon ✓	Marrakesh
Mexico City	Moscow	Prague	Rio	Vienna	Warsaw	

▶ 'I'd like to visit Portugal.' ...'Let's go to Lisbon.'...........................

1 'I'd like to visit Greece.' 'Let's go to ....'

2 'It would be nice to see Denmark.' 'Let's go ....'

3 'I want to see Austria.' 'Let's ....'

4 'I've always wanted to see the Czech Republic.' ....

5 'I'm interested in seeing Poland.' ....

6 'What about a holiday in Russia?' ....

7 'Morocco sounds interesting.' ....

8 'I've never been to Turkey.' ....

9 'What about Thailand this year?' ....

10 'I'd love to see China.' ....

11 'It's time to see Mexico.' ....

12 'Brazil this summer, OK?' ....

1 **Put in the correct preposition or – (= no preposition).**

1 What's happened .... Bill? He's an hour late.
2 I usually arrive .... the station at 8.30.
3 'Have you lost something?' I'm looking .... my keys.'
4 'You look happy.' 'Yes, I'm thinking .... my holiday.'
5 I had to wait .... the bus for half an hour this morning.
6 Have you paid .... the tickets?
7 Could you look .... the children for half an hour?
8 Who's paying .... the bill for lunch?
9 My parents don't like me to ask .... money.
10 I got .... the bus and sat down.

2 **Write the questions for these answers, using prepositions (*from, for* etc).**

1 .... 'I'm from Japan.'
2 .... 'I'm waiting for a phone call.'
3 .... 'I'm writing to Alex.'
4 .... 'I'm looking at some photos.'
5 .... 'We're talking about you.'

3 **Which is/are correct? Circle the letter(s) of the correct sentence(s). One, two or more answers may be correct for each question.**

1 A He picked up the plate.
   B He picked the plate up.
   C He picked up it.
   D He picked it up.
2 I don't repair my car myself. I ...
   A repair it in the garage.
   B let it repair in the garage.
   C let repair it in the garage.
   D have repaired it in the garage.
   E have it repaired in the garage.
   F have it repair in the garage.
3 A I sent some flowers to my mother.
   B I sent some flowers my mother.
   C I sent to my mother some flowers.
   D I sent my mother some flowers.

4 A DO NOT OPEN THIS WINDOW
   B NOT OPEN THIS WINDOW
   C DON'T OPEN THIS WINDOW
   D OPEN NOT THIS WINDOW
5 A Let's to play cards.
   B Let's playing cards.
   C Let's play cards.
6 A Let's not go home.
   B Let's don't go home.
   C Not let's go home.
   D Let's go not home.

4 **Put in the missing words.**

1 Hurry ....! We're late.
2 Don't turn ...., but somebody is following us.
3 Can you .... in this form?
4 The radio's too loud. Can you .... it down?
5 It's dark. I'll switch .... the lights.
6 It's cold. .... on your coat.
7 Shall I wash .... these plates?
8 She borrowed my shoes and never brought them ....
9 Be .... when you're driving. There's a lot of ice on the roads.
10 .... in and sit down.
11 Don't .... Everything will be all right.
12 Goodbye! .... a good journey.
13 Look ....! There's a car coming.
14 .... yourself at home.

grammar summary

A/an shows that we are talking about **one person or thing**. We often use *a/an*:

- in **descriptions**
    She's **an** interesting person.   He's got **a** loud voice.
- when we say **what something is**, or what somebody's **job** is
    This is **a** return ticket.   I'm **an** engineer.

The usually means '*You know which one(s) I'm talking about*.'
    Can I use **the** phone? (The hearer knows that this means '*your phone*'.)

Nouns used **without articles** often have a special meaning.
    I dislike **cats**. (This means '*all cats*'.)

Most Western European languages have articles. So if you speak (for example) French, German, Spanish or Greek, you will not have too many problems with *a/an* and *the*: they are used mostly in the same way as your articles. There are a few differences: see pages 150–155. If you speak a non-Western-European language (for example Russian, Polish, Arabic, Chinese, Japanese), you may find articles more difficult. Study all of this Section, especially pages 148–149.

pre-test: which units do you need?

Try this small test. It will help you to decide which units you need. The answers are on page 283.

1 *A* or *an*?

▶ ..*an*.... egg   ▶ ...*a*..... dog   1 .... house   2 .... hour   3 .... idea
4 .... university

2 Correct (✓) or not (✗)?

▶ a day ✓.   ▶ a days ✗.   1 a book ...   2 a milk ...   3 a films ...

3 No article (–), *the* or *a*?

▶ Where did you put ..*the*.... butter?   ▶ I speak ...–.... French.   1 I often listen to .... music.
2 .... phone's downstairs in .... kitchen.   3 Canada is .... big country.
4 My sister's .... hairdresser.   5 She's got .... nice face and .... blue eyes.
6 This table is made of .... glass.

4 Correct (✓) or not (✗)?

1 She's from the Texas. ...   2 I'm at Oxford Station. ...   3 He was in the bed at 10.00. ...

An Englishman, an Irishman, a Scotsman and a Welshman went into a pub. The Englishman ...

Shut the door and turn off the lights when you go, will you?

We've got offices in Australia, Canada and the United States.

He's a doctor and she's an engineer.

I'll meet you at the Palace Hotel in Clark Street at 8.00.

He's got a very nice smile.

You have beautiful eyes.

a and *an*; pronunciation of *the*

We use *a* before a consonant sound (for example, the normal sound of *b, c, d, f, g, h*).

a book   a coat   a house   a letter   a new idea

We use *an* before a vowel sound (for example, the normal sound of *a, e, i, o, u*).

an address   an egg   an idea   an old house

---

1 **Put in *a* or *an*.**

▶ ..*a*... ticket   ▶ ..*an*.. afternoon   1 ...... bicycle   2 ...... airport   3 ...... shop
4 ...... holiday   5 ...... exercise   6 ...... day   7 ...... American   8 ...... student

---

We choose *a* or *an* because of pronunciation, not spelling.

• *a house, a hand, a head* BUT *an hour* /aʊə/ (the *h* is silent, so *hour* is like *our*)
• *an uncle, an umbrella,* BUT *a university* (pronounced *'you-niversity'*), *a European* (pronounced *'you-ropean'*), *a uniform* (pronounced *'you-niform')*, *a useful book*
• *an orange, an opera, an office* BUT *a one-pound stamp* (pronounced *'wun ...'*)

---

2 **Put in adjectives.**

▶ a car (*expensive*) ...*an expensive car*........   5 an uncle (*rich*) ....
▶ an address (*new*) ....*a new address*............   6 a job (*easy*) ....
1 a friend (*old*) ....   7 an exercise (*hard*) ....
2 an apple (*big*) ....   8 a language (*European*) ....
3 a child (*unhappy*) ....   9 a book (*small*) ....
4 a train (*early*) ....

Before a consonant sound we pronounce *the* as /ðə/ (like the end of *mother*).
Before a vowel sound we say /ði/ (it rhymes with *see*).

---

3 **Pronounce:**

the beginning   the woman   the child   the time   the place   the house   the horse
the end   the old man   the office   the address   the American
the hour   the one   the university   the European   the uniform

---

4 **GRAMMAR AND VOCABULARY: seven useful things**
Complete the sentences with words from the box. Use *a* or *an*.

| alarm clock ✓   calculator   torch   envelope   hammer   knife   tin-opener ✓ |

▶ You use ...*a tin-opener*........... to open tins.   3 You can see at night with
▶ ..*An alarm clock*..... wakes you up   ....
  in the morning.   4 You can put nails into wood with
1 You can use .... when you   ....
  send a letter.   5 .... is useful for
2 .... is useful for mathematics.   cutting things.

---

countable and uncountable *a car, cars; petrol*

Countable nouns are words like *car, book, chair*. They are the names of things that you can count: you can say '*one car*', '*two books*', '*three chairs*'. They can be singular (*a cat, one book*) or plural (*two chairs, lots of books*).

Uncountable nouns are words like *smoke, rice, water, petrol*. These are things that you can't count: you can say '*smoke*', but not '~~one smoke~~' or '~~two rices~~' or '~~three waters~~'. Uncountable nouns are only singular. (For more information, see page 190.)

1 Fill in the table with the words from the box.

| bird ✓ | bottles ✓ | blood ✓ | children ✓ | flower ✓ | love ✓ | meat | mountains |
| music | nose | oil | photos | piano | river | snow | songs | table | windows |

SINGULAR COUNTABLE	PLURAL COUNTABLE	UNCOUNTABLE
bird	*bottles*	*blood*
flower	*children*	*love*
....	....	....
....	....	....
....	....	....
....	....	....

We use *a/an* only before singular countable nouns.
(*A/an* is a bit like *one*: you can't say ~~one houses~~ or ~~one air~~.)

SINGULAR COUNTABLE	PLURAL COUNTABLE	UNCOUNTABLE
a house	*houses* (NOT ~~a houses~~)	*air* (NOT ~~an air~~)
a car	*cars*	*petrol*

We often use an **uncountable noun (without *a/an*)** to say what something is **made of**.

*The walls in the house were all **made of glass**.*   *This sweater is **made of silk**.*

2 Put in *a/an* or nothing (–).

▶ Jake's father makes ...–...... films.
▶ I need ..*a*........ new bicycle.
1 I never drink .... milk.
2 Jane is .... old friend.
3 Their house is made of .... wood.
4 I often listen to .... music.

5 The police are looking for him with .... dogs.
6 My room has got .... really big window.
7 That child wants .... new shoes.
8 She was wearing .... orange skirt.
9 The table is made of .... glass.

We use *one* instead of *a/an* when the **exact number** is important. Compare:

*Can I have **a** cheese sandwich?* (NOT ~~Can I have one cheese sandwich?~~)
*No, I asked for **one** sandwich, **not two**!*   *I only want **one** sandwich.*

3 Put in *a/an* or *one*.

▶ She's got ..*a*........... nice coat.
▶ She's only got *one*........... coat.
1 Can I have .... boiled egg?
2 No, I said .... egg, not two.

3 I've got .... problem. Can you help?
4 She's only got .... child.
5 John's got .... beautiful sister.
6 .... girlfriend is enough.

the and *a/an*   *Let's see a film. I didn't like the film.*

We use *the*, not *a/an*, to talk about somebody or something, when the speaker and hearer both know about this person or thing; when they both know which one(s). In other cases we use *a/an*.

THE	A/AN
Could you close the door?	*Could you open a window?*
(You know which door.)	(I don't mind which window.)
I'm going to the post office.	*Is there a post office near here?*
(You know which one - the one near here.)	
Can I use the phone? (= 'your phone')	*Have you got a phone?*
I didn't like the film. (= 'the one that we saw')	*Let's go and see a film.*
He looked at the moon. (There's only one.)	*He looked at a tree.*
She's in the front room.	*I need a room for tonight.*
(You know which room – I'm telling you.)	
She came on the 8.15 train.	*She arrived in an old taxi.*
(You know which train – I'm telling you.)	
How much is the red coat?	*I've just bought a new coat.*
(You know which coat – I'm telling you.)	

1 Put in *a/an* or *the*.

▶ I walked up to her house, rang .the..... bell and opened ...the.... door.

▶ He lives in ....a..... small village.

1 Look – that's John walking across .... street.

2 Can I use .... bathroom?

3 I need .... English-French dictionary – have you got one?

4 I know .... good restaurant – shall I reserve .... table for tonight?

5 Where's .... teacher? She's very late.

6 I want .... long holiday in .... sun.

7 Who's .... man in your office?

8 I'm leaving on .... 4.30 bus.

9 'Which is your coat?' '............ green one.'

10 Ann's looking for .... new job.

11 Why are you looking at .... sky?

12 I'll meet you at 4.30 at .... bus stop outside .... police station.

We use *the* before *only*; *first, second* etc; and **superlatives** like *oldest, most* (see page 208).

*She's **the only woman** for me.*   *I live on **the second** floor.*
*It's **the oldest restaurant** in Glasgow.*   *He bought **the most expensive one**.*

2 Put the beginnings and ends together, and put in *a/an* or *the*.

1 Sarah's .the...........	A cup of coffee? ...
2 I've got	B first train tomorrow morning? ...
3 John's	C hottest day of the year. ...
4 What time is	D most intelligent person in our family. .1.
5 Yesterday was	E only boy in the class. ...
6 Would you like	F present for you. ...

We often use *a/an* to talk about a person or thing **for the first time**; and *the* when we talk about **the person or thing again**.

A man walked up to a policeman. The man took out a map and asked the policeman ...

3 **Put in *a/an* or *the*.**

A BAG IN A BAG

This is ▶ ..a........ true story. Last year I went into 1 .... big sports shop because I wanted
2 .... sports bag. 3 .... assistant came up to me, and I told him what I wanted. 4 ....
assistant brought me three different bags. I chose 5 .... smallest one and paid for it. 6 ....
assistant put 7 .... bag in 8 .... large plastic bag. I told him one bag was enough, and asked
him to take 9 .... bag out of 10 .... other bag. He did so, but he looked very unhappy as I
walked out of 11 .... shop.

Remember: we **don't** use *a/an* with **plurals**. We can use *the* with **plurals**.
*She's wearing **black shoes**.* (NOT ...~~a black shoes~~.) *She bought **the shoes** last week.*

4 GRAMMAR AND VOCABULARY: animals, birds and other creatures
Make sure you know the words in the box. Use a dictionary if necessary. Then look at the groups of pictures and complete the sentences. Put in *a/an* or *the*.

| ant | camel ✓ | eagle | frog | monkey | mouse (*plural* mice) |
| parrot | pigeon | snake | spider | | |

GROUP A

▶ This is a ..camel....... It's .....the....... biggest animal in ....the......... group.
1 This is .... It's .... smallest animal in .... group.
2 This is .... It's .... most intelligent ....
GROUP B
3 This is .... It's .... fastest bird in .... group.
4 This is .... It's .... only blue and yellow .... in ....
5 This is .... It's .... smallest ....
GROUP C
6 This is .... It's .... only creature with eight legs in ....
7 This is .... It's .... creature with six legs in ....
8 This is .... It's .... with no legs ....
9 This is .... It's .... green creature ....

a/an   *She's a doctor.*

We use *a/an* when we say **what** something is, or **what job** somebody does.

*A pony is **a** small horse.*   *Canada is **a** big country.*   *My sister is **an** electrician.*

Remember: we don't use *a/an* with plurals.

*Ponies are small **horses**.* (NOT ... ~~a small horses.~~)

1 Say what these people's jobs are. Use the words in the box.

builder   cook   dentist   doctor ✓   driver   hairdresser
musician   photographer   shop assistant   teacher

▶ *She's a doctor.*
1 He's a ....
2 He's ....
3 She's ....
4 He...
5 She...
6 She...
7 He...
8 She...
9 He...

2 Complete the sentences with your own ideas.

1 .... is a good film.
2 .... is a bad film.
3 .... is a terrible singer.
4 ....is an interesting book.
5 .... is a great man/woman.
6 .... are beautiful animals.
7 .... is a/an ....

3 GRAMMAR AND VOCABULARY: **kinds of things**
Look up these words in a dictionary if necessary:
building, (musical) instrument, vehicle, tool, container.
Now change these to true singular sentences.

▶ Cars are buildings. *A car is a vehicle.*
▶ Houses are instruments. *A house is a building.*
1 Bags are vehicles. ....
2 Hammers are containers. ....
3 Pianos are buildings. ....
4 Buses are tools. ....
5 Screwdrivers are containers. ....
6 Guitars are tools. ....
7 Boxes are instruments. ....
8 Hotels are vehicles. ....

a/an: describing people   *She's got a nice smile.*

We often use *a/an* in **descriptions**.

*She's got **a** quiet voice.* (NOT *... the quiet voice.*)   *He's got **a** friendly face.*

Remember: we **don't** use *a/an* with **plurals** or **uncountable nouns**.

*She's got **blue eyes**.* (NOT *... a blue eyes.*)   *He's got **long hair**.* (NOT *... a long hair.*)

1 Look at the pictures and complete the sentences. Use the words in the box, and add *a/an* if necessary.

big beard	big ears	big nose ✓	long neck	loud voice	nice smile ✓	dark hair

▶ She's got *a nice smile.*
▶ He's got *a big nose.*
1 She's got ....
2 He's got ....
3 She's got ....
4 He's got ....
5 She's got ....

2 Here are two descriptions of the same person. Put in *a/an* or nothing (–).

A 'My name's Sandra. I'm tall and slim. I've got ▶ ..––.. blue eyes, ▶ ..a.. small nose, 1 ...... big mouth and 2 ...... dark hair. I think I've got 3 ...... nice smile. I wear 4 ...... glasses.'

B 'Sandra's got 1 ...... very friendly face with 2 ...... big smile. She's got 3 ...... long dark hair and 4 ...... blue eyes. She's got 5 ...... long legs, and she's very pretty. She's wearing 6 ...... blue dress today. She's got 7 ...... nice voice.'

3 Write a short description (two or three sentences) of a friend of yours. Use some words from Exercises 1 and 2.

....
....
....

DESCRIPTIONS WRITTEN BY ENGLISH 7-YEAR-OLDS

my Dad

He's got green eyes like me.
He has got light brown hair
in some places.

My Friend

My friend is Annie Lydford. Annie's got short
hair and loves horses. Annie has blue
eyes and a round head with a short
haircut down to her forehead. Annie's
always happy and she makes a really good friend.

talking in general without *the*   *People are funny.*

> We do not normally use *the* to talk about people or things **in general**. *The* does not mean '*all*'. We use *the* to talk about particular people or things (see page 148).

GENERAL	PARTICULAR
People are funny.	*The people in that house are funny.*
I like music.	*The music's too loud – can you turn it down?*
Sugar is fattening.	*Could you pass the sugar?*
She's interested in dogs and horses.	*'Why are the dogs barking?' 'There's somebody outside.'*

1 **Make some sentences from the words in the boxes.**

Artists Builders Cats
Dogs Horses
Photographers Pianists
Shop assistants
Students Teachers

build don't eat don't like
eat learn like
paint play sell take
teach

cats dogs grass
houses meat
music photos
pictures things

▶ *Dogs don't like cats.* ....   4 ....

▶ *Teachers teach things.* ....   5 ....

1 ....   6 ....

2 ....   7 ....

3 ....   8 ....

2 **Circle the correct forms.**

▶ *The old people /* (*Old people*) often forget *the things /* (*things.*)

▶ I like talking to (*the old ladies*)*/ old ladies* who live in that house.

1 *The books / Books* are expensive in my country.

2 'Where shall I put *the books / books*?' 'On the floor.'

3 Japanese is a difficult language for *the English people / English people.*

4 *The flowers / flowers* are beautiful. Thank you very much!

5 *The life / Life* is sometimes hard.

6 I don't understand *the words / words* of that song.

7 *The food / food* in this restaurant is very expensive.

8 *The water / Water* turns into *the ice / ice* at 0°C.

9 Why are *the windows / windows* open in this room?

3 **Here are some common sayings about men and women (not all true!). Complete the sentences with words from the box, and give your opinion.**

drivers   lost ✓   money   things   things   think   think   understand   understand

▶ Men never ask the way when they're ...*lost*........................ TRUE / NOT TRUE

1 Men are better .... than women. TRUE / NOT TRUE

2 Women are more careful with .... than men. TRUE / NOT TRUE

3 Women .... men. Men don't .... women. TRUE / NOT TRUE

4 Women .... that men will change, but they don't. TRUE / NOT TRUE

5 Men don't .... that women will change, but they do. TRUE / NOT TRUE

6 Men pay too much for .... that they want. Women buy .... that they don't want because they're cheap. TRUE / NOT TRUE

4 Read the two texts and then write one yourself.

I love snow.
I like poetry, art and walking.
I don't like football, big dictionaries or hot weather.
I hate telephones, banks, vegetable soup, pop music and small dogs.

I hate writing letters.
I don't like swimming or opera.
I like children, apples, sport, television and cheese.
I love computers, history, dancing, cats, nice clothes and shopping.

....

....

....

....

5 GRAMMAR AND VOCABULARY: interests

Choose some words from the box to complete the sentences. Use a dictionary if necessary. Don't use *the*!

art	chess	dancing	football	history	music	opera	photography
poetry	politics (*singular*)	skating	swimming	tennis	travel		

1 I like ....

2 I don't like ....

3 I like .... better than ....

4 I love ...., but I hate ....

5 I enjoy ....

6 I think .... is interesting, but .... is boring.

7 .... is difficult.

8 I'm good at ...., but I'm not so good at ....

9 I prefer .... to ....

10 I'm not interested in ....

11 Most people are interested in ....

12 Not many people are interested in ....

names *Mary, Africa, the USA*

- people: ~~the~~

  Mary works for **Dr Andrews**. (NOT ~~The Mary ... the Dr Andrews.~~)
  General Parker   Prince Charles   Aunt Elizabeth

- languages: ~~the~~

  Sorry, I don't speak **Russian**. (NOT ~~... the Russian.~~)

- most place-names (for example continents, countries, states, lakes, mountains, towns, streets): ~~the~~

  Barry's from **Texas**. (NOT ~~... the Texas.~~)
  Africa   Cuba   Queensland   Dublin   Lake Geneva   Mount Everest
  Wall Street   Piccadilly Circus   Hyde Park   Times Square

1 **Complete the sentences with words from the boxes.**

Lake Superior	London	Oxford Street	Peru	Queensland ✓	Spanish	Uncle Eric

▶ ~~Queensland~~............... is in Australia.

1 They speak .... in ....

2 Here's a postcard from .... He's been swimming in ....

3 .... is in the centre of ....

Africa	France	Kilimanjaro	Napoleon	Switzerland

4 .... was a very small man.

5 .... is the highest mountain in ....

6 .... is next to ....

- deserts, rivers, seas and oceans (but not lakes!): *the*

  the Sahara Desert   the Thames   the Rhine   the Mediterranean   the Atlantic

- plural names: *the*

  the Netherlands   the United States / the USA   the Alps

- expressions with *Republic/Kingdom/etc*: *the*

  the Czech Republic   the United Kingdom

- large areas of the world: *the*

  the West   the Middle East   the Far East

2 **Circle the correct answers.**

▶ I once went on a boat on the (Rhine) / Lake Victoria.

▶ We're going to drive right across (Europe) / Sahara Desert.

1 Ann's just come back from the *Himalayas / Mount Everest*.

2 My sister works in *Netherlands / Denmark*.

3 I'd like to learn *Japanese / the Japanese*.

4 My parents are on holiday in the *South Africa / People's Republic of China*.

5 Here's a photo of Max in *USA / Trafalgar Square*.

6 Alan's living in a small town near the *Barcelona / Mediterranean*.

7 We have friends in *Ireland / Republic of Ireland*.

8 Wales is the smallest country in the *Great Britain / United Kingdom*.

9 There are a lot of Spanish-speaking people in the *USA / America*.

Edinburgh Castle

BUILDINGS WITH *THE*

● most names of buildings: *the*

the Hilton Hotel   the Old Mill Restaurant
the Globe Theatre   the British Museum
the Eiffel Tower   the Taj Mahal
the Great Pyramid

EXCEPTIONS

● place-name + *Airport, Station, Cathedral, University, Palace, Castle, School:* ~~the~~

Oxford Airport   Glasgow Central Station
Exeter Cathedral   Cambridge University
Buckingham Palace   Didcot Junior School

● name + possessive *'s:* ~~the~~

St Paul's Cathedral   McDonald's

the Tower of London

the Globe Theatre

the Taj Mahal

❸ Put *the* before five of these buildings, and nothing (–) before three.

▶ the...... Taj Mahal   ▶ ....─.... Halloran's Restaurant   1 .... Old Steak House

2 .... National Gallery of Modern Art   3 .... Central Museum   4 .... Birmingham Airport

5 .... Sheraton Hotel   6 .... New Theatre   7 .... Jenner's Hotel

8 .... Canterbury Cathedral

❹ Put in *the* or nothing (–).

1 .... American English   2 .... Asia   3 .... Blue Train Restaurant

4 .... Dominican Republic   5 .... Florida   6 .... Gobi Desert

7 .... Lake Michigan   8 .... Metropolitan Museum   9 .... Mississippi (River)

10 .... Mount Kenya   11 .... New York   12 .... North Sea   13 .... Paris

14 .... Regent Street   15 .... Rocky Mountains   16 .... Trafalgar Square

17 .... Egypt   18 .... White House   19 .... Whitehall Theatre   20 .... Far East

special cases   *in bed; after lunch; a hundred; ...*

- meals: ~~the~~

  to have breakfast/lunch/dinner; before/at/after/for breakfast etc

- days, months and public holidays: ~~the~~

  on Tuesday(s); in July; at Christmas

- *next/last* + a period of time: ~~the~~

  next month; last year

1 **Complete the sentences with words from the box.**

breakfast ✓   Easter   lunch   next   September   Tuesday

▶ I usually just have toast and coffee for breakfast..........

1 Let's have .... together on ....

2 We usually go to Scotland at .... and in ....

3 I'm working at home .... week.

- places and activities: ~~the~~

  to/at/from school/university/college; to/in/out of church/prison/hospital/bed; at home; to/at/from work; on holiday

- transport: expressions with *by*: ~~the~~

  by car/bus/bicycle/plane/train/underground/boat AND *on foot*

2 **Complete the sentences with words from the box.**

bed   car   church   hospital   university   work

1 I usually stay in .... late at the weekend.

2 Jake's going to .... to study business.

3 Most of the people in our village go to .... on Sundays.

4 I've never been in .... in my life.

5 If I go to .... by .... it takes half an hour.

3 **Write descriptions under the pictures using the words *boat, hospital, school* and *work*.**

   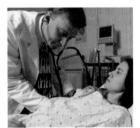

1 ....   2 ....   3 ....   4 ....

A/AN

We use *a/an* (before singular countable nouns):

- **after *with*, *without* and *as*: *a/an***

  *I did the translation **with a** dictionary.* (NOT *... ~~with dictionary.~~*)
  *You can't get in **without a** ticket.* (NOT *... ~~without ticket.~~*)
  *She's working **as a** bus-driver.*

- **after *haven't/hasn't got*: *a/an***

  *We **haven't got a** fax.* (NOT ~~*We haven't got fax.*~~)

- **in exclamations with *What ...!*: *a/an***

  ***What a** crazy idea!*

- **before *hundred/thousand/million*: *a/an***

  ***a hundred** days*   ***a thousand** people*   ***a million** dollars*

4 Put the beginnings and ends together, and put in *a/an*.

1 What	A .... American passport. ...
2 I didn't listen to the programme; I haven't got	B .....*a*..... terrible day! *1.*
3 I want a house with	C .... garden. ...
4 I went to sleep on the sofa and used my coat as	D .... hundred times. ...
5 I've told you	E .... million people in our city. ...
6 There are about	F .... blanket. ...
7 You can't work there without	G .... radio. ...

THE: COMMON EXPRESSIONS WITH *THE*

the same; the country/sea/mountains; on the right/left; at the top/bottom/side/front/back; in the middle; at the cinema/theatre; on the radio (BUT *on TV*)

*Her hair is **the same** colour as her mother's.* (NOT ~~*Her hair is same colour ...*~~)   *We live in **the country**.*
*I prefer **the mountains**; she prefers **the sea**.*   *Our house is the second **on the right**.*
*Write your name **at the top** of the page.*   *I don't often go to **the cinema**.*

5 Make sentences.

▶ Anne's house / the first /left   ..*Anne's house is the first on the left.*...........................
1 Pat and I work / same office   ....
2 We / going / theatre / tonight   ....
3 My room / top / house   ....
4 Would you like / live / country?   ....
5 We usually go / mountains / Christmas   ....

POSSESSIVES

We **don't** use *a/an* or *the* with *my, your* etc (see page 182).

***your** address* (NOT ~~*the your address*~~)   ***my** friend / a friend of mine* (NOT ~~*a my friend*~~)

test yourself   articles: *a/an* and *the*

1 **Put in *a* or *an*.**

1 ...... address   2 ...... student   3 ...... English student   4 ...... university student
5 ...... bus   6 ...... old woman   7 ...... house   8 ...... hour's lesson
9 ...... one-pound coin

2 **How many countable and uncountable nouns can you find in these advertisements?**

A DIAMOND IS
for ever

Beautiful hair
✂ today!

Learn to take better photos!
For information, call 13462
■ ■ ■

You'll find all
the music you
love at our
London shop.

We have the best **coffee**

For a great snow holiday at a
great price, call us **now**!

COUNTABLE: ....
UNCOUNTABLE: ....

3 **Put in *a, an, the* or nothing (–).**

1 My sister lives in .... big flat.
2 'Where's .... phone?' 'In .... kitchen.'
3 My brother has got .... loud voice.
4 Most people like ...... animals.
5 Do you play .... tennis?
6 .... music's too loud – please turn it down.

7 Have you ever seen .... Eiffel Tower?
8 My brother is .... doctor.
9 Andy works at .... Apollo Theatre.
10 .... River Rhone runs into ....
   Mediterranean Sea.
11 All our furniture is made of .... wood.

4 **Put in *a, an, the* or nothing (–).**

A TRUE STORY
In 1 .... 1969, in 2 .... Portland, 3 .... Oregon, 4 .... man went to rob 5 .... bank.
He didn't want 6 .... people in 7 .... bank to know what was happening, so he walked up
to one of 8 .... cashiers, wrote on 9 .... piece of 10 .... paper 'This is 11 .... robbery
and I've got 12 .... gun', and showed 13 .... paper to 14 .... cashier. Then he wrote 'Take
all 15 .... money out of your drawer and put it in 16 .... paper bag.' 17 .... cashier read
18 .... message, wrote at 19 .... bottom of 20 .... paper 'I haven't got 21 .... paper bag'
and gave 22 .... paper back to 23 .... robber. 24 .... robber ran out of 25 .... bank.

5 **Put in *a/an* or *the*.**

♪ There is 1 .... mountain far away.
And on 2 .... mountain stands 3 .... tree.
And on 4 .... tree there is 5 .... branch.
♩ And on 6 .... branch there is 7 .... nest. ♪
And in 8 .... nest there is 9 .... egg.
♪ And in 10 .... egg there is 11 .... bird. ♪
One day 12 .... bird will fly.
One day we will be free.
(old folk song) ♭

◼ More difficult questions

SECTION 12 determiners

grammar summary

this, that, these, those	some, any, no	enough	all, each, every, both, either, neither
much, many, a little, a few	a lot, lots	(a/an, the	my, your etc)

Determiners are words that come at the beginning of noun phrases, before adjectives. Determiners help to show **which** or **how many** people/things we are talking about.

this old coat   *some* strange ideas   *all* English words   *enough* people

Most determiners are explained and practised in this section. *A/an* and *the* have a separate section on pages 145–158. *My, your* etc are explained together with pronouns on pages 182–183.
Somebody, anything, nowhere etc are included here. These are not determiners, but it is more convenient to deal with them in this section.

pre-test: which units do you need?

Try this small test. It will help you to decide which units you need. The answers are on page 284.

1 Circle the correct answer.

▶ Come here and look at *this* / *these* photos.
1 Could you pass me *this* / *that* plate?
2 I don't need *some* / *any* help.
3 Everything *is* / *are* very difficult.
4 He's got *dark* / *some dark* hair.
5 Would you like *little* / *a little* more coffee?

6 This tea is *too* / *too much* hot.
7 I think you're driving *too* / *too much* fast.
8 *All* / *Every* foreign language is difficult.
9 I like *all* / *every* kinds of music.
10 I can write with *both* / *either* hand – let me show you.

2 Correct (✓) or not (✗)?

▶ This is my brother. ✓.   ▶ I understand all. ✗   1 I haven't got no time. ...
2 I've got any time. ...   3 Could I have some water? ...   4 You can come on any day. ...
5 She has much money. ...   6 There aren't many girls here. ...   7 A lot of us was there. ...
8 Most of people think so. ...   9 He was carrying a heavy bag in every hand. ...

3 Put the words in the correct order.

1 petrol got enough haven't we ....
2 driving not enough fast you're ....

this, that, these and *those*

We can use *this* and *these* to talk about things that are here, near to us.
We can use *that* and *those* to talk about things that are there, not near.

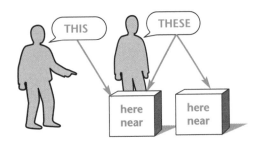
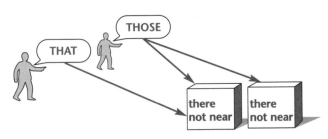

1 **Put in *this* or *these*.**

▶ Do you like ..this.......... dress?
1 Do you like .... shoes?
2 .... cat sleeps all day.
3 .... tomatoes are not very good.
4 .... letters are for you.
5 I don't understand .... word.

2 **Put in *that* or *those*.**

▶ Ann lives in ..that.......... house over there.
1 Who are .... people?
2 Could you pass me .... papers?
3 I don't think .... train is ours.
4 .... glasses look very nice.
5 Why is she running after .... man?

3 GRAMMAR AND VOCABULARY: **cutlery and crockery**
Use the words in the box to make ten or more sentences about the colours of the things in the picture. Use a dictionary if necessary.

| cup | plate | saucer | knife ✓ | fork | spoon | glass | napkin | jug | bowl |

This knife is black. Those knives are silver. ....
....
....
....

We can use *this* and *these* to talk about things that are happening now or starting now.
We can use *that* and *those* to talk about things that are finished.

I like this music.   *Listen to these sentences.*
That lesson was boring.   *Did you answer those letters yesterday?*

4 Circle the correct answer.

▶ *Do /* (*Did*) *you like that film?*
1 *I'm enjoying / I enjoyed* these lessons.
2 This game *was / will be* hard.
3 *These / Those* potatoes weren't very nice.
4 That holiday *is / was* great!

We can use *this, that, these* and *those* **without nouns**.

*I don't like **this**.*   *Look at **these**.*   *Who said **that**?*   ***Those** are pretty.*

We can use *this* to **introduce** people, and to introduce ourselves on the telephone.

***This** is my friend Doris.*   ***This** is Alex. Can I speak to Fred?*

5 Put in *this, that, these* or *those*.

▶ I don't like living in .this................... country.
1 Could you bring .... box to me, please?
2 Why did you say ....?
3 .... is Peter – is Mary at home?
4 Who are .... people over there?
5 Listen – you will like .... story.
6 Wait – I can't walk fast in .... shoes.
7 '........................... is my sister Helen.' 'How do you do?'
8 .... was a wonderful meal – thanks.
9 I'm not enjoying .... conversation.
10 Do you remember .... people that we met in Greece?

'It's no use, Cyril, I don't understand this camera. I can only see your feet.'

some and *any* *I need some sugar. Have you got any?*

He's got some problems.

She hasn't got any problems.

We use *some* and *any*, not *a/an*, with uncountable and plural nouns.
They mean 'a limited number or quantity'.
We use *some* in affirmative (➕) sentences.
We use *any* in negative (➖) sentences, and in most questions.

I'd like some water.	*Here are some flowers for you.*
I haven't got any money.	*There aren't any trains today.*
Have you got any sugar?	*Do you speak any other languages?*

❶ Circle the correct answers.

▶ I'd like (some) / any help.

1 There aren't *some / any* letters for you.

2 Have you got *some / any* brothers or sisters?

3 We need *some / any* more milk.

4 She's got *some / any* interesting friends.

5 Are there *some / any* restaurants near here?

6 I'm having *some / any* problems with my car.

7 I didn't have *some / any* breakfast today.

8 He hasn't done *some / any* work for ten years.

9 Do you know *some / any* Americans?

❷ Complete the sentences with *any* and words from the box.

English newspapers   games   foreign languages   help ✓   more to drink   sleep

▶ Ann likes to do things by herself: she doesn't want ...*any help.*.........................

1 No, I'm not thirsty – I don't want ....

2 Joe doesn't speak ....

3 Our team hasn't won .... this year.

4 I didn't get .... last night.

5 I couldn't find .... at the shop.

We use *some* in questions which expect the answer 'Yes' – for example offers or requests

Would you like some more coffee?   *Could I have some bread?*

❸ Write sentences with *some*.

1 (*Ask for coffee*) Could I have ....

2 (*Offer bread*) Would you like ....

3 (*Offer rice*) ....

4 (*Ask for tomatoes*) ....

5 (*Offer more potatoes*) ....

6 (*Ask for more milk*) ....

We use *any* with words like *never, without* or *hardly,* which have negative meanings.

They never give me any help.   I got there without any difficulty.
You made hardly any mistakes.

4 **Put the beginnings and ends together.**

1 I finished the work without	A any rain. ...
2 I was tired, so I went to bed without	B some rain. ...
3 I'm going to do	C any work in the garden. ...
4 In August we had	D some work in the house. ...
5 In July we hardly had	E any supper. ...
6 She never does	F some supper. ...
7 You're hungry. I'll make you	G any help. 1.

We can use *some* and *any* **without nouns** if the meaning is clear.

'Can you lend me some money?' 'Sorry, I haven't got any.'
'I need some more envelopes.' 'I'll bring you some.'

5 **Complete the answers with words from the box and put in *some* or *any*.**

buy   good   got ✓   more ✓   put   tomorrow   want   you

▶ 'How many children has he got?' 'He hasn't ...*got any*............'
▶ 'This is wonderful soup.' 'Have ....*some more*............'
1 'How much did the flowers cost?' 'I didn't ....'
2 'We need light bulbs.' 'I'll get ....'
3 'Where's the sugar?' 'There's .... in front of ....'
4 'Why didn't you buy any cheese?' 'Because I didn't ....'
5 'Shall we go to the cinema?' 'There aren't .... films.'
6 'The car needs oil.' 'But I've just .... in.'

6 GRAMMAR AND VOCABULARY: possessions
Have you got any of the things in the box? Use a dictionary if necessary. Write some sentences with *some* or *any*.

aspirins   ballpoint pens   dollars   jewellery   keys   love letters
make-up   red shoes   stamps   string   ties   white socks

I've got some ballpoint pens.   I haven't got any red shoes.........................
....
....
....
....
....

→ For *of* after *some* and *any*, see page 177.

any, not any, no and *none*

> *Any* is used in negative sentences, but is **not negative**. *Not ... any* is negative.
>
> *Sorry, I haven't got **any** time now.* (NOT ~~Sorry, I've got any time now.~~)

❶ Complete the sentences with negative past-tense verbs. Use words from the box.

ask	be	do	find	get ✓	have

▶ I *didn't get* .... any letters today.

1 There .... any fruit in the shops.

2 John .... any work at university.

3 The hotel .... any free rooms.

4 The policeman .... me any questions.

5 We .... any open petrol stations.

> We can use *no* instead of *not ... any*. *No* is more emphatic – stronger. Note the sentence structure.
>
> *Sorry, I've got **no** time.* (NOT ~~I haven't got no time.~~)

❷ Change *not ... any* to *no*, or *no* to *not ... any*.

▶ I haven't got any American friends. *I've got no American friends.* ....

▶ There's no bread. *There isn't any bread.* ....

1 She speaks no German. She doesn't ....

2 He's written no letters to her. ....

3 We don't get any rain here. ....

4 There isn't any post on Sundays. ....

5 She hasn't got any brothers or sisters. ....

> In conversation, we often make short incomplete sentences with *any* and *no*.
>
> *'Can you help me?' 'Sorry, **no** time.'*   *'**Any** letters for me?' 'Yes.'*

❸ Make short sentences.

▶ *news* ❓
  Any news? ....

▶ *'It's dark.' 'electricity'* ➖
  'No electricity.' ....

1 *Sorry, milk* ➖
  ....

2 *phone calls for me* ❓
  ....

3 *more money* ➖
  ....

4 *problems today* ❓
  ....

> Before *of* (see page 177), we use *none*, not *no*. And we use *none*, not *no*, without a noun.
>
> ***None** of them phoned.* (NOT ~~No of them ...~~)   *There's **none** in the house.* (NOT ~~There's no ...~~)

❹ Put in *no* or *none*.

▶ *None* ... of these telephones work.

▶ I had ...*no*.... difficulty understanding her.

1 'How many children has he got?' ....

2 There are .... trains after midnight.

3 Did you buy milk? There's .... in the fridge.

4 .... of us can play the piano.

5 There are .... palm trees in Antarctica, and there are .... in Greenland.

somebody, anything, nowhere, ...

somebody	someone	something	somewhere	anybody	anyone	anything	anywhere
nobody	no one	nothing	nowhere	everybody	everyone	everything	everywhere

Somebody and *someone* mean the same; so do *anybody* and *anyone*, etc.
The difference between *somebody* etc and *anybody* etc is the same as the difference between *some* and *any* (see pages 162–163). For *every*, see page 174.

Somebody telephoned for you.   *Has anybody seen my keys?*   *She didn't speak to anyone.*
I've got something for you.   *Do you want anything from the shops?*   *I didn't say anything.*
He lives somewhere in London.   *Have you seen John anywhere?*   *She never goes anywhere.*
Nothing *happened.*   *Everyone knew that.*

After *nobody/no one*, *everybody/everyone*, *everything* and *nothing* we use **singular** verbs.

*Everybody **knows**.* (NOT ~~Everybody know.~~)   *Everything **is** OK.*   *Nothing **happens** here.*

1 Complete the words.

▶ Is ....*any*.body at home?

1 'What did you say?' 'No..................'
2 I haven't seen Ann ....where.
3 There's ....one at the door.
4 Can I do any................ to help?
5 You can find Coca-Cola every................
6 No................ understands me.

7 'Where did you go at the weekend?'
   '................where – we stayed at home.'
8 I want to tell you some................
9 Every................ in my family has blue eyes.
10 I don't know ....body who plays rugby.
11 Every................ in this shop is expensive.
12 I want to live ....where warm.

2 These are sentences from real conversations. Can you complete them with *somebody, anything* etc?

1 Does .... want to speak about that?
2 The poor woman has .... to go.
3 It doesn't cost ....
4 .... said 'thank you': not one man.
5 Ten people in one room with no bath, no water, ...
6 What can you buy for a woman who has ....?

3 GRAMMAR AND VOCABULARY: word order with *somebody* etc; common adjectives
Do you know all the adjectives in the box? Use a dictionary if necessary.

boring	hot	intelligent	interesting	nice	sour ✓	sweet	useful	useless	warm

Write your own examples for:

▶ something sour   ..*a lemon*..................
1 something sweet   ....
2 something interesting   ....
3 something boring   ....
4 somewhere warm   ....
5 somewhere very hot   ....
6 something useful   ....
7 something useless   ....
8 somebody nice   ....
9 somebody intelligent   ....

One negative word (like *nothing, never, not*) is normally enough (see page 114).

*She **never** says **anything**.* (NOT ~~She never says nothing.~~ OR ~~She doesn't never ...~~)

Note the difference between *no one* and *none*. *No one* means 'nobody'; *none* means 'not any'.

No one can help me.   *I wanted some plums, but there were **none** in the shop.*

some/any or no article   *Have some toast. I don't like toast.*

We use *some* and *any* to talk about **limited numbers or quantities**. Compare:

LIMITED NUMBERS/QUANTITIES	NOT LIMITED
'Have some toast.' *('one or two pieces')* *I need some new clothes.* *Is there any water in the fridge?*	*'No thanks. I don't like toast.'* *('toast in general')* *She always wears nice clothes.* *Is there water on the moon?*

We **don't** normally use *some* in **descriptions**.

She's got black hair. (NOT ~~She's got some black hair.~~)

We **don't** use *some* when we **say what people/things are**.

Andy and John are students. (NOT ~~Andy and John are some students.~~)

❶ Join the beginnings and ends.

1 'What are those?'	A 'Chocolates.' *1*
2 'What did she give you?'	B any money with you? ...
3 Cheese is made from	C some milk in my coffee? ...
4 Could I have	D 'Some chocolates.' ...
5 Why does she always talk about	E milk. ...
6 Have you got	F money? ...
7 Her children are both	G air. ...
8 In the pub we met	H doctors. ...
9 Let me show you	I good photos. ...
10 Open the window and let in	J some fresh air. ...
11 This camera takes	K some photos of the children. ...
12 You can't live without	L some students. ...

❷ GRAMMAR AND VOCABULARY: buying food
A man went shopping and bought some food. Complete the sentences.
Learn the words for food. Use a dictionary if necessary.

cheese   pepper   vinegar   cornflakes

grapes   mustard   carrots   rice   oil   mushrooms

▶ *grapes* ➕ He bought some grapes, because he likes ...*grapes.*.........................
▶ *cheese* ➖ He didn't buy .....*any cheese*........., because he doesn't like cheese.
1 *mustard* ➕ He bought some mustard, because he likes ....
2 *mushrooms* ➕ He bought ...., because
   he likes ....
3 *carrots* ➖ He didn't buy any carrots, because he doesn't like ....
4 *vinegar* ➖ ....
5 *rice* ➕ ....
6 *pepper* ➖ ....
7 *cornflakes* ➕ ....
8 *oil* ➖ ....

any = 'one or another – it's not important which'

We can use *any* to mean *'one or another – it's not important which'*.
With this meaning, *any* is common in **affirmative (⊕) sentences.**

*'When shall I come and see you?' 'It doesn't matter – **any** time.'*
*'What newspaper do you want?' 'I don't mind. **Any** paper is OK.'*
*You can get a passport form in **any** post office.*

GRAMMAR AND VOCABULARY: two useful expressions

It doesn't matter.   I don't mind.

---

1 **Complete each sentence with *any* and a word from the box.**

| bank   boy   bus   colour   day   doctor ✓   problems   question   supermarket |

▶ *Any doctor*........................... will tell you to stop smoking.
1 He gets angry with .... who talks to his girlfriend.
2 'Would you like red, blue, ...?' 'It doesn't matter. .... is OK.'
3 You can get this kind of rice in ....
4 I think she knows everything. She can answer ....; it doesn't matter
   how difficult it is.
5 If you have .... come and ask me for help.
6 'When shall we meet?' 'I don't mind. .... this week.'
7 'Where can I change money?' 'In ....'
8 'Which bus should I get to the station?' '.. – they all go there.'

We can use *anybody*, *anything* and *anywhere* to mean *'it's not important who/what/where.'*

*It's easy. **Anybody** can do it.   That dog eats **anything** – meat, bread, shoes, ...*
*'Where shall I sit?' '**Anywhere** you like.'*

---

2 **Put the beginnings and ends together and put in *anybody*, *anything* or *anywhere*.**

1 It's not hard to dance.	A 'I don't mind. I'm so hungry
2 'Where would you like to live?'	I'll eat ....' ...
3 'What would you like for lunch?'	B 'It's true. Ask ....' ...
4 'I don't believe you.'	C 'Yes. Put it .... you like.' ...
5 'Can I park the car behind your	D ..*Anybody*........................... can do it. 1̲.
house?'	E He can play ....
6 Joe's a brilliant pianist.	F '.. in America.' ...

---

much and *many* *How much milk? How many languages?*

We use *much* with singular (uncountable) nouns, and *many* with plurals.

Do you listen to much *music?*   *Do you go to* many *concerts?*

1 **Put in *much* or *many*.**

► She doesn't speak ....*much*.......... English.
► She doesn't buy ...*many*.......... clothes.
1 I haven't got .... time.
2 Do you play .... football?
3 There aren't .... people here.
4 Are there .... Americans in your company?
5 We don't have .... rain in summer.
6 I don't eat .... meat.
7 Have you travelled to .... countries?
8 We don't go to .... films.
9 Was there .... traffic on the road?
10 Not .... tourists visit our town.
11 Do you know .... songs?

> So many worlds,
> so much to do,
> so little done.
>
> (Alfred Lord Tennyson)

We use *how much* with singular (uncountable) nouns, and *how many* with plurals.

How much milk *do you want?*   *How many languages* *are there in the world?*

2 **Write the questions. Do you know the answers? (See the bottom of the page.)**

► plays / Shakespeare / write ...*How many plays did Shakespeare write?*.............................
1 symphonies / Beethoven / write ....
2 cents / in a dollar .... are there ....
3 kilometres / in a mile ....
4 states / in the USA ....
5 blood / in a person's body .... is there ....
6 air / we breathe / every minute .... do we ....

We can use *much* and *many* **without nouns** if the meaning is clear.

'Have you got any money?' 'Not **much.***'*   *'How many people were there?' 'Not* **many.***'*

Much and *many* are used mostly in **questions** and **negatives**. They are unusual in affirmative (➕) sentences. In an informal style, we prefer expressions like *a lot of* (see page 169).

'Do you get **much** *snow in winter?' 'Not* **much,** *but we get* **a lot of** *rain.'* (NOT ...~~we get much rain.~~)
'Have you got **many** *English friends?' 'No, I haven't got* **many** *English friends. But I've got* **a lot of** *American friends.'* (NOT USUALLY ... *I've got many American friends.*)

➔ For *too much* and *too many*, see page 172.
➔ For *of* after *much* and *many*, see page 177.

► thirty-seven 1 nine 2 a hundred 3 1.6 4 fifty 5 five/six litres 6 six/seven litres

a lot of and *lots of*

A lot of and **lots of** are common in an informal style. They mean the same.

*I haven't got **a lot of** time just now.*   *He's got **lots of** money and **lots of** friends.*

We can use both expressions before singular (uncountable) or plural nouns.

- **a lot of** / **lots of** + singular subject: singular verb

  A lot of his work is good.   **Lots of** his work is good. (NOT ~~Lots of his work are good.~~)

- **a lot of** / **lots of** + plural subject: plural verb

  A lot of his ideas are good. (NOT ~~A lot of his ideas is good.~~)   **Lots of** his ideas are good.

1 (Circle) the correct answer.

1 Lots of people *have / has* computers now.
2 There *is / are* lots of cinemas near here.
3 Lots of snow *has / have* fallen today.

4 A lot of my friends *work / works* in London.
5 There *is / are* lots of food in the fridge.
6 A lot of things *need / needs* to change.

In affirmative (➕) sentences in conversation, **a lot of** and **lots of** are more natural than *much/many* (see page 168).

*This car uses **lots of** petrol.*
  (NOT ~~This car uses much petrol.~~)
*We eat **a lot of** vegetables.*
  (NOT ~~We eat many vegetables.~~)

not much hair   *not many teeth*

a lot of / lots of hair   *a lot of / lots of teeth*

2 Make these expressions affirmative (➕).

▶ not much time .a lot / lots of time.............
▶ not many people .a lot / lots of people...........
1 not much work ....
2 not many ideas ....

3 not much football ....
4 not many languages ....
5 not many houses ....
6 not much sleep ....

3 GRAMMAR AND VOCABULARY: towns
  Make sure you know the words in the box. Use a dictionary if necessary. Then write three sentences about a town, using *a lot of* / *lots of* / *not much* / *not many*.

| bookshops | cinemas | hotels | industry | libraries | markets | nightlife |
| parks | restaurants | theatres | traffic | | | |

▶ In Oxford there are a lot of museums; there is not much industry.
1 In ....
2 ....
3 ....

If we use *a lot* or *lots* **with a noun**, we **always** use *of*.
If we use *a lot* or *lots* **without a noun**, we **don't** use *of*.

*'Have you got **a lot of** work?'* (NOT ...~~a lot work.~~) *'Yes, **a lot**.'* (NOT *'~~Yes, a lot of.~~'*)

a little and *a few*   *a little English; a few words*

> We use *a little* with **singular** (uncountable) nouns, and *a few* with **plurals**.
> If you're hungry, we've got **a little soup** and **a few tomatoes**.

① **Put in *a little* or *a few*.**

1 I know .... English.
2 And I speak .... words of Spanish.
3 I'll be on holiday in .... days.
4 Can you give me .... help?
5 Ann will be ready in .... minutes.
6 Could I have .... more coffee?
7 I'd like to ask you .... questions.
8 I'm having .... trouble with the police.
9 The soup needs .... more salt.
10 I'm going away for .... weeks.

> *Little* and *few* (without *a*) have a rather **negative** (■) meaning (like *not much/many*).
> *A little* and *a few* have a more positive (■) meaning (like *some*).

> We've got *a little* food in the house if you're hungry. (= 'some, better than nothing')
> There was *little* food in the house, so we went to a restaurant. (= 'not much, not enough')
> His lesson was very difficult, but *a few* students understood it. (= 'more than I expected')
> His lesson was so difficult that *few* students understood it. (= 'not many, hardly any')

② **Circle the correct answer.**

▶ I have (*little*) / *a little* time to read newspapers and no time at all to read books.
1 Come about 8 o'clock; I'll have *little* / *a little* time then.
2 There was *little* / *a little* water on the mountain, and we all got very thirsty.
3 Foreign languages are difficult, and *few* / *a few* people learn them perfectly.
4 I'm going to Scotland with *few* / *a few* friends next week.
5 I've brought you *few* / *a few* flowers.
6 Life is very hard in the Arctic, so *few* / *a few* people live there.

> *Little* and *few* are rather formal; in conversation we use **not much/many** or **only a little/few**.
> There wasn't **much** food in the house. OR There was **only a little** food in the house.
> The lesson was so difficult that **not many / only a few** students understood it.

③ **Make these sentences more conversational.**

▶ I speak little English. *I only speak a little English.* OR *I don't speak much English.*
1 There was little room on the bus. ....
2 Few people learn foreign languages perfectly. ....
3 She has few friends. ....
4 We get little rain here in summer. ....
5 This car uses little petrol. ....
6 There are few flowers in the garden. ....

> We can use (*a*) **little** and (*a*) **few** without nouns if the meaning is clear.
> 'Have you got any money?' '**A little**.'   'Did you buy any clothes?' '**A few**.'

→ For *of* after *little* and *few*, see page 177.

enough money; fast enough

We put *enough* before singular (uncountable) or plural nouns.

Have you got enough money for the bus?   There aren't enough plates for everybody.

1 **Look at the pictures and complete the descriptions.**

1 not .... food   2 .... strings   3 .... seats   4 ....

2 **Use *enough* with words from the box to complete the sentences.**

buses ✓   chairs   girls   money   salt   time   work

▶ You need a car in our village, because there aren't .*enough buses*....................
1 Have you got .... to finish the work?
2 There were plenty of boys at the party, but not ....
3 We couldn't sit down because there weren't ....
4 I won't pass the exam because I haven't done ....
5 I've got just .... for a ticket to America.
6 This soup isn't very nice. There's not .... in it.

We put *enough* after adjectives and adverbs

*This room isn't **big** enough.* (NOT ... ~~enough big~~)   *You're not walking **fast** enough*

3 GRAMMAR AND VOCABULARY: common adjectives
Make sure you know the words in the box. Use a dictionary if necessary. Then complete the list with *not ... enough*.

bright   clear   comfortable   deep   easy   fresh   interesting ✓   loud

	POSSIBLE PROBLEMS		POSSIBLE PROBLEMS
▶ a book	*not interesting enough*	4 an exercise	....
1 an alarm clock	....	5 an explanation	....
2 a chair	....	6 eggs	....
3 a lamp	....	7 a swimming pool	....

4 **Put *enough* with each word.**

▶ old .*old enough*..............	2 beds	5 milk ....
▶ people .*enough people*.........	3 often	6 help ....
1 warm	4 quiet	7 sweet ....

We can use *enough* without a noun if the meaning is clear.

*'More coffee?' 'No, thanks. I've got **enough**.'*

too, too much/many and *not enough*

> We use *too* with adjectives and adverbs. We use *too much/many* with nouns.
> This coffee's too cold. (NOT ... ~~too much cold~~ ...)   He drives too fast.
> I've got too much work and not enough time.   You ask too many questions.

not hot enough   *too hot*

1 **Put in *too*, *too much* or *too many*.**

1	.... old	6	.... work
2	.... trouble	7	.... hot
3	.... problems	8	.... students
4	.... money	9	.... cars
5	 ill	10	.... difficult

2 GRAMMAR AND VOCABULARY: **common adjectives**
Make sure you know the words in the box. Use a dictionary if necessary. Then change the expressions.

cheap	dry	expensive	fast ✓	hard	heavy	high	light	low
narrow	short	slow ✓	soft	tall	thick	thin	wet	wide

▶ not fast enough = ...*too slow*...........................   4 not hard enough = ...
▶ too slow = ..*not fast enough*.........................   5 too narrow = ...
1 not high enough = ...   6 too expensive = ...
2 not tall enough = ...   7 too dry = ...
3 not heavy enough = ...   8 too thick = ...

3 **A man is going walking in the mountains for three days. Look at the things that he is taking and give your opinion, using (*not*) *enough* or *too much/many*. Use a dictionary if necessary.**

HE IS TAKING	YOUR OPINION
1 packet of soup	▶ *not enough soup*....
1 camera	▶ *enough cameras*.......
50 films	▶ *too many films*........
5 pairs of socks	1 ....
1 pair of boots	2 ....
3 pocket torches	3 ....
1 tube of sun-cream	4 ....
2 waterproof jackets	5 ....
2 pairs of sunglasses	6 ....
10 kg of bread	7 ....
2 kg of cheese	8 ....
100 cl of water	9 ....
1 orange	10 ....
1 bar of chocolate	11 ....
1 small bar of soap	12 ....
3 toothbrushes	13 ....

→ For infinitives after *enough* and *too* (for example *old enough to work, too tired to speak*), see page 126.
→ For the difference between *much* and *many*, see page 168.   → For *enough*, see page 171.

all (of) my friends; all of them; they are all ...

We can often **drop** *of* after *all*.

ALL WITHOUT OF before (adjective +) noun	ALL (OF) before the, my/your etc, this/that etc	ALL OF before it/us/you/them
All birds lay eggs. (NOT All of birds ...) *I like all good music.*	*Did you eat all (of) the rice?* *All (of) my friends like music.*	*I didn't eat all of it.* *She's invited all of us.*

❶ Put in *all*, *all (of)* or *all of*.

▸ <u>All</u> .... cars break down sometimes.
▸ I've read <u>all (of)</u> .... these magazines.
▸ He wants <u>all of</u> .... us to be there at ten o'clock.
1 Have you finished .... your work?
2 I wrote to .... them.
3 .... babies cry.
4 She telephones .... her friends every day.
5 This is a present for .... you.
6 I like nearly .... music.
7 .... us felt the same.
8 .... the restaurants were full.

> All human beings are born free and equal in dignity and rights.
> (*Universal Declaration of Human Rights*)

> Justice is open to all people in the same way as the Ritz Hotel.
> (*Judge Sturgess*)

> All animals are equal but some are more equal than others.
> (*George Orwell*)

All can also go **with a verb.**

*The trains **all stop** at Cardiff.*   *We usually **all work** on Saturdays.*

❷ Change the sentences to put *all* with the verb.

▸ All my family like travelling. <u>My family all like travelling.</u>
1 All the buses run on Sundays. ....
2 All the films start at 7 o'clock. ....
3 All our secretaries speak Arabic. ....
4 All these coats cost the same. ....

All goes **after auxiliary verbs** (*will, have, can* etc) and after *are* and *were*.

*The visitors **have all arrived**. (NOT ... all have arrived.) You **are all** late. (NOT You all are late.)*

❸ Change the sentences.

▸ All the lessons will start on Tuesday. <u>The lessons will all start on Tuesday.</u>
1 All these children can swim. ....
2 All our windows are dirty. ....
3 Sorry, all the tickets have gone. ....
4 All the shops will be open tomorrow. ....

We don't normally use *all* without a noun to mean '*everybody*' or '*everything*'.

***Everybody** knows that. (NOT All know that.)*
*I've forgotten **everything**. (NOT I've forgotten all.)*   *'What did you tell him?' '**Everything**.'*

→ For *everybody, everything* etc, see page 165.   → For *all* and *every*, see page 174.

all children; every child

We can use *all* and *every* with similar meanings, but the grammar is different.

ALL + PLURAL	EVERY + SINGULAR
All children are different. *All teachers make mistakes.*	**Every child is different.** (NOT ~~All child~~ ...) *Every teacher makes mistakes.*

We can use other determiners (*the, my, this* etc) after *all*, but not after *every* (see page 175).

All the shops were closed. *all my friends all these bills*	**Every shop was closed.** (NOT ~~Every the shop~~ ...) *every friend* (NOT ~~every my friend~~) *every bill*

1 **Rewrite the sentences with *every*.**

▶ All the buses were late. *Every bus was late.*...

1 All animals breathe air. ....

2 She's read all the books in the library. ....

3 I paid all the bills. ....

4 All the computers are working today. ....

5 All languages have verbs. ....

6 All London trains stop at Reading. ....

2 **Put in *all* or *every*.**

1 Not .... birds can fly.

2 Not .... mistake is important.

3 I played in nearly .... match.

4 We lost nearly .... the matches.

5 .... office in this building has central heating.

6 .... babies cry.

7 .... the clocks in the house are wrong.

8 I play tennis for an hour .... day.

9 .... cup in the house is broken.

10 .... languages are difficult.

11 .... his children have left home.

12 'Do you believe me?' 'I believe .... word.'

> All women become like their mothers.
>   That is their tragedy.
> No man does. That's his.
>
> *(Oscar Wilde)*

> Every day, in every way, I am getting
>   better and better.
>
> *(Emile Coué)*

All + singular means '*every part of*'; it is **different** from *every* + singular.

*She was there **all day**.* (= 'from morning to night')

*She was there **every day**.* (= 'Monday, Tuesday, Wednesday, ...')

GRAMMAR AND VOCABULARY: useful expressions with *all* and *every*

*all day/morning/afternoon/evening/night/week   She's been crying **all evening**.*

*every day (= 'on Mondays, Tuesdays, Wednesdays, etc')   I play tennis **every day**.*

*every three days, every two weeks, etc   I go to see my father **every two weeks**.*

*every other day/week/etc (= 'every two days/weeks/etc')   I phone her **every other day**.*

*all the time   She worries about him **all the time**.*

*all my life   **All my life** I've wanted to go to Peru.*

*all right = (= 'OK')   'I'm going home now.' '**All right**.'*

every and *each*; *every one*

Every and *each* mean the same. They are both used with singular nouns and verbs.
Every is more common.

Every/Each day brings *a new problem.*

We often use *each* when we want to say that things are separate or different. Compare:

> *We asked every politician the same question.*   *Each politician gave a different answer.*

We use *every* for three or more. We use *each* for two or more.

She had a ring on every finger.   *She had a bag in each hand.* (NOT ... *in every hand.*)

1 Circle the best answer.

▶ I work *each* / *every* day except Sunday.
1 *Each* / *Every* day is new and different.
2 Not *each* / *every* Canadian speaks English.
3 I looked for my keys in *each* / *every* pocket, one after the other.
4 She wrote a personal answer to *each* / *every* letter.
5 The doctor examined *each* / *every* patient very carefully.
6 *Each* / *Every* house in this street looks the same.
7 But inside, *each* / *every* house is quite different.
8 There's a shop at *each* / *every* end of the street.

Before *of* (see page 177), or with **no noun**, we use *every one*, not *every*.

She knows every one of her students by name. (NOT ... *every of her students* ...)
He's got hundreds of books, and he's read every one. (NOT ... *he's read every.*)

2 Put in *every* or *every one*.

1 .... of these oranges is bad.
2 I learnt Latin for seven years at school, but I've forgotten .... word.
3 'Can I have one of those chocolates?' 'Sorry, I've eaten ....'
4 .... of his teachers said he was stupid; but he did well in ....
   of his exams.
5 When the soldiers left the town they burnt down .... house.
6 The questions were easy: I could answer ....

➔ *Every one* is **not the same** as *everyone* meaning 'everybody' – see page 165.

both, either and neither

We use *both*, *either* and *neither* to talk about **two** people or things.
Both (● + ● = 'one and the other') has a plural noun.
Either (● / ● = 'one or the other') has a singular noun.
Neither (✖ ✖ = 'not either, not one and not the other') has a **singular** noun.

'Are you free on Monday or Wednesday?' 'I'm free on both days.'
'Which day is better for you?' 'Either day is OK.'
'About four o'clock?' 'No, sorry, I'm not free on either afternoon.'
'What about Thursday or Saturday, then?' 'No, neither day is any good.'

1 Put in *both, either* or *neither*.

1 .... children are very tall.
2 I'm busy on .... afternoons.
3 'Which room shall I use?' 'Number 6 or number 8: .... room is OK.'
4 .... students tried the exam, but .... student passed.
5 I'm lucky – I can write with .... hand.
6 It's very heavy: use .... hands to carry it.
7 .... coat will look good on you. Why don't you buy one?'
8 'No, ... colour really looks good. I don't like .... coat.
   And .... coats are very expensive.'

2 GRAMMAR AND VOCABULARY: things that come in twos
**Make sure you know all these words. Use a dictionary if necessary. Then complete the
sentences, using *both*.**

ankle ✓	direction	ear-ring	end	knee	parent	side	sock	team

▶ I hurt *both ankles* .... playing football.
1 Cars are parked on .... of the road.
2 .... of her .... are doctors.
3 Traffic on the road was very slow in ....
4 .... are playing really badly.
5 She hurt .... skiing.
6 I've lost .... of my ....
   – have you seen them anywhere?
7 Police were stopping cars at .... of the bridge.
8 That child has got holes in .... of his ....

We can use *both of* before *the, my/your* etc and *these/those*, but we often leave out *of* or *of the*.
both of the children OR **both the** children OR **both** children   **both (of) my** parents
We always use *both of* before *us/you/them.*
both of us (NOT ~~both us~~)

3 Rewrite the expressions without *of* or *of the* if possible.

▶ both of my parents *...both my parents...*
▶ both of the houses *..both houses..*
▶ both of them *..both of them..*
1 both of these books ....
2 both of the doors ....
3 both of you ....
4 both of our jobs ....
5 both of the shops ....
6 both of my uncles ....

determiners and *of* *most people; most of us*

Sometimes we use **determiners** (*some, any, much, many, few, enough* etc) with **of**.

DETERMINER + *OF*	DETERMINER WITHOUT *OF*
• before *the*: *some of the people here*	*some people* (NOT ~~some of people~~)
• before *this* etc: *too many of those books*	*too many old books*
• before *my* etc: *a few of our friends*	*a few friends*
• before *it, us* etc: *enough of it* *most of them*	*enough milk* *most students*

1 **Change the expressions.**

▶ some houses (*those*) ..*some of those houses*...

1 not much time (*the*) ....

2 any friends (*my*) ....

3 enough meat (*that*) ....

4 some big plates (*the*) ....

5 a few ideas (*her*) ....

6 most mistakes (*these*) ....

2 **Put in *of* or nothing (–).**

▶ Some ..—.. people don't like her.

▶ Some ..*of*. the people in the class don't like her.

1 Can you lend me some more ...... money?

2 I've lost some ...... the addresses.

3 I don't like many ...... his books.

4 She knows a few ...... those people.

5 There wasn't enough ...... food for everybody.

6 I didn't have much ...... time to talk to her.

7 A few ...... us want to change things.

8 I spend a lot ...... my time in Scotland.

9 We haven't got any more ...... eggs.

10 She didn't eat much ...... it.

Note the difference between *most people/things* (in general) and *most of the people/things* (particular ones).

Most people like dancing.
You can pay by credit card in most shops.

Most of the people at the party were dancing.
Most of the shops here are open on Sundays.

3 **Put in *most* or *most of the*.**

1 .... people talk to themselves.

2 I know .... people in our village.

3 .... people on the bus had no tickets.

4 .... people like music.

5 .... cars are expensive.

6 There are students in .... houses in this street.

7 .... cats eat fish.

8 Our cat eats .... things: fish, meat, biscuits, cheese, ...

9 I understand .... words in this book.

10 She's very friendly: she gets on well with .... people.

→ For *a lot of*, see page 169.
→ For *both* (*of*), see page 176.
→ For *all* (*of*), see page 173.
→ For *no* and *none* (*of*), see page 164.
→ For *every* and *every one* (*of*), see pages 174–175.

1 **Put in *this, that, these* or *those.***

1 Listen to .... You'll love it!
2 I didn't like .... film yesterday.
3 Who are .... people in John's car?
4 '..................... is my friend Pat.' 'How do you do?'

2 (Circle) **the correct answers.**

1 *I need / I don't need* some help.
2 There are *no letters / any letters* for you.
3 'What's the problem?' *'Any.' / 'Anything.' / 'Nothing.'*
4 'Where shall I sit?' *'Anywhere.' / 'Everywhere.'*
5 She's got *beautiful eyes / some beautiful eyes*.
6 She didn't eat *much / many* breakfast.
7 Were there *much / many* people at the party?
8 James always has *much / lots of* money.
9 A lot of my friends *think / thinks* I'm wrong.
10 There *is / are* lots of time before the shop closes.
11 I don't go to *a lot / many* parties.
12 Am I driving *too / too much* fast?
13 Are those shoes *big enough? / enough big?*
14 *Is / Are* everybody ready?

3 **Put in *all, each, every, everybody* or *everything.***

1 Not .... bird can fly.
2 I pronounced .... word separately, very slowly.
3 We'll start when .... student has arrived.
4 There's a pub at .... end of our street.
5 Tell me ....
6 She stayed in bed .... day yesterday.
7 Do you know .... here?

4 **Put in the correct answers.**

1 .... roads are closed. (*Either / Neither / Both*)
2 'Which car can I take?' 'It doesn't matter – .... car is OK.' (*either / neither / both*)
3 The police questioned .... of the students. (*every / every one*)
4 .... people like animals. (*Most / Most of the*)
5 I didn't like .... those books. (*many / many of*)
6 'How many books have you got to read?' '................................' (*A lot / A lot of*)
7 Can I give you my answer tomorrow? I need .... time to think. (*little / a little*)
8 His ideas are so difficult that .... people understand them. (*few / a few*)

5 **Make these sentences more conversational.**

1 She has little money. ....
2 I have many friends in Edinburgh. ....

◉ More difficult questions

SECTION 13 personal pronouns; possessives

● grammar summary

> I, you, he, she, it, we, they   me, you, him, her, it, us, them
> my, you, his, her, its, your, their   mine, yours, his, hers, yours, theirs
> myself, yourself, himself, herself, itself, ourselves, themselves   each other

We use **pronouns** when it is not necessary, or not possible, to use a more exact noun phrase.

> *Mrs Parker phoned.* **She** *said ...* (The speaker uses the personal pronoun *she* because it is not necessary to repeat *Mrs Parker*.)
>
> *Ann talks to* **herself** *all the time.* (It is unnecessary to repeat *Ann*.)

In this section we explain **personal pronouns** (*I, me, you* etc); **possessives** (*my, your* etc and *mine, yours* etc);
reflexive pronouns (*myself, yourself* etc), and *each other*.
Indefinite pronouns (*somebody, anything* etc) are explained in Section 12 together with *some* and *any*,
on page 165.
Relative pronouns (*who, which* etc) are explained in Section 18 on pages 237–244.

● pre-test: which units do you need?

Try this small test. It will help you to decide which units you need. The answers are on page 284.

1 Correct (✓) or not (✗)?

▶ We were early. ✓

▶ Them were all late. ✗

1 'Did you like France?' 'I thought it was wonderful.' ...

2 'Where are your gloves?' 'I've lost it.' ...

3 'Shall we go out?' 'No, is snowing.' ...

4 'Where's John?' 'That's he over there.' ...

5 'Who said that?' 'It was me.' ...

6 Where's mine car? ...

7 This isn't my coat. It's her. ...

8 Joe and Pat think our house is nicer than theirs. ...

9 Ann and Peter write to themselves every week. ...

10 Joe and Mary telephone each other every day. ...

11 I'm teaching myself to play the guitar. ...

12 The President himself answered my letter. ...

2 *His,* *her* or *their*?

▶ Ann lives with ...*her*...... mother.

1 Mary's gone to see .... brother.

2 Cathy's lost .... keys.

3 John needs to phone .... wife.

4 Joe and Pat want to sell .... house.

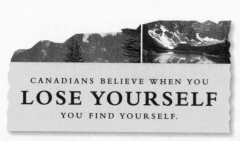

CANADIANS BELIEVE WHEN YOU
LOSE YOURSELF
YOU FIND YOURSELF.

Presents for him, her, you and them!

KENZO
FOR HIM. FOR HER.

"IT'S NOT JUST HAIR,
IT'S YOUR HAIR"

charles
worthington
LONDON

personal pronouns: *I* and *me* etc

SUBJECTS	*I*	*you*	*he*	*she*	*it*	*we* –	*they*
OTHER USES	*me*	*you*	*him*	*her*	*it*	*us*	*them*

SUBJECTS: *I, HE* ETC | *I like Mary.*   *He needs help.*   *They want your address.*
OBJECTS: *ME* ETC | *Mary doesn't like me.*   *Help him.*   *Don't tell them anything.*
AFTER PREPOSITIONS: *ME* ETC | *Look at me.*   *Why is Jane with him?*   *Is that for us?*
AFTER *BE*: *ME* ETC | *'Who's there?' 'It's me.'* (NOT USUALLY *'It is I.'*)
 | *'Is that Joe?' 'Yes, that's him.'*
INFORMAL ANSWERS: *ME* ETC | *'Who said that?' 'Me.'*   *'I'm tired.' 'Me too.'*

❶ Circle the correct answer.

▶ (*I*)/ *Me* don't understand.

1 'Who said that?' 'It was *she / her*.'
2 Tell *we / us* your address.
3 This isn't for you, it's for *he / him*.
4 I don't think *they / them* are here today.

5 'Where's your brother?' 'That's *he / him* over there.'
6 Where are the children? Can you see *they? / them?*
7 Ask *she / her* why *she / her* is crying.

❷ Put in *he, him, she, her, they* or *them*.

1 'Does your father speak English?' '................. understands a little.'
2 'I'm seeing Lucy and Pete on Tuesday.' 'Oh, give .... my love.'
3 'Mr Carter's here.' 'Ask .... to wait downstairs.'
4 Where are your friends? ....'re very late.
5 'Have you spoken to Mrs Lewis?' 'Not yet. I'm going to phone .... this evening.'
6 'Where's Ann?' '.................'s in Germany all this week.'

We use *it, they* and *them* for **things**, including (usually) **countries** and **animals**.

I like Scotland, but it's cold in winter.   *She sold her horse because it cost too much.*

---

❸ Put in *it, they* or *them*.

1 'Where are my keys?' '.................'re on that chair.'
2 'Where did that cat come from?' '................. came in through the window.'
3 'What did you think of the film?' '.................'s not very good.'
4 'What shall I do with these letters?' 'Just put .... on the table.'
5 'Can I have John's address?' 'I'll give .... to you this afternoon.'
6 'Did you enjoy your holiday in Ireland?' 'Yes, ...'s a wonderful place.'
7 'Where are your glasses?' 'I've lost ....'
8 'Would you like tickets for the concert?' 'How much do .... cost?'

We use *it* to talk about **times, dates, distances** and the **weather**.

It's five o'clock.   *It's Tuesday.*   *It's December 17th today.*   *It's my birthday.*
It's 20 miles from my house to the centre of Oxford.   *It's cold today.*   *It's raining.*

---

❹ Write true answers to these questions beginning *It's ...*

1 What time is it? It's ....
2 What day is it? ....

3 What's the date? ....
4 How far is it to London? ....

We **don't** usually **leave out** personal pronouns. (For exceptions in spoken English, see page 271.)

Jan arrived in America in 1976. ***He*** *found a job in a clothes shop.* (NOT ~~*Found a job*~~ ...)
'What languages do you know?' ***'I*** *can speak some German.'* (NOT '~~*Can speak*~~ ...')
'Is your room OK?' *'Yes, I like* ***it***.*'* (NOT '~~*Yes, I like.*~~ ')

5 **Write answers, using *I*, *you*, etc.**

▶ 'What time is the next train?' (*8.30, leaves, at*)
   'It leaves at 8.30.' ....

1 'Where's John?' (*has, London, to, moved*)
   ....

2 'Have you seen my glasses?' (*on, chair, are, that*)
   ....

3 'What do you think of my new shoes?' (*like*)
   ....

4 'What's Elisabeth going to do?' (*medicine, study, going to, is*)
   ....

5 'I'm learning Greek.' 'Is it easy?' (*No, difficult, is*)
   ....

6 **GRAMMAR AND VOCABULARY: weather**
**Make sure you know the adjectives and verbs in the box. Use a dictionary if necessary.
Then label the pictures.**

| ADJECTIVES: cloudy cold foggy ✓ hot sunny warm windy |
| VERBS: hail ✓ rain snow |

▶ *It's hailing.* ...... ▶ *It's foggy.* .... 1 .... 2 .... 3 ....

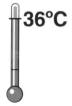   

4 .... 5 .... 6 .... 7 .... 8 ....

In conversation, we often use *me* after *and* in subjects. Many people feel this is incorrect.
John and me *saw a great film last night.* (More 'correct': ***John and I*** ...)

possessives: *my, your* etc   *This is my coat.*

I	→ **my**	This is **my** coat.
you	→ **your**	That's **your** problem.
he	→ **his**	John's visiting **his** mother.
she	→ **her**	Ann looks like **her** brothers.
it	→ **its**	The club has **its** meetings on Tuesdays.
we	→ **our**	**Our** friends Joe and Pat are staying with us.
they	→ **their**	The children have spent all **their** money.
who?	→ **whose?**	**Whose** coat is this?

Possessives **don't change** for singular and **plural**.

our friend   *our* friends (NOT ~~ours friends~~)

Note how we use *his* and *her*: if a boy or man has something, we use *his*; if a girl or woman has something, we use *her*.

I saw John and his sister yesterday. (NOT ... ~~John and her sister~~ ...)
Mary and her brother are students. (NOT ~~Mary and his brother~~ ...)

We often use **possessives** with **parts of the body** and **clothes**.

Phil has broken his arm. (NOT ~~Phil has broken the arm.~~)
She stood there with her eyes closed and her hands in her pockets.

1 Put in the correct possessives.

▶ Ann's lost ......*her*....... keys.
▶ Would you like to wash ....*your*..... hands?
1 Peter says .... wife is ill.
2 We're taking .... holiday in June.
3 .... car is that outside?
4 My bank has changed .... name.
5 I'm going to sell .... motorbike.
6 My students have got .... exam next week.
7 John writes to .... girlfriend every day.
8 Ann lives with .... father in Portugal.
9 Please put .... coats upstairs.
10 Robert broke .... leg skiing last winter.
11 'What film did you see?' 'Sorry, I've forgotten .... name.'

'Your loving son,'

2 **Who sold what to who? Make sentences.**

ANN: car → JOHN: bike → PETER: dog → MARY: house → PAT AND SAM: motorbike → BILL: piano →
ALICE: coat → MICHAEL: camera → HELEN: guitar → MARILYN: hair-dryer → TOM: dictionary → ANN

▶ Ann sold her car to John. ....   6 ....
1 John sold .... to Peter.   7 ....
2 Peter ....   8 ....
3 ....   9 ....
4 ....   10 ....
5 ....

3 **Look at the picture and complete the text.**

▶ .Ann........................ and ▶ .her husband Bill.... went on holiday with 1 ....
and 2 .... in 3 .... There's room for six in the van, so Ann invited
4 .... to go with them, but she didn't ask 5 ...., because Bill
doesn't get on with Lucy. Bill asked 6 ...., but she said no, because she doesn't like
Frank. Then Bill asked 7 ...., but he wasn't free. However, 8 ....
was happy to go with them, so everything was OK.

▶ Ann

▶ Ann's husband Bill

1 Bill and Ann's son Joe

2 Bill and Ann's daughter Emma

3 Bill and Ann's camper van

4 Ann's brother Frank

5 Ann's sister Lucy

6 Bill's sister Mary

7 Bill's brother Eric

8 Bill and Ann's friend Pete

We **don't** use *a/an, the, this* or *that* **before possessives**.

my car (NOT ~~the my car~~)   *this* idea OR *my* idea (NOT ~~this my idea~~)

Don't confuse *its* (possessive) and *it's* (= 'it is' or 'it has' – see page 277). Compare:
*The company had **its** annual meeting yesterday. **It's** losing a lot of money.*

possessives: *mine, yours* etc   *This is mine.*

DETERMINER	PRONOUN
my coat	*mine*
your car	*yours*
his chair	*his*

DETERMINER	PRONOUN
her book	*hers*
our house	*ours*
their problem	*theirs*

We use *mine, yours* etc without nouns. Compare:

*That's not **my** coat. This is **mine**.* (NOT *This is the mine.*)   *Is that **your** car? I thought **yours** was a Ford.*
*Their garden is much bigger than **ours**.*

We can use the question word ***whose*** with or without nouns.

***Whose** coat is that?*   ***Whose** is that coat?*

1 Change the sentences.

▶ That's *my newspaper*.   ...*That's mine.*...............................

1 I prefer our house to *their house*.   I prefer our house to ....

2 Her hair looks better than *your hair*.   Her hair ....

3 *Your hair* looks terrible.   ....

4 That dog looks like *our dog*.   ....

2 GRAMMAR AND VOCABULARY: the bathroom
Look at the pictures of John and Mary's bathroom, and use the words in the box to make sentences with *his, hers* or *theirs*. Use a dictionary if necessary.

dressing-gown	hair-dryer	make-up	razor	shampoo	soap	toothbrush
toothbrush	toothpaste	towel	washcloth ✓	washcloth		

▶ *The red washcloth is his.*...............................   6 ....

1 The .... is not theirs.   7 ....

2 ....   8 ....

3 ....   9 ....

4 ....   10 ....

5 ....   11 ....

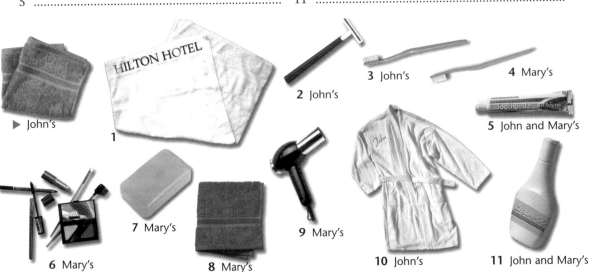

▶ John's   1   2 John's   3 John's   4 Mary's   5 John and Mary's

6 Mary's   7 Mary's   8 Mary's   9 Mary's   10 John's   11 John and Mary's

reflexive pronouns: *myself, yourself* etc

I → **myself**	you → **yourself**	he → **himself**	she → **herself**	it → **itself**
we → **ourselves**	you → **yourselves**	they → **themselves**		

We use **myself, yourself** etc when an **object** is the **same** person/thing as the **subject**.

I cut myself shaving this morning. (NOT ~~I cut me~~...)   *We must ask ourselves some questions.*
He tried to kill himself. (Different from *He tried to kill him*.)

1 (Circle) **the correct answer.**

1 She doesn't love *him / himself*.
2 She likes looking at *her / herself* in the mirror.
3 Old people often talk to *them / themselves*.

4 I'm going out tonight, so you will all have to cook for *yourself / yourselves*.
5 I like Bill, but I don't understand *him / himself*.

2 **Put in *myself, yourself* etc.**

1 I'm teaching .... to play the guitar.
2 'Who's John talking to?' ....
3 Get a drink for ....
4 We really enjoyed .... last night.

5 Mary talks about .... all the time.
6 Find chairs for .... and sit down.
7 They just want to make money for ....

We can also use **myself** etc to emphasise – to say *'that person/thing and nobody/nothing else'*.

*It's best if **you** do it **yourself**.*   *I want to speak to **the manager himself**, not his secretary.*

3 **Put in *myself, yourself* etc.**

1 Did you cut your hair ....?
2 Peter and Ann built their house ....
3 I answer all my letters ....

4 Can you repair this, or must we do it ....?
5 We got a letter from the Queen ....

Note the difference between **ourselves** etc and **each other**.

They're looking at themselves.

They're looking at each other.

4 *Each other* **or** *-selves*?
1 Henry and Barbara write to .... every week.
2 Joe and Pat have bought a flat for ....
3 Do you and Mary tell .... everything?
4 You'll need photos of .... for your passports.
5 Ann and I have known .... for years.

GRAMMAR AND VOCABULARY: some common expressions with reflexive pronouns

by myself/yourself etc (= 'alone')   *enjoy myself/yourself* etc   *Take care of yourself.*
Help yourself. (= 'Take what you want.')   *Make yourself comfortable.*

1 **Complete the table.**

I	me	my	mine	myself
	you			
he		his		
			hers	
	it		—	
		our		
				yourselves
they				

2 (Circle) **the correct answers.**

1 John and *his / her / their* wife have gone to Greece.
2 Ann's lost *his / her / its* keys.
3 That's not *me / my / mine* coat.
4 This coat is *me / my / mine*.
5 Their house is much bigger than *our / ours / my*.
6 *Who / Who's / Whose* is this bag?
7 That dog has hurt *it's / its / their* ear.
8 They've taken my car: *they / their / theirs* isn't running.
9 'Who did that?' 'It was *I / me*.'
10 'What about this music?' '*I like*.' / '*I like it*.'

11 'Which is your sister?' 'That's *she / her* in the red dress.'
12 *There are / It is* five miles to the nearest station.
13 *It is / We are* Tuesday.
14 I *got up / got myself up* very late this morning.
15 Ann and I write to *ourselves / each other* every week.
16 Let's *meet / meet ourselves / meet each other* at 8.00 this evening.
17 I really *enjoyed / enjoyed myself* at your party.
18 Don't help me – I want to do it *I / me / myself*.
19 Peter's here with *his / her / their* two sisters.
20 *Its / It's / They are* five o'clock.

3 **Choose words from the boxes to complete the text.**

each other	her	his	its	themselves	they	your

My brother and 1 .... girlfriend have known 2 .... for about five years,
but 3 .... 've only been going out together for six months.

he	her	him	she	their	they	we

Before that, he didn't like 4 .... and 5 .... didn't like him, but later
6 .... became good friends, and started going out together.

her	hers	his	its	it's	our	their	they	they're

7 .... both have small flats. His flat is in the centre, and 8 .... very comfortable.
9 .... is a long way out, and it's not so nice. So they spend most of 10 .... free
time at 11 .... place.

he	her	hers	herself	him	himself	its	it's	she's

He works in a garage, and 12 .... a teacher, but she doesn't let 13 ....
touch 14 .... car – she looks after it 15 ....

each other	I	my	they	them	their	themselves	they're

I like 16 .... both very much, and I think 17 .... good for 18 ....,
so 19 .... hope 20 .... will stay together.

SECTION 14 nouns

grammar summary

Nouns are mostly words for things and people – for example *house, tree, driver, child, water, idea, lesson*. Most nouns can come after *the*.

English nouns can be **countable** (we can say *two houses*) or **uncountable** (we can't say ~~two waters~~). **Countable** nouns have **plurals** (*houses*), and we can use *a/an* with them (*a house, an idea*). **Uncountable** nouns have **no plurals**, and we **can't** use *a/an* before them. Some English uncountable nouns are countable in some other languages (like *furniture*).

We can **join** two nouns:
- with a **possessive 's or s'** (for example *my **brother's** wife, my **parents'** house*).
- with a **preposition** (for example *a **piece of** cake*).
- directly one after the other (for example ***chocolate** cake, a **shoe** shop*).

The differences between these three structures are hard to learn – this is one of the most difficult points in English grammar. There are some basic rules in this section.

pre-test: which units do you need?

Try this small test. It will help you to decide which units you need. The answers are on page 284.

1 **Write the plurals.**

dog *dogs*.................... home .... day .... family ....
woman .... child .... leaf ....

2 **Correct (✓) or not (✗)?**

▶ There are two mans outside. ✗.
▶ This is my father's house. ✓.
1 My family have moved to Manchester. ...
2 I bought two new blue jeans yesterday. ...
3 People are all different. ...
4 I'd like a one with pockets. ...

5 I don't like the ones without pockets. ...
6 Here's a photo of my parent's wedding. ...
7 I think that's the John's car. ...
8 Do you have the address of Mary? ...
9 Have you got the telephone's book? ...
10 This shoe shop is very expensive. ...

3 **A/an or some?**

▶ .*a*............... chair   ▶ .*some*......... furniture   1 .... information
2 .... baggage   3 .... journey   4 .... petrol
5 .... bread   6 .... idea

singular and plural nouns   *cat, cats; box, boxes*

Countable nouns have different forms for **singular** and **plural**.

one **car**   four **cars**   one **day**   ten **days**   one **baby**   four **babies**   one **child**   six **children**

HOW TO MAKE PLURALS

- **most nouns:** + -s   book → books   home → homes   car → cars
- **-s, -sh, -ch, -x:** + -es   bus → buses   wish → wishes   church → churches   fox → foxes

1 Write the plurals.

| apple ✓ | boss ✓ | box | brush | cat | chair | church | class | dress | garden |
| gas | glass | hotel | plane | ship | table | time | tree | watch | wish |

+ -S: ..apples............   ....

....

+ -ES: ..bosses............   ....

....

NOUNS ENDING IN -Y

- -ay, -ey, -oy, -uy: + -s   day → days   monkey → monkeys   toy → toys
- -by, -dy, -fy, -gy, etc: -y → -ies   baby → babies   lady → ladies   lorry → lorries

2 Write the plurals.

| boy ✓ | city ✓ | copy | country | family | guy | holiday | key | party | way |

+ -S: ..boys............   ....

-Y → -IES: ..cities............   ....

COMMON IRREGULAR PLURALS

mouse → mice	child → children	half → halves	shelf → shelves
foot → feet	penny → pence	knife → knives	thief → thieves
tooth → teeth	person → people	leaf → leaves	wife → wives
man → men		life → lives	
woman → women	potato → potatoes	loaf → loaves	sheep → sheep
	tomato → tomatoes	self → selves	fish → fish

Simple present verbs have different forms after **singular** and **plural** nouns (see page 14).

*This **bus runs** at weekends.*   *Most of the **buses run** at weekends.*
*My **brother has** a small flat.*   *Both my **brothers have** good jobs.*

3 Put in plural nouns or simple present verbs.

▶ Their homes .....are..... in Scotland. (*be*)
1 Our .... play a lot of football. (*child*)
2 Those .... don't look English. (*student*)
3 Some people .... to talk to you. (*want*)
4 Big .... are always dirty. (*city*)
5 Their .... are travelling with them. (*wife*)
6 These knives ....n't cut very well. (*do*)
7 My .... are giving me trouble. (*tooth*)
8 Those .... cost too much. (*watch*)
9 Most .... cry at night. (*baby*)
10 The .... are all wet. (*match*)
11 Who are those ....? (*guy*)
12 My parents .... at home. (*work*)
13 How many .... live here? (*person*)

singular/plural *team, family; jeans, scissors*

Words for **groups of people** can have **singular or plural verbs** in British English.
We often use **plural verbs** when we talk about **personal actions** (for example *play, want, think*).

*The **team is/are playing** badly.   My **family want/wants** me to study.*
*The **government think/thinks** taxes are too low.*

Note the difference between *England* (the country) and *England* (the football team).

*England **has** got a new prime minister.   England **have** got a new manager.*

Police is always **plural**.

*The **police are** looking for a tall 30-year-old woman.* (NOT ~~The police is looking~~ ...)

❶ Group nouns (✓) or not (✗)?

army ✓   audience ✓   beach ✗   class   club   Communist Party   company
crowd   idea   lunch   question   room   school   train

❷ Put the beginnings and ends together, and put in plural verbs from the box.

haven't   need ✓   play   say   want

1 The club	A .... her to go to university. ...
2 The company	B only .... classical music. ...
3 Her family	C .... scored a goal this year. ...
4 The orchestra	D .... that they're losing money. ...
5 This team	E ...*need*........... a bigger room for their meetings. *1.*

Some nouns are **always plural**. Some common examples:
trousers   jeans   tights   shorts   pants   pyjamas   glasses   scissors
***Those** trousers **are** too short.* (NOT ~~That trouser~~ ...)   *Where **are** my glasses?*

❸ Complete the sentences. Use the words in the box.

blue jeans ✓   dark glasses   silk pyjamas   scissors   shorts   black trousers

▶ Every time I see her she's wearing ...*blue jeans*.........................

1 I can't see very well with these ....

2 It's hot today. I'm going to put on ....

3 These .... don't cut very well.

4 You'd better put on your best .... for the interview.

5 She always sleeps in ....

We can also use the expression *a pair of* with these nouns.

*three **pairs of** jeans* (NOT ~~three jeans~~)   *two **pairs of** pyjamas* (NOT ~~two pyjamas~~)
*There is **a pair of** scissors on your chair.* (NOT ... ~~a scissors~~ ...)

more about countable and uncountable nouns

→ For an introduction to countable and uncountable nouns, and some basic exercises, see page 147.

Countable nouns are words like *car, book, chair*. They can be singular or plural.
Uncountable nouns are words like *petrol, rice, water*. They are only singular.

1 Revision. (Circle) the uncountable nouns.

cup   dog   flower   guitar   love   meat   music   ear   oil   photo   river
salt   snow   sugar   women   wool

The following words are uncountable in English (but countable in some other languages). They are
normally **only singular**, and we **cannot** use *a/an* with them. (NOT *a travel, a furniture*)
*advice   baggage   bread   furniture   hair   information   knowledge   luck   luggage
news   spaghetti* (and *macaroni* etc)   *travel   work*
This furniture is *too expensive.*   *His* **hair is** *very long.*   **Travel teaches** *you a lot.*

2 Put *a* with the countable nouns and *some* with the uncountable nouns.

..some... bread   ..a........ cheque   .... baggage   .... fridge   .... furniture
.... handbag   .... holiday   .... knowledge   .... luck
.... newspaper   .... problem   .... station   .... travel   .... work

3 Put in suitable uncountable nouns from the box.

| advice | baggage | furniture | information ✓ | news | spaghetti | travel | work |

▶ Can you give me some ...*information*............... about the school?
1 'Have you got much ....?' 'No, just one small bag.'
2 I live 50 kilometres from my work, so I spend a lot of money on ....
3 This .... isn't very good. You cooked it for too long.
4 I've stopped reading the papers. The .... is always bad.
5 I don't know what to do. Can you give me some ....?
6 All this .... is from my mother's house.
7 I've got too much .... and not enough free time.

To give a **countable** meaning, we usually use a **longer expression** or a **different word**.
Can you give me **a piece of advice**?   *Did you have* **a good journey**?

4 Put in words or expressions from the box.

| a piece of advice   a piece of baggage ✓   a piece of information   a piece of news   a job   a journey |

▶ a suitcase   ...*a piece of baggage*...............................
1 selling newspapers   ....
2 driving from London to Edinburgh   ....
3 'Don't marry him, dear.'   ....
4 'The next train leaves at 10.15.'   ....
5 'There has been a big train crash.'   ....

Some words can be countable or uncountable, with **different meanings.**

A light was on in the house. (= 'a lamp')   *Light travels at 300,000 km a second.*
I've seen that film three times.   *Time goes fast when you're having fun.*
I had a strange experience yesterday.   *We need a secretary with experience.*
Three coffees, please. (= 'cups of coffee')   *I drink too much coffee.*

5 Look at the pictures and put in descriptions from the box.

a chicken	chicken	a chocolate	chocolate	a glass	glass	an iron
iron	a paper	paper		

1 ....   2 ....   3 ....   4 ....   5 ....

6 ....   7 ....   8 ....   9 ....   10 ....

6 GRAMMAR AND VOCABULARY: containers
Make sure you know the words in the box. Use a dictionary if necessary. Then use them to complete the descriptions under the pictures.

bag	bottle	box	can	cup	glass	jar	jug	mug	packet

1 a ....   2 a ....   3 a ....   4 a ....   5 a ....
of water   of water   of chocolates   of tea   of coffee

 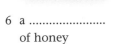    

6 a ....   7 a ....   8 a ....   9 a ....   10 a ....
of honey   of soup   of onions   of orange juice   of biscuits

one and ones   *a big one; the ones on the chair*

We often use *one* instead of repeating a countable noun.

'What sort of car would you like?' 'A big one.' (= *'A big car.'*) (NOT *'A big.'*)
That was a great party. Let's have another one soon.

The plural is *ones*.

'Which are your gloves?' 'The ones on the chair.'

❶ Complete the sentences with *one(s)*, using words from the box.

another	green ✓	blue	last	new	this	small

▶ I bought a blue shirt and two .*green ones*.
1 That shop isn't as good as ....
2 My TV's broken. I must get ....
3 She's finished her apple. She wants
   ....

4 That bus is the .... tonight.
5 'Another piece of cake?'
   'Just a ....'
6 I don't like the red shoes. I prefer
   the ....

❷ Look at the picture and answer the questions. Use words from the box.

big	black	blue	fast	glass ✓	green	red
slow	small	white	wooden ✓	yellow		

▶ Which table do you prefer? .*The glass one.*...........................
   OR .*The wooden one.*...........................
1 Which house do you prefer? ....
2 Which sweater do you prefer? ....
3 Which car do you prefer? ....
4 Which dog do you prefer? ....
5 Which flower do you prefer? ....

maximum speed
250 km/h

maximum speed
50 km/h

We say *one*, **not** *a one*, when there is **no adjective**.

'What sort of cake would you like?' 'One with a lot of cream.' (NOT *'A one with …'*)
'Is there a garage near here?' 'There's one in Weston Street.'

❸ Write some true sentences. Use the expressions in the box.

I've already got one.   I haven't got one.   I need one.   I need a new one.
I don't need one.   I'd like one.   I don't want one.

▶ a computer .*I don't need one.*...........................
1 a bicycle ....
2 a fast car ....
3 a camera ....

4 a cup of coffee ....
5 a tennis racket ....
6 a raincoat ....
7 a rich uncle ....

We only use *one* for **countable** nouns (see page 190).

'Would you like some coffee?' 'Yes, black (coffee), please.' (NOT *'Yes, black one …'*)

's and s' possessive: forms *son's, sons', men's*

1 **Make possessive forms by adding *'s* or *'*.**

▶ my mother.'s nose
▶ my sisters.'.. names
1 Alice and John... house
2 artists... ideas
3 my dog... ears
4 those dogs... ears
5 those men... faces
6 his girlfriend... piano
7 their grandchild... birthday
8 their grandchildren... school
9 ladies... hats

10 my aunt and uncle... shop
11 Patrick... books
12 a photographer... job
13 our postman... cat
14 postmen... uniforms
15 Joyce... pen
16 the thief... bag
17 the thieves... car
18 that woman... brother
19 most women... desks
20 your mum and dad... bedroom

2 **'Police are looking for two young girls.' Complete the news story. Don't forget to add *'s* or *'*.**

The two girls disappeared from (*their grandmother*) ▶ ....their grandmother's...... garden in Ilkley yesterday evening. Josie and Cara Sharp, aged 7 and 9, were staying at (*their grandparents*) 1 .... house for a week. They were in Ilkley for a (*children*) 2 .... theatre course. The police have asked the course teachers for (*the other children*) 3 .... names and addresses, and they have also put Josie (*and Cara*) 4 .... photos on local television. (*The two girls*) 5 .... mother, Mrs Jenna Sharp, has appeared on TV as well. A shopkeeper thinks she saw Josie and Cara getting into (*a man*) 6 .... car; police officers have asked for (*the shopkeeper*) 7 .... help with a photofit picture of the man. The police have also got (*local people*) 8 .... help in looking for the girls near the town.

3 **Write the possessive expressions.**

▶ My son has got a teacher. She has got a husband. *my son's teacher's husband* ....
1 My sister has got a secretary. She has got an office. ....
2 Jane has got children. They have got bicycles. ....
3 Rob has got a family. They have got a holiday flat. ....

's and s' possessive: use   *Ian's car; the boss's car*

Possessive nouns with *'s* or *s'* **take the place** of *the*.

the car that belongs to Ian → Ian's car (NOT ~~Ian's the car~~)
the shoes that belong to Jo → Jo's shoes

But a possessive noun can have **its own article**.

the car that belongs to the boss → the boss's car
the shoes that belong to the children → the children's shoes

---

1 Make *'s* or *s'* possessive structures.

▶ The dog belongs to Joe. ...Joe's dog...........................
▶ The dog belongs to the postman. ...the postman's dog.....................
1 The house belongs to Ann. ....
2 The house belongs to the doctor. ....
3 The book belongs to Oliver. ....
4 The car belongs to the teacher. ....
5 The money belongs to the children. ....
6 The money belongs to Susan. ....

2 Change the sentences.

▶ *The* classes are using the new books. (*the French teachers*)
  The French teachers' classes are using the new books. ....
1 *The* car is parked in front of *the* house. (*the builder; Anna*)
  .... car is parked in front of .... house.
2 Do you know *the* address? (*the tall woman*)
  ....
3 *Their* bedtime is eight o'clock. (*the children*)
  ....
4 *The* brothers are both in the army. (*Alice and Pat*)
  ....

We use **possessive** *'s* and *s'* mostly to talk about **possession, experience** and **relationships** (family, friends etc). We usually put *'s* or *s'* after the names of **people** and **animals**.

Ann's purse   *Ann's English lessons*   *Ann's husband*   *Ann's friend*   *Ann's boss*
my dad's book (NOT ~~the book of my dad~~)   *my horse's ears* (NOT ~~the ears of my horse~~)
BUT *the roof* **of the house** (NOT ~~the house's roof~~)   *the top* **of my desk** (NOT ~~my desk's top~~)

---

3 Write two sentences for each item.

▶ Is *the door* open? (*Paul; the library*)
  Is Paul's door open? Is the door of the library open? ....
1 What's *the name*? (*your brother; that book*)
  ....
2 Is there anything in *the pockets*? (*the children; that coat*)
  ....
3 You can see the church from *the window*. (*Emma; the living room*)
  ....
4 Why are *the arms* so dirty? (*John; your chair*)
  ....

With some **common time words, we** add *'s* to say **how long** something takes.

a second's thought   a minute's silence

4 Choose a time expression for each sentence. Use the words in the box.

second ✓   minute   hour   day   week   year

▶ 'Who was it?' I asked. There was *a pause* before she answered. <u>a second's pause</u>
1 After university, Eric took *a course* to become a teacher. ....
2 Lin had *a holiday* with her mother earlier this year. ....
3 Oxford is nearly 600 km from Edinburgh – that's *a journey*. ....
4 Sita's new job will mean *a drive* to work every morning. ....
5 There was *a wait* while the computer started up. ....

We can use **noun + 's or s'** without another noun, if the meaning is **clear**.

'Whose coat is that?' 'Harry's.'   *My hair is dark, but* **my children's** *is fair.*

We also use **noun + 's or s'** without other nouns for **offices, churches** and **some shops**.

I bought this at **Allder's**.   *I hate going to the* **dentist's**.   *She sings at* **St. John's**.

5 Look at the pictures and complete the sentences.

▶ The green skirt is ...<u>Tamsin's.</u>... ...<u>She</u>... bought it at <u>Selfridge's.</u>
1 The grey pullover is .... bought it at ....
2 The black leather jacket ....
3 The blue shirt ....
4 The brown leather jacket ....
5 The navy blue pullover ....
6 The red shirt ....
7 The yellow scarf ....

Tamsin   Simon

We often **noun + 's or s'** without other nouns to talk about **people's homes**.

I saw Monica **at June and Barry's** *on Friday.*   *Lee is going* **to his sister's** *next weekend.*

6 Other people's homes: write about two or more things in your past. Use *at ...'s* or *at ...s'*.

<u>I met my girlfriend at Judy's.   I went to my grandparents' for Easter.</u>
....
....

noun + noun   *Milk chocolate is a kind of chocolate.*

We can put one noun before another when we are talking about a **kind** of thing or person.
The **first noun** is usually singular.

milk chocolate = a kind of chocolate, with **milk** in it   chocolate **milk** = a kind of milk, with **chocolate** in it
flower shop = shop that sells **flowers** (NOT ~~flowers shop~~)   **corner** shop = a shop on a **corner**
hotel receptionist = a receptionist in a **hotel**   **history** teacher = a teacher who teaches **history**

1 Use the words in the box to make noun + noun structures. You can use some of the
words more than once.

army	aspirin	business	corner	e-mail	flower	garden	home
jazz	kitchen	milk	opera	perfume	police	pop	prison	village

▶ 3 kinds of shop *flower shop, corner shop, village shop* ....

1 3 kinds of address ....

2 3 kinds of bottle ....

3 3 kinds of singer ....

4 3 kinds of wall ....

5 3 kinds of uniform ....

6 2 kinds of chair ....

2 Change the expressions in the box to noun + noun structures, and put the beginnings
and ends together. Remember: don't make the first noun plural.

clothes for babies	make-up for eyes ✓	building with offices in it	food for dogs
engineer who works on computers	school of languages	drawer for knives

1 Judy wears too much ...*eye make-up*.. to the office	A but he couldn't repair it. ...
2 They're going to put a big	B I want to learn Japanese. ...
3 Our dog won't eat ....;	C – does she think she's at a party? 1̶
4 The .... looked at my printer,	D he only wants fresh meat or fish. ...
5 Do you know of a good ....?	E when my brother was born. ...
6 My aunt made some lovely	F at the corner of our street. ...
7 Why are the spoons in the ....?	G And who put them there? ...

We often use **noun + noun structures** to talk about what things are **made of**.

3 Write noun + noun names for these.

▶ soup with chicken in it ...*chicken soup*...........................

1 a box made of metal ....

2 cakes with chocolate in them ....

3 a fork made of plastic ....

4 soup made of vegetables ....

5 a jacket made of leather ....

6 shirts made of cotton ....

7 a plate made of paper ....

8 salad with tomatoes in it ....

9 a wall made of stones ....

We often use **noun + noun structures** when the second noun is made from a verb + *er*

a truck driver = *a person who drives a truck*   *a hair dryer* = *a machine for drying hair*

4 **What do we call these people or things?**

▶ This person drives a bus. .*a bus driver*.............................

1 This person manages an office. ....

2 This machine makes coffee. ....

3 This person drinks coffee. ....

4 This person loves animals. ....

5 This stuff cleans floors. ....

6 This person plays tennis. ....

7 This thing opens letters. ....

8 This person smokes cigars. ....

9 This person climbs mountains. ....

NOUN + NOUN STRUCTURE OR '*s* / *s*' POSSESSIVE STRUCTURE

We mostly use '*s* or *s*' when the **first noun** **possesses, experiences** or **has a relationship** with the second noun. We use a **noun + noun structure** for **other** kinds of meaning. So **things** do **not usually** take '*s* / *s*'. Compare:

the dog's name (possession: the dog has a name)   *Rita's accident* (experience: Rita had an accident)
Ed's brother (relationship: Ed has a brother)   *Annie's secretary is Ellen's best friend.* (relationships)
BUT *a shoe brush* (the shoe doesn't possess or experience the brush; shoes don't have relationships)

5 (Circle) **the correct answers.**

1 Could I borrow your *telephone's book / telephone book* for a minute?

2 Is that your *teacher's book / teacher book*, or is it yours?

3 *Elizabeth's journey / Elizabeth journey* took her to five continents.

4 The *train's journey / train journey* from Huntsville to Victoria was very boring.

5 My *aunt's home / aunt home* is full of beautiful furniture.

6 Our *holiday's home / holiday home* is in the French Alps.

7 My *brother's interview / brother interview* with the president will be on the radio today.

8 I was very nervous about my *job's interview / job interview*.

GRAMMAR AND VOCABULARY: one-word noun + noun structures

Some noun + noun structures are so common that we write them as **one word**, for example:
armchair   bathroom   bedroom   bookshop   businessman   businesswoman   hairbrush
handbag   raincoat   postman   postwoman   schoolchild   suitcase   toothbrush   toothpaste

test yourself   nouns

1 **Write the plurals.**

bus _buses_ .... fox .... journey .... country ....

match .... book .... table .... foot ....

person .... knife .... mouse ....

2 **Correct (✓) or not (✗)?**

▶ My friends are playing well. ✓

1 He buys too much clothes. ...

2 He's bought two new trousers. ...

3 the Peter's house ...

4 the mother of James ...

5 That building is a boy's school. ...

6 She writes children's books. ...

3 **Countable or uncountable? Put in _a/an_ or _some_.**

▶ We need _a_ .... new bed.

▶ We need _some_ .... new furniture.

1 Can you give me .... advice?

2 I found .... money in the street this morning.

3 I've got .... difficult job to do today.

4 Ann gave me .... good news.

5 I need a taxi, because I've got .... heavy luggage.

6 Did you have .... good journey?

4 **Which nouns can be plural? Write the plural or ✗.**

▶ note _notes_ ....

▶ money _✗_ ....

1 information ....

2 bread ....

3 idea ....

4 luck ....

5 knowledge ....

6 journey ....

7 furniture ....

8 government ....

9 class ....

10 traffic ....

5 **Put in three different nouns.**

1 a pair of .... 2 a pair of .... 3 a pair of ....

6 **Correct (✓) or not (✗)?**

1 The team are playing well. ...

2 The police don't usually carry guns in Britain. ...

3 How much are the blue ones? ...

4 I'd like a one with a radio. ...

5 the house's door ...

6 the teacher's book ...

7 the telephone book ...

8 a journey of a day ...

9 two shoes shops ...

10 We're going round to Jan and Peters place. ...

11 I like eating chocolate milk. ...

12 I've bought a new leather jacket. ...

7 **What are these people?**

▶ _a hockey player_ ......   1 ....   2 ....   3 ....

◉ More difficult questions

SECTION 15 adjectives and adverbs

grammar summary

Adjectives are words like *easy, slow, sorry, important*. They usually tell you more about **people** or **things**. They can go **before nouns**, or **after** *be, seem, look*, etc.

Adverbs are words like *easily, slowly, yesterday, there*. Adverbs tell you, for example, **how, when** or **where** something happens.

We can **compare** people and things with *as ... as, -er than* or *more ... than*.
   *Joe's **as tall as** me.*   *Jane's **taller than** me.*   *She works **more carefully than** me.*

We can use *-est* or *most* to compare people and things with **all of their group**.
   *Mary's the **most intelligent** person in the class.*   *John is the **oldest** of his children.*

We use *-er* and *-est* with **shorter adjectives** and some short adverbs.

pre-test: which units do you need?

Try this small test. It will help you to decide which units you need. The answers are on page 284.

1 **Write the adverbs.**

nice *nicely*......................   complete ....   easy ....
beautiful ....   probable ....

2 **Correct (✓) or not (✗)?**

▶ She asked some difficults questions. ✗   4 I often play tennis. ...
1 She was wearing a green, beautiful dress. ...   5 I'm not as tall as my sister. ...
2 You are certainly right. ...   6 Can you drive slowlier, please? ...
3 He speaks very well Russian. ...   7 I'm very interesting in politics. ...

3 **Circle the correct words.**

▶ He talks very (fast) / *fastly*.   5 He doesn't work very *hard / hardly*.
1 I'm *terrible / terribly* sorry.   6 This is the *more / most* expensive hotel *in / of*
2 It looks *beautiful / beautifully*.   the country.
3 I drove very *careful / carefully* on the snow.   7 Ann is much older *as / than / that / of* her
4 She spoke to me in *perfect / perfectly* English.   husband.

4 **Write the comparatives.**

old *older*......................   fat ....   happy ....
late ....   good ....   interesting ....

Great books for young readers!

London's wildest nightclub

'Best sports car of the year' – it's bigger, lighter, stronger and faster.

For smaller kitchens, the smallest dishwasher in the world

100% organic soup. Nothing could be more comforting.

adjectives   *a beautiful little girl who was not stupid*

Adjectives go before, not after **nouns**.

1   2   1   2
a *long* journey (NOT *a journey long*)   *loud* music (NOT *music loud*)

Adjectives **don't change** for **singular** and **plural**.

a *fast* car   *fast* cars (NOT *fasts cars*)

Before nouns, we **don't** usually put *and* between adjectives.

a *big bad* wolf (NOT *a big and bad wolf*)

Colour adjectives usually come **after others**.

beautiful red apples (NOT *red beautiful apples*)

1 **Put in the adjectives and write the story.**

One day, a time ago, (*long   fine*)   ▶ *One fine day, a long time ago.*........................
a girl (*beautiful   little*)   1 ....
in a coat (*red*)   2 ....
was walking though a forest (*dark*)   3 ....
with a bag (*big*)   4 ....
of apples (*red   wonderful*)   5 ....
to see her grandmother. (*old*)   6 ....
Under a tree (*tall   green*)   7 ....
she saw a wolf (*big   bad*)   8 ....
with teeth. (*white   long*)   9 ....

2 **Put the words in the correct order and continue the story.**

'good little, girl morning', said   1 'Good ....
big the bad wolf.   2 ....
'going you where are   3 ....
that with bag heavy   4 ....
day this fine on?'   5 ....
'going my see to grandmother I'm old'   6 ....
girl the said little.   7 ....
'lives small she in house a   8 ....
new the supermarket near.'   9 ....

3 **Put in adjectives from the box to finish the story.**

big	friendly	stupid	little

'OK,' said the wolf in a 1 .... voice.
'I'll see you later.' 'I don't think so,' said
the 2 .... girl, who was not
3 .... She took a 4 ....
pistol out of her bag and shot the wolf dead.

(from an idea by James Thurber)

'I don't think so,' said the little girl.

Adjectives can go after *be, become, get, seem, look* (= '*seem*') and *feel*.

*The water **is** cold.*   *Everything **became** clear.*   *It's **getting** late.*   *You **seem** tired.*
*She **looks** happy.*   *I **feel** hot.*

After these verbs, we put ***and** before the last* of two or more adjectives.

*He was tall, dark **and** handsome.* (NOT ~~He was tall, dark, handsome.~~)   *You look well **and** happy.*

---

4 **Look at the pictures and complete the sentences, using words from the box.**

| and   and   beautiful   cold   hungry   intelligent   tired |

1 She is ....   2 He looks ....

---

5 **Make sentences.**

▶ 'Bill / be / very / tall.' *'Bill's very tall.'* .... 'Yes, he's nearly 2 metres.'
1 'That car / look / expensive.' .... 'No, it's cheap.'
2 'Jane / seem / happy.' .... 'She's in love again.'
3 'I / feel / ill.' .... 'Shall I call the doctor?'
4 It / get / dark / very early here in winter. ....
5 My parents / getting / old. ....

---

6 **Make sentences with adjectives from the box.**

| Australian   bad   beautiful   hot ✓   late   rich |

▶ This water / not be very / ... *...This water isn't very hot...*
1 'The train / be / ...' .... 'No, it's on time.'
2 'He / look / ...' .... 'No, he's American.'
3 'Your hair / look / ...' .... 'Oh, thanks.'
4 My memory / getting very / ... .
5 I want / become ... / and famous ....

We don't usually use adjectives without nouns.

*'Ann's ill.' 'The **poor girl**.'* (NOT ~~'The poor.'~~)

→ For word order in sentences like *Is Bill very tall?*, see page 106.

adverbs *He ate quickly. It was badly cooked.*

Adjectives are connected with **nouns** and **pronouns**. They usually tell you more about **people** or **things**.
They can go before nouns, or after *be, seem, look,* etc (see pages 200–201).
Adverbs are connected with **other words** – for example **verbs**.
Some adverbs tell you **how something happens**. These often end in *-ly.*

It's an **easy** **language**.   You can **learn** this language *easily.*

The **music** is **slow**.   The pianist is **playing** *slowly.*

Her **ideas** are **interesting**.   She **spoke** *interestingly* about her ideas.

Joe looked **hungry**.   Joe **ate** *hungrily.*

① Choose an adjective or an adverb.

▶ Could I have a *quick* .... quick word with you? (*quick / quickly*)
▶ She walked away *quickly.* .... (*quick / quickly*)
1 This is a .... train – it stops everywhere. (*slow / slowly*)
2 He talked very .... about his work. (*interesting / interestingly*)
3 You've cooked the meat .... (*beautiful / beautifully*)
4 I've got an .... job for you. (*easy / easily*)
5 She writes in .... English. (*perfect / perfectly*)
6 I sing very .... (*bad / badly*)
7 I feel .... today. (*happy / happily*)
8 You seem very .... (*angry / angrily*)
9 Anne's a .... swimmer. (*strong / strongly*)
10 Could you talk more ...., please? (*quiet / quietly*)

● **usually: adjective + *-ly*:**   *quick → quickly*   *real → really* (NOT ~~realy~~)   *complete → completely*
● ***-y → -ily*:**   *easy → easily*   *happy → happily*
● ***-ble → -bly*:**   *possible → possibly*

② Write the adverbs.

▶ wrong *wrongly* ....   4 thirsty ....   8 wonderful ....
1 final ....   5 probable ....   9 cold ....
2 sincere ....   6 usual ....   10 unhappy ....
3 loud ....   7 nice ....   11 comfortable ....

Some **adverbs** tell you **when** or **where** something happens.

*I'm going **away tomorrow**.*   *We ran **downhill**.*   *The accident happened **there**.*

Others tell you **how much**: for example *much* (especially in negatives and questions – see page 168), *a lot, a bit* (conversational), *a little*.

*We don't go out **much**.*   *I watch TV **a lot**.*   *I play the guitar **a bit**.*   *He sings **a little**.*

Adverbs that say **how, where, when** or **how much** often come **at the end of a sentence**. (Some can also come at the beginning.) They do **not** come **between the verb and the object**.

	VERB	OBJECT	ADVERB	
She	speaks	English	well.	(NOT ~~She speaks well English.~~)
They	make	very good bread	here.	(NOT ~~They make here very good bread.~~)
I	bought	a lot of clothes	yesterday.	(NOT ~~I bought yesterday a lot of clothes.~~)
We	didn't enjoy	the holiday	much.	(NOT ~~We didn't enjoy much the holiday.~~)

3 Make sentences with adverbs from the box. (Different answers are possible.)

carefully   clearly   correctly   perfectly   slowly   tomorrow   much   yesterday

▶ soup / cook / the   *Cook the soup slowly.* OR *Cook the soup carefully.*
1 the / read / I / letter ....
2 computer / bought / a / I ....
3 name / your / write ....
4 see / must / the / doctor / you ....
5 languages / speaks / he / four ....
6 the / you / write / address / didn't ....
7 skiing / don't like / I ....

Very much can be used in affirmative (🖶) sentences as well as negatives and questions. Be careful of the word order.

*I like sport **very much**.* (NOT ~~I like very much sport.~~)

4 Write about four things that you like very much.

1 I like .... very much.   3 ....
2 ....   4 ....

Adverbs can go before **adjectives**, and before **past participles** (for example *broken, finished*).

terribly sorry (NOT ~~terrible sorry~~)   *nearly ready*   *completely finished*

5 Complete the sentences with words from the box.

cooked   empty   finished   interesting   married ✓   sorry   tired   written

▶ Joe and Ann have been happily *married* .... for twenty-five years.
1 I'm terribly .... to tell you that we have no more tickets.
2 There's nothing to eat – the fridge is completely ....
3 The book's very well ...., but it's not terribly ....
4 After walking all day, Peter was extremely ....
5 The food here is very well ...., but they don't give you enough.
6 'Is your new house ready yet?' 'It's nearly ....'

adverbs with the verb   *often, certainly,* etc

Some adverbs, for example *always* or *certainly*, usually go **with the verb**.

how often:	*always*	*often*	*usually*	*sometimes*	*ever*	*hardly ever* (= 'almost never')	*never*
how certainly:	*certainly*	*definitely*	*probably*			
other:	*already*	*also*	*just*	*still*	*even*	*only*

These adverbs go before **most verbs**, but after **auxiliary verbs** (*have, will, can, must* etc) and after
am/are/is/was/were.

She *always* **comes** here at weekends.	I **have** *already* read that book.
I *certainly* **like** London.	It **will** *probably* rain tomorrow.
Andy *often* **gets** ill.	She **can** *certainly* help you.
We *already* **know** each other.	I **am** *only* here to see Barbara.
She *hardly ever* **sees** him.	You **are** *certainly* right.

1 **Put the adverbs in the correct places.**

▶ I speak French, but people know that I'm English. (*often; always*)

  I often speak French, but people always know that I'm English.

1 Jake eats fish. He eats fish for breakfast. (*always; even*)

  ....

2 Ann plays tennis, but she plays in the evenings. (*often; only*)

  ....

3 Ed puts tomato sauce on everything. He puts it on ice cream. (*usually; probably*)

  ....

  ....

4 Your sister is a good singer. She is a very interesting person. (*certainly; also*)

  ....

  ....

5 My mother is asleep. I think she is ill. (*still; probably*)

  ....

6 I get to the station on time, and the train is late. (*always; always*)

  ....

In questions, **these adverbs** usually go **after auxiliary verb + subject**.

Do you *ever* write poems?   **Has Mary** *always* lived here?   **Are you** *often* in London?

2 **Put the adverbs in the correct places.**

1 Do you play cards? (*often*) ....

2 Have you been to Tibet? (*ever*) ....

3 Are you happy? (*always*) ....

4 Does the boss take a holiday? (*ever*) ....

5 Do you eat in restaurants? (*usually*) ....

6 Is Barbara ill? (*still*) ....

3 Look at the table and make some sentences with *often, once a day* etc.

ACTIVITY	ANN	BILL
goes swimming	1/d*	1/m
plays football	–	3/w
plays tennis	1/w	1/y
goes skiing	5–6/y	–
goes to the theatre	1/w	2–3/y
goes to the cinema	3–4/y	2/m
goes to concerts	–	1/w

*1/d = once a day;
2/m = twice a month; etc

Ann often goes swimming.
Ann goes swimming once a day / every day.
Bill goes to the theatre two or three times a year.
....
....
....
....
....
....
....
....
....
....
....
....
....

4 GRAMMAR AND VOCABULARY: *go* with spare-time activities
Look at the pictures, and put the correct numbers with the activities. Use a dictionary if necessary.

IN YOUR SPARE TIME YOU CAN:
go walking ..*6*..
go climbing ......
go swimming ......
go sailing ......
go wind-surfing ......
go skiing ......
go skating ......
go fishing ......
go shopping ......
go to the opera ......
go to the theatre ......
go to concerts ......

5 Write some sentences about your spare-time activities. Use words from Exercises 1–4.

▶ *I never go climbing.*
▶ *I go swimming every day.*
1 ....
2 ....
3 ....
4 ....
5 ....
6 ....

interested and *interesting*, etc

Interested, bored, excited etc say how **people** feel.
Interesting, boring, exciting etc describe the **things** (or people) that cause the feelings.
She's very interested in the lessons. (NOT ~~She's very interesting in the lessons.~~)
The lessons are always interesting. *(NOT ~~The lessons are always interested.~~)*
I'm often bored at work, because I've got a boring job.

1 **Write these words under the pictures:** *interested, interesting, bored, boring*

1 .... 2 .... 3 .... 4 ....

2 **Put in words from the box.**

annoyed (= 'a little angry') ✓ annoying excited exciting frightened
frightening surprised surprising

1 Somebody phones you late at night. You are .*annoyed*................. He/she is ....
2 A woman hears noises at night. She is .... The noises are ....
3 A family makes .... holiday plans. The children are very ....
4 Your exam mark is very good. This is .... And you are ....

3 **Here are the beginnings of five books. Write what you think of the books. Use** *very
interesting, quite interesting, not very interesting, quite boring* **or** *very boring.*

1 After King Leofric died in 1342, ...
  I think this book is probably ....
2 The moment Olga walked into Alan's office, he realised his life had changed for ever ...
  I think ....
3 Since the beginning of history, cats ...
  ....
4 The man in black had already killed five people that morning. The sixth ...
  ....
5 Four billion years ago, our world ...
  ....

4 GRAMMAR AND VOCABULARY: **adverbs of degree; subjects of study**
**Make sure you know the words in the box. Use a dictionary if necessary. Then write how
interested you are in some of the subjects. You can use** *extremely* **(= +++),** *very, quite, not
very, not* **or** *not at all* **(= – – –).**

art   biology   economics   history   literature   mathematics   philosophy   physics   politics

I'm extremely interested in .... I'm ....
I'm very bored by ....
I'm not at all ....

fast, hard, hardly, well, friendly, ...

> *Fast, hard, late, early, daily, weekly and monthly* are **adjectives** and adverbs.
>
> | | | | |
> |---|---|---|---|
> | He's got a **fast** car. | He drives fast. | I got an **early** flight. | I went home early. |
> | It's **hard** work. | She works hard. | It's a **weekly** paper. | I buy it weekly. |
> | The train was **late**. | Trains are running late. | | |
>
> *Hardly* and *lately* have different meanings from *hard* and *late*.
> *Hardly* = 'almost not'; lately = 'recently', 'not long ago'
>
> He hardly works these days – maybe one day a week.   Have you heard from John **lately**?
>
> *Well* can be an **adjective** (the opposite of *ill*) or an adverb (the opposite of *badly*).
>
> 'How are you?' 'Very **well**, thanks.'   The team are playing well.

1 These are sentences from real conversations. Put in words from the boxes.

early   hard   hardly   weekly   well

1 And I really understand Italian quite ....
2 You've got no playschool tomorrow so you haven't got to get up ...., have you?
3 Why should I work .... when you never do anything?
4 Departures from the UK are ...., mid-morning on Sundays from Dover.
5 She was really, you know, nervous, and .... came out of her flat at all.

2 Choose the best answer.

▶ You look .well..............., Mike. (*early / lately / well*)
1 Your father read the .... Express when he was alive. (*hardly / Daily / lately*)
2 You haven't seen the window cleaner ...., have you? (*lately / hard / weekly*)
3 I ran as .... as I could, along the Tottenham Court Road. (*early / fast / hardly*)
4 I .... sleep – an hour at a time. (*well / hard / hardly*)
5 I got up .... to finish some work. (*well / hardly / early*)

> *Friendly, lonely, lovely, silly* are **adjectives**, not adverbs.
>
> She gave me a **friendly** smile. (BUT NOT *She smiled friendly.*)
> He was very **lonely**. (BUT NOT *He walked lonely through the streets.*)
> Her voice is **lovely**. (BUT NOT *She sings lovely.*)   Don't be **silly**.
>
> There are no adverbs *friendlily, lovelily* etc. Instead, we use other words or expressions.
>
> She spoke **in a friendly way**.   She sings **beautifully**.

3 Put in adjectives and adverbs from the box.

daily   early ✓   fast   friendly   hard   hardly   late   lonely   silly

I don't like getting up ▶ .early........... so I usually stay in bed too long, and then have to eat
breakfast very 1 .... and run for my train. On the train I read the 2 .... paper,
because after I get to work there's no more time for reading. The boss is nice, but she makes us work
very 3 ...., and I often have to stay 4 .... to finish everything. There's a nice
new secretary in the office. I 5 .... know her, but she always gives me a 6 ....
smile when I arrive. She hasn't lived here long. Perhaps it's a 7 .... idea, but I wonder if
she's 8 .... I think I'll ask her out.

comparative and superlative adjectives: forms

Comparative adjectives are forms like *colder, more famous*.
Superlative adjectives are forms like *coldest, most famous*.

- **most short** (one-syllable) **adjectives:** + *-er, -est*   *old → older, oldest*
- **short adjectives** ending in *-e*: + *-r, -st*   *nice → nicer, nicest*

1 Write the comparative and superlative adjectives.

▶ cold ..*colder, coldest*........................   5 strange ....
▶ late ..*later, latest*...........................   6 fine ....
1 green ....   7 high ....
2 safe ....   8 wide ....
3 rich ....   9 near ....
4 small ....   10 white ....

- **short adjectives** ending in **one vowel + one consonant:**
  double consonant + *-er, -est*   *fat → fatter, fattest*   *thin → thinner, thinnest*
  BUT **don't double** *w*:   *low → lower, lowest*

2 Write the comparative and superlative adjectives.

▶ red ..*redder, reddest*............   2 hot ....   4 wet ....
▶ slow ..*slower, slowest*..........   3 new ....   5 slim ....
1 big ....

- **two-syllable adjectives** ending in *-y*: *y → i* + *-er, -est*   *happy → happier, happiest*

3 Write the comparative and superlative adjectives.

▶ friendly ..*friendlier, friendliest*.............   3 sleepy ....
1 lazy ....   4 angry ....
2 hungry ....   5 dirty ....

- **most other longer adjectives:** + *more, most*   *hopeful → more hopeful, most hopeful*

4 Write the comparative and superlative adjectives.

▶ famous ..*more famous, most famous*..........   4 dangerous ....
1 careful ....   5 important ....
2 beautiful ....   6 boring ....
3 intelligent ....   7 interested ....

- **irregular adjectives:**   *good → better, best*   *bad → worse, worst*
  far → further, furthest OR *farther, farthest*

5 Put in irregular comparative adjectives.

▶ I know that my handwriting is bad, but Jenny's is ..*worse*...............
1 I'm so tired. Is the bus stop much ....?
2 I don't enjoy train travel here, but I do in France – the trains are .... there.
3 'How's your toothache today?' 'It's ....' 'You should see a dentist.'

comparative or superlative?

We use comparatives to compare people and things with **other people and things**.

A is bigger than B.   *A is bigger than B and c.*   John *is a more careful driver than Robin.*

 ◄ *Dawn is tall.*

 ◄ *Dawn is taller than Leah.* ►

 ◄ *Dawn is taller than all the other players.* ►

We use superlatives (usually with *the*) to compare people and things with **all of the group that they are in**.

A is the biggest of the three letters A, B and c.   John *is the most careful driver in the family.*

 ◄ *Dawn is the tallest player in the team.*

1 **Circle the correct answer.**

► Dawn is (*older*) / *the oldest* than all of her sisters.
► Leah is *taller* / (*the tallest*) person in her family.
1 All of your friends are nice, but George is certainly *the nicer* / *the nicest*.
2 This is *the better* / *the best* women's basketball team in the country.
3 Basketballs are *more expensive* / *the most expensive* than footballs.
4 Ice hockey is a *more dangerous* / *most dangerous* sport than basketball or tennis.
5 Of all the sports in the Olympics, which sport is *more dangerous?* / *the most dangerous?*
6 A basketball court is usually *bigger* / *the biggest* than a tennis court.

2 **Choose a comparative or a superlative. Remember to use *the* before the superlatives.**

► 'The Marriage of Figaro' is ...*the most beautiful*............... of all Mozart's operas. (*beautiful*)
► My new car is ...*faster*.................................... than my old one. (*fast*)
1 My mother and her sisters are all .... than their children. (*short*)
2 I think Annie is .... person in our class. (*intelligent*)
3 Let's meet in the library – it's .... than all the other rooms. (*quiet*)
4 My bedroom is .... room in the house. (*cold*)
5 A 3-year-old's voice is .... than 200 people in a busy restaurant. (*loud*)
6 Brazil is .... South American country. (*big*)

comparatives: use   *brighter than the moon*

We use *than* after comparative adjectives.

*Russia is **bigger than** China.* (NOT ... ~~that China.~~)   *Rob and Tina are **older than** Emma.*

1 Compare each pair of things in the box. Write two sentences for each pair.

> COMPARE: the sun and the moon ✓   dogs and cats   train travel and air travel
>   the Sahara and the Himalayas
>
> ADJECTIVES: bright ✓   cheap   cold   fast   friendly   hot   intelligent   small ✓

▶ *The sun is brighter than the moon.*   3 ....
▶ *The moon is smaller than the sun.*   4 ....
1 ....   5 ....
2 ....   6 ....

2 Use comparative adjectives with *... than all the other ...*

▶ Alaska's area is 1,518,700km^2. No other US state is so large.
  Alaska is larger than all the other US states.

1 The Amazon is 6,670km long. No other river in South America is so long.

  ....

2 Blue whales can weigh 120 tonnes. No other whales are so heavy.

  ....

3 Mont Blanc is 4,807m high. No other mountain in the Alps is so high.

  ....

4 Cheetahs can run 110km/h. No other big cats are so fast.

  ....

blue whale

whales

cheetah

big cats

With comparatives, we can say *... than I am / than you are / than John is* etc.
But in informal **spoken English**, we usually prefer *... than me/you/him/her/it/us/them.*

3 Write two endings for each sentence: one with *than me, than you* etc and one with *than I am, than you are* etc.

▶ Bob was angry, but I .... *was angrier than him / than he was.*
1 John's very careful with money, but Maria ....
2 I'm hungry, but you must be ....
3 You're not very short. Tony's ....
4 We're excited, but our children ....
5 My girlfriend is so beautiful. No other woman ....

We can use *a lot / a bit* (more conversational) or *much / a little* before comparatives.

*Your cooking is **much better** than my sister's.* (NOT ... ~~very better~~ AND NOT ... ~~too better~~ ...)
*This book is **a lot more interesting** than that one.*   *You sound **a bit happier** today.*

a bit longer

much longer

4 Use the table. Write sentences about Mark and Simon with *a bit / a little* and *a lot / much* with the adjectives from the box.

short ✓ / tall   old / young   rich   fast / slow   comfortable   quiet / noisy

	How tall?	How old?	How rich?		How fast?	How comfortable?	How quiet?
Mark	1m95	35	€900,000/year	Mark's car	190km/h	★★★	★★
Simon	1m85	36	€250,000/year	Simon's car	130km/h	★★	★★★★★

▶ *Simon is a bit (OR a little) shorter than Mark.*

1 ....
2 ....
3 ....
4 ....
5 ....
6 ....
7 ....
8 ....
9 ....

Simon   Mark

We can use *more than* and *less than* without adjectives.

*Liz spent **more than a week's pay** on that dress.*   *It took us **less than ten minutes** to get home.*

5 GRAMMAR AND VOCABULARY: time
Make sure you know the words in the box. Use a dictionary if necessary. Then answer the questions.

century   day   decade   fortnight   hour   minute   month   second   week   year

▶ How much is a minute? ....*More than a second and less than an hour*...

1 How much is a decade? ....

2 How much is a month? ....

3 How much is a fortnight? ....

4 How much is a week? ....

superlatives   *the highest mountain in the world*

After **superlatives**, we normally use *in* before the names of **places**.

*Everest is the **highest** mountain **in the world**.*
*Jan is the **most intelligent** person **in the office**.*
*Sirius is the **brightest** star **in the sky**.*

After **superlatives**, we also use *in* before **singular** words for **groups** of people.

*Sam is the **youngest** player **in the orchestra**.*
*Wilkins is the **oldest** minister **in this government**.*

In most **other cases**, we use *of* after superlatives.

*Ann's the **tallest of the three sisters**.*   *This is the **shortest** day **of the year**.*

1 Put the beginnings, middles and ends together.

1 Jonathan is	A the biggest state ...	m in the group. ...
2 My great-great-aunt is	B the longest river ...	n in my family. ...
3 London is	C the best musician ...	o in the team. 1.
4 Alaska is	D the fastest runner 1.	p in Africa. ...
5 The guitar player is	E the biggest city ...	q in Britain. ...
6 The Nile is	F the oldest person ...	r in the USA. ...
7 My parents' room is	G the most expensive ...	s of the four bedrooms. ...
8 The Mercedes is	H the longest day ...	t of the five girls. ...
9 Sarah is	I the youngest ...	u of the three cars. ...
10 June 21st is	J the biggest ...	v of the year. ...

2 Write sentences with superlatives.

▶ In my job, Friday / busy day / week
  In my job, Friday is the busiest day of the week. ....

1 In the 1970s, the Beatles / rich musicians / world

   ....

2 Eric says that Eleanor / good singer / group

   ....

3 When I was a child, my father / tall man / our town

   ....

4 In this country, February / cold month / year

   ....

5 Who / old / your three aunts?

   ....

6 Helen is very intelligent, but she / quiet person / my class

   ....

> There is so much good in the worst of us,
> and so much bad in the best of us.
>
> (*Author unknown*)

comparison of adverbs   *More slowly, please.*

To make the **comparative** of most **adverbs**: *more* + adverb (... *than*)

*Can you speak **more quietly**, please?   I'm working **more slowly** today **than** yesterday.*
*Angela writes **more clearly than** Ellie.*

---

1 Write sentences with comparative adverbs and *than*.

▶ Jo drives / dangerously / Sam   *Jo drives more dangerously than Sam.*...............

1 Lee talks to people / politely / Ben   ....

2 Liam works / carefully / John   ....

3 Simon goes swimming / often / Karen   ....

4 My car runs / quietly / my sister's car   ....

5 Annie talks / slowly / Rob   ....

Early, late, fast, hard, near and ***soon*** have comparatives with ***-er***, like adjectives.

*I got to the station **earlier** than Mary.   Bill lives **nearer** to school than Pete, so he gets up **later**.*

Irregular comparatives and superlatives: *well → **better**   **badly** → **worse**   **far → further/farther***
                                        *little → **less**   a lot / much → **more***

*My mother drives **better** than my father.   He sings badly, but I sing **worse**.*
*She talks **less** than he does, but she thinks **more**.   I live **further** from the centre than you.*

---

2 Use the comparatives of the adverbs in the box to complete the advice.

early	fast	hard ✓	late	little	much	near

▶ 'I want to earn more money.' 'Work ..*harder*.....'

1 'I want to eat my breakfast slowly in the morning.' 'Get up ....'

2 'I want to get more sleep.' 'Get up ....'

3 'I want to be stronger.' 'Exercise ....'

4 'I hate driving to work.' 'Live .... to your work and walk.'

5 'I get a lot of headaches.' 'Try to worry ....'

6 'I'm afraid I'm going to miss the train.' 'Walk ....'

Sentences with superlative adverbs (for example *John drives **the most dangerously***) are not very common.

1. *Annie*   AN–Y–THING YOU CAN DO, I   can do bet – ter,

From *Annie Get Your Gun.*
Words and music by Irving Berlin

(not) as ... as   *Your hands are as cold as ice.*

We use (*not*) *as ... as* to say that people and things are (**not**) **the same in some way.**

I don't think Tom is going to be **as tall as** *his sister.*   *Your hands are* **as cold as** *ice.*
Can you read this for me? My eyes aren't **as good as** *yours.*

❶ Read the sentences and decide: which picture is Jean and which picture is Cassie?

Jean isn't as old as Cassie.   Cassie's hair isn't as long as Jean's.
Jean's hands aren't as small as Cassie's.   Jean isn't as fair as Cassie.

Picture A is ....   Picture B is ....

Now write some more sentences about Jean and Cassie with *not as ... as*.

1 slim ....
2 tall ....
3 skirt / long ....
4 bag / big ....
5 coat / heavy ....
6 glass / big ....

With *as ... as*, we can say ... *as I am / as you are / as John is* etc. But in informal **spoken English**, we usually prefer ... *as me/you/him/her/it/us/them*.

❷ Change the sentences in two ways, but keep the same meaning.

▶ Joan's prettier than her sister. ...*Joan's sister isn't as pretty as her.*......................
...*Joan's sister isn't as pretty as she is.*..
1 You're nicer than the other doctor. The other doctor ....
....
2 He's more interesting than his boss. ....
....
3 I'm slimmer than my mother. ....
....
4 We're more careful than the Browns. ....
....

We can put *just, nearly, not quite* and *half, twice, three times* etc **before** as ... as.

He's **just as** handsome as his brother.   My hair is **not quite as** fair as my sister's hair.
The twins are **nearly as** tall as their mother.   Brazil is **half as** big as Russia.

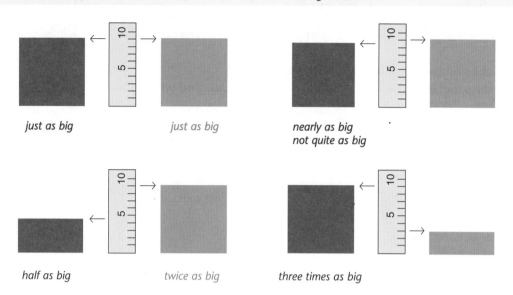

just as big	just as big	nearly as big not quite as big

half as big	twice as big	three times as big

3 **Think of a member of your family. Compare yourself to him or her, using** *as ... as* **and some of the words and expressions from the box. Write five sentences.**

BEFORE *AS*:	just	nearly	not quite	half	twice	three times etc		
ADJECTIVES:	dark	fair	friendly	handsome	happy	intelligent	kind	nice
	old	pretty	quiet	short	slim	tall		

▶ *I'm nearly as tall as Annie.*   3 ....
▶ *I'm not quite as old as her.*   4 ....
1 ....   5 ....
2 ....   6 ....

We can use *as much as* and *as many as* with nouns.

Deborah doesn't work **as many hours as** *I do, but she makes just* **as much money as** *me.*

4 **Make sentences with** *as ... as* **or** *not as ... as,* **and some of the expressions from Exercise 3.**

▶ Alice has $200 and Matt has $100.   *Alice has twice as much money as Matt.*
....

1 Eric has 20 cousins, and Tony has 10.   Eric ....
....

2 Ben eats 3 sandwiches every day; Jo eats 1.   ....
....

3 Helen has 23 computer games and Adrian has 25.   ....
....

4 Liz drinks 6 cups of coffee a day; Chris drinks 12.   ....
....

5 Mike has 600 books, and David has 600 too.   ....
....

6 Nedjma only has a little free time; Ali has a lot.   ....
....

test yourself   adjectives and adverbs

1 Write the adverbs.

quick *quickly*   real ....   complete ....   possible ....   happy ....

2 Write the comparatives and superlatives.

tall ..... *taller, tallest* ....   easy ....

interesting ....   bad ....

thin ....   far ....

cheap ....   good ....

3 These sentences are all wrong (✗). Can you correct the mistakes?

▸ She was wearing a red beautiful coat. ...... *a beautiful red coat.* ....

1 There are films interestings on TV tonight. ....

2 There's a good and cheap restaurant in Dover St. ....

3 He's tall, dark, good-looking. ....

4 She's the best pianist of the world. ....

5 My sister is much taller that me. ....

6 Anna is the more beautiful person here. ....

7 I am very interesting in the lessons. ....

4 Where do the adjectives and adverbs go?

▸ I am ready. (*nearly*)

1 He was wearing dirty trousers. (*black*)

2 She speaks Chinese. (*very well*)

3 I lost my keys. (*yesterday*)

5 Circle the correct answers.

1 You are making a *terrible / terribly* mistake.

2 She walked up the steps *slow / slowly*.

3 I cook very *bad / badly*.

4 Ann looks very *unhappy / unhappily*.

6 Where do the adverbs go?

1 They've been married for 15 years. (*happily*)

2 We go to New York. (*often*)

3 Ann and Simon are late. (*always*)

4 She's an interesting person. (*certainly*)

7 Circle the correct answers.

1 It was raining *hard / hardly* when I got up.

2 The boss is a really *friend / friendly* person.

3 I'm *terrible / terribly* sorry I arrived so *late / lately*.

4 Please drive *slowlier / more slowly*.

8 Look at the pictures and make sentences.

▸ B / fast / A   *B is faster than A.* ....

1 A / fast / B   A is not as ....

2 C / expensive / A   ....

3 A / expensive / B   ....

4 B / expensive   B is the ....

5 B / big / C   ....

6 C / big / A   ....

7 C / big   ....

A   £14,999
Maximum speed
120 km/h

B   £29,999
Maximum speed
200 km/h

C   £19,999
Maximum speed
150 km/h

◉ More difficult questions

SECTION 16 conjunctions

● grammar summary

> after   although   and   as soon as   because   before   but   so   until   when   while
> both ... and   either ... or   neither ... nor   (➔ For *if*, see Section 17.)
> (If necessary, use a dictionary to check the meanings of these conjunctions.)

We use **conjunctions** to **join** sentences together.
   *I went to Germany **because** Emma was there.*   *We went home **after** the concert finished.*

Some conjunctions (and the words that follow them) can go in **two places**.
   *I cleaned my room **before** I went out.*   ***Before** I went out, I cleaned my room.*

We use **present tenses** to talk about the **future** with **time-conjunctions**.
   *I'll phone you **when** I arrive.*   *Let's wait here **until** somebody comes.*

We can use ***and*** to join sentences, shorter expressions or single words. We **don't** need to **repeat unnecessary words** with *and*.
   *I went downstairs **and** (I) opened the door.*   *I've got friends in Canada **and** (in) Australia.*
   *Could I have a knife **and** (a) fork?*

● pre-test: which units do you need?

Try this small test. It will help you to decide which units you need. The answers are on page 284.

❶ Correct (✓) or not (✗)?

▶ We started without her because of she was late. ✗.
1 Although it was raining, I went out. ...
2 I went to London soon after I got to England. ...
3 After Jake will get here, we'll all go out. ...
4 Will you still love me when I'm old? ...
5 Because it was cold, so I put on a coat. ...
6 I got the job in spite of my English was bad. ...
7 You are beautiful, intelligent, kind. ...
8 You can either come in my car or walk home. ...
9 I need a knife and I need a fork. ...

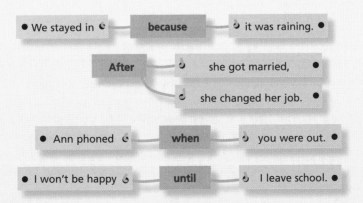

We stayed in ◡ — **because** — ◡ it was raining. ●

After — ◡ she got married, ●
                   ◡ she changed her job. ●

● Ann phoned ◡ — **when** — ◡ you were out. ●

● I won't be happy ◡ — **until** — ◡ I leave school. ●

conjunctions: introduction   *and, but, because ...*

> **Conjunctions** are words like *and, but, because, although, if, while, so, until.*
> We use conjunctions to **join sentences together.**
>
> | | | |
> |---|---|---|
> | It was cold | **and** | I wanted to go home. |
> | I like him | **but** | I don't like her. |
> | He got up | **although** | he was ill. |
> | I didn't buy it | **because** | it was too expensive. |
> | I'll phone you | **if** | the train is late. |
> | Andrew called | **while** | you were out. |
> | It was raining | **so** | I took my umbrella. |
> | I waited | **until** | Mary was ready. |
> | Let's go out | **as soon as** | Peter arrives. |

1 **Circle the best conjunction.**

> ▶ I'll phone you *although / so /* (*when*) I arrive.
1 The party was boring, *although / because / so* I went home.
2 The weather was nice, *although / or / until* it was a bit cold.
3 She speaks good French, *after / because / but* she has a strong English accent.
4 I enjoyed my month in Argentina, *although / and / but* I learnt a lot of Spanish.
5 I'll tell you my plans *because / so / while* we're having lunch.
6 I helped him *after / because / or* he was a good friend.

2 **Choose the best conjunction to join the sentences. Use a dictionary if necessary.**

> ▶ I lived in Liverpool. I left school. (*if, although, until*)
> I lived in Liverpool until I left school.
1 I'll be glad. This job is finished. (*when, or, while*)
....
2 I'll be very angry. You do that again. (*and, if, but*)
....
3 I'd like to talk to you. You go home. (*before, and, although*)
....
4 I watched TV. John came home. (*if, until, or*)
....
5 I'll see you again. We come back from holiday. (*while, after, and*)
....

3 **Put conjunctions from the box into the text.**

although   although   and   and   and   because   because   before   so   until   when

Andy Probert was bored at school, 1 .... he left 2 .... he was sixteen
3 .... got a job in a travel agency. He did not stay there very long, 4 .... he liked
the work. He decided to move 5 .... the pay was very low 6 .... the hours were
too long. His next job was in an import-export company. He liked that much better, 7 ....
he travelled to America a lot 8 .... the work was very well paid. He worked there for three
years, 9 .... he really understood the business; then he started his own company. Now he
is doing very well, 10 .... the work is sometimes very hard. He says he wants to make
enough money to stop working 11 .... he is 50.

position of conjunctions   *If you need help, ask me.*

When we use **conjunctions**, there are often **two possibilities**.

1 **Start** with the conjunction (and the part that follows it).	2 Put the conjunction **between** the two parts of the sentence.
CONJUNCTION bbbbb, **aaaaa**	**Aaaaa**(,) CONJUNCTION bbbbb
*IF you need help, **please ask me.***	***Please ask me** IF you need help.*
*WHEN you are in London, **phone us.***	***Phone us** WHEN you are in London.*
*ALTHOUGH it was raining, **I went out.***	***I went out,** ALTHOUGH it was raining hard.*
*AS SOON AS she could, **she went to bed.***	***She went to bed** AS SOON AS she could.*

Note that we often put **commas** (,) in sentences with conjunctions, especially in longer sentences.
We **usually** use a **comma** if we **start** with the conjunction.

1 **Put these sentences together in two ways.**

▶ I enjoyed the film. The beginning was boring. (*although*)
I enjoyed the film, although the beginning was boring.
Although the beginning was boring, I enjoyed the film.

1 I put on two sweaters. It was very cold. (*because*)
....
....

2 I'm going to work in Australia. I leave school. (*when*)
....
....

3 I go and see Felix. I want to talk to somebody. (*if*)
....
....

4 Ann made coffee. Bill fried some eggs. (*while*)
....
....

5 I was interested in the conversation. I didn't understand everything. (*although*)
....
....

6 We went to a restaurant. There was no food in the house. (*because*)
....
....

7 We'll have a big party. John comes home. (*when*)
....
....

8 I stayed with friends. My parents were travelling. (*while*)
....
....

9 I go for long walks at the weekend. The weather's fine. (*if*)
....
....

10 Come and see us. You arrive in Scotland. (*as soon as*)
....
....

before and *after*   *I talked to John before I phoned Peter.*

Note how we use *before* and *after*.
(1) A HAPPENED, THEN (2) B HAPPENED.
A happened before B happened.   OR   Before B happened, A happened.
After A happened, B happened.   OR   B happened after A happened.

*I talked to John before **I phoned Peter.***   *Before **I phoned Peter,** I talked to John.*
(Both sentences say that I talked to John first.)
Ann moved to York** after she got married.*   *After Ann got married, **she moved to York.
(Both sentences say that Ann got married first.)

❶ Put these sentences together in two ways with *before* or *after*.

▶ (1) I have tea. (2) I go to bed. (*before*)
    I̲ ̲h̲a̲v̲e̲ ̲t̲e̲a̲ ̲b̲e̲f̲o̲r̲e̲ ̲I̲ ̲g̲o̲t̲ ̲t̲o̲ ̲b̲e̲d̲.̲ ̲ ̲ ̲B̲e̲f̲o̲r̲e̲ ̲I̲ ̲g̲o̲ ̲t̲o̲ ̲b̲e̲d̲,̲ ̲I̲ ̲h̲a̲v̲e̲ ̲t̲e̲a̲.̲...

1 (1) We get back from holiday. (2) There's always a lot of work. (*after*)
....
....

2 (1) I usually clean the house. (2) My mother comes to visit. (*before*)
....
....

3 (1) I listen to music for half an hour. (2) I start work. (*before*)
....
....

4 (1) I left school. (2) I got very ill. (*after*)
....
....

5 (1) I stopped playing football. (2) I started playing hockey. (*after*)
....
....

6 (1) We moved to London. (2) We got married. (*before*)
....
....

❷ GRAMMAR AND VOCABULARY: wars
Make sure you know the words in the box; then read the sentences and put in 1 and 2 to show what happened first.

ally	army	attack	battle	declare war (on)	defeat	general	invade

▶ The Moronians prepared for war (.2.) after Fantasia invaded Kayland (.1.).

1 Before the Moronians declared war on Fantasia (....), the Moronian President went to Fantasia (....) for talks with General Zunk.

2 After the President returned from Fantasia (....), Moronia declared war on Fantasia (....).

3 The Fantasian army invaded Zedland (....) soon after Moronia declared war on Fantasia (....).

4 Before Moronia attacked Fantasia (....), the Moronians defeated Fantasia's ally Beeland (....).

5 Zunk flew to Ruritania (....) after Moronia defeated Fantasia at the battle of Quark (....).

➜ For *-ing* forms with *before* and *after*, see page 133.

tenses with time conjunctions   *I'll see you before you go.*

We use the **simple present** with a **future** meaning after *before, after, while, until, when* and *as soon as*.
*I'll see you **before** you **go**.* (NOT ...~~before you will go.~~)   *We'll talk about it **after** I **get** back.*
*You can use my car **while** I'm in Ireland.*   *Don't move **until** I **tell** you.*
*He'll phone you **when** he **arrives**.* (NOT ... ~~when he will arrive.~~)
*We'll start the party **as soon as** Justin **gets** here.*

1 Put in verbs from the box. Use the simple present.

| hear   leave   make   open ✓   write |

▶ Wait here until Jane ...*opens*......... the door.
1 Call me as soon as you .... about the exam.
2 Can you hold the baby while I .... coffee?
3 What's John going to do when he .... school?
4 Give my love to Sue when you .... to her.

2 Put in verbs from the box (simple present or *will*).

| find   give ✓   help   start   travel |

▶ I'll *give*.......... you my address before I say goodbye.
1 Ann's going to live here until she .... a job.
2 We're going to look after Sue's flat while she .... round America.
3 I .... you after I get back from work.
4 We're early – we've got half an hour before the lesson ....

3 Look at Bill and Ann's summer dates and complete the conversation.

BILL AND ANN'S SUMMER DATES
The children will get out of school at midday on July 8th.
Bill's brother will be in England from July 12th to July 14th.
Bill and Ann's new car will be ready on July 17th.
Eric will go back to work on July 20th.
Ann's father will go into hospital on July 25th.

BILL: Let's go to Eric's from the 4th to the 30th.
ANN: No, we can't leave until the 8th. The children, remember?
BILL: OK. We'll leave (*at midday on the 8th*) as soon as the children 1 .... out of school.
ANN: That won't work, because we'll have to be here (*from the 12th to the 14th*)
         while 2 ....
BILL: Then we'll go from the 15th to the 30th.
ANN: No, we'll have to be back (*before the 25th*) before 3 ....
BILL: OK. The 15th to the 24th it is.
ANN: Well, in that case, let's wait (*until the 17th*) until 4 ....
BILL: The 17th to the 24th. Right.
ANN: But we can't stay with Eric (*after the 20th*) after 5 ....
BILL: Fine. The 17th to the 20th.
ANN: No, because ...

➔ For tenses with *if* see page 229.

because and *so*; *although* and *but*

We can say **why** things happen with *because* or *so* (but not both).

Because *Sue was tired, she went to bed.* / *Sue went to bed* ***because*** *she was tired.*
OR *Sue was tired,* ***so*** *she went to bed.* (BUT NOT ~~Because Sue was tired, so she went to bed.~~)

We usually put a comma (,) before *so*. For more about commas with conjunctions, see page 219.

❶ Join the sentences with *because* (twice) and with *so*.

▶ He passed the exam. He had a good teacher.
Because he had a good teacher, he passed the exam.
He passed the exam because he had a good teacher.
He had a good teacher, so he passed the exam.

1 I changed my hotel. The rooms were dirty.

....

....

....

2 The taxi was late. We missed the train.

....

....

....

3 I didn't like the film. I walked out of the cinema.

....

....

....

We can say that things are **not as we expect** with *although* or *but* (but not both).

Although *Pete was tired, he didn't go to bed.* / *Pete didn't go to bed,* ***although*** *he was tired.*
OR *Pete was tired,* ***but*** *he didn't go to bed.* (BUT NOT ~~Although Pete was tired, but he didn't go to bed.~~)

We usually put commas before *although* and *but*.

❷ Join the sentences with *although* (twice) and with *but*.

▶ She passed the exam. She had a bad teacher.
Although she had a bad teacher, she passed the exam.
She passed the exam, although she had a bad teacher.
She had a bad teacher, but she passed the exam.

1 I felt ill. I went on working.

....

....

....

2 She was very kind. I didn't like her.

....

....

....

3 He's a big man. He doesn't eat much.

....

....

....

Because (conjunction) and *because of* (preposition) are **different**.

*We stayed in **because it was raining**.*   *We stayed in **because of the rain**.*
*He was able to go to university **because his uncle helped him** / **because of his uncle's help**.*

Although (conjunction) and *in spite of* (preposition) are **different**.

*We went out, **although it was raining**.*   *We went out **in spite of the rain**.*
*I got the job, **although my English was bad** / **in spite of my bad English**.*

3 Join the beginnings and ends.

1 Although I knew her well,	A a problem at the airport. ...
2 Although it was cold,	B but he went out without a coat. ...
3 Ann arrived late because of	C he went out without a coat. ...
4 Ann only arrived at 11 o'clock because	D her plane was late. ...
5 It was very cold,	E she never talked to me about her problems. *1.*
6 Because I was an old friend,	F so he asked me to help him. ...
7 We were old friends,	G the bad pay and conditions. ...
8 She stayed in the company, although	H she asked me to help her. ...
9 She went on working there in spite of	I the pay and conditions were bad. ...

4 GRAMMAR AND VOCABULARY: **related nouns, verbs and adjectives**
The words in the boxes are all nouns. Make sure you know them. Use a dictionary if necessary. Then change the sentences.

heat	hunger	illness ✓	rain	snow ✓	unhappiness

▶ We drove slowly because it was snowing.
~~We drove slowly because of the snow.~~

▶ She went on working, although she was ill.
~~She went on working in spite of her illness.~~

1 Because I was unhappy, I didn't want to see anybody.
Because of my ....

2 Although she was hungry, she didn't eat anything.
....

3 We had to drink a lot because it was hot.
....

4 We had to stop playing because it was raining.
....

cold	interest (in something)	thirst	tiredness	work

5 She kept all the windows open, although it was cold.
....

6 I couldn't go away last weekend because I was working.
....

7 Although he was interested in the lesson, he went to sleep.
....

8 I couldn't understand her because I was tired.
....

9 Although I was thirsty, I didn't drink anything.
....

and   *I speak Russian, English and Swahili.*

We can use *and* to **join** sentences, shorter expressions or single words.

*Sylvia won the first game **and** Pete won the second.*
*'What's she interested in?' 'Scottish dancing **and** mountain climbing.'*
*'What shall we have for supper?' 'Fish **and** chips.'*

In **lists**, we usually put *and* between the **last two things**, and **commas** (,) between the **others**.

*We need soap, bread, orange juice, tomatoes **and** sugar.*
*She was beautiful, intelligent **and** kind.* (NOT *... ~~beautiful, intelligent, kind.~~*)

1 Write the sentences using *and* and commas.

▶ She speaks (*French   German   Japanese   Arabic*).
~~She speaks French, German, Japanese and Arabic.~~ ....

1 My company has offices in (*London   Tokyo   New York   Cairo*).
....

2 I've invited (*Paul   Alexandra   Eric   Luke   Janet*).
....

3 I'll be here on (*Tuesday   Thursday   Friday   Sunday*).
....

4 She's got (*five cats   two dogs   a horse   a rabbit*).
....

5 He plays (*golf   rugby   hockey   badminton*).
....

6 She (*addressed   stamped   posted*) the letter.
....

When we use *and*, we do **not** usually repeat **unnecessary words**.

*She sings and **she** plays the violin.*	→	*She sings and plays the violin.*
*He plays tennis and **he plays** badminton.*	→	*He plays tennis and badminton.*
*They have offices in Britain and **in** America.*	→	*They have offices in Britain and America.*
*We stayed with my brother and **my** sister.*	→	*We stayed with my brother and sister.*
*The house and **the** garden were full of people.*	→	*The house and garden were full of people.*
*I've been to Greece and **I've been to** Turkey.*	→	*I've been to Greece and Turkey.*
*I washed **my shirt** and **I** dried my shirt.*	→	*I washed and dried my shirt.*

2 Cross out the unnecessary words, and put in commas if necessary.

▶ I speak Russian, ~~and I speak~~ English and ~~I speak~~ Swahili.

1 She has painted the kitchen and she has painted the living room and she has painted the dining room.

2 Bob was wearing a pink shirt and Bob was wearing blue jeans and Bob was wearing white trainers.

3 Can you give me a knife and can you give me a fork and can you give me a spoon, please?

4 Many people speak English in India and many people speak English in Singapore and many people speak English in South Africa.

5 I've written six letters and I've posted six letters this morning.

We use *or* in similar ways.

*You can come with me **or** wait here.*   *I don't speak German, French **or** Spanish.*

double conjunctions *both ... and; (n)either ... (n)or*

We can make *and* more emphatic ('stronger') by using **both ... and**.

He's **both** a top sportsman **and** a famous writer.   She **both** sings **and** dances.

We can make *or* more emphatic by using **either ... or**.

You can **either** come with me now **or** find your own way home.
We have time to see **either** the museum **or** the cathedral, but not both.

Neither ... nor means 'not one and not the other'.

The lessons were **neither** interesting **nor** useful.   He speaks **neither** English **nor** French.

1 Make sentences with *both ... and, either ... or* or *neither ... nor*.

▶ She speaks (*Chinese* ➕ *Japanese* ➕)
  She speaks both Chinese and Japanese.

▶ You can have (*coffee / tea*)
  You can have either coffee or tea.

▶ I can (*draw* ➖ *sing* ➖)
  I can neither draw nor sing.

1 I think that she's (*Scottish / Irish*)
  ....

2 I'd like to work with (*animals / children*)
  ....

3 He did well in (*mathematics* ➕ *history* ➕)
  ....

4 This car is (*fast* ➖ *comfortable* ➖)
  ....

5 She (*looked at me* ➖ *said anything* ➖)
  ....

6 I've got problems (*at home* ➕ *in my job* ➕)
  ....

2 GRAMMAR AND VOCABULARY: musical instruments
Look at the table and make sure you know the names of the instruments. Then make sentences. Put *the* with the names of the instruments.

▶ (*Steve, trumpet, violin*) Steve plays both the trumpet and the violin.
▶ (*Joanna, David, trombone*) Neither Joanna nor David plays the flute.
1 (*Karl, trombone, saxophone*) ....
2 (*Melanie, cello, drums*) ....
3 (*Steve, Karen, violin*) ....
4 (*Joanna, Charles, guitar*) ....
5 (*Karen, piano, trumpet*) ....
6 (*Sophie, guitar, trumpet*) ....
7 (*Charles, Steve, saxophone*) ....
8 (*Sophie, Steve, trumpet*) ....

	cello	drums	trombone	guitar	piano	saxophone	trumpet	violin
Joanna	✓	✓	✗	✗	✗	✗	✗	✗
Karl	✗	✗	✓	✗	✗	✓	✗	✗
David	✓	✗	✗	✓	✗	✗	✗	✗
Steve	✗	✗	✗	✗	✗	✗	✓	✓
Melanie	✗	✗	✓	✗	✓	✗	✗	✗
Sophie	✗	✗	✗	✓	✗	✗	✓	✗
Karen	✗	✗	✗	✗	✗	✓	✗	✓
Charles	✗	✓	✗	✗	✓	✗	✗	✗

test yourself   conjunctions

1 **Put in the correct tenses (simple present or *will*).**

▶ *I'll phone* .... you when I ..... *arrive* .... (*phone; arrive*)

1 I think I .... some tea before I .... to bed. (*have; go*)

2 I .... here until your train .... (*wait; come*)

3 When you .... again, Ann .... here. (*come; be*)

4 We .... sorry when Anne .... back home. (*be; go*)

2 **Complete the sentences with words from the box. You don't need to use all the words.**

| although | because | but | so | until | when | while |

1 .... she spoke very fast, I understood nearly everything.

2 I couldn't read .... it was too dark.

3 The food wasn't very good, ... he ate everything.

4 The lesson finished early, ... we went for a walk.

5 .... I got his letter I went round to see him.

3 **Use the conjunctions to put these sentences together in two ways.**

▶ The weather's good. I go fishing at weekends. (*if*)
If the weather's good, I go fishing at weekends.
I go fishing at weekends if the weather's good.

1 The teacher was ill. The children had a holiday. (*because*)
....
....

2 I was in China. I made a lot of friends. (*when*)
....
....

3 They built the new road. It was difficult to get to our village. (*until*)
....
....

4 **Circle the correct answers.**

1 I had a drink with Andrew *before / after* he left.

2 *Before / After* I took my examinations, I studied very hard.

3 Lucy went out with her friends *although / in spite of* she wasn't feeling well.

4 I went into the house *although / in spite of* there was nobody there.

5 *Although / In spite of* the rain, the streets were full of people.

6 *Because / Because of* the bad weather, we couldn't play the match.

7 I couldn't understand them *because / because of* their accent.

5 **Correct (✓) or not (✗)?**

1 You can either stay here or come with me. ...

2 He plays neither the piano nor he plays the guitar. ...

3 Carol went on working in spite of her illness. ...

4 Although the train was late, but I got there in time. ...

5 The house was small, cold, dirty. ...

6 The table and chair were very dirty. ...

SECTION 17 *if*

● grammar summary

Most tenses are possible in sentences with *if*.

If you're happy, I'm happy.   *He won't come tomorrow if he came yesterday.*
If you've been to Paris, you've seen the Eiffel Tower.

Note the following **three important structures**:

- **present tenses for future:**
  With *if*, we use **present tenses** to talk about the future.
  I'll phone you if I have time. (NOT ... *if I will have time.*)

- ***if* + past, ... would ...**
  We can use **past tenses** with *if* to show that something is **not real** or **not probable now**.
  (We normally use *would* in the other part of the sentence.)
  If I had more money, I would buy a car now.

- ***if* + past perfect, ... would have ...**
  To talk about **unreal past** events – things that did not happen – we use *if* + **past perfect**.
  (We normally use *would have* + **past participle** in the other part of the sentence.)
  I'm sorry you had all those problems. If you had asked me, I would have helped you.

● pre-test: which units do you need?

Try this small test. It will help you to decide which units you need. The answers are on page 284.

① Correct (✓) or not (✗)?

▶ If I would have gone to London, I had seen Alex. ✗
1 If I'm sleepy, I drink a cup of coffee. ...
2 If I could drive, I could get a better job. ...
3 We'll go and see Max and Chris if we'll be in Berlin. ...
4 If he's from Switzerland, he probably understands French. ...
5 If we left early tomorrow morning, we would arrive before 12.00. ...
6 You can't come in here unless you don't have a ticket. ...
7 If he would work harder, he passed his exams. ...
8 I wouldn't do that if I were you. ...
9 If you didn't help me, I would have been in trouble. ...

If it's Tuesday, this must be Belgium.
(*Title of film about American tourists in Europe*)

If you can keep your head when all
about you are losing theirs,
... you'll be a man, my son.
(*Rudyard Kipling*)

If you were the only girl in the world,
and I were the only boy ...
(*Song by Clifford Grey*)

If you can keep your head when all
about you are losing theirs,
you just don't know what's going on.
(*British Army saying*)

if: position; *unless*

1 Use *if* to put these sentences together in two ways.

▶ Joe works at Brown's. He probably knows Annie.
If Joe works at Brown's, he probably knows Annie.
Joe probably knows Annie if he works at Brown's.

1 I can't sleep. I get up and read.

....

....

2 You take books from my room. Please tell me.

....

....

3 You're hungry. Why don't you cook some soup?

....

....

4 She arrived this morning. She will probably phone us this evening.

....

....

5 We catch the first train. We can be in London by 9.00.

....

....

We can use *unless* to mean '*if ... not*', '*except if*'.
You can't come in **unless** *you have a ticket.* (= 'You can't come in *if you don't* have a ticket.')
Unless *I'm very tired, I go to bed about midnight.* (= '*Except if I'm very tired ...*')

2 Rewrite these sentences with *unless*.

▶ Children can't go in if they are not with an adult.
Children can't go in unless they are with an adult.

▶ If you don't give me my money, I'm going to the police.
Unless you give me my money, I'm going to the police.

1 You can't park here if you don't live in this street.

....

2 If you are not over 15, you can't see this film.

....

3 I don't drive fast except if I'm really late.

....

4 If I'm not going fishing, I get up late on Sundays.

....

5 We usually go for a walk after supper if there isn't a good film on TV.

....

➔ For the difference between *if* and *when*, see page 280.

if: future   *I'll phone you if I hear from Alice.*

Most tenses are possible in sentences with *if*.

If you're happy, I'm happy.   *He won't come tomorrow if he came yesterday.*
If you've been to Paris, you've seen the Eiffel Tower.

But after *if*, we normally use a present tense to talk about the future.

If it is sunny tomorrow, we'll eat in the garden.   *I'll phone you if I hear from Alice.*
I'll be sorry if I don't pass this exam.

1 Make sentences with *if*.

I'm afraid the bus will be late.
▶ → get to work late again   *If the bus is late, I'll get to work late again.*
▶ → lose my job   *If I get to work late again, I'll lose my job.*
1 → not find another job   ....
2 → lose my flat   ....
3 → move back to my parents' house   ....
4 → get very bored   ....
5 → go swimming every day   ....
6 → look very good   ....
7 → meet interesting people   ....
8 → go to lots of parties   ....
9 → have a wonderful time   ....

2 Put in the correct verb forms.

▶ If it ...*rains*......, we ...*will have*..... the party inside. (*rain; have*)
1 I .... happy if I .... my exam. (*be; pass*)
2 If you .... now, you .... the train. (*leave; catch*)
3 John says he .... as a taxi-driver if he .... money. (*work; need*)
4 If I .... free tomorrow evening, I .... you on Friday. (*not be; see*)
5 Mary .... Chinese next year if she .... time. (*study; have*)
6 I .... you to the station if I .... find my car keys. (*drive; can*)
7 If he .... her, he .... a happy life. (*marry; not have*)
8 .... you .... smoking if the doctor .... you that you must? (*stop; tell*)
9 If we .... to the boss very politely, ... he .... to us? (*talk; listen*)

3 GRAMMAR AND VOCABULARY: names of languages
Anna is going to work in another country next year. See if you can make sentences with the correct language names. Use a dictionary if necessary.

Arabic	Chinese ✓	Dutch	German	Greek	Portuguese	Swahili

▶ (*China*) ..*If she goes to China, she will have to learn Chinese.*..
1 (*Egypt*) If she ....
2 (*Brazil*) ....
3 (*Holland*) ....
4 (*Kenya*) ....
5 (*Greece*) ....
6 (*Austria*) ....

→ We also use **present tenses** for the **future** after **time conjunctions**: see page 221.

not real / not probable   *If dogs could talk, ...*

We use *if* + past tense + *would* to talk about things that are not real or not probable now.

IF ... + PAST TENSE	WOULD + INFINITIVE (WITHOUT *TO*)
If I *had* a million dollars,	I *would build* a big swimming pool.
If you *were* the President,	what *would* you *do*?
If dogs *could* talk,	they *would tell* some interesting stories.
If he *didn't travel* so much,	*he'd have* more money.

Contractions (see page 277): I would → I'd, you would → you'd, etc

---

1 Put in the correct forms of the verbs.

▶ If people ..*had*...... four arms, life ..*would be*.. easier. (*have; be*)

1 If my cat .... open the fridge, it .... all my food. (*can; eat*)

2 If Ann and Bill .... here, they .... what to do. (*be; know*)

3 If I .... the answer, I .... you. (*know; tell*)

4 If your boss .... you to work on Sunday, ... you .... it? (*ask; do*)

5 If you .... read people's thoughts, what .... you .... ? (*can; do*)

---

2 Complete each sentence with the correct forms of the correct verbs.

1 I .... a car if I .... enough money. (*have, buy*)

2 If I .... you to marry me, what .... you ....? (*say, ask*)

3 Alex .... his work on time if he .... so much. (*finish, not talk*)

4 I .... Chinese if I .... more time. (*have, study*)

5 If the programmes .... better, I .... more TV. (*be, watch*)

6 This .... a nice country if it .... so much. (*not rain, be*)

7 I .... Carola better if she .... about herself all the time. (*not talk, like*)

---

3 Make sentences in two ways.

▶ My parents don't live near here, so I don't see them at weekends.
If my parents lived near here, I would see them at weekends.................
I would see my parents at weekends if they lived near here.................

1 We won't play cards because Jane and Peter aren't here.
If Jane and Peter were here, we would play cards.................
We ....

2 We haven't got enough money so we won't buy a new car.
....
....

3 Fred doesn't answer letters, so I don't write to him.
....
....

4 I won't take your photo because I can't find my camera.
....
....

5 I don't enjoy opera because I can't understand the words.
....
....

4 QUESTIONNAIRE: WHAT WOULD YOU DO IF ...?
Write sentences. Use a dictionary if necessary.

1 If you heard a strange noise in your house in the night, would you:
A go and look?   **B** phone the police?   **C** hide under the bedclothes?
If I heard a strange noise in my house in the night, I would ....
....

2 If you found a lot of money in the street, would you:
A keep it?   **B** try to find the person who had lost it?   **C** take it to the police?
....
....

3 If you saw a child stealing from a shop, would you:
A tell the child to stop?   **B** tell a shop assistant?   **C** do nothing?
....
....

4 If a shop assistant gave you too much change, would you:
A tell him/her?   **B** take the money and say nothing?
....
....

5 If you found a dead mouse in your kitchen, would you:
A throw it out?   **B** ask somebody to throw it out?   **C** run?
....
....

6 If you found a suitcase on the pavement outside a bank, would you:
A take it into the bank?   **B** take it to the police?   **C** take it home?   **D** leave it?
....
....

7 if you found a friend's diary, would you:
A read it?   **B** give it to him/her without reading it?
....
....

5 **What would you do if you had a free year and a lot of money? Write three or more sentences.**

travel round the world   study ....   go to ....   (other answers)

1 If I ....
....
2 If I ....
....
3 If I ....
....

After *I* and *we*, we can use **should** with the same meaning as *would* in British English.
*If I had more time, I **should**/**would** learn the saxophone.*

If I go ..., I will ...; If I went ..., I would ...

The difference between *if I go* and *if I went* (for example) is **not** a difference of **time**.
We can use both *if I go/see* etc and *if I went/saw* etc to talk about the **present or future**.
With *if*, a past tense does not mean 'past time'; it means 'not real' or 'not probable'.

PROBABLE/POSSIBLE	NOT REAL/NOT PROBABLE
If I go to London, I'll visit Tony.	*If I went to the moon, I would take a lot of photos.*
If I see Ann, I'll give her your address.	*If I saw the Prime Minister, I would say 'hello'.*

1 **Choose the best sentence-beginning.**

▶ If I (live) / lived to be 75, ...
1 If I *live / lived* to be 175, ...
2 If dogs *can / could* talk, ...
3 If I *go / went* shopping next week, ...
4 If Switzerland *starts / started* a war against Australia, ...
5 If the government *gives / gave* everybody a month's holiday with pay, ...
6 If you *need / needed* help one day, ...
7 If everybody *gives / gave* 10% of their money to poor countries, ...
8 If everybody *thinks / thought* the same as me, ...
9 If I *am / was* the most intelligent person in the world, ...
10 If prices *go / went* up next year, ...

2 **Choose the best way to continue the sentences.**

▶ I'm not going to open the window. If I *open* /(opened) the window, it *will* /(would) be too noisy.
▶ Maybe I'll open a window. But if I (open) / *opened* a window, it(will) / *would* be very noisy.
1 I'm going to get up early tomorrow. If I *have / had* time, I'll / I'd walk to work.
2 If I *have / had* time, I'll / I'd walk to work, but it's just not possible.
3 'I may get a job in Germany.' 'If you *get / got* it, what *will / would* your boyfriend say?'
4 'There's a job in Germany, but I don't think I'll get it.' 'If you *get / got* it, what *will / would* your boyfriend say?'
5 We never leave food on the table. If we *do / did*, the cat *will / would* eat it.
6 'Shall I put this on the table?' 'If you *do / did*, the cat *will / would* eat it.'
7 I'll probably go to university. But if I *go / went*, I *won't / wouldn't* earn any money for three years.
8 I'm not going to go to university. If I *go / went* to university, I *won't / wouldn't* earn any money for three years.

> ## The laws of work
>
> 1. If anything can go wrong, it will go wrong.
> 2. If a job looks easy, it's difficult. If it looks difficult, it's impossible.
> 3. If you think a job will take two hours, it will take four days. If you think it will take four days, it will take eight weeks. And so on.
> 4. If you throw something away, you will need it the next day.
> 5. If you do what everybody wants you to do, somebody won't like it.
> 6. If you explain so clearly that nobody can misunderstand, somebody will.

If I were you, ...

We sometimes use *were* instead of *was* after *if*. This is usually rather formal.

*If I **were** taller I would play basketball.*   *If John **were** here, he would know what to do.*

We often say *If I **were** you, I would / I'd ...*, when we want to give people **advice**.

*If I **were** you, I'd get a new car.*   *I **wouldn't** stand there if I **were** you.*

1 **Write sentences with *if I were you*, using the expressions in the box.**

call the police at once   fly   not sell it   join a club   see a doctor ✓ take a holiday

▶ 'I feel ill.' *'If I were you, I'd see a doctor.'* ....
1 'I'm really tired.' 'If ....,'
2 'I haven't got any friends.' 'If ....,'
3 'Shall I take the train to Scotland?' 'I would ....,'
4 'Somebody has stolen my car.' 'If ....,'
5 'John wants to buy my motorbike.' 'I ....,'

2 **John Baker has won a lot of money in the lottery. His family and friends are giving him advice. Look at the pictures and use the words in the box to complete the sentences.**

buy a sports car   buy a house ✓   give the money away   have a big party
put the money in the bank   start a business   stop work   travel round the world

▶ JOHN'S GIRLFRIEND: *If I were you, I'd buy a house.* ....
1 HIS MOTHER: ....
2 HIS FATHER: ....
3 HIS BROTHER: ....
4 HIS GRANDMOTHER: ....
5 HIS SISTER: ....
6 HIS FRIEND JOE: ....
7 HIS FRIEND STEPHANIE: ....

could = 'would be able to'   *We could go cycling if ...*

We can use **could** to mean '**would be able to**'.

*If you arrived early, we **could** talk about the meeting.*   *If Joe came, he **could** help with the dog.*

Sometimes we use *could* twice: once as a past tense (to say that something is not real / not probable), and once for *would be able to*.

If I could sell my car, I could buy a computer.

1 Complete the sentences with *could* and expressions from the box.

| ask her to help ✓   get up late   go and see him   go cycling   go to the cinema more often |
| have breakfast in the garden   read the paper ✓   watch a film   write to Henry |

▶ If Alice was here, ..we could ask her to help.............................

▶ If I could find my glasses, ...I could read the paper...........................

1 If John was at home, we ....

2 If the TV was working, we ....

3 If we had bikes, ...

4 If it was Saturday, I ....

5 If it was warmer, we ....

6 If I could find my address book, ...

7 If we lived in a town, ...

2 Andy is reading the job advertisements. Unfortunately he can't do much (see the box).
Look at the advertisements and write sentences with *if he ... he could ...*

| Andy doesn't speak Japanese ✓   he doesn't have a passport   he can't drive |
| he can't cook   he doesn't like children   he doesn't like animals   he can't swim |

▶ If he spoke Japanese, he could get a job.................... at the Grand Hotel.

1 If he could drive, ... at Calloway Ltd.

2 .... at Patterson Travel.

3 .... at Fred's Café.

4 .... at Crowndale School.

5 .... at the City Zoo.

6 .... at the Leisure Centre.

RECEPTIONIST
required immediately
at the Grand Hotel.
Must speak Japanese.
Phone 69423.

Calloway Ltd
needs energetic young
SALES ASSISTANT.
Must have driving
licence. Phone 33446.

Courier needed by
PATTERSON TRAVEL.
Must have passport.
Phone 44576.

ASSISTANT COOK
needed at Fred's
Cafe. Phone 65712.

Welfare Officer
required at
Crowndale School.
Must like children.
Phone 88759.

The CITY ZOO requires
Assistant Keeper.
No experience necessary,
but must like animals.

The Leisure Centre
needs Attendant,
starting immediately.
Must be able to swim.

unreal past *If a had happened, b would have happened.*

When we use *if* to talk about **unreal past** events – things that **didn't happen** – we use the **past perfect** and *would have* + **past participle**.

IF ... + PAST PERFECT	WOULD HAVE + PAST PARTICIPLE
If the weather had been better,	*we would have gone to the sea.* (But it wasn't, so we didn't.)
If you had asked me,	*I would have helped you.* (But you didn't, so I didn't.)
If Mary had seen you	*what would you have said?* (But she didn't.)
If she hadn't gone skiing,	*she wouldn't have fallen and broken her leg.* (But she did.)

1 **Put in the correct verb forms.**

1 If I .... here yesterday, I would have come to see you. (*be*)

2 If Joe .... harder, he would have passed his exams. (*work*)

3 If you .... a map with you, you wouldn't have got lost. (*take*)

4 We would have won the game if we .... so badly. (*not play*)

5 If I had gone to university, I .... medicine and become a doctor. (*study*)

6 .... you .... if you had driven more slowly? (*crash*)

7 You .... badly if you hadn't drunk all that coffee. (*not sleep*)

8 If you .... on holiday with us, you .... a wonderful time. (*come; have*)

9 If my car ...., I .... here at 8 o'clock. (*not break down; be*)

10 .... you .... harder at school last year if you .... the teachers? (*study; like*)

11 She .... married if she .... to leave home. (*not get; not want*)

12 .... you .... me if I .... you? (*help; ask*)

2 **Getting up early is bad for you. Read the text in the box and make sentences.**

> get up early → catch the 8.15 train → sit by a beautiful foreign woman
> → fall in love and marry her → go to live in her country → work in her father's diamond business
> → become very rich → go into politics → die in a revolution

▶ *If I had got up early, I would have caught the 8.15 train.* ....

1 If I had caught ....

2 .... and married her.

3 ....

4 ....

5 ....

6 ....

7 ....

3 **Hot weather is good for you. Read the text and complete the sentences.**

> It was hot, so my mother opened the door. A cat came in and ate her supper, so she went to the shop to buy food. In the shop she saw an advertisement for a secretary. So she got a new job, and met my father. I'm glad it was a hot day!

▶ *If it hadn't been* hot, *my mother wouldn't have opened* .... the door.

1 If she hadn't opened the door, the cat .... her supper.

2 .... her supper, ... the shop.

3 .... the shop, ... the advertisement.

4 .... the advertisement, ... a new job.

5 .... a new job, ... my father.

1 Use *if* to put these sentences together in two ways.

I need help. I ask my brother.
1 If ....
2 .... if ....

2 Put in the correct verb forms.

▶ I'm sure John ..*will help*............ you if you ask him. (*help*)
1 If you .... your glasses, you would see much better. (*clean*)
2 I .... and see you tomorrow if I have time. (*come*)
3 If she spoke more slowly, perhaps I .... her. (*understand*)
4 If you .... at 12.00, you will arrive at 3.20. (*leave*)
5 I .... my car if I needed money. (*sell*)

3 Correct (✓) or not (✗)?

▶ I get up and watch TV if I can't sleep. ✓
1 I'll be very happy if I'll pass the exam. ...
2 If she's from Greece, she speaks Greek. ...
3 If he would eat more, he wasn't so thin. ...
4 If I don't see you today, I see you tomorrow. ...

4 Choose the best way to continue the sentences.

1 I'm not going to buy a car. If I *buy / bought* a car, I *will / would* spend all my money on it.
2 Maybe I'll go and see Sandra. But if I *go / went* and *see / saw* her, *I'll / I'd* have to talk to her stupid brother.
3 My parents live a long way away. If they *live / lived* nearer, I *will / would* see them more often.
4 We're going to stay at home this evening. If we *go / went* out, we *won't / wouldn't* do anything interesting.

5 Rewrite these sentences with *unless*.

1 You can't go there if you don't have a visa. ....
2 If you don't go now, I'll call the police. ....

6 Correct (✓) or not (✗)?

1 If I could cook, I could get a job in a restaurant. ...
2 You won't catch the bus unless you don't run. ...
3 If it didn't rain, I would have played tennis. ...
4 I would put on a sweater if I were you. ...
5 Everything would have been OK if I hadn't lost my keys. ...

7 Put in the correct verb forms.

1 If I .... coffee last night, I .... better. (*not drink; sleep*)
2 If my parents .... more money, I .... to university after I left school. (*have; go*)
3 Annie .... to Brazil last year if she .... Pete. (*go; not meet*)

◧ More difficult questions

grammar summary

who	(whom)	which	that	what

We use **relative pronouns** to **join sentences** to **nouns**.

The man was Welsh. He won the prize.   *The man who won the prize was Welsh.*

We use *who* for **people** and *which* for **things**. We can also use *that* for **people and things**.
*There's **the man who/that** sold me my bike.*   *She said **a word which/that** I didn't hear.*

We often leave out **object pronouns**.
*Do you remember those photos **(that)** I showed you?*

Prepositions can often go in **two places**.
*The woman **about whom** we were **talking** walked into the room. (formal)*
*The woman **that** we were **talking about** walked into the room. (conversational)*

We can use *what* to mean 'the thing(s) which'.
*The children always eat **what** I cook.*

pre-test: which units do you need?

Try this small test. It will help you to decide which units you need. The answers are on page 284.

1 Correct (✓) or not (✗)?

▶ We stayed in a hotel who had a beautiful garden. ✗

1 I didn't like the man which my sister married. ...

2 Did I tell you about the film which we saw? ...

3 Eric said a word which I couldn't understand it. ...

4 People that live in London are called 'Londoners'. ...

5 Is the book you're reading interesting? ...

6 I'm spending the day with some people I know. ...

7 The people came to dinner stayed very late. ...

8 The girl I work with gave me some flowers. ...

9 I don't believe anything what she says. ...

10 Have you got what you need? ...

---

art·ist /ˈɑːtɪst; *AmE* ˈɑːrt-/ *noun* **1** a person who creates works of art, especially paintings or drawings: *an exhib*

bee /biː/ *noun* **1** a black and yellow flying insect that can sting. Bees live in large groups and make HONEY (=

builder *noun* **1** a person who builds things, esp one whose job is building houses, etc. **2** (in compounds) a person who

burg·lar /ˈbɜːglə(r); *AmE* ˈbɜːrg-/ *noun* a person who enters a building illegally in order to steal ⇨ note at

bus /bʌs/ *noun* (*pl* **buses**, *US* also **busses**) a large vehicle that carries passengers, esp one that travels along a fixed route, stopping

cheese /tʃiːz/ *noun* **1** [U, C] a type of food made from milk that can be either soft or hard and is usually white or yellow in colour; a particu

plant¹ /plɑːnt, *US* plænt/ *noun* **1** [C] a type of living thing that grows in the earth and usu has a stem, leaves and roots:

sau·cer /ˈsɔːsə(r)/ *noun* a small shallow round dish that a cup stands on; an object that is shaped like this:

(Oxford Advanced Learner's Dictionary)

relative *who* and *which* *the keys which I lost*

We can use **sentences** to **describe nouns**.
To join sentences to nouns, we use **relative pronouns**: *who* (for people) and *which* (for things).

The man *plays* golf. **He** lives at No 10.   The man **who** lives at No 10 *plays* golf.

The letter *is* for me. You *saw* **it**.   The letter **which** you *saw* is for me.

I *like* the girl. **She** works with Ann.   I *like* the girl **who** works with Ann.

I've got those books. You *wanted* **them**.   I've got those books **which** you *wanted*.

❶ Put in *who* or *which*.

1 The people .... live downstairs are Irish.
2 The shop .... sells that good bread is closed today.
3 The dictionary .... I bought yesterday isn't very good.
4 That cheese .... you like comes from Scotland.
5 Do you know the girls .... are standing by the window?
6 I can't find the key .... opens this door.
7 I've lost the ear-rings .... Harry gave me.
8 The police are looking for three men .... robbed the National Bank yesterday.
9 We know the woman .... teaches French at Jane's school.

We use *who* or *which* instead of *he, him, she, it* etc. **Don't** use **both**.

The woman **who** ~~she~~ *teaches me French is ill.*   *Here's the address* **which** *you wanted* ~~it~~.

❷ Circle the correct answer.

1 There's the man who *took / he took* your coat.
2 Do you know the people who *live / they live* next door?
3 I like that woman; *she is / is* very kind.
4 I've found the keys which I *lost / lost them*.
5 Do you like the new dress which I *bought / bought it* yesterday?
6 The car which *is parked / it is parked* outside belongs to Susan.
7 This is a new kind of knife: *cuts / it cuts* everything.
8 The poems which Mark *writes / writes them* are very hard to understand.

> The man who makes no mistakes
> does not usually make anything.
>
> *(E J Phelps)*

3 Look at the picture and the information, and write sentences with *who.*

▶ ~~The man and woman who live in flat 8 are from Scotland.~~ ....

1 ....

2 ....

3 ....

4 ....

5 ....

6 ....

7 ....

FLAT	INFORMATION
1	play loud music all night
2	broke her leg skiing
3	play golf all day
4	haven't got much money
5	has three children
6	drives a Rolls-Royce
7	are hiding from the police
8	are from Scotland

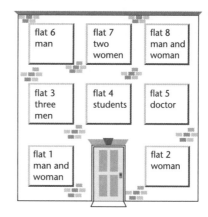

4 Join the sentences in the place marked *. Change *he, it* etc to *who* or *which.*

▶ Most of the people* speak German. They live in Austria.
~~Most of the people who live in Austria speak German.~~ ....

▶ I know a shop*. It sells really good meat.
~~I know a shop which sells really good meat.~~ ....

1 The bus* isn't running today. It goes to Oxford.
....

2 Yesterday I met a man*. He works with your brother.
....

3 The child* was ill. She didn't come to the party.
....

4 Can you pick up the papers*? They are lying on the floor.
....

5 The eggs* were bad. I bought them yesterday.
....

6 Here's the book*. You asked me to buy it for you.
....

7 I don't like the man*. He is going out with my sister.
....

We can use *whom* for people when the relative pronoun is the **object** of the following verb.
*I've just got a postcard from a woman **whom** I met on holiday last year.*

But *whom* is formal and unusual. In spoken English, we more often use *that* (see page 240), *who* or **nothing** (see page 241).

*I've just got a postcard from a woman **who/that** I met on holiday last year.*
OR *I've just got a postcard from a woman **I met** on holiday last year.*

relative *that*   *a bird that can't fly*

> We can use *that* instead of *who* or *which*.
>
> *The man **that** lives at number 8 is getting married.*   *You haven't drunk the tea **that** I made for you.*

1 Join the sentences in the place marked *, using *that*.

▶ I'd like to speak to the person*. She wrote this letter.
I'd like to speak to the person that wrote this letter.

▶ The tomatoes* are all bad. I bought them yesterday.
The tomatoes that I bought yesterday are all bad.

1 Joe's got a motorbike*. It can do 200 km an hour.
....

2 Is that the computer*? It doesn't work.
....

3 Those are the trousers*. I use them for gardening.
....

4 A man* wants to marry my sister. He lives in New York.
....

5 The doctors* all said different things. They looked at my leg.
....

6 The flowers* are beautiful. You gave them to Aunt Sarah.
....

7 The children* have gone on holiday. They play football with Paul.
....

2 GRAMMAR AND VOCABULARY: **things that fly**
Write descriptions with *that*. Use a dictionary if necessary.

| can fly straight up   flies at night and hears very well   can't fly   doesn't have an engine |
| eats small animals and birds   can fly to the moon   makes honey ✓ |
| doesn't make honey and can bite you |

▶ an insect .*that makes honey*............................
1 an insect ....
2 a bird ....
3 a bird ....
4 an animal ....
5 a machine ....
6 a plane ....
7 a thing ....

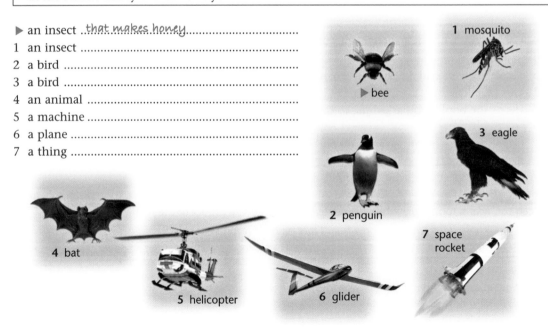

1 mosquito
▶ bee
3 eagle
2 penguin
7 space rocket
4 bat
5 helicopter
6 glider

leaving out relative pronouns   *the car (that) you bought*

When a relative pronoun (*who/which/that*) is the **object** of the following verb, we often leave it out.
But we can't leave out a relative pronoun when it is the **subject** of the following verb.

(*I phoned a man.*)
The man **that I phoned** spoke Spanish.
  → The man **I phoned** spoke Spanish.

The train **that you want** leaves at 10.00.
  → The train **you want** leaves at 10.00.

(*A man phoned me.*)
The man **that phoned** me spoke Greek.
  (NOT ~~The man phoned me spoke Greek.~~)

The train **that stops at York** goes at 8.00.
  (NOT ~~The train stops at York goes at 8.00.~~)

1 **Is the relative pronoun the subject (S) or object (O) of the following verb?**

▶ the woman *who* wrote this letter S
▶ the film *that* I saw O
1 the languages *that* she spoke ...
2 a woman *who* helped me ...

3 a man *who(m)* I helped ...
4 the weather *that* we have had ...
5 a machine *that* makes paper ...
6 that car *which* you bought ...

2 **Look at Exercise 1. Find the expressions with object relative pronouns and rewrite them without *who(m)*, *which* or *that*.**

▶ the film I saw ....
1 ....
2 ....

3 ....
4 ....

3 **Join the sentences in the place marked * without using *who, which* or *that*.**

▶ The cup of coffee* is on the table. You wanted it.
  The cup of coffee you wanted is on the table. ....

1 I'm working for a man*. I've known him for twenty years.
  ....

2 They played a lot of music*. I didn't like it.
  ....

3 The campsite* was very dirty. We found it.
  ....

4 I'm going on holiday with some people*. I know them.
  ....

5 That book* is very good. You suggested it to me.
  ....

6 The ring* belonged to her grandmother. She lost it.
  ....

4 **Write three sentences beginning *Everybody I know ...***

▶ Everybody I know likes rock music. ....
1 ....
2 ....
3 ....

prepositions *the man that she works for*

Some **verbs** have **prepositions** with them (see page 136) – for example *look at, listen to.*
When **relative pronouns** are the **objects** of these verbs, there are **two possibilities:**
- preposition before *whom/which* (very formal)

  *The woman smiled. I was **looking at** her.* → *The woman at whom I was looking smiled.*
  *The flat was dirty. He **lived in** it.* → *The flat in which he lived was dirty.*

- preposition after verb (more informal; we can leave out *who(m)/which/that.*)

  *The woman (whom/that) I was **looking at** smiled.* ⌐ *The flat he **lived in** was dirty.*

❶ Change these expressions to make them more conversational. Use *that.*

▶ a boy with whom I went to school *a boy that I went to school with* ....

1 the girl about whom I was talking ....

2 the people for whom I work ....

3 the house in which I live ....

4 the music to which you are listening ....

5 the bus on which I go to work ....

❷ Rewrite the expressions from Exercise 1, but leave out *that.*

▶ *a boy I went to school with* .... 3 ....

1 .... 4 ....

2 .... 5 ....

❸ Look at the information about Helen, and then make sentences (like the example) about the people in her life.

> Helen lives in a big flat with a friend called Pam. She works for a man called Eric. At weekends
> she plays tennis with a woman called Monica. Sometimes she reads to an 80-year-old woman
> called Karen, or baby-sits for people called Ann and Joe. She is in love with a man called Bill.

▶ Pam is *the friend she lives with.* ....

1 Eric is ....

2 Monica is ....

3 Karen is ....

4 Ann and Joe are ....

5 Bill is ....

❹ Now write sentences (like the example) about Helen's birthday presents.

> For Helen's birthday, Pam gave her a handbag, Eric gave her chocolates, Monica gave her a clock,
> Karen gave her theatre tickets, Ann and Joe gave her a picture, and Bill gave her flowers and ear-rings.

▶ The friend she lives *with gave her a handbag.* ....

1 The man she works ....

2 The woman ....

3 The 80-year-old woman ....

4 The people ....

5 The man ....

relative *what*   *It was just what I wanted.*

> We can use **what** to mean '*the thing(s) which/that*' or '*anything that*'.
>
> *Have you got **what** you need for your journey? (= '... **the things that** you need ...')*
> *I'm sorry about **what** happened.*   *'Can I have something to eat?' 'Take **what** you like.'*
>
> We use **what** with a **singular** verb.
>
> ***What** I bought **was** mostly very cheap.* (NOT ~~What I bought were~~ ...)

❶ Change the words *in italics* to *what*.

▶ *The things that* she said weren't true. ..What she said wasn't true. ....

1 *The things that* he did made everybody angry. ....

2 Take *anything that* you want. ....

3 Soap – that's *the thing that* I forgot to pack! ....

4 She gave me a watch. It was just *the thing that* I wanted. ....
   ....

5 That child does *anything that* he likes. ....

6 *The thing that* I need is some food. ....

❷ Write a sentence beginning *What I need is ...*

   ....

> We use **that**, not *what*, after **anything, something, nothing, everything, all** and **the only thing**.
>
> *You can take **anything that** you want.* (NOT ... ~~anything what you want.~~)
> *The shop had **nothing that** I wanted.*   ***All that** I could do was stand and watch.*
> *Money is **the only thing** in the world **that** matters to him.*

❸ Put in *that* or *what*.

1 I believe everything .... she says.

2 .... she did surprised everybody.

3 I can't give you .... you want.

4 He said nothing .... was important.

5 I can't eat .... I like.

6 I can't eat everything .... I like.

7 The only thing .... I forgot
   was toothpaste.

8 Ask Peter – he'll tell you .... you need
   to know.

❹ GRAMMAR AND VOCABULARY: jewellery
Read the text and complete the sentences. Use a dictionary if necessary.

> Ann, Mary, Sally, Jane, Barbara and Helen have all got rich boyfriends. For Christmas, Ann
> wanted a gold watch, Mary wanted a diamond brooch, Sally wanted sapphire ear-rings, Jane
> wanted a pearl necklace, Barbara wanted a ruby ring and Helen wanted a silver bracelet. But:

▶ Ann got a diamond brooch.   .Ann got what Mary wanted. ....

1 Mary got a ruby ring.   ....

2 Sally got a silver bracelet.   ....

3 Jane got a gold watch.   ....

4 Barbara got a pearl necklace.   ....

5 Helen got sapphire ear-rings.   ....

test yourself relative pronouns

1 Correct (✓) or not (✗)?

1 The people which live next door have got five children. ...
2 Do you know a shop who sells good cheese? ...
3 I didn't understand the language which she was speaking. ...
4 I didn't understand the language that she was speaking. ...
5 I've found the dictionary that I lost it yesterday. ...
6 The girls that I work with gave me flowers for my birthday. ...
7 Where's the paper you wrote the address on? ...
8 You can have anything what you like. ...
9 What she said made me very angry. ...

2 Join the sentences in the place marked *, using *who* or *which*.

1 I know a man*. He writes film music.

....

2 Yesterday I saw a film*. You would like it.

....

3 The bus* got to London twenty minutes late. I took it.

....

4 The car* isn't very good. I bought it last month.

....

3 Join the sentences in the place marked *, using *that*.

1 The tickets* were very expensive. I got them.

....

2 These are the scissors*. I use them for cutting paper.

....

3 The woman* is from Brazil. She gives me tennis lessons.

....

4 The man* is always very friendly. He works in the corner shop.

....

4 Rewrite the sentences without relative pronouns if you can. If you can't, write 'can't change'.

▶ Where's the book which I was reading? *Where's the book I was reading?* ....
▶ The people who live next door are Italian. *can't change* ....
1 The clock that I bought doesn't work. ....
2 I didn't like the film which I saw last night. ....
3 Here's the letter that came for you. ....
4 It was a journey that took twelve hours. ....

5 Change these expressions to make them more conversational.

1 a boy to whom I talked ....
2 the people for whom I work ....
3 the hotel in which we stayed ....
4 the place to which I drove ....

SECTION 19 indirect speech

● grammar summary

When we tell people **what somebody said or thought**, we often use **indirect speech**.
Tenses, here-and-now words (like *this, here, today*) and **pronouns** (like *I, you*) **may change** in indirect speech. This is because the time, place and speaker may be different.
  *'I really **like** it **here**.'*   Bill said that **he** really **liked** it **there**.

We often **leave out** *that*, especially after common verbs like *say* and *think*.
  Bill **said** he really liked it there.

Indirect questions have a **different structure** from direct questions.
  *'What **is** your phone number?'*   He asked me what **my phone number was**.
  *'**Do** you **like** cherries?'*   She asked me **if I liked** cherries.

We can use **object + infinitive** (with *to*) after *ask* and *tell*.
  *I **asked him to make** some coffee.*   She **told the children not to make** a noise.

● pre-test: which units do you need?

Try this small test. It will help you to decide which units you need. The answers are on page 284.

1 Correct (✓) or not (✗)?

▶ I said Peter where was he going. ✗

1 A man asked me where the post office was. ...
2 I said I'm really tired. ...
3 John asked how did I feel. ...
4 I asked somebody where was the station? ...
5 Can you say me what the time is? ...
6 Mary asked me to help her. ...

7 I didn't know if I was late. ...
8 I didn't know whether I was late. ...
9 I told Ann to not worry. ...
10 Jake told that he wanted a holiday. ...
11 Do you know where all those people work? ...
12 Joe phoned me on Sunday and said he went to a great party yesterday. ...

They told me, Heraclitus, they told me
  you were dead,
They brought me bitter news to hear
  and bitter tears to shed.
I wept, as I remembered how often you
  and I
Had tired the sun with talking and sent
  him down the sky.

                  (William Cory)

There are so many kinds of awful men –
One can't avoid them all. She often said
She'd never make the same mistake again:
She always made a new mistake instead.

                  (Wendy Cope)

tenses and pronouns   *Bill said he was really happy.*

When we tell people **what somebody said or thought,** we often use **indirect speech.**
Tenses and **pronouns** (*I, you* etc) **change** in indirect speech if the **time** and **speaker** are **different.**
For example, **present** tenses become past; *I* may become *he* or *she; my* may become *his* or *her.*

SOMEBODY SAID/THOUGHT	INDIRECT SPEECH
'I'm happy.'	*Bill said that he was happy.* (NOT ~~Bill said that I'm happy.~~)
'I have a problem.'	*I thought that I had a problem.* (NOT ~~I thought to have a problem.~~)
'She likes me.'	*He knew that she liked him.*
'My feet are cold.'	*She said her feet were cold.*

We often **leave out** *that,* especially after common verbs like *say, think.*

*Bill **said** he was really happy.*   *I **thought** it was a great party.*

1 Put in the correct pronouns (*I* etc) or possessives (*my* etc).

▶ 'She likes me.' He knew she liked *him.*..........
1 'I speak French.' He said .... spoke French.
2 'I'm sorry.' She said .... was sorry.
3 'Ann phoned me.' She said Ann had phoned ....
4 'We want our money.' They said .... wanted .... money.

We can use both *say* and *tell* in indirect speech. *Tell* must have a **personal object:** we *tell somebody something. Say* doesn't need a personal object: we *say something* (*to somebody*).

*She **told me** I was late.* (NOT ~~She told I was late.~~)
*They **told Ann** the wrong time.* (NOT ~~They told the wrong time to Ann.~~)
*She **said** I was late.* (NOT ~~She said me I was late.~~)
*I **said** nothing to the police.* (NOT ~~I said the police nothing.~~)

2 Circle the correct answer.

1 I *said / told* the driver I wanted to stop.
2 My mother *said / told* there was a letter for me.
3 Everybody *said / told* I looked beautiful.
4 Why did you *say / tell* the lessons were expensive?
5 Eric *said / told* the waiter he couldn't pay.
6 I didn't *say / tell* Peter that I was going away.
7 Nobody *said / told* me that the shop was closed.
8 Ann *said / told* that she would wait at the bus stop.

3 Put the beginnings and ends together, and look at the use of tenses.

1 In 1896 Lord Kelvin said	A aeroplanes were impossible. *1*
2 In 1937 Hitler's nephew Willi said	B he would never be a scientist. ...
3 When Columbus got to America he thought	C his uncle was not interested in war. ...
4 When Albert Einstein was 10, a teacher told him	D the sun went round the earth. ...
5 Hundreds of years ago, people believed	E he had reached India. ...

When we tell people what somebody **said in the past**, there is a **time difference**.
(For example, somebody said something on Sunday, and I tell you about it on Monday.)
Because of this, **tenses usually change as follows**:

DIRECT SPEECH ON SUNDAY	TENSE CHANGE	INDIRECT SPEECH ON MONDAY
The children are in Ireland.	AM/ARE/IS → WAS/WERE	*Karen said her children were in Ireland.*
My TV isn't working.		*He said his TV wasn't working.*
I have a meeting at 4.00.	HAVE/HAS → HAD	*She said she had a meeting at 4.00.*
Sue has passed her exam.		*Sally told me Sue had passed her exam.*
I will probably be late.	WILL → WOULD	*I thought I would probably be late.*
You can have three tickets.	CAN → COULD	*The man said I could have three tickets.*
It doesn't matter, Martin.	DO/DOES → DID	*I told Martin it didn't matter.*
The train leaves at 6.00.	SIMPLE PRESENT → SIMPLE PAST	*The timetable said the train left at 6.00.*
We all speak English.		*She said they all spoke English.*
I forgot my keys.	SIMPLE PAST → PAST PERFECT	*He said he had forgotten his keys.*

4 Rewrite the sentences in indirect speech, changing the tenses. Begin *He/She/They said* ...

▶ SALLY: 'I'm tired.' *She said (that) she was tired.* ....

1 ANN: 'My sister needs a car.' ....

2 BILL: 'I have to phone Andrew.' ....

3 MARY: 'Nobody wants to help me.' ....

4 HELEN: 'The radio doesn't work.' ....

5 JOHN: 'I will be in Paris in July.' ....

6 MIKE: 'I like the red sweater.' ....

7 DAVID: 'I can't swim.' ....

8 ALICE: 'My parents are travelling.' ....

9 MARIA: 'The lessons are very good.' ....

10 ERIC AND SUE: 'We haven't heard from Joe.' ....

5 Look at the picture to see what John thought when he was small. Write his thoughts in indirect speech.

He thought animals could talk. ....

....

....

....

....

....

....

ANIMALS CAN TALK.   CATS HAVE NINE LIVES.
MY FATHER KNOWS EVERYTHING.
SPAGHETTI GROWS ON TREES.
THE TEACHER LIVES IN THE SCHOOL.
I WILL BE RICH ONE DAY.
MY MOTHER HAS ALWAYS BEEN OLD.

6 What did you think when you were small? Write one or two sentences.

1 ....

2 ....

If somebody said something that is **still true** when it is reported, tenses don't always change.

*'My parents **don't** write to me.'* → *She told me that her parents **didn't/don't** write to her.*

→ For tenses after present reporting verbs (for example *She says that she's tired*) see page 249.

indirect questions   *She asked him what his name was.*

Indirect questions have a **different word order** from direct questions, and no question marks: ̶?̶

DIRECT QUESTION:	Monica said, 'Where is John?'	I said, 'When can you come?'
INDIRECT QUESTION:	Monica asked where John was.	I asked when she could come.
	(NOT ~~Monica asked where was John?~~)	

We **don't** use *do* in indirect questions.

DIRECT QUESTION:	'What do you want?'	'Where does Andrew live?'
INDIRECT QUESTION:	She asked me what I wanted.	I asked him where Andrew lived.
	(NOT ~~She asked me what did I want.~~)	

1 A policewoman stopped a driver in London and asked him some questions. Write the questions in indirect speech.

▶ 'What is your name?' ...*She asked him what his name was.*......

1 'Where do you live?' ....

2 'Where do you work?' ....

3 'Where are you going?' ....

4 'Where have you been?' ....

5 'What is the number of your car?' ....

....

6 'Why are you driving on the right?' ....

....

With indirect *yes/no* questions we use *if* or **whether**. They mean the same.

DIRECT QUESTION:	Do you know Tim?	Are you French?
INDIRECT QUESTION:	He asked me if/whether I knew Tim.	She asked if/whether I was French.

2 The policewoman asked some more questions. Write them in indirect speech with *if* or *whether*.

▶ 'Are you British?'   She asked him if ...*he was British.*....................................

1 'Is it your car?'   She asked him whether ....

2 'Do you have a driving licence?' ....

3 'Do you have it with you?' ....

4 'Do you always drive with the door open?' ....

....

5 'Are you listening to me?' ....

3 These are some of the questions from a woman's job interview. Write them in indirect speech.

▶ 'How old are you?' ...*They asked her how old she was.*..................................

1 'Are you married?' ....

2 'Do you have children?' ....

3 'Where have you worked before?' ....

4 'Why do you want to change your job?' ....

....

5 'Can you speak any foreign languages?' ....

....

6 'What exams have you passed?' ....

present reporting verbs *She says she comes from London.*

After **present** verbs (for example *she says, I think*) we **don't change** the tenses.

DIRECT SPEECH: *'Well, yes, I come from London.' 'Funny – she has a Scottish accent.'*

INDIRECT SPEECH: *She says she comes from London, but I think she has a Scottish accent.*

❶ Complete the indirect speech sentences.

▶	'I'm Irish.'	He says .he's Irish.
▶	'Where is Peter?'	She wants to know .where Peter is.
▶	'Did John phone?'	I don't know .if John phoned.
1	'We live in Greece.'	They say ....
2	'I went to Belfast yesterday.'	She says ....
3	'I've been ill.'	He says ....
4	'It's going to rain.'	She thinks..
5	'I'll ask my sister.'	She says ....
6	'We're going to be rich.'	They believe ....
7	'Is lunch ready?'	He wants to know ....
8	'Where did I put my keys?'	I don't remember ....

We can ask questions politely by saying *Do you know ...?* or *Can you tell me ...?* + indirect question (see page 248).

Where does she live? → Do you know where she lives?
Is he at home? → Can you tell me if he's at home?

❷ Rewrite the questions.

▶	What does this word mean?	Do you know ..what this word means?
▶	Is there a lesson today?	Can you tell me .if there's a lesson today?
1	Where can I buy tickets?	Can you ....
2	How much does it cost?	Do ....
3	Has John phoned?	Can ....
4	Must I pay now?	Can ....
5	Does Maria like steak?	Can ....
6	Where did I park the car?	Do ....

We can also use indirect questions in answers.

Sorry, I don't know where she lives.   I can't remember if he's married.

❸ Don't give the answers! But write sentences beginning *I know, I don't know, I'd like to know, I don't want to know, I don't care* or *I can't remember*.

▶ Who built the Eiffel Tower?	..I know who built the Eiffel Tower.
1 What languages do Irish people speak?	....
2 What do elephants eat?	....
3 Does the British Museum open on Christmas Day?	....
	....
4 Was King William II a tall man?	....
5 Do birds dream?	....

here and *now* → *there* and *then*

When we tell people what somebody said, we may have to **change** words like *here, this, today* and *now*. This is because the **place and time have changed** since the words were spoken.

BILL IN IRELAND IN DECEMBER	JOE IN LONDON IN MARCH
*I like it **here**.*	*Bill said he liked it there / in Ireland.*
*I'm going fishing **this week**.*	*He said he was going fishing that week.*
*I'm not working **today**.*	*He said he wasn't working that day.*
*What do you want to do **now**?*	*He asked what I wanted to do then/next.*

1 Match the direct and indirect speech expressions.

DIRECT SPEECH: *'here* and *now'* words		INDIRECT SPEECH: *'there* and *then'* words	
1 here	6 today	A that day ...	F the next day ...
2 now	7 tonight	B that night ...	G there _1_
3 this	8 last week	C that ...	H the week before ...
4 tomorrow	9 next week	D the day before ...	I then ...
5 yesterday		E the next week ...	

2 A friend of yours said these sentences a month ago in another country.
Now you are telling somebody what she said.
Complete the sentences with the correct *'there* and *then'* words.

▶ 'I'm not happy here.'   She said she wasn't happy ....there...

1 'I hate this place.'   She said she hated ....

2 'I left home last week.'   She said she had left home ....

3 'I wrote to my father yesterday.'   She said she had written to her father ....

4 'Are you leaving today?'   She asked me if I was leaving ....

5 'Where will you be tonight?'   She asked where I would be ....

6 'I'll phone you tomorrow.'   She said she would phone me ....

3 Another friend of yours said these sentences two weeks ago in another town.
Now you are telling somebody what he said. Write the sentences with the correct tenses
and *'here* and *now'* words.

▶ 'I'm really happy here.'   He said he ...was really happy there...

1 'I love this place.'   ....

2 'I saw a great film yesterday.'   ....

3 'I'm going to another party tonight.'   ....
....

4 'Do you want to play tennis tomorrow?'   ....
....

5 'My girlfriend will be here next week.'   ....
....

infinitives   *She told me to get out.*

We use *ask* or *tell* + object + infinitive (with *to*), to say what people want(ed) us to do.

DIRECT SPEECH	INDIRECT SPEECH
'Please close the door.'	She **asked me** to close the door.
'Could you phone Angela?'	I **asked John** to phone Angela.
'Get out!'	She **told me** to get out.
'Don't worry.'	The doctor **always tells her** not to worry.

① Write past indirect speech sentences.

▶ JOHN: Peter, could you close the window? (*ask*)
   John asked Peter to close the window.

▶ THE TEACHER: Andrew, don't talk so loud. (*tell*)
   The teacher told Andrew not to talk so loud.

1 ERIC: Sue, please give me your phone number. (*ask*)
   ....

2 THE BOSS: Joe, I'd like you to work late. (*tell*)
   ....

3 MARY: Sue, don't tell Karen about Bill. (*ask*)
   ....

4 MR SANDERS: Fred, please don't smoke in my car. (*ask*)
   ....

5 THE GENERAL: Colonel Walker, take 100 men and cross the river. (*tell*)
   ....

6 ANN: Mary, you mustn't study so hard. (*tell*)
   ....

② Joe left home for university. His family gave him
lots of advice. Look at the picture and complete
the sentences.

▶ His mother ...*told him to write*................... every week.
▶ His grandmother ...*told him not to forget*.....................
   to brush his teeth.
1 His girlfriend told .... every day.
2 His mother .... clean.
3 His father .... hard.
4 His sister .... parties.
5 His brother .... exercise.
6 His mother .... every day.
7 His father .... late.
8 His brother .... with money.
9 His sister .... for money.
10 His grandmother .... properly.

We **don't** use **object + infinitive** after *say* or *suggest*.

I told her to phone me. (BUT NOT ~~I said her to phone me.~~)
I suggested that he should take the train. OR *I suggested taking the train.*
   (BUT NOT ~~I suggested him to take the train.~~)

→ For other verbs with **object + infinitive**, see page 122.

test yourself   indirect speech

1 Correct (✓) or not (✗)?

1 Shakespeare told his wife that you don't understand my work. ...

2 I don't know what does this word mean. ...

3 Please tell me what you want. ...

4 I asked what the time was. ...

5 Mary asked me where Bill lived? ...

2 Read the letter and then complete the text.

> Dear all,
>
>   Sorry I haven't written for a few weeks. I've been too busy.
> I'm having a great time; I'm going to parties every night. I'm
> doing a bit of work too. We had an exam last week. I hope I'll
> get good marks.
>   I only have one shirt – I've lost the others. Mum, can you buy
> me six more? And I can't find my raincoat. Is it at home?
>   My room here isn't very nice – I'll have to look for a better one.
> And the food here in college isn't much good, so I'm living on
> hamburgers. I've spent nearly all my money. Dad, can you
> send some more?
>   Can you give me Aunt Ellen's address? And I haven't heard
> from Sarah. Where is she living? And does John want to come
> and spend two or three days down here with me?
>   That's all for now. Love to everybody.
>
>   Joe

In his letter Joe ▶ *said* .... he was sorry that he ▶ *hadn't written* .... for a few weeks. It was because he 1 .... too busy. He 2 .... his family that he 3 .... a great time, but he 4 .... some work too. He said he 5 .... an exam 6 .... week ...., and he hoped he 7 .... get good marks.

   Joe 8 .... that he only 9 .... one shirt, because he 10 .... the others. He asked his mother 11 .... him six more. And he asked 12 .... his raincoat 13 .... at home.

   His room 14 .... not very nice, he said, so he 15 .... have to look for a better one. And because of the bad college food he 16 .... on hamburgers.

   He said he 17 .... nearly all his money, and asked his father 18 .... him some more.

   Joe also asked his family 19 .... him his Aunt Ellen's address. And he 20 .... them that he 21 .... from Sarah, and asked 22 .... she 23 ....

   At the end of the letter, Joe asked 24 .... John 25 .... to go and spend a few days with him.

SECTION 20 prepositions

grammar summary

above	across	against	along	at	behind	between	by	down	during
for	from	in	in front of	into	near	off	on	opposite	out of	over
past	round	through	to	under	until/till	up			

Some prepositions are difficult, because they have more than one meaning. (A preposition in one language often has several different translations into another language.)

In this section, we explain and practise the most important prepositions: those that we use to talk about **time**, **place** and **movement**.

→ For *since* and *for*, see page 61.
→ For the **place** of prepositions in **questions**, see page 137; in **passives**, see page 101; with **relative pronouns**, see page 242.
→ For *-ing* **forms** after prepositions, see page 132.
→ For **verbs** followed by prepositions, see page 136.
→ For lists of **common expressions** with prepositions, see pages 278–279.

pre-test: which units do you need?

Try this small test. It will help you to decide which units you need. The answers are on page 284.

1 Correct (✓) or not (✗)?

▶ I'll see you on Tuesday afternoon. ✓..
1 What are you doing on next Thursday? ...
2 Are you going away at Christmas? ...
3 She was born at April 6, 1998. ...
4 We played tennis from 2.00 till 6.00. ...
5 Can you clean this jacket until Saturday? ...
6 What time does the lesson start? ...
7 Can I speak to you during a few minutes? ...
8 She felt ill during the journey. ...
9 There was a notice in the door that said 'CLOSED'. ...
10 I'll wait for you at the cinema. ...
11 When did you arrive to the station? ...
12 There's a supermarket in front of our house. ...
13 I walked across the street and into the station. ...
14 A bird flew through my window. ...

BOOK TITLES

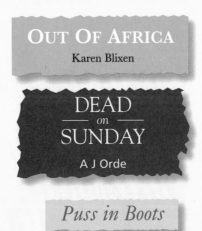

at, *in* and *on* (time)

We use *at* with **clock times**.

I'll see you at 4.15.   *The plane leaves at six.*   *Call me at lunchtime.*

But we say **What time...?**, NOT USUALLY *At what time ...?*

What time *is the film?*

We use *on* with **days, dates** and expressions like **Monday morning** and **Friday afternoon**.

I'll be at home on Tuesday.   *We get up late on Sundays.*
The meeting's on June 23rd.   *I'm always sleepy on Monday mornings.*
I had to work on Christmas Day.

1 Put in *at* or *on*.

1 What are you doing .... Saturday?
2 Can you wake me .... 6.30?
3 The classes start .... September 8th.
4 I'll be at work late .... Tuesday morning.
5 I have my guitar lessons .... 10.00 .... Wednesdays.
6 She got married .... Easter Monday.
7 My new job starts .... April 17th.
8 Can we meet .... lunchtime .... Tuesday?

We say *in the morning, in the afternoon, in the evening*, but *at night*.

She was born at 6.16 in the morning.   *I work best in the evening.*
This street is very quiet at night.

We use *in* with **weeks, seasons, months, years** and **centuries**.

We're going to Denmark in the first week of May.
I always get unhappy in the winter.   *My birthday's in March.*
Shakespeare died in 1616.
There were terrible wars in the 17th century.

William
Shakespeare
1564 – 1616

We say *at the weekend, at Christmas, at Easter*.

What are you doing at the weekend?   *Did you go away at Christmas?*

2 Put in *in, at* or *on*.

1 We all went to Wales .... the weekend.
2 I usually go skiing .... February.
3 She finished school .... 1996.
4 My mother usually comes to stay .... Christmas.
5 I don't like driving .... night.
6 Our garden looks wonderful .... the spring.
7 I usually stop work .... 5.00 .... the afternoon.
8 I'll finish university .... June.
9 I last saw her .... 1998.
10 Carola was born .... 8.25 .... the evening ....
    Thursday 17th April 2000.
11 I'm never hungry early .... the morning.
12 It gets very hot here .... the summer.

We **don't** use **prepositions** before common expressions with *this, next, last* and *every*.

*What are you doing **this afternoon**?*   *Goodbye. See you **next week**.*
*Bill was here **last Tuesday**.*   *We go on holiday to the same place **every year**.*

3 **Today is Wednesday March 15th 2002. Rewrite the sentences using *this, next, last* and *every*.**

▶ I met her *in 2001*. ...*I met her last year*...
1 I'll see you *on March 22nd*. ....
2 It rained non-stop *from March 6th to March 12th*. ....
3 Business was bad *in February 2002*. ....
4 Shall we go out *on March 15th in the evening*? ....
5 We're going to America *in April 2002*. ....
6 Ann had a car crash *on March 8th*. ....
7 I'm going to change my job *in 2003*. ....
8 My holiday is in August *2002, 2003, 2004, 2005, 2006* etc. ....
9 I've spent too much money already *in March*. ....
10 The new school will be open *in March 2003*. ....

To say **how long** it takes to **finish** something, we use *in*.

*They built our house **in three months**.*   *Your soup will be ready **in ten minutes**.*

4 **My Australian friend Sheila is saving money because she wants to buy a sports car. She is saving $1 a day, starting tomorrow.**

▶ When will she have $2 in her savings account? ...*In two days*.....................
1 When will she have $5? ....
2 When will she have $7? In a ....
3 When will she have $14? ....
4 When will she have $30? ....
5 When will she have $365? ....
6 The car costs $36,500. When will she have it? ....

GRAMMAR AND VOCABULARY: dates

WE WRITE	WE SAY
1999	nineteen ninety-nine
17(th) March 2002	the seventeenth of March, two thousand and two
OR March 17(th) 2002	March the seventeenth, two thousand and two
OR 17.3.(20)02	
OR 17/3/(20)02	
American English: 3.17.2002	March (the) seventeenth, two thousand (and) two

5 **Say these dates:**

  1 *21.3.1999*   2 *14 February 1960*   3 *July 28 1846*   4 *6/5/03*   5 *May 9 1984*

from ... to, until and *by*

We use *until* or *till* (informal) to say when an action or situation **ends**.
*We played football **until** 5 o'clock.*   *I'll be in London **till** Thursday.*

1 Complete the sentences with *until* or *till* and expressions from the box.

the age of 14   July   lunchtime   six o'clock in the morning ✓   Saturday   the end

▶ It was a great party. We danced *until six o'clock in the morning.*...
1 I'm going to have a sandwich now. I can't wait ....
2 Granny's coming on Monday for a few days. She's going to stay ....
3 When I was young, you had to go to school ....
4 I didn't like the film, so I didn't stay ....
5 I'm doing a three-month computer course; it goes on ....

We can give the **beginning and end** of an action or situation with *from ... to/until/till*.
*I worked **from** 8.00 **to** 6.00 yesterday.*   *We'll be away **from** July 16 **until/till** August 4.*

2 Make sentences about John's Sunday morning with *to, till* or *until*.
▶ read paper / 7.30 / 8.00   *He read the paper from 7.30 to 8.00.*...
                                  OR He read the paper from 7.30 until/till 8.00.................................
1 washed car / 8.00 / 9.00   ....
2 talked to woman next door / 9.00 / 9.15   ....
3 played tennis / 10.00 / 11.00   ....
4 talked to friends / 11.00 / 11.30   ....
5 went for a walk / 11.30 / 12.45   ....

3 Write two sentences with *from ... to/till/until* about things you did yesterday.
1 ....
2 ....

We use *by* (= '*not later than*') to say that something happens at or before a certain moment.

UNTIL
You can keep the car until Sunday.

BY
You really must bring it back by 12.00 on Sunday.

4 Put in *by* or *until*.
1 This book must go back to the library .... Tuesday.
2 The film goes on .... 9.30.
3 Can you finish painting the room .... Friday?
4 If I give you this coat to clean, can you do it .... tomorrow?
5 I must find some money .... the end of the week.
6 Can you wait for my answer .... tonight?

for, during and *while*

1 Put in *for* or *during*.

1 I lived in Mexico .... six years.
2 I got a headache .... the examination.
3 We visited Kyoto .... our holiday in Japan.
4 The electricity went off .... two hours .... the afternoon.
5 Alex and his wife met .... the war.
6 Could I talk to you .... a few minutes?
7 I usually get a lot of phone calls .... the morning.
8 She and her boyfriend have been together .... a long time.

2 Change the expressions.

▶ during the meal (*I / eat*)   .while I was eating.............................
▶ while I was travelling (*journey*)   .during the journey.............................
1 during the game (*they / play*)   ....
2 while we were listening (*lesson*)   ....
3 while they were fighting (*war*)   ....
4 during her lesson (*she / teach*)   ....
5 during his speech (*he / speak*)   ....
6 during the conversation (*they / talk*)   ....
7 while she was in hospital (*illness*)   ....
8 during the snowstorm (*it / snow*)   ....

3 GRAMMAR AND VOCABULARY: useful expressions with *for*
Look at the expressions in the box, and choose suitable ones to complete the sentences.
Different answers are possible.

for a moment   for a minute or two   for a few minutes   for an hour or so (= 'about an hour')
for a couple of hours   for a long time   for ages   for years and years   for ever   for life

1 They waited ...., but the bus didn't come.
2 I will love you ....
3 Could I talk to you ....?
4 I played tennis .... and then went home.
5 I went to sleep .... during the opera.
6 She usually stops work at 11 o'clock .... and has a cup of coffee.
7 I often watch TV .... before I go to bed.
8 They put him in prison ....

in and *on* (place)

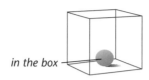

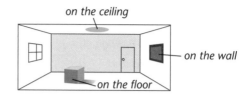

in the box

on the ceiling

on the wall

on the floor

We use *in* with 3-dimensional spaces like boxes, rooms, towns or countries.
We use *on* with 2-dimensional surfaces like floors, tables, walls or ceilings.

'Where's Joe?' 'In the kitchen.'   There's nothing *in the fridge*.   Ann's *in Poland*.
Why are all those papers on the floor?   *The church has wonderful paintings on the ceiling.*
She had photos of all her family on the wall.

People are *in* clothes. **Clothes and jewellery** (ear-rings etc) are *on* people.

Who is the man in the grey suit?   *That sweater looks good on you.*   *She had a ring on every finger.*

---

1 Put in *in* or *on*.

1 .... a bath   2 .... a roof   3 .... a tree   4 .... a table   5 .... a cup

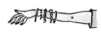

6 .... her arm   7 .... a plate   8 .... your head   9 .... your head   10 .... a door

---

We say *in a book*, *in the newspaper*, *in a story* (BUT *on a page*); *in a street*.

Is there anything interesting in the paper?   *Her photo is on page 4.*   *They live in Park Street.*

---

2 Put in words from the boxes with *in* or *on*.

children's stories ✓   her first finger   my diary   the office   the roof of the car   the cupboard

▶ *In children's stories* ...., animals can talk.

1 'Are you free next Tuesday?' 'Just a minute. I'll look ....'

2 Is Sandra .... today?

3 She had a wonderful diamond ring ....

4 'Where's the salt?' ....

5 The cat likes to sleep ....

a little village   his T-shirt   my pocket   a piece of paper   the wall   your car

6 Don't leave your keys .... when you get out.

7 .... it said 'Aberdeen University Football Club'.

8 She had pictures of pop singers .... in her room.

9 They live .... near Belfast.

10 I wrote her address .... and put it

....

Note that we say *in a car* BUT *on a bus/train/plane/ship*.

Granny arrived in a taxi, as usual.   *I'm leaving on the 4.15 train.*

at (place)

*I'll meet you **at** the cinema.*

OK

Operator	TE	GW 🚂
LONDON Paddington ⊖	1743	1803
Ealing Broadway ⊖	...	...
Slough	1800	1822
Maidenhead	...	...
Twyford	...	...
Reading . . . . *dep*	1820	1838
Tilehurst	...	...
Pangbourne	...	...
Goring & Streatley	...	...
Wallingford 🚌		
Cholsey	...	...
Didcot Parkway . . *arr*	1835	1853

*The train stops
at Slough, Reading
and Didcot.*

We often use *at* to show where **something happens** – for example, with **meeting places** or **points on a journey**.

*I'll see you this evening **at Sarah's house**.   You have to change planes **at Karachi**.
I saw Ann waiting **at the bus stop**.   Turn left **at the next corner**.*

We often use *at* with words for **things that people do**, or the **places where they do them**.

at a football match   at breakfast, lunch etc   *at a restaurant   at work   at the office
at the theatre   at the cinema   at the station   at a party   at (the) college/university*

---

1 Put in words from the box with *at*.

a Chinese restaurant   a theatre   breakfast   the cinema
work   the party   the station   the traffic lights ✓

▶ Paul crashed his car because he didn't stop .at the traffic lights.....................................
1 Are there any good films .... this week?
2 Her train was terribly late – I spent hours waiting ....
3 Will you be .... at Mike's house on Saturday?
4 We had a really good meal .... in Park Street last night.
5 I saw my first Shakespeare play .... in a small town in Ireland.
6 The boss doesn't let us take personal phone calls ....
7 Helen never says anything .... because she's still asleep.

We often use *at* with *the top, the bottom, the side, the beginning* and *the end*.

*My room's **at the top** of the house.   Begin **at the beginning**.*

---

2 Put in *at the top, at the bottom* etc.

1 Their house is down .... of the hill.
2 I never have any money .... of the month.
3 I stopped for a minute .... of the stairs to have a rest.
4 The best fruit is always .... of the tree, where you can't get it.
5 Maria wasn't there .... of the lesson; she came in late.

Sometimes *in* and *at* are **both possible**. We prefer *at* when we are thinking about **the activity** – what we do in the place – and *in* when we think about the place itself.

*We **had lunch at** the station restaurant. It was very hot in the big dining room.*

---

other prepositions of place

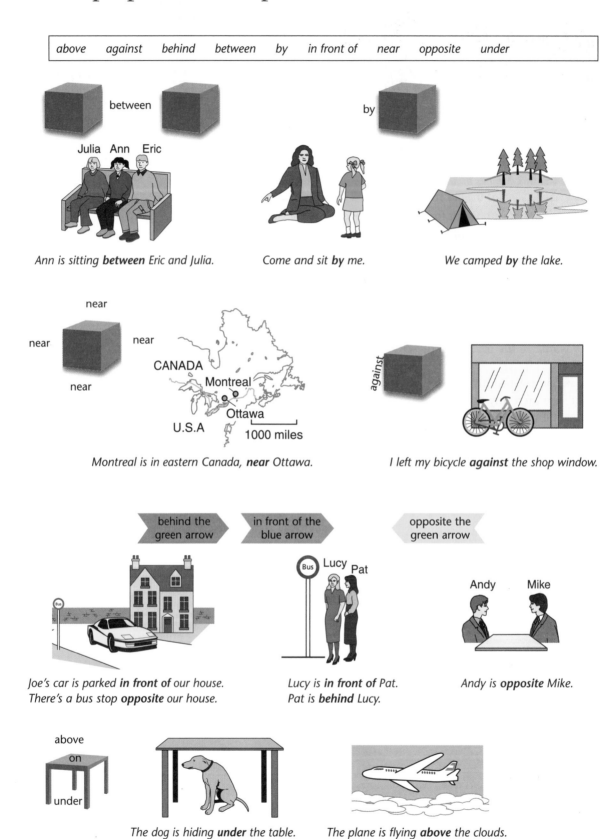

| above | against | behind | between | by | in front of | near | opposite | under |

between

by

Julia Ann Eric

*Ann is sitting **between** Eric and Julia.*

*Come and sit **by** me.*

*We camped **by** the lake.*

near
near
near
near

CANADA
Montreal
Ottawa
U.S.A
1000 miles

against

*Montreal is in eastern Canada, **near** Ottawa.*

*I left my bicycle **against** the shop window.*

behind the
green arrow

in front of the
blue arrow

opposite the
green arrow

Bus Lucy Pat

Andy   Mike

*Joe's car is parked **in front of** our house.*
*There's a bus stop **opposite** our house.*

*Lucy is **in front of** Pat.*
*Pat is **behind** Lucy.*

*Andy is **opposite** Mike.*

above
on
under

*The dog is hiding **under** the table.*

*The plane is flying **above** the clouds.*

1 Choose the correct prepositions.

▶ I usually sit ......<u>by</u>.......... a window in class, so I can look out if I get bored. (*behind, by, in front of*)

1 There was a big bird flying high up .... the trees. (*above, against, opposite*)

2 They live in a beautiful old house .... a river. (*above, by, under*)

3 There's a big clock .... the door of the station. (*above, against, between*)

4 I sat down .... Mary and looked into her eyes. (*above, behind, by*)

5 You can park your car .... the house. (*against, behind, between*)

6 I'll meet you at the station .... the clock. (*against, between, under*)

7 The door wouldn't stay shut, so I put a chair .... it. (*above, against, near*)

2 Put in the correct prepositions.

1 She put the money at the bottom of her suitcase, ... her clothes.

2 Our house is .... a bank and a supermarket, and just .... the police station.

3 Please don't put your bicycle .... our wall.

4 Sorry we're late – we were driving .... a slow bus all the way.

5 I work in a small town .... Birmingham.

6 In the theatre I couldn't see anything because there was a very tall man .... me.

7 We usually have lunch in a little café .... the school, about five minutes' walk away.

3 Look at the picture and put in the prepositions.

▶ ...<u>above</u>...................... the travel agent's.   5 .... the two women.

1 .... the supermarket.   6 .... the window.

2 .... the banks.   7 .... the car.

3 .... the National Bank.   8 .... the travel agent's.

4 .... the travel agent's.   9 .... the man.

prepositions of movement

across	*along*	*down*	*into*	*off*	*over*
out of	*past*	*round*	*through*	*under*	*up*

1 **Write the expressions under the correct photos. Use a dictionary if necessary.**

across the river   along the yellow line   down the mountain   into the water
off the bike   over the fence   out of the shop   past the café
round the corner   through the gate   under the bridge   up the steps

1 ....

2 ....

3 ....

4 ....

5 ....

6 ....

7 ....

8 ....

9 ....

10 ....

11 ....

12 ....

2 Cross out the words that are wrong.

▶ across *the road /* ~~*the church*~~

1 along *the corner / the road*
2 up *the mountain / the table*
3 down *the church / the stairs*
4 over *the corner / the wall*
5 into *the bank / the bridge*
6 round *the corner / the road*

7 through *the door / the railway line*
8 off *the police station / the table*
9 out of *the church / the stairs*
10 under *the bridge / the people*
11 past *the floor / the bank*
12 across *the river / the wall*

3 Choose the correct prepositions and put them in the correct places.

▶ I went ..*up*.............. the stairs and ..*along*......... the passage. (*along, into, out of, up*)

1 Mrs Andrews got .... the taxi and ran .... Oxford Street. (*across, round, out of, over*)

2 Alice walked .... the steps to the river and .... the bridge. (*along, down, through, over*)

3 He walked slowly .... the road for a few minutes, then he stopped and went .... a small door .... a garden. (*across, along, into, through*)

4 Mary went .... the stairs and .... her office, took a letter .... the table and started to read it. (*into, off, out of, over, up*)

5 Go .... the supermarket, ... the railway bridge, ... the first corner, and the police station is on your right. (*along, down, past, round, under*)

We use **to** for **movement**, and *at* or *in* for **position** – where somebody/something is (see pages 258–259).

*I went **to** the bus stop to meet Helen.   I waited **at** the bus stop for twenty minutes.*

We can use *from* ... before *to* ...

*He took five days to cycle **from** London **to** Edinburgh.*

We **get to** a place, but we **arrive at** a place, or **arrive in** a big place (NOT ~~*arrive to*~~).

*It took three hours to **get to** Cambridge.   I was tired when I **arrived at** the station.*
*We **arrived in** London very early in the morning.*

---

4 Put in *from, to, at* or *in*.

1 Let's go .... the country this weekend.
2 She spends hours .... the bathroom.
3 Shall we drive .... Scotland or go by train?
4 We flew directly .... Berlin .... Tokyo.
5 What time do we arrive .... Paris?
6 After six days' walking, they got .... a river.
7 I saw Annie standing .... the bus stop.
8 When we arrived .... her house she had already left.

Note that we get *into* and *out of cars* BUT *on(to)* and *off buses/trains/planes/ships*.

test yourself   prepositions

1 Put in *in, at, on* or nothing (–).

▶ I'll be here again ..–.. this afternoon.
1 I saw her ...... Tuesday.
2 We usually play golf ...... the weekend.
3 My birthday is ...... January.
4 The meeting is ...... June 18th.

5 Do you go away ...... Christmas?
6 Let's go to Scotland ...... next weekend.
7 We always get up late ...... Sunday morning.
8 I can't work ...... night.
9 The lesson starts ...... 9.45.

2 Put in *in, at, to* or *on*.

▶ We live *in*.. a small town near Edinburgh.
1 'How do you know that?' 'I read it ......
   the newspaper.'
2 The train stopped ...... every station.
3 I'll meet you ...... the bus stop outside
   the station.
4 Please don't put your feet ...... the table.
5 What's that black mark ...... the ceiling?
6 You will find the information ...... page 16.

7 I thought she was going to walk from the
   station, but she arrived ...... a taxi.
8 Please write your name ...... the bottom of the
   paper.
9 She has a ring ...... the third finger of her
   left hand.
10 What time does this bus get ...... London?
11 She posted the letter in April; it arrived ......
   my house in June.

3 Put in *in, from, by* or *until*.

1 I'm going to stay in this job .... next year.
2 I have classes tomorrow .... 9.30 .... 4.00.
3 You can borrow my bicycle, but I must have it back .... Friday.
4 Do you think you can learn English .... two months?
5 Can you clean these trousers .... tomorrow afternoon?
6 The train leaves .... ten minutes.

4 Put in *for, during* or *while*.

1 We travelled round America .... two months last year.
2 I couldn't sleep .... the night, so I got up and read a book.
3 Somebody got into the house and stole the TV .... we were asleep.
4 I'd like to see you .... a few minutes.
5 I went to sleep .... the lesson.

5 Put in the correct prepositions. (More than one answer may be possible.)

▶ He sat ..*by/near*............. the window, and looked out from time to time.
1 C comes .... B and D in the alphabet.
2 I couldn't see the plane, because it was high .... the clouds.
3 I had to wait a long time at the post office, because the woman .... me wanted a lot
   of different things.
4 There's a garage on the other side of the street just .... our house.
5 Please don't put bicycles .... the shop window.
6 He turned round and walked away .... the trees.
7 We cycled .... a little road .... the river for about five kilometres.
8 Ann came .... the church and walked slowly .... the square.
9 'Where's the swimming pool?' 'Drive .... the police station, ...
   the railway bridge and .... the corner, and you'll see it on your left.'

▣ More difficult questions

SECTION 21 spoken grammar

grammar summary

In **spoken English**, we often **leave words out** if the meaning is clear. This often happens **after auxiliary verbs**.
*She said she would phone, but she **didn't**. (= '... she didn't phone.')*
*I'll finish the work as soon as I **can**. (= '... as soon as I can finish the work.')*

There are several common kinds of **short spoken sentence** made with **subject + auxiliary verb**:

- **question tags:** *You're from Scotland, **aren't you?***
- **short answers:** *'Did you see Patrick?' 'No, I **didn't**.'*
- **reply questions:** *'I've got a headache.' '**Have you?** I am sorry.'*
- **so do I, nor can I** etc: *'I was really cold on that bus.' '**So was I**.'*

We also often **leave out infinitives** (and other words) **after to**.
*I've never seen the Taj Mahal, but I'd like **to**. (= '... I'd like to see the Taj Mahal.')*

And we may **leave out small words** (pronouns, articles, auxiliary verbs) **at the beginning of sentences.**
*Don't know. (= '**I** don't know.')*   *Train's late. (= '**The** train's late.')*
*Been waiting long? (= '**Have you** been waiting long?')*

pre-test: which units do you need?

Try this small test. It will help you to decide which units you need. The answers are on page 284.

1 Correct (✓) or not (✗)?

1 Are you English, are you? ...
2 Eric passed his exam, didn't he? ...
3 There weren't enough chairs, were there? ...
4 'I didn't like the party much.' 'Didn't you?' ...
5 'Can you swim?' 'Yes, I do.' ...
6 'My father plays a lot of tennis.' 'So mine does.' ...
7 The President didn't answer my letter, and neither did the Foreign Minister. ...
8 I haven't seen many films this year, but my sister has seen. ...
9 'Can you walk a bit faster?' 'I'm trying to.' ...
10 Lost your key? ...

'Forgotten your key again, George?'

'It's all coming back to me now.
We were married once, weren't we?'

question tags *This music isn't very good, is it?*

Question tags are short questions that can follow sentences, especially in **spoken** English.
We make question tags with **auxiliary verb** (*have, be, can* etc) + **pronoun** (*I, you* etc).
We use question tags to **ask if something is true**, or to **ask** people **to agree** with us.

You haven't got my keys, **have you?**   *Ann will be here tomorrow,* **won't she?**
This music isn't very good, **is it?**   *That child can run fast,* **can't he?**

Question tags are usually **negative** (■) after **affirmative** (✚) sentences, and **not negative** after **negative** sentences. We **don't** put question tags **after questions**.

It is warm, isn't it?   *It isn't cold, is it?* (BUT NOT *Is it cold, isn't it?*)

Negative tags are usually **contracted** (see page 277) – for example **isn't it?** (NOT USUALLY *is it not?*)
The negative tag for *I am* is **aren't I?** (see page 277)

I'm late, aren't I?

---

① **Question tag or nothing (–)? Circle the correct form.**

▶ I'm late, *am I?* / (*aren't I?*) / – ?
▶ You can't swim, (*can you?*) / *can't you?* / – ?
▶ Has Ann phoned *has she?* / *hasn't she?* / (– ?)

1 You'll be here tomorrow,
   will you? / *won't you?* / – ?
2 The postman hasn't come,
   has he? / *hasn't he?* / – ?

3 Are you ready *are you?* / *aren't you?* / – ?
4 It's dark in here, *is it?* / *isn't it?* / – ?
5 He can't speak Greek, *can he?* / *can't he?* / – ?
6 The train's late, *is it?* / *isn't it?* / – ?
7 The food wasn't bad, *was it?* / *wasn't it?* / – ?
8 Have you done it *have you?* / *haven't you?* / – ?

If the sentence has an **auxiliary verb** or *be*, we use this in the question tag.

You would like coffee, wouldn't you?   *I'm not talking too fast, am I?*
Ann doesn't eat meat, does she?   *You aren't angry with me, are you?*

If there is **no auxiliary verb**, we use *do/does/did* in the tag.

They went to Spain, didn't they?   *The lesson starts at 6.00, doesn't it?*

---

② **Here are some sentences from real conversations. Put in the question tags.**

▶ You're playing football tomorrow, *aren't you?*
1 That's the answer, ...
2 We're seeing Rebecca again tomorrow, ...
3 She's a lovely baby, ...
4 You'll be OK, ..., Roger?
5 Your brother can tell us that, ...
6 Margaret likes brown bread, ...
7 This house gets hot in summer, ...

---

③ **Here are some negative sentences. Put in the question tags.**

▶ They weren't at home, *were they?*
1 But he's not at school now, ...
2 You can't remember anything, ...
3 They don't use much electricity, ...
4 She doesn't look happy, ...
5 Those flowers don't need much water, ...

4 **Change these questions into statements with question tags.**

▶ Do you work at Smith's? *You work at Smith's, don't you?* ....

1 Have they lived in France? They've ....

2 Did they all go home early? ....

3 Did it rain all last week? ....

4 Does her brother write for the newspapers? ....

5 Do I need a visa? ....

6 Would you like a holiday? ....

7 Was the train late? ....

8 Did Sarah forget your birthday? ....

We can use *there* as a **subject** in question tags.

There's a letter for me, **isn't there?**   *There weren't any problems,* **were there?**

---

5 **Put in the question tags.**

1 There was a phone call for me, ...

2 There are six more lessons this year, ...

3 There's a meeting this afternoon, ...

4 There hasn't been any snow this year, ...

5 There weren't many people at the party, ...

If a tag asks a real question, we say it with a rising intonation: the music of the voice goes ^{up}.

If a tag just asks for agreement, we use a falling intonation: the voice goes _{down}.

We're meeting in Oxford, _{aren't} ^{we}?   *Nice day,* ^{isn't} _{it}?

---

6 **Try to pronounce these tags.**

1 The lesson begins at twelve, doesn't it?

2 Your sister's gone to America, hasn't she?

3 Bill's a good singer, isn't he?

4 It's cold, isn't it?

5 You're from Scotland, aren't you?

6 She looks good in red, doesn't she?

---

7 GRAMMAR AND VOCABULARY: **seven things from the office**
What would you ask if you were not sure of the names of the things in the pictures?

▶ *It's a stapler, isn't it?* ....   4 ....

1 They're ....   5 ....

2 ....   6 ....

3 ....

▶ stapler   1 paper clips   2 diary   3 hole-punch   4 address book   5 rulers   6 calculators

short answers   *Yes, I have.   No, they didn't.*

To answer just '*Yes*' or '*No*' is **not** always very **polite**.
We often prefer answers with **pronoun** (*I, you* etc) + auxiliary verb (*be, have, can* etc).
The auxiliary verb in the **answer** is usually **the same** as the one in the **question**.

'*Are you coming?*' '*Yes, I am.*'   '*Have you phoned home?*' '*Yes, I have.*'
'*Can Ellie speak Spanish?*' '*No, she can't.*'   '*Did you watch the match?*' '*No, I didn't.*'

Negative (–) short answers are usually **contracted** (see page 277): *can't, didn't* etc.
Affirmative (+) short answers are **not contracted**: we don't say ~~Yes, I'm~~ or ~~Yes, she's~~, for example.

1 Write short answers to these questions.

▶ 'Do you like jazz?' 'Yes, *I do.*'
▶ 'Are they coming home?' 'No, *they aren't.*'
1 'Is it raining?' 'No, ...'
2 'Has Joe phoned?' 'No, ...'
3 'Do the children understand?'
  'Yes, ...'
4 'Can I go now?'
  'No, ...'
5 'Does your brother like sport?'
  'No, ...'
6 'Do you want tickets?' 'Yes, ...'
7 'Would your mother like coffee?'
  'No, ...'
8 'Was the film interesting?'
  'No, ...'
9 'Are you ready?' 'No, ...'

2 Give your own personal short answers to these questions.

▶ 'Do you like coffee?' *'Yes, I do.' / 'No, I don't.'*
1 'Are you thinking in English now?' ....
2 'Do you live in a town?' ....
3 'Do you speak French?' ....
4 'Is it raining now?' ....
5 'Is your English getting better?' ....
6 'Have you been to New York?' ....
7 'Did you watch TV yesterday?' ....
8 'Can you swim?' ....

We can use short answers to **agree** or **disagree** with things that people say.

'*It's hot today.*' '*Yes, it is.*'   '*You didn't buy bread.*' '*Yes, I did.*'   '*The train's late.*' '*No, it isn't.*'

If there is **no auxiliary verb**, we use *do/does/did* in the short answer.

'*Her hair looks nice.*' '*Yes, it does.*'

3 Write short answers to agree or disagree.

1 'You're early.' 'No, ...'
2 'It's cold.' 'Yes, ...'
3 'She sings really well.' 'Yes, ...'
4 'The lesson starts at 5.00.' 'No, ...'
5 'Bill didn't phone.' 'Yes, ...'

4 GRAMMAR AND VOCABULARY: things that people can do
Answer with '*Yes, I can*' or '*No, I can't*'.

1 Can you knit? ....
2 Can you cook? ....
3 Can you skate? ....
4 Can you repair cars? ....
5 Can you dive? ....
6 Can you draw? ....
7 Can you shoot? ....
8 Can you ride a horse? ....

knit   cook   skate   repair cars   dive   draw   shoot   ride a horse

reply questions *Oh, yes? Did they really?*

In conversation, we often ask **short questions** (auxiliary verb + pronoun) **to show interest**.

'I've just had a letter from Eric.' 'Have you?' 'Yes. He says he's coming back ...'

These **'reply questions'** are not really questions: they mean *'Oh, yes? That's interesting.'*
Some more examples:

'John's getting married.' 'Is he really? Who to?'
'Ann and Peter had a lovely time in Greece.' 'Did they?' 'Yes. They went ...'

We answer **negative** sentences with **negative** reply questions.

'I can't see very well with these glasses.' 'Can't you? Maybe you should get new ones.'

1 Put the beginnings and ends together, and put in reply questions.

1 'Oliver didn't eat much.'	A 'Didn't he?.......... Perhaps he's ill.' *1*
2 'I don't like this bread at all.'	B '.......................... I hope they're having a good time.' ...
3 'The Smiths are in America.'	C '.......................... I'll get a different kind next time.' ...'
4 'My French is getting very bad.'	D '.......................... When's he going to bring it back?' ...
5 'John's taken the car.'	E '.......................... I'll have a look at them.' ...
6 'I can't understand these papers.'	F '.......................... You need to go to France for a few weeks.' ...

2 GRAMMAR AND VOCABULARY: showing our feelings
Complete the sentences with reply questions and expressions from the box. Use a dictionary if necessary. Different answers are possible.

Congratulations.	Good luck.	I am sorry.	I don't believe it. ✓
Say 'hello' to him/her for me.		That's interesting.	That's terrible.
That's a surprise.	What a nuisance.	What a pity.	

▶ 'The Swiss have declared war on America.' *'Have they? I don't believe it.'* ....
1 'I've just passed my exams.' ....
2 'I'm seeing Mary next week.' ....
3 'My job interview is tomorrow.' ....
4 'Some trees can live for thousands of years.' ....
5 'John didn't get into university.' ....
6 'My computer has crashed again.' ....
7 'I don't feel well.' ....
8 'Andy and Paula are getting married.' ....
9 'I haven't got enough money to buy food.' ....

revision of spoken question and answer structures

QUESTION TAGS	SHORT ANSWERS	REPLY QUESTIONS
It is ..., **isn't it?**	'Are you ...?' **'No, I'm not.'**	'I'm ...' **'Are you?'**
I am ..., **aren't I?**	'Has she ...?' **'Yes, she has.'**	'He's ...' **'Has he?'**
She has ..., **hasn't she?**	'Do they ...?' **'Yes, they do.'**	'They like ...' **'Do they?'**
They like ..., **don't they?**	'Are we ...?' **'No, we aren't.'**	'We're ...' **'Are we?'**
We aren't ..., **are we?**	'He wasn't ...' **'No, he wasn't.'**	'She wasn't ...' **'Wasn't she?'**
He didn't ..., **did he?**	'She didn't ...' **'Yes, she did.'**	'He didn't ...' **'Didn't he?'**

1 Circle the best answer.

▶ Ann can't sing at all, (can she?) / she can't.

1 'I'm worried about Peter.' *'You are?'* / *'Are you?'* / *'Aren't you?'*

2 *'Joe didn't phone yesterday.'* / *'Joe phoned yesterday.'* 'Didn't he?'

3 *'I'm feeling ill.'* / *'I'm not feeling well.'* 'Are you?'

4 *'Does John need help?'* / *'John needs help.'* 'Does he?'

5 *Do you remember David,* / *You don't remember David,* do you?

6 'I've got a headache.' *'You haven't.'* / *'You have.'* / *'Have you?'*

7 They can stay with us, *they can't?* / *can't they?* / *can they?*

2 Read the conversation, and put in question tags (QT), short answers (SA) or reply questions (RQ).

QT	'Hello, Carol. Lovely day, ▶ ~~isn't it?~~...............'
SA	'▶ ...~~Yes, it is.~~........... How are you?'
	'Well, I've got a problem.'
RQ	'▶ ...~~Have you?~~......... What's the matter?'
QT	'You remember my brother's boy Bill, 1 ....'
SA; QT	'2 .... He went to Australia, 3 ....'
SA	'No, 4 .... He went to Canada. Anyway, he's coming back to England.'
RQ	'5 .... That's nice.'
	'Well, yes, but he wants to stay with me.'
RQ	'Oh, 6 .... Is that the problem?'
SA	'7 .... I'm not very happy about it.'
RQ; QT	'8 .... Why? You like Bill, 9 ....'
SA	'10 .... – very much.'
QT	'And you've got a lot of room in that big house, 11 ....'
SA	'12 .... But would you like to have a young man living in your house all the time?'
	'No, I suppose not.'
	'Well, I don't know what to do. I'm really very worried.'
RQ	'13 .... Would you like some advice?'
SA	'14 ....'
	'Tell him the truth. Say you like him a lot, but you don't want people in your house.'
QT	'I can't say that, 15 ....'
SA	'16 .... He'll understand. I'm sure of it.'
RQ	'17 .... I don't know. Anyway, I'll think about it.'

leaving out words   *Don't know if she has.*

We often use just **an auxiliary verb** **instead of repeating a longer expression**, if the meaning is clear. This happens in question tags, short answers and reply questions (see pages 266–269), and in other sentences too.

'Get up!' 'I am.' (= *'I am getting up.'*)   *Come round tomorrow evening, if you* **can**
I haven't seen that film, but my brother **has**. (NOT ... ~~but my brother has seen.~~)

We use *do/does/did* if there is no other auxiliary verb to repeat.

David said he knew the address, but he **didn't** *really.*

1 **Make these sentences more natural by crossing out unnecessary words.**

▶ You said it wasn't raining, but it is ~~raining~~.
1 He thinks I don't understand, but I do understand.
2 'You'd better eat something.' 'I have eaten something.'
3 Alice said she would lend me her car, but I don't think she will lend me her car.
4 Eric was sure he would pass his exam. I hope he has passed his exam.
5 'Will you write to me every day?' 'Of course I will write to you every day.'
6 I can't help you today, but I can help you tomorrow.

We often use *to* **instead of a longer expression**, if the meaning is clear.

'Would you like to stay with us next weekend?' 'I'd love **to**.' (= *'I'd love to stay with you.'*)
I don't play tennis, but I used **to**.   *'Are you going to Scotland this summer?' 'We hope* **to**.'

2 **Complete the sentences, using the words in the box with *to*.**

I'd like   It's starting   I'm trying ✓   I used   she didn't want   Sorry, I forgot   They hope

▶ 'Can't you go faster?' .*.'I'm trying to.'*...............
1 'Are Sue and Dave getting married this year?' ....
2 I asked her to dance, but ....
3 I've never learnt to ski, but ....
4 I don't speak German very well now, but ....
5 'Did you remember to phone Liz?' ....
6 'Is it raining?' ....

In conversation, people may **leave out 'small words'** (for example pronouns, articles, auxiliary verbs) **at the beginnings of sentences.**

Must go now.   Can't help you, sorry.   Don't know.   Car's not going well.
Seen Bill? (= *'Have you seen Bill?'*)   *Nobody here.* (= *'There's nobody here.'*)

3 **Write the complete sentences.**

1 Couldn't understand what he wanted from me. ....
....
2 Doesn't know what she's doing. ....
3 Bus is late again. ....
4 Speak French? ....
5 Haven't seen them. ....
6 Don't think so. ....

→ For sentences where we leave out *that*, see pages 241 and 246.

So am I.   Nor can Pat.

To say that A is/does the same as B, we can use *so* + auxiliary verb (*be, have, can,* etc) + subject (note the word order).

'I'm hungry.' 'So am I.' (NOT ~~'So I am.'~~)   *Sue's stopped her lessons, and so has Eric.*

If there is **no auxiliary verb** to repeat, we use *do/does/did*.

'My brother works in the theatre.' 'So does my cousin.'

1 Complete the sentences, using *so*.

▶ 'My job's boring.' (➕ *mine*) 'So is mine.'......................

▶ 'My room gets very cold at night.' (➕ *mine*) 'So does mine.'........................

1 'Ann is very interested in history.' (➕ *Alice*) ....

2 'My grandfather plays golf all day.' (➕ *my father*) ....

3 'I can swim under water.' (➕ *I*) ....

4 'Peter wants a bicycle for Christmas.' (➕ *Mary*) ....

5 'Joe has just got married.' (➕ *Eric*) ....

In **negative** sentences we use *neither* or *nor* + auxiliary verb + subject.

'I'm not working today.' 'Neither am I.'   *'Mary can't drive.' 'Nor can Pat.'*
Bill doesn't like the boss, and neither does Jan.

2 Complete the sentences, using *neither/nor*.

▶ Joe didn't play very well, and (➖ *the others*) nor did the others OR neither did the others...............

1 The soup wasn't very good, and (➖ *the meat*) ....

2 'Bill hasn't phoned yet.' (➖ *Annie*) ....

3 'This dictionary doesn't show pronunciation.' (➖ *this one*) ....

4 'I can't cook.' (➖ *I*) ....

5 His parents won't help him, and (➖ *his friends*) ....

We can use short sentences (subject + auxiliary verb) to say that A is not the same as B.

'I'm not going to school today.' 'I am.'   *Some people don't like modern art, but I do.*
'I like this music.' 'I don't.'   *The food was cheap, but the drinks weren't.*

3 Complete the sentences with expressions from the box.

| her second one | her sister | my car | my father ✓ |
| our dog | the back door | the green ones ✓ | the train |

▶ 'My father works too hard.' 'My father doesn't.'........................

▶ 'The red apples aren't very sweet.' 'The green ones are.'........................

1 'My car doesn't use a lot of petrol.' ....

2 'Mary has passed all her exams.' 'Yes, but ....

3 Most dogs can swim, but ....

4 'The bus takes a long time to get to London.' ....

5 The front door wasn't open, but ....

6 'Her first book didn't sell very well.' ....

4 Look at the table and write sentences.

	LIKES DANCING	HAS BEEN TO AMERICA	PLAYS TENNIS	CAN SKI	IS TALL	LAUGHS A LOT
ERIC	✓	✗	✓	✓	✗	✓
JULIE	✓	✓	✗	✗	✗	✓
PAUL	✗	✗	✗	✓	✗	✗
DAN	✓	✓	✓	✓	✓	✓
DENISE	✗	✓	✗	✗	✓	✗
RACHEL	✓	✓	✗	✗	✓	✓

▶ (Eric, Dan, dancing) ...*Eric likes dancing, and so does Dan.*...............

▶ (Julie, Rachel, ski) .....*Julie can't ski, and nor can Rachel.*.............

▶ (Julie, Denise, laugh) ...*Julie laughs a lot, but Denise doesn't.*.............

▶ (Eric, Julie, America) ...*Eric hasn't been to America, but Julie has.*..........

1 (Eric, Dan, tennis) ....

2 (Julie, Denise, tall) ....

3 (Denise, Paul, laugh) ....

4 (Dan, Rachel, ski) ....

5 (Julie, Denise, America) ....

6 (Eric, Paul, tall) ....

7 (Julie, Dan, tennis) ....

8 (Paul, Rachel, dancing) ....

5 Here are some facts about Mike and Katy. Are you the same as them, or different? Write your answers, using *So am I, Neither/Nor do I, I have, I can't*, etc.

▶ Katy has got blue eyes. ...*So have I.* OR *I haven't.*.....

▶ Mike doesn't like fish. .....*I do.* OR *Nor do I.*..............

1 Katy is interested in politics. ....

2 Mike has been to Texas. ....

3 Katy can sing. ....

4 Mike likes old music. ....

5 Katy speaks French. ....

6 Katy isn't very tall. ....

7 Mike hasn't got much hair. ....

8 Katy can't drink milk. ....

9 Mike doesn't like hot weather. ....

10 Mike doesn't understand computers. ....

We can also use *too* or *not either* to say that **A is/does the same as B.**

'I'm hungry.' '*I am too.*'   Lucy hasn't written, and **Carol hasn't either.**

In informal conversation we often say *Me too* instead of *So do I, I do too* etc.

'I've got a headache.' '*Me too.*' (NOT *~~I also.~~*)

test yourself   spoken grammar

1 **Put in the question tags.**

▶ It's a nice day, *isn't it?*......

1 You can play the piano, ...

2 Ann will be here tomorrow, ...

3 You haven't got the keys, ...

4 Peter likes fishing, ...

5 There wasn't much rain in the night, ...

2 **Change these questions into statements with question tags.**

▶ Do you live in Dublin? *You live in Dublin, don't you?* ....

1 Have they gone home? They've ....

2 Do we need tickets? ....

3 Would you like some more coffee? ....

4 Was Mike away yesterday? ....

3 **Write short answers.**

▶ 'Do you like swimming?' 'Yes, *I do.*......'

1 'Was Mary at home?' 'No, ...'

2 'Does Bill play cards?' 'No, ...'

3 'Would your sister like some tea?'
   'No, ...'

4 'The plane arrives at 6.45.' 'No, ...'

4 **Write reply questions.**

▶ 'I've just passed my exam.' '*Have you?*.......... Congratulations.'

1 'Mary's getting a new job.' '.................. I hope she likes it.'

2 'Joe and Pat moved to London in March.' '.................. I didn't know.'

3 'My father can speak four languages.' '.................. He must be very clever.'

4 'We were all ill after the club dinner.' '.................. That's terrible.'

5 'I won't be here next week.' '.................. Come and see us the week after.'

5 **Complete the sentences with *So am I, Nor/Neither do I,* etc.**

▶ Arthur has gone home, and (➕ *Jane*) *so has Jane*..................

1 Oliver can run very well and (➕ *Susan*) ....

2 The 3.15 train hasn't arrived yet, and (➖ *the 3.45*) ....

3 'I wasn't happy at school.' (➖ *I*) ....

4 Ken didn't come to the lesson, and (➖ *Sally*) ....

5 Peter likes travelling, and (➕ *his brother*) ....

6 **Make these sentences more natural by crossing out unnecessary words.**

▶ You said you weren't late, but you were ~~late.~~

1 She says I don't love her, but I do love her.

2 'You should phone Aunt Lucy.' 'I have phoned Aunt Lucy.'

3 Robert thought that he would get rich fast, but I don't think he will get rich fast.

4 'Help me.' 'I'm trying to help you.'

7 **Write the complete sentences.**

1 Car won't start. Don't know why. *The car won't start.* ....

2 'Seen my mother today?' 'Don't think so.'
   '..................' '..................'

3 Sorry, can't come in here. ....

appendix 1 common irregular verbs

(These are the most common irregular verbs. For a complete list, see a good dictionary.)

INFINITIVE	SIMPLE PAST	PAST PARTICIPLE	INFINITIVE	SIMPLE PAST	PAST PARTICIPLE
be	was/were	been	let	let	let
become	became	become	lie	lay	lain
begin	began	begun	lose	lost	lost
break	broke	broken	make	made	made
bring	brought	brought	mean	meant	meant
build	built	built	meet	met	met
buy	bought	bought	pay	paid	paid
catch	caught	caught	put	put	put
choose	chose	chosen	read /riːd/	read /red/	read /red/
come	came	come	ride	rode	ridden
cost	cost	cost	run	ran	run
cut	cut	cut	say	said	said
do	did	done	see	saw	seen
draw	drew	drawn	sell	sold	sold
dream	dreamt/dreamed	dreamt/dreamed	send	sent	sent
drink	drank	drunk	show	showed	shown
drive	drove	driven	shut	shut	shut
eat	ate	eaten	sing	sang	sung
fall	fell	fallen	sit	sat	sat
feel	felt	felt	sleep	slept	slept
fight	fought	fought	speak	spoke	spoken
find	found	found	spell	spelt	spelt
fly	flew	flown	spend	spent	spent
forget	forgot	forgotten	stand	stood	stood
get	got	got	steal	stole	stolen
give	gave	given	swim	swam	swum
go	went	gone/been*	take	took	taken
have	had	had	teach	taught	taught
hear	heard	heard	tell	told	told
hit	hit	hit	think	thought	thought
hold	held	held	throw	threw	thrown
keep	kept	kept	understand	understood	understood
know	knew	known	wake	woke	woken
lead	led	led	wear	wore	worn
learn	learnt/learned	learnt/learned	win	won	won
leave	left	left	write	wrote	written
lend	lent	lent			

* See page 55.

appendix 2   active and passive verb forms

	ACTIVE		PASSIVE: TENSE OF *BE* + PAST PARTICIPLE	
INFINITIVE	*(to) watch*	*(to) write*	*(to) be* **watched**	*(to) be* **written**
-ING FORM	*watching*	*writing*	*being* **watched**	*being* **written**
SIMPLE PRESENT	*I watch*	*I write*	*I am* **watched**	*It is* **written**
PRESENT PROGRESSIVE	*I am watching*	*I am writing*	*I am being* **watched**	*It is being* **written**
SIMPLE PAST	*I watched*	*I wrote*	*I was* **watched**	*It was* **written**
PAST PROGRESSIVE	*I was watching*	*I was writing*	*I was being* **watched**	*It was being* **written**
PRESENT PERFECT	*I have watched*	*I have written*	*I have been* **watched**	*It has been* **written**
PAST PERFECT	*I had watched*	*I had written*	*I had been* **watched**	*It had been* **written**
WILL FUTURE	*I will watch*	*I will write*	*I will be* **watched**	*It will be* **written**
GOING TO FUTURE	*I am going to watch*	*I am going to write*	*I am going to be* **watched**	*It is going to be* **written**
MODAL VERBS	*I can watch*	*I can write*	*I can be* **watched**	*It can be* **written**
	I must watch	*I must write*	*I must be* **watched**	*It must be* **written**
	I should watch	*I should write*	*I should be* **watched**	*It should be* **written**
	etc	etc	etc	etc

→ For the use of the different tenses, see Sections 2–5.
→ For the use of passives, see Section 7.
→ For the spelling of *-ing* forms, see page 21.
→ For the spelling of third-person present forms (*writes, watches, sits, goes* etc), see page 14.

appendix 3   capital letters (A, B, C etc)

We use CAPITAL LETTERS to begin the names of **people, places, nationalities, languages, days, months** and **holidays.**
   Abraham Lincoln   New York   American   Arabic   Thursday   September   Christmas

We also use CAPITAL LETTERS for the most important words in the titles of **books, films** etc.
   War and Peace   Gone with the Wind

And we use a CAPITAL LETTER for the first word in a sentence, and for the pronoun *I*.
   Yesterday I went for a long bike ride.

appendix 4   contractions

Contractions like *he's*, *isn't* show the pronunciation of informal speech.
They are common and correct in informal writing (for example, friendly letters), but are unusual in formal writing.

AFFIRMATIVE (➕) CONTRACTIONS: PRONOUN + *'M, 'RE, 'S, 'VE, 'D, 'LL*	NEGATIVE (➖) CONTRACTIONS: *BE, HAVE* OR OTHER AUXILIARY + *N'T*	
I am → I'm *we are → we're* *she is → she's* *he has → he's* *I have → I've* *you had → you'd* *you would → you'd* *they will → they'll*	*are not → aren't* *is not → isn't* *have not → haven't* *has not → hasn't* *had not → hadn't* *do not → don't* *does not → doesn't* *did not → didn't* *will not → won't*	*shall not → shan't* *would not → wouldn't* *should not → shouldn't* *cannot → can't* *could not → couldn't* *might not → mightn't* *must not → mustn't* *need not → needn't*

- With *be*, two negative forms are common: *you're not / you aren't, she's not / she isn't*, etc.
  With *have, had, will* and *would*, the forms with *n't* are more common: we usually say *I haven't, I hadn't* etc, not *I've not, I'd not* etc.

- There is no contraction *amn't*, BUT *am not → aren't* in questions.
  I'm late, aren't I? (BUT *I'm not late,* NOT *I aren't late.*)

- The contraction *'s* (= *is* or *has*) can be written after pronouns, nouns, question words, *here* and *there*.
  It's late.   Your mother's gone home.   Mary's got a headache.   How's Joe these days?
  Here's your money.   There's the telephone.

- We don't use affirmative (➕) contractions at the ends of sentences.
  'You're early.' 'Yes, we are.' (NOT *Yes, we're.*)
  'I think she's gone home.' 'Yes, I think **she has***.'* (NOT *... I think she's.*)

  Negative (➖) contractions are possible at the ends of sentences.
  'It's raining.' 'No, it **isn't***.'*

- Don't confuse *it's* (= *it is/has*) with *its* (possessive – see page 182).
  The cat isn't hungry. It's only eaten half of its food.

  Don't confuse *who's* (= *who is/has*) with *whose* (possessive – see page 182).
  Who's the woman in the green coat?   Whose car is that?

- In very informal speech, *going to, want to* and *got to* are often pronounced like *gonna, wanna* and *gotta*.
  They are sometimes written like this, especially in American English.

appendix 5   expressions with prepositions
prepositions after verbs, adjectives and nouns

We use prepositions (*at, in* etc) after some verbs, adjectives and nouns. This is a list of the most common examples.

afraid of
*She's **afraid of** dogs.*

agree with
*I don't **agree with** you.*

angry about something
*We're all **angry about** the new working hours.*

angry with somebody
*Mary's very **angry with** you.*

arrive at/in a place
*I usually **arrive at** school at 8.30.*
*What time do we **arrive in** London?*

ask for
*If you want anything, just **ask for** it.*

bad at
*I'm **bad at** games.*

believe in (= 'believe that something is real')
*Do you **believe in** ghosts?*

belong to
*This book **belongs to** me.*

depend on
*We may arrive late this evening. It **depends on** the traffic.*

different from/to
*You're **different from** (OR **to**) your sister.*

difficulty in doing something
*I have a lot of **difficulty in** understanding her.*

discuss something **with** somebody
*We **discussed** our plans **with** the manager.*

divide into
*I **divided** the cake **into** four parts.*

dream about something or somebody;
dream of doing something
*I often **dream about** horses.*
*When I was young, I **dreamt of** becoming a pilot.*

dressed in
*She was **dressed** completely **in** black.*

example of
*Can you show me an **example of** your work?*

explain something **to** somebody
*Can you **explain** this word **to** me?*

get into/out of a car;
get on(to)/off a bus, train, plane, ship
*I picked up my case and **got into** the taxi.*
*She **got off** the bus at the wrong stop.*

get to a place
*How do you **get to** Southport from here?*

good at
*He's **good at** tennis.*

happen to
*What's **happened to** Alice? She's an hour late.*

the idea of doing something
*We had **the idea of** starting a small business.*

interested in
*Are you **interested in** animals?*

kind to
*They have always been very **kind to** me.*

laugh at
*Please don't **laugh at** my French pronunciation.*

listen to
*I like to **listen to** music while I'm working.*

look after children etc
*Can you **look after** the children for half an hour?*

look at
***Look at** that wonderful old car!*

look for (= 'try to find')
*'What are you **looking for**?' 'My keys.'*

married to
*He's **married to** Jane Gordon, the novelist.*

nice to
*You weren't very **nice to** my mother.*

pay somebody **for** something; **pay** a bill
*Have you **paid** John **for** the tickets?*
*I forgot to **pay** the electricity bill.*

pleased with
*We are very **pleased with** his work.*

polite to
*It's best to be **polite to** policemen.*

reason for
*What was the **reason for** his change of plans?*

smile at
*In this job you have to **smile at** people all day.*

talk about
*Were you **talking about** me?*

think about/of
*I **think about** you all the time.*
*We're **thinking of** going to America.*

translate into/from
*I've got to **translate** this letter **from** French **into** German.*

typical of
*She went out without saying 'Thank you'. That's just **typical of** her.*

wait for
*I **waited for** her for half an hour, and then went home.*

wrong with
*What's **wrong with** the car?*

→ For more about prepositions, see Section 20.
→ For more about prepositions with verbs, see page 136.

common expressions beginning with prepositions

at a party   *at* the cinema   *at* the theatre
at the top   *at* the bottom   *at* the side
at the beginning   *at* the end of something   *in* the end (= 'finally', 'after a long time')

by car/bus/train etc (BUT *on* foot)
a book *by* Dickens   an opera *by* Mozart

in a raincoat/dress/hat
in the rain/snow
in the sky   *in* the world
in a picture
in the middle
in a loud/quiet voice
write *in* pen/pencil
in my opinion
in time (= 'not late')   *on* time (= 'at just the right time; not late or early')

on the phone   *on* the radio   *on* TV
on page 22

→ For expressions without articles like *in hospital, at university*, see page 156.

appendix 6   word problems

This section tells you about some words that are difficult to use correctly. We explain some other word problems in other sections of the book: see the Index.

after   We **don't** usually say *and after, X happened*. We prefer *afterwards* or *after that*.
   *We had a pizza, **and afterwards / after that** we went skating.* (NOT *...~~and after, we went~~ ...*)

ago   *Ago* goes **after** a time expression. Compare *ago* with *for* and *since* (see page 61).
   *It's August 1st. I came here **three months ago**. I've lived here **for three months, since May**.*

another is one word.
   *Would you like **another** glass?* (NOT *... ~~an other glass.~~*)

as and *like* (similarity)   To say that things are **similar**, we normally use *like*. But before **subject + verb**, we prefer *as* in a **formal** style.
   *Your sister looks **like** you.*   *Pronounce it **like I do** (informal) / **as I do** (formal).*

as, not *like* (jobs)   To talk about the **jobs** that people or things do, use *as*, not *like*.
   *He's working **as** a waiter.* (NOT *~~He's working like a waiter.~~*)   *I used my shoe **as** a hammer.*

born   We say that somebody *is/was born* (passive).
   *I **was born** in London.*   *Thousands of deaf children **are born** every year.*

do and *make*   Common expressions with *do* and *make*:
   ***do** work, a job, shopping, washing, ironing, business;* ***do** something, nothing, anything, everything*
   ***make** a suggestion, a decision, a phone call, a noise, a journey, a mistake, money, a bed, a fire, love*

do + ...ing   Common expressions:
   ***do** the shopping;* ***do** some (a lot of / a bit of) walking, swimming, reading, climbing, sailing, skiing*

else   We use *else* to mean *other* after *something, anything, somebody, nobody* etc.
   ***Something else** to drink?*   ***Nobody else** cooks like you.*

ever is used mostly in **questions**, or with **present perfect + superlative**.
   *Do you **ever** play golf?*   *Have you **ever** been to Ireland?*
   *This is the **best** film I've **ever seen**.*   *She says he's the **nicest** boy she's **ever met**.*

explain is **not** used with **two objects** (see page 140).
   *Can you **explain** this word **to me**?* (NOT *~~Can you explain me this word?~~*)

get   *get* + adjective = 'become'   *get* + noun = 'receive', 'take' etc
      get + preposition/adverb = 'move', 'change place'
   *She's **getting** old.*   *I **got** a letter today.*   *We **get off** the bus here.*   ***Get out!***

get + past participle   Common expressions: *get married, get dressed, get lost*
   *Ann and Bill are **getting married** next week.*   *I **got lost** on my way back from the station.*

hear and *listen to*   We can **hear** something **without trying**. When we **listen to** something, we **want** to hear it.
   *Suddenly I **heard** a noise in the garden.*   *Are you **listening to** me?* (NOT *... ~~listening me?~~*)
We often use *can* with *hear*.
   *I **could hear** Mary and John talking in the kitchen.*

home   We **leave out** *to* before *home*.
   *Well, goodnight, I'm going **home**.* (BUT *Is anybody **at home**?*)

hope   We often use *so* and *not* after *hope*.
   *'Is David coming tomorrow?' 'I **hope so**.'*   *'Do you think it will rain?' 'I **hope not**.'*

if and *when*   We use *if* for things that **may** happen, and *when* for things that **will** happen.
   ***If** I live to be 100 ...*   ***If** it rains today ...*   ***When** I die ...*   ***When** it gets dark ...*

just has several meanings: 1) **right now**   2) **a short time ago** (with present perfect, see page 60)
3) **exactly**   4) **really**   5) **only**
  1) *I'll phone you later. We're **just** having lunch.*   2) *Aunt Daphne has **just** arrived.*
  3) *It's **just** four o'clock.*   4) *I **just** love your dress.*
  5) *'Put those chocolates down!' 'I was **just** looking at them, Mum.'*

let and *make*   If I ***let you do something***, I say that you **can** do it. If I ***make you do it***, I say that you **must**.
After *let* and *make*, we use **object + infinitive without** *to*.
  *Her parents **let her go** to the party. But they **made her come** home at midnight.*

remember and *forget* + infinitive (with *to*) look towards the **future**.
remember and *forget* + *-ing* form look back to the **past**.
  *I must **remember to buy** bread.   She always **forgets to close** the door.*
  *I **remember seeing** the Queen when I was six.   I'll never **forget meeting** you.*

same   We normally use **the** with *same*; and we say **the same as** ... (NOT ~~the same like~~ ...).
  *We had **the same** idea. (NOT ... ~~a same idea~~ OR ... ~~same idea~~)   Her shoes are **the same as** mine.*

see and *hear* + object + infinitive (without *to*)/...*ing*   If you ***see/hear somebody do something***, you see/hear
a **complete** action. If you ***see/hear somebody doing something***, they are **in the middle** of doing it.
  *I **saw her go** into John's house.   I **heard her play** Beethoven's violin concerto on the radio.*
  *I looked up and **saw Bill talking** to Sue.   I walked past Ann's room and **heard her crying**.*

see, look and *watch*   We can **see** something **without trying**. When we **look at** something, we **want** to
see it.
  *I **saw** Bill in the supermarket yesterday.   **Look at** that bird! (NOT ~~Look that bird!~~)*
We often use **can** with *see*.
  *On the left of the photo you **can see** my grandmother.*
We **watch** things that **move, change** or **happen**.
  *We **watch** TV most evenings.   Did you **watch** the football match?*
  *The police **are watching** him to see where he goes.*

so and *such*   We use **so + adjective without a noun**, and *such* when there is **a noun**.
  so kind   so big   such kind people   such a big mistake   such a fool

still, yet and *already*   We use *still* to say that something **is continuing**; *yet* to ask if it **has happened**
(or to say it **hasn't**); *already* to say it has happened **earlier than we expected**.
  *Granny's **still** on the phone.   'Has the postman come **yet**?' 'No, not **yet**.'*
  *I've **already** spent the week's money, and it's only Tuesday.*

than, as and *that*   Use *than* after **comparatives** (see page 210); *as* in the structure **as ... as** (see page 214);
that after *say, think* etc and as a **relative pronoun** (see page 240).
  *She's **taller than** me.   It's **as cold as** ice.   The boss **says that** you're right.*
  *Who's the woman **that** just came in?*

think   We often use *so* after *think*. **Don't** use an **infinitive** after *think*.
  *'Are you coming to the party?' 'I **think so**.'   'Is it raining?' 'I don't **think so**.'*
  *I'm **thinking of going** to America. (NOT ~~I'm thinking to go~~ ...)*

try   After *try* we can use an **infinitive** (with *to*) or an *-ing* form. We prefer an **infinitive** when we are talking
about trying **difficult** things.
  ***Try to stop** smoking – it's bad for you.   'It's really hot in here.' '**Try opening** a window.'*

very and *too*   *Too* means 'more than we want'; *very* doesn't.
  *'It's **very** warm today.' 'Yes, a bit **too** warm for me.' 'Oh, it's OK for me.'*

wait   We often use **wait for** with **object + infinitive** (with *to*).
  *I'm **waiting for** the postman **to come**.*

which? and *what?*   We prefer *which* when we are **choosing** between a **small number** of things, and *what*
when there is a **wider choice**.
  *'I'd like a pair of those shoes.' '**Which** ones – the blue or the red? And **what** size?'*

whom   In a very **formal** style, we use ***whom*** as an **object** in questions and relative clauses.
   Whom *did they elect?*   *With* ***whom*** *did she go?*   *She hated the man for* ***whom*** *she worked.*

In an **informal** style, ***who*** is more normal in questions, and ***that*** (or nothing) in relatives.
   Who *did they elect?*   ***Who*** *did she go with?*   *She hated the man (****that****) she worked for.*

why and *because*   **Why** **asks for** a reason. ***Because*** **gives** a reason.
   *'****Why**** are you late?' '****Because**** I missed the train.'*

pre-test answers

SECTION 1 *be* and *have*

1 1 is   (page 2)   2 Are (page 3)   3 There is
(pages 6-7)   4 Did you have (page 11)
2 1 ✓; ✗; ✓; ✓ (page 3)   2 ✗ (pages 8-9)   3 ✗
(page 10)   4 ✗ (page 4)   5 ✓ (page 8)
3 1 Will all the family be at home? (page 5)
2 Will there be a meeting tomorrow?
(page 7)
3 Has Phil got a headache? (page 10)
4 Did Ann have a lesson yesterday? (page 8)

SECTION 2 present tenses

1 1 ✗ (page 21)   2 ✗ (pages 15, 22, 26)   3 ✓
(pages 21, 24)   4 ✗ (page 14)   5 ✗ (page 14)
6 ✓ (page 18)   7 ✗ (page 16)   8 ✗ (page 16)
9 ✓ (page 16)   10 ✓ (page 17)   11 ✗ (page 24)
12 ✗ (page 28)

SECTION 3 talking about the future

1 1 ✗ (page 37)   2 ✓ (page 35)   3 ✗ (page 37)
4 ✗ (pages 32, 38)   5 ✓ (page 37)   6 ✓ (pages
34, 38)   7 ✓ (page 39)   8 ✓ (pages 32, 38)
9 ✗ (page 34)   10 ✗ (page 38)   11 ✗ (page 36)

SECTION 4 past tenses

1 1 B (page 42)   2 B (page 42)   3 A (page 43)
4 A (page 44)   5 B (page 44)   6 A (page 45)
7 B (pages 46-49)   8 A (page 49)   9 A, B (page
49)

SECTION 5 perfect tenses

1 1 B (page 52)   2 A (page 53)   3 B (pages 54-
56)   4 B (page 56)   5 A (pages 54, 56)   6 B
(page 58)   7 B (page 58)   8 A, B (page 55)
9 B (page 61)   10 A (page 61)   11 B (page 68)
12 A, B (pages 58, 60)   13 B (pages 62-64)

SECTION 6 modal verbs

1 1 ✗ (page 72)   2 ✓ (page 80)   3 ✗ (page 74)
4 ✓ (page 73)   5 ✗ (pages 73, 76)   6 ✓ (page
75)   7 ✓ (page 76)   8 ✗ (page 87)   9 ✗ (page
74)   10 ✓ (page 89)   11 ✗ (page 89)   12 ✗
(page 88)   13 ✓ (page 86)   14 ✓ (page 90)

2 1 Can/Could/May (pages 84-85)
2 Can/Could (page 83)   3 must (page 82)
4 can't (page 82)   5 should (page 77)
6 will be able (page 79)

SECTION 7 passives

1 1 ✗ (page 94)   2 ✗ (pages 94, 96)   3 ✗ (page
95)   4 ✓ (page 98)   5 ✓ (page 99)   6 ✗ (page
97)   7 ✗ (page 101)   8 ✓ (page 100)   9 ✗
(page 96)
2 1 B (page 102)   2 A (page 102)

SECTION 8 questions and negatives

1 1 ✗ (page 106)   2 ✓ (page 107)   3 ✗ (page
106)   4 ✗ (page 106)   5 ✗ (page 108)   6 ✓
(page 108)   7 ✓ (page 109)   8 ✓ (page 109)
9 ✗ (page 110)   10 ✓ (page 112)   11 ✗ (page
114)   12 ✓ (page 115)   13 ✓ (page 115)

SECTION 9 infinitives and *-ing* forms

1 1 ✓ (page 128)   2 ✗ (page 118)   3 ✗ (page
119)   4 ✓ (page 122)   5 ✗ (pages 132-133)
6 ✗ (page 126)   7 ✗ (page 130)   8 ✓ (page
130)   9 ✗ (pages 120-121)   10 ✗ (page 124)
11 ✓ (page 125)   12 ✓ (page 127)   13 ✓ (page
129)

SECTION 10 special structures with verbs

1 (page 136) 1 with   2 to   3 at
2 1 'Where are you from?' (page 137)
3 1 A, B, D (pages 138-139)   2 A, B (page 140)
3 A (page 141)   4 C (page 142)   5 A (page
143)

SECTION 11 articles: *a/an* and *the*

1 (page 146) 1 a   2 an   3 an   4 a
2 (page 147) 1 ✓   2 ✗   3 ✗
3 1 – (page 150)   2 the; the (page 148)   3 a
(page 151)   4 a (page 150)   5 a; – (page 151)
6 – (page 147)
4 1 ✗ (page 154)   2 ✓ (page 155)   3 ✗ (page
156)

SECTION 12 determiners

1   1 that (page 160)   2 any (page 162)   3 is (page 165)   4 dark (page 166)   5 a little (page 170)   6 too (page 172)   7 too (page 172)   8 Every (page 174)   9 all (page 174) 10 either (page 176)

2   1 ✗ (page 164)   2 ✗ (page 164)   3 ✓ (page 162)   4 ✓ (page 167)   5 ✗ (pages 168-169) 6 ✓ (page 168)   7 ✗ (page 169)   8 ✗ (page 177)   9 ✗ (page 175)

3   1 We haven't got enough petrol. (page 171) 2 You're not driving fast enough. (page 171)

SECTION 13 personal pronouns; possessives

1   1 ✓ (page 180)   2 ✗ (page 180)   3 ✗ (pages 180-181)   4 ✗ (page 180)   5 ✓ (page 180) 6 ✗ (page 182)   7 ✗ (page 184)   8 ✓ (page 184)   9 ✗ (page 185)   10 ✓ (page 185) 11 ✓ (page 185)   12 ✓ (page 185)

2   (page 182)   1 her   2 her   3 his   4 their

SECTION 14 nouns

1   (page 188)   homes; days; families; women; children; leaves

2   1 ✓ (page 189)   2 ✗ (page 189)   3 ✓ (page 188)   4 ✗ (page 192)   5 ✓ (page 192)   6 ✗ (page 193)   7 ✗ (page 194)   8 ✗ (page 194) 9 ✗ (pages 195-196)   10 ✓ (page 195)

3   (pages 190-191)   1 some   2 some   3 a 4 some   5 some   6 an

SECTION 15 adjectives and adverbs

1   (page 202)   completely; easily; beautifully; probably

2   1 ✗ (page 200)   2 ✓ (pages 202, 204)   3 ✗ (page 203)   4 ✓ (page 204)   5 ✓ (page 214) 6 ✗ (page 213)   7 ✗ (page 206)

3   1 terribly (page 202)   2 beautiful (page 203) 3 carefully (pages 202-203)   4 perfect (pages 200, 202)   5 hard (page 207)   6 most; in (page 209)   7 than (page 210)

4   (page 208)   fatter; happier; later; better; more interesting

SECTION 16 conjunctions

1   1 ✓ (pages 219, 222)   2 ✓ (page 220) 3 ✗ (page 221)   4 ✓ (page 221)   5 ✗ (page 222)   6 ✗ (page 223)   7 ✗ (page 224) 8 ✓ (page 225)   9 ✗ (page 224)

SECTION 17 if

1   1 ✓ (page 228)   2 ✓ (page 234)   3 ✗ (page 229)   4 ✓ (page 228)   5 ✓ (pages 230, 232) 6 ✗ (page 228)   7 ✗ (page 230)   8 ✓ (page 233)   9 ✗ (page 235)

SECTION 18 relative pronouns

1   1 ✗ (page 238)   2 ✓ (page 238)   3 ✗ (page 238)   4 ✓ (page 240)   5 ✓ (page 241) 6 ✓ (page 241)   7 ✗ (page 241)   8 ✓ (page 242)   9 ✗ (page 243)   10 ✓ (page 243)

SECTION 19 indirect speech

1   1 ✓ (page 248)   2 ✗ (page 247)   3 ✗ (page 248)   4 ✗ (page 248)   5 ✗ (pages 246, 249) 6 ✓ (page 251)   7 ✓ (page 248)   8 ✓ (page 248)   9 ✗ (page 251)   10 ✗ (page 246) 11 ✓ (page 248)   12 ✗ (page 250)

SECTION 20 prepositions

1   1 ✗ (page 254)   2 ✓ (page 254)   3 ✗ (page 254)   4 ✓ (page 256)   5 ✗ (page 256) 6 ✓ (page 254)   7 ✗ (page 257)   8 ✓ (page 257)   9 ✗ (page 258)   10 ✓ (page 259) 11 ✗ (page 263)   12 ✗ (page 260)   13 ✓ (page 262)   14 ✓ (page 262)

SECTION 21 spoken grammar

1   1 ✗ (page 266)   2 ✓ (page 266)   3 ✓ (page 267)   4 ✓ (page 269)   5 ✗ (page 268) 6 ✗ (page 272)   7 ✓ (page 272)   8 ✗ (page 271)   9 ✓ (page 271)   10 ✓ (page 271)

answer key

pages 2–3

1 1 are 2 is 3 are 4 am 5 are 6 is

2 1 We're all tired. 2 They're here.
3 I'm sorry. 4 My name's Peter.
5 You're early. 6 The shop's closed.

3 1 Is Marie from Paris? 2 Are we very late?
3 Is John in bed? 4 Is the boss in Japan?
5 Is his car fast?

4 1 What's 2 Where are 3 Who's 4 Why are
5 When's 6 How's

5 1 she isn't / she's not ill. 2 they aren't /
they're not in London. 3 you aren't /
you're not too tall. 4 we aren't / we're not
very late. 5 it isn't / it's not hot. 6 I'm not
at university.

6 1 He is thirsty. 2 She is cold. 3 They are
hot. 4 It is cold.

7 1 right 2 size 3 colour 4 interested

page 4

1 1 were; was 2 was; were 3 were 4 was;
were 5 was; were 6 Were; was 7 was; was

2 1 Was the party good? 2 Were the people
interesting? 3 Was your father a teacher?
4 Was everybody late? 5 Was John's brother
at school with you? (… with you at school?)

3 1 weren't late. 2 wasn't a teacher. 3 wasn't
with Anna 4 weren't well 5 weren't in
England

page 5

1 It will be hot in Rio. It will be warm in Paris.
It will be cold in London. It will be very cold
in Moscow.

2 1 I won't be sorry. 2 It will be hot.
3 We'll be at home. 4 The shops won't
be closed. 5 He won't be in Scotland.
6 Ann won't be at school.

3 1 When will your father be in England?
2 Will Ann be at the party with John?
3 Will everybody be here at 8.00?
4 Will the train be late again?
5 When will Joe and Mary be in the office?
6 Will the weather be good tomorrow?
7 Where will you be on Tuesday?

pages 6–7

2 1 Is there a doctor here? 2 Are there any
trains to London this evening? 3 Is there
much money in your bank account?
4 How many students are there in your class?
5 Was there a special price for students?
6 Were there any mistakes in my letter?
7 Were there many children at the swimming
pool? 8 How many people were there at
the party?

4 1 Will there be trains? 2 Will there be
computers? 3 Will there be good food?
4 Will there be different countries? 5 Will
there be governments?

5 1 There's 2 It's 3 there 4 There isn't
5 It's 6 It's

6 1 There is a large living room. 2 There is
a small study. 3 There is a downstairs
cloakroom. 4 There are two bathrooms.
5 There are four bedrooms. 6 There is gas
central heating. 7 There is a double garage.
8 There is a large garden.

pages 8–9

1 1 My father 2 We all 3 had 4 has 5 Paul
6 have 7 has 8 last year

2 1 We don't have a garden. 2 Do they have
any children? 3 Does Peter have a cold?
4 My aunt doesn't have a dog. 5 Does Mary
have any brothers or sisters? 6 I don't have
enough money. 7 Does Sally have
a boyfriend? 8 Why do you have two cars?

3 1 She didn't have a computer. 2 She had
very fair hair. 3 Did she have lots of friends?
4 She didn't have many nice clothes.
5 Did she have her own room?

5 1 He will have a job. 2 He won't have
a bicycle. 3 He will have a car. 4 Will he
have a house? 5 Will he have a girlfriend?
6 He won't have old clothes. 7 He will have
a suit. 8 Will he have a guitar?

6 1 nephews. 2 uncles; aunts.
3 eight cousins.

In these answers, we usually give **either** contracted forms (for example *I'm, don't*)
or full forms (for example *I am, do not*). Normally both are correct.

ANSWER KEY 285

page 10

1 1 He's got two brothers.   2 He hasn't got
a car.   3 He's got three dogs.   4 He's got
a dictionary.   5 He hasn't got long hair.
6 He hasn't got any sisters.

3 1 Have they got a big garden?   2 Has Ann
got a good job?   3 Has Bill got a big car?
4 Have they got a plane?   5 Have they got
any horses?

page 11

1 1 had dinner   2 has coffee   3 have a baby
4 have a shower   5 have toast   6 have a game

2 1 do you have lunch   2 She didn't have
a good trip.   3 didn't have a shower.
4 Did you have a good flight?   5 Did you
have a good game?   I don't have coffee

page 12

1 1 They weren't ready.   2 We're all here.
3 I'm not a student.   4 Where's your house?
5 Ann isn't English. OR Ann's not English.
6 She won't be late.

2 1 Where   2 I   3 Are   4 has   5 is   6 am
7 won't

3 1 Is there a taxi outside?   2 Has Chris got
a headache?   3 Joe doesn't have a car.
4 Did Ann have a meeting yesterday?
5 I didn't have coffee for breakfast.
6 Will there be an English lesson tomorrow?
7 I'm not hungry.   8 Ann hasn't got a new
car.   9 Did she have a nice time at the
party?   10 Has the house got a big garden?

4 1 ✗   2 ✗   3 ✓   4 ✗   5 ✗   6 ✓   7 ✓

5 1 is   2 is   3 is   4 are   5 has   6 was   7 were
not   8 did not have   9 was   10 is   11 has
12 has   13 is   14 is   15 is   16 has   17 does
not have   18 has   19 has   20 has

page 14

1 + -s: cooks, drinks, lives, reads, runs,
smokes, stands, starts, writes
+ -es: fetches, fixes, misses, pushes, touches,
watches, wishes

2 + -s: enjoys, plays, stays
-y → -ies: copies, fries, marries, studies, tries

3 1 I live in that house.   2 Ann works in
a bank.   3 Susan plays the violin very badly.
4 Those children come from Scotland.
5 You look very young.

4 1 The boss   2 I   3 Bread   4 Andy   5 Mary
and Ian   6 You   7 Our cat   8 That child
9 All those buses   10 My father

page 15

1 1 play   2 speaks   3 ask   4 goes   5 make
6 washes   7 says   8 sits   9 tries   10 watches

2 2 C; makes   3 D; keep   4 B; keeps
5 A; wash   6 E; make   7 G; takes

pages 16–17

1 1 Does   2 Do   3 Do   4 Does   5 Does   6 Do

2 1 Does the Oxford bus stop here?   2 Do the
teachers know her?   3 Do you play the
piano?   4 Does John work in a restaurant?
5 Does this train stop at York?   6 Do we
need more eggs?   7 Does Mary like parties?
8 Does Peter speak Spanish well?

3 1 your children   2 the lesson   3 you
4 the holiday   5 those women   6 you

4 1 Where do   2 What does   3 When do
4 Why does   5 How many; does

5 1 What do you want?   2 What does this
word mean?   3 What time does the film
start?   4 How much do those shoes cost?
5 Why does she need money?   6 How does
this camera work?   7 Where do you buy
your meat?   8 Who do you want to see?

6 1 When do Peter and Ann's children play
football?   2 What time does the film about
skiing in New Zealand start?   3 What does
the second word in the first sentence mean?
4 Why does the man in the flat downstairs
want to change his job?   5 How much does
a ticket for Saturday's concert cost?

pages 18–19

1 1 You do not speak Chinese.   2 Bill does not
play the guitar very well.   3 We do not agree
about holidays.   4 George and Andrew
do not live near me. OR Alan and John do not
live near George and Andrew.   5 My father
does not write poetry.   6 Barbara does not live
in London.   7 Henry does not like parties.

2 1 I don't like pop music.   2 The train
doesn't stop at Cardiff.   3 Peter doesn't
remember faces very well.   4 We don't know
his wife.   5 Alice doesn't teach mathematics.
6 The children don't play hockey on Mondays.
7 The shops don't open on Sunday afternoons.

3 1 Our cat doesn't like fish. 2 Ann doesn't speak Russian. 3 I don't remember your phone number. 4 Oranges don't grow in Britain. 5 The postman doesn't come on Sundays. 6 We don't play much tennis.

4 1 don't like 2 doesn't speak 3 don't remember 4 don't know 5 doesn't want 6 don't want 7 doesn't work 8 don't think

page 20

1 C

2 1 does 2 My cats 3 doesn't 4 stops 5 do English people 6 open 7 your holiday start 8 play 9 That café 10 say

3 1 I don't like getting up early. 2 Do you want something to drink? 3 Joe plays football on Saturdays. 4 Do you remember her phone number? 5 That clock doesn't work. 6 She often flies to Paris on business. 7 It doesn't rain much here in summer. 8 Do elephants eat meat? 9 Does he think he can sing? 10 We need a new car.

page 21

1 1 are talking 2 is eating 3 is cooking 4 am not enjoying 5 am reading 6 is not raining 7 are not listening 8 am feeling 9 is not going 10 are learning

2 cleaning, coming, dying, enjoying, going, living, making, playing, singing, starting, washing, writing

3 getting, feeling, putting, hitting, jumping, raining, robbing, shopping, shouting, sitting, slimming, dreaming, standing, talking, turning, answering, opening, visiting, forgetting

pages 22–23

1 1 The baby's crying again. 2 It's snowing again. 3 You're looking very beautiful today. 4 Your coffee is getting cold. 5 I'm playing a lot of football this year. 6 We're waiting for a phone call. 7 Chris and Helen are spending a week in France.

2 1 She's washing her face. 2 She's brushing her teeth. 3 She's listening to the radio. 4 She's drinking coffee. 5 She's reading the newspaper. 6 She's brushing her hair. 7 She's reading letters. 8 She's opening the door. 9 She's going to work.

3 1 He isn't / He's not listening to me. 2 I'm not working today. 3 It isn't / It's not raining now. 4 She isn't / She's not wearing a coat. 5 They aren't / They're not learning very much. 6 We aren't / We're not enjoying this film. 7 You aren't / You're not eating much these days.

4 (*Possible answers*:) Ann is wearing a black blouse, a red jacket, a red skirt with a black belt, a grey raincoat and black shoes. She is not wearing a hat. Sandra is wearing a pink dress, a pink cardigan, grey boots, a black coat and a grey hat. She is not wearing glasses. David is wearing a green shirt with a green tie, a grey suit, a black belt, green socks, black shoes and glasses. He is not wearing a coat. (*Other answers are possible.*)

page 24

1 1 Are you waiting for somebody? 2 Is your boyfriend enjoying the concert? 3 Are those men taking our car? 4 Are you talking to me? 5 Is it snowing? 6 Are we going too fast?

2 1 is he writing? 2 is it stopping? 3 are they eating? 4 are they playing? 5 are you going?

3 1 Why are all those people laughing? 2 What is that big black dog eating? 3 Is everybody in your family going to Scotland for Christmas? 4 What game are those children playing? 5 Where are Ann and her friends studying?

page 25

1 1 Are you getting up? 2 What are you drinking? 3 You are not listening. 4 Where are you going? 5 Am I talking too fast? 6 I am not enjoying this film. 7 What are all those people looking at? 8 I am not cooking this for you.

2 1 Peter is trying to save money. 2 Why are those children crying? 3 Are all your friends playing football this afternoon? 4 She is not looking very well today. 5 I think she is making a big mistake. 6 You are not wearing your usual glasses. 7 I am hoping to get a new job. 8 Is the 10.15 train from London to Edinburgh running today?

3 1 is snowing 2 is looking 3 is wearing 4 is not wearing 5 is walking 6 are looking 7 are trying 8 are stopping 9 is returning 10 is kissing 11 is … saying

In these answers, we usually give **either** contracted forms (for example *I'm, don't*) or full forms (for example *I am, do not*). Normally both are correct.

ANSWER KEY 287

pages 26–27

1 SIMPLE PRESENT: nearly always, on Fridays, very often, when I'm tired

PRESENT PROGRESSIVE: just now, these days, this afternoon, today

2 1 eat; is not eating   2 fly; plane is not flying   3 rains; it is not raining   4 works; he / John is not working hard   5 plays; she / Ann is not playing tennis   6 speaks; he / John is not speaking English now.   7 drives; he / Bill is not driving a bus now.   8 sells; this shop / it is not selling books now.   9 plays; is not playing the piano now.   10 writes; he / Simon is not writing poetry now.   11 chase; dog is not chasing cats now.

3 1 is she working   2 Does it rain   3 don't speak   4 is getting   5 Do you play   6 are you writing   7 She's coming   8 I'm going   9 boils   10 Is that water boiling

4 1 He often reads poems, but now he is reading an autobiography.   2 She often reads comics, but now she is reading a grammar.   3 He often reads short stories, but now he's reading a cookery book.   4 I often read biographies, but now I'm reading a newspaper.   5 They often read newspapers, but now they're reading a notice.   6 He often reads magazines, but now he's reading a poem.

pages 28–29

1 1 don't understand.   2 prefer   3 like   4 seems   5 Do ... need

2 1 What does this word mean?   2 Rob doesn't want to see the doctor.   3 I think she loves me.   4 Peter seems tired.   5 We don't need a new car.   6 Do you know that man?   7 I hate cold weather.

3 1 doesn't matter.   2 don't remember   3 don't recognise   4 don't believe   5 don't mind

4 1 are seeing   2 think; see   3 are you thinking   4 is that woman looking   5 looks like   6 feel

5 1 'I don't understand.'   2 'I see.'   3 'I hope not.'   4 'I think so.'   5 'I don't think so.'   6 'I don't know.'   7 'I know.'   8 'It depends.'   9 'It doesn't matter.'   10 'I don't remember.'   11 'I don't mind.'

page 30

1 lives, passes, plays, stands, teaches, tries, washes

2 flying, holding, making, playing, sitting, stopping

3 1 Do you drive to school?   2 Granny doesn't drink coffee.   3 I travel a lot in Europe.   4 Alex wants to be a doctor.   5 The fast train doesn't stop at this station.   6 Do you speak English to your children?

4 1 's cooking   2 's snowing   3 aren't listening / 're not listening   4 's selling

5 1 She's coming   2 'Do you smoke?'   3 every Sunday   4 these days   5 most Tuesdays

6 1 Why are all those people looking at me?   2 Does the 7.15 train to London run on Saturdays?   3 Where are you and Ann having lunch today?   4 Does that man in the dark coat at the bus-stop work in your office?

7 1 ✓ 2 ✗ 3 ✗ 4 ✓ 5 ✗ 6 ✗

pages 32–33

1 1 The woman is going to eat breakfast.   2 He is going to read a letter.   3 She is going to play the piano.   4 The cars are going to crash.   5 He is going to drink coffee.   6 The ball is going to break the window.

2 1 Is Ann going to change her school?   2 Where are you going to put that picture?   3 What are you going to buy for Bill's birthday?   4 Is Eric going to play football tomorrow?   5 When are you going to stop smoking?   6 Is Alice going to go to university?

3 1 I'm going to stay in a nice hotel.   2 I'm going to swim a lot.   3 I'm not going to do any work.   4 I'm going to take photos.   5 I'm not going to read English newspapers.   6 I'm going to learn some Italian.   7 I'm not going to write postcards.   8 I'm not going to visit museums.

4 1 She is going to switch off the radio.   2 She is going to turn up the radio.   3 She is going to turn down the radio.   4 She is going to turn on the TV.   5 She is going to turn off the TV.   6 She is going to turn on the tap.   7 She is going to turn off the tap.   8 She is going to plug in the iron.   9 She is going to unplug the iron.   10 She is going to plug in the hair-dryer.   11 She is going to unplug the hair-dryer.

page 34

1 1 No, he's seeing John Parker on Sunday morning.   2 No, he's going to the Birmingham office by train.   3 No, he's having lunch with Stewart on Tuesday.
4 No, he's going to the theatre on Wednesday evening.   5 No, his new secretary is starting on Thursday.   OR No, he's going to Berlin on Friday.   6 No, he's going to Phil and Monica's wedding on Saturday.

2 1 Where are you staying?   2 How long are you staying?   3 How are you travelling?
4 Are you taking the/your dog?   5 Who's going with you?   6 When are you coming back?

3 1 She's seeing her bank manager on Monday.
2 She's seeing her doctor on Tuesday.
3 She's seeing her dentist on Wednesday.
4 She's seeing her accountant on Thursday.
5 She's seeing her solicitor on Friday.

page 35

1 1 The class will begin   2 They'll be home
3 I think the examination will be difficult.
4 We'll walk to the party.   5 I will not speak to her.

2 1 won't be; will she be   2 won't have; Will you have   3 won't find; will I find   4 won't go; will they go   5 won't get; will he get

3 1 What time will tomorrow evening's concert start?   2 When will you and the family get back from Paris?   3 Will you be here tomorrow?   4 Will you and your mother be here tomorrow?   5 Where will you be this evening?   6 Will the children have enough money for the journey?   7 How soon will you know the answer?   8 Will John and Susan want to play golf tomorrow?

page 36

1 1 'll start   2 will change   3 won't snow
4 'll go to sleep soon.   5 will tell

3 1 old house   2 'll come to   3 bridge
4 'll come to   5 'll see   6 house   7 'll recognise   8 door   9 apple trees   10 'll find
11 key   12 'll have   13 great time.

page 37

1 1 'll wash   2 'll do   3 won't start.
4 won't stop   5 'll go shopping.   6 'll help

3 1 A   2 B   3 A   4 A   5 A   6 A

page 38

1 1 will   2 will   3 is going to   4 will
5 's going to

2 1 I'll   2 I'll   3 I'm going to   4 I'll   5 I'll

3 1 Jack is arriving at 4.00.   2 I'm flying to Glasgow tomorrow.   3 We're spending next week in Ireland.

page 39

1 1 The next lesson starts at 2.00.   2 This term ends on March 12th.   3 When does the concert finish?   4 We don't have a lesson next Thursday.   5 Does this train stop at Reading?   6 The play starts at 8.00.
7 What time do you arrive in Rome?
8 The banks close at 3.00 tomorrow.
9 The 7.15 train stops at every station.

2 The flight leaves at 8.15.   2 The concert starts at 10.00/10pm.   3 The train arrives at Oxford at 12.58.

page 40

1 1 I'll   2 She'll   3 It won't

2 1 Is Mary going to phone this evening?
2 I'm going to stop smoking.   3 Peter is going to marry his boss.   4 It's not/It isn't going to rain.   5 I'm going to cook steak this evening.   6 When are you going to have a haircut?   7 When are you and your wife going to come and see us?

3 1 I'll be here next week.   2 We won't have enough money for a holiday.   3 Where will I find the key?   4 John won't pass his exams.
5 I think the train will be late.
6 Will all this money change your life?

4 I'm seeing Andrew tonight.   2 How are you travelling to Ireland?   3 I'm not using the car tomorrow.   4 John and Sylvia are staying with us tomorrow.   5 What time are the people from London arriving?

5 1 is going to   2 will see   3 'I'll go.'
4 I'll tell   5 am seeing   6 is going to
7 I'll   8 I'm going to   9 I'll take

In these answers, we usually give **either** contracted forms (for example *I'm, don't*) or full forms (for example *I am, do not*). Normally both are correct.

ANSWER KEY   289

pages 42–43

1 arrived, changed, cooked, hated, lived, passed, shaved, watched

2 stayed, studied, cried, annoyed, carried, hurried, prayed

3 shopped, rained, started, robbed, slimmed, jumped, shouted, slipped, fitted, turned, visited, regretted, developed, galloped, opened, answered, referred

5 1 worked 2 know 3 feel 4 came 5 see
6 write 7 arrive 8 like

6 1 We didn't speak Arabic together.
2 My uncle didn't teach science.
3 Bill didn't cook the fish. 4 I didn't take my father to the mountains. OR My father didn't take my mother to the mountains.
5 We didn't tell the police everything. OR The police didn't tell our parents everything.
6 I didn't write to my brother. OR My brother didn't write to my sister. 7 I didn't like the music. 8 We didn't know her phone number.

7 1 he changed his shirt. 2 she didn't answer the others. 3 he didn't go to her house.
4 I brought some chocolates. 5 she bought a very nice dress. 6 I didn't eat the meat.
7 we didn't keep the letters. 8 they spoke German. 9 he didn't shave at weekends.

page 44

1 1 bring 2 start 3 saw 4 leave 5 speak
6 keep 7 learnt 8 forgot

2 1 did she remember it? 2 did you pay the others? 3 did you like the film? 4 did he play well? 5 did you give them any money?

3 1 Where did he go? 2 What did he buy?
3 Who did she marry? 4 What did she break? 5 Where did he stay?

4 1 When did Mrs Potter's two boys play football? 2 Why did all the people in the class feel tired? 3 What did the big man with the grey beard say? 4 Why did the people who were sitting at the back of the bus start to sing?

page 45

1 1 said 2 made 3 did she ask 4 told 5 fell
6 did you put

2 1 did you phone? 2 wrote to you? 3 broke the window? 4 did you break? 5 did she play? 6 fell off the table?

3 1 built 2 invented 3 painted 4 directed
5 composed

page 46

1 2 A; forgot 3 D; read 4 E; spoke 5 C; like, stopped 6 F; learn

3 1 stood 2 heard 3 opened 4 came 5 did not see 6 said 7 took 8 gave 9 held
10 did not read 11 said 12 did not speak
13 wrote 14 ran 15 turned

page 47

1 1 I learnt/learned a lot of Latin. 2 I didn't remember to buy the milk. 3 I didn't speak to her mother. 4 'Did he phone this morning?'
5 I took the train. 6 did you go to Malaysia?
7 it didn't stop at Glasgow. 8 'They saw two films.' 9 'Did you eat my chocolates?'

2 1 When did Sarah and her baby come out of hospital? 2 Why did Peter's friends from the office give him a bicycle? 3 What did the small woman with long hair say?
4 What did the children buy? 5 Who left a bicycle in the garden? 6 What fell off the table? 7 Who found a cat in his office?

3 A

page 48

1 1 were dancing 2 was cooking supper
3 was driving home 4 was not watching TV

2 1 'Was she writing letters?' 2 'Where was he shopping?' 3 'What was she cooking?'
4 'Why were they crying?' 5 'Were they driving to Scotland?'

page 49

1 1 was having 2 watched 3 was watching
4 worked 5 were studying 6 drove 7 walked

2 1 was reading; jumped 2 met; was travelling
3 broke; was skiing. 4 was shopping; stole

3 1 was shopping. 2 stopped. 3 said 4 were talking. 5 broke. 6 was working.

page 50

1 brought, cried, felt, stayed, stopped

2 1 What did all those people want? 2 Did all your brothers send birthday cards? 3 The baby ate some toothpaste this morning.
4 The teacher didn't answer my question.

3 1 Why did Peter telephone? 2 What did Mary expect? 3 What happened? 4 Who took the car?

4 1 we were watching TV. 2 he wasn't reading (it). 3 were they speaking English?

5 1 went; was raining 2 read 3 Did … watch 4 walked; were talking 5 was swimming

6 1 were singing 2 were standing 3 opened 4 drove 5 turned 6 started 7 was passing 8 ran 9 pulled

pages 52–53

2 1 She has forgotten my address. 2 I have made a mistake. 3 You haven't shut the door. 4 Alan has worked very hard. 5 I haven't heard from Mary. 6 John hasn't learnt/learned anything. 7 I've broken a cup. 8 We have remembered Ann's birthday. 9 The rain has stopped. 10 I haven't seen a newspaper today.

3 1 Have we paid? 2 Has Bill phoned? 3 Have you heard the news? 4 Have the dogs come back? 5 What has Barbara told the police? 6 Why have Andy and Sarah brought the children? 7 What have you said to Mike?

4 1 Have the Sunday newspapers arrived? 2 Have all those people gone home? 3 Has the secretary from your father's office telephoned? 4 Where has/have the family in the upstairs flat gone? 5 Why have all the students in Mr Carter's class given him presents?

5 No, sorry, I haven't seen your ball. OR No, I haven't seen your ball, sorry.

pages 54–55

1 1 probably not 2 yes 3 don't know 4 yes 5 don't know 6 yes 7 no 8 don't know 9 don't know 10 no

2 1 has sent 2 have bought 3 have cut 4 has stopped.

3 2 C; has lost 3 B; has left 4 A; have forgotten 5 D; have seen

4 1 gone 2 been 3 been 4 gone 5 been 6 gone

5 1 made 2 polished 3 washed 4 ironed 5 washed up 6 put 7 tidied 8 did

6 1 Have you swept 2 Have you made 3 Have you polished 4 Have you washed 5 Have you ironed 6 Have you washed up 7 have you put 8 Have you tidied 9 haven't done

page 56

1 1 's eaten 2 's gone 3 've won 4 's stolen 5 's come 6 has died

2 1 has married OR has left 2 has died OR has married 3 has stopped 4 has left 5 has closed

3 last week, then, yesterday, in 1990

4 1 ✗ 2 ✗ 3 ✓ 4 ✗ 5 ✓ 6 ✗ 7 ✗ 8 ✓

page 57

1 1 has left; didn't like 2 have bought; found 3 have sold; got 4 has found; did … find 5 has gone; went; sent 6 has had; fell 7 have heard; sent 8 have told; did … say 9 have died; lost 10 have not arrived; took

2 1 'Did he get good marks?' 2 'When did she go?' 3 'When did he tell you?' 4 'Where did he stay?' 5 'Why did he sell it?' 6 'How much did it cost?' 7 'Where did he meet her?' 8 'Why did you stop?'

pages 58–59

1 1 have drunk eight 2 have written six 3 have read five 4 has driven 40,000 5 have lived … eight 6 has eaten twenty

2 1 Joe has changed his job twice this year. 2 Have you ever written a poem? 3 I have never climbed a mountain. 4 How often has she asked you for money? 5 I have often tried to stop smoking. 6 Alex has phoned me six times this week. 7 Has Charles spoken to you today? 8 Mary has not told me her new address. 9 Have you ever broken your leg? 10 We have not played football this year.

3 1 B 2 A 3 B 4 A 5 B

4 1 Have you ever been 2 have never read 3 stayed 4 have wanted 5 this year 6 last week

In these answers, we usually give **either** contracted forms (for example *I'm, don't*) or full forms (for example *I am, do not*). Normally both are correct.

page 60

1 1 have already paid.   2 has already left.
3 has already got up.   4 have already cooked
5 has already finished.

2 1 Bill hasn't found a job yet.   2 Have you
finished that book yet?   3 I haven't started
work yet.   4 Have you had supper yet?

3 1 I have just looked at the floor.   2 I have
just thought about my home.   3 I have just
moved my feet.   4 I have just put my hand
on my head.

4 1 She has already written three letters.
2 She has just telephoned her mother.
3 She has already cleaned the kitchen.
4 She hasn't read the newspaper yet.
5 She has just made some toast.
6 She hasn't listened to the radio yet.

page 61

1 1 for   2 since   3 since   4 for   5 since
6 since   7 for   8 for   9 since   10 since
11 for   12 since

4 1 How long have you known Mike?
2 How long have you been a student?
3 How long has your brother been a doctor?
4 How long has Andrew had that dog?
5 How long have David and Elizabeth been
together?

pages 62–63

1 1 Mary has been painting the house for four
days.   2 We have been driving for four
hours.   3 Ann has been working at Smiths
since January.   4 Joe has been building boats
for twenty years.   5 We have been waiting
for the bus since 8.30.   6 Prices have been
going up since last year.

2 1 How long has Jane been talking on the
phone?   2 How long has your brother been
working in Glasgow?   3 How long has Eric
been driving buses?   4 How long has that
man been standing outside?   5 How long
have you been playing the piano?

4 1 ✓ 2 ✗ 3 ✓ 4 ✓ 5 ✗ 6 ✓

5 1 She has been playing the piano.   2 He has
been playing football.   3 She has been
teaching.   4 He has been writing letters.
5 She has been swimming.

page 64

1 1 been raining   2 broken   3 told
4 been driving   5 read   6 been waiting
7 been playing   8 played

2 1 has been snowing   2 have had   3 has been
working   4 has been   5 have ... known

3 1 been living   2 lived   3 worked   4 been
working

pages 66-67

1 1 began   2 broken   3 come   4 drunk   5 ate
6 fell   7 forgotten   8 given   9 knew
10 taken

2 1 Did all those people go home?   2 Peter
hasn't told us everything.   3 Has the
postman been?   4 Has Pat been working all
day?   5 Eric and Angela didn't buy a new
house.   6 Did Mary's boyfriend forget her
birthday?

3 1 Why has everybody gone home?
2 How long has Ann been learning Chinese?
3 Why did George close the door?
4 Where have the people in the big house
gone on holiday?   5 When did the President
and his family visit Russia?   6 How long
have Jan's father and mother been travelling
in Scotland?   7 What has happened?

4 1 yes   2 don't know   3 yes   4 don't know
5 don't know   6 yes   7 no   8 yes

5 1 had   2 spent   3 lost   4 did not pass
5 happened.   6 has been   7 has changed
8 have bought   9 has opened   10 have had
11 have passed

6 1 have changed; didn't like   2 have found;
did ... find   3 has already lost   4 lost
5 Has ... spoken   6 has been snowing
7 have finished   8 studied   9 have passed
10 have ... known   11 Have ... written
12 waited   13 has just gone   14 haven't
tried   15 has been eating

7 1 have been   2 ago   3 came   4 has been
doing   5 have opened   6 have just asked
7 hasn't decided   8 has never lived
9 bought   10 talked

pages 68-69

1 1 had worked   2 hadn't rained.   3 had
happened   4 had seen   5 hadn't got
6 had they been   7 had paid   8 hadn't done

2 1 understood; had got 2 didn't play; had hurt 3 had looked; started 4 had never travelled; went 5 arrived; had already closed 6 didn't have; had paid

3 1 got; had eaten 2 met; had been 3 started; remembered; had not closed 4 found; had ... opened 5 told; had ... bought

4 1 When George had eaten all the chocolate biscuits, he started eating the lemon ones.
2 When I had turned off the lights in the office, I locked the door and left.
3 I borrowed Karen's newspaper when she had read it. 4 Mark had a long hot shower when he had done his exercises. 5 When Barry had phoned his mother with the good news, he went to bed.

page 70

1 1 broken, brought, come, drunk, eaten, forgotten, given, left, made, stood, stayed, stopped, taken, thought, tried

2 1 We haven't been walking. 2 They've phoned. 3 I hadn't spoken to her before.
4 Has she been to Chicago? 5 He's bought a car. 6 Has she been studying Italian?

3 1 has lost; lost 2 Have you ever driven 3 has never had 4 Did you see; has just phoned 5 yet 6 eight weeks ago 7 I've been; for 8 'It's already started.'

4 1 We've known; for 2 I've been working 3 has passed; Did he get 4 has gone; did she leave 5 stood

5 1 saw; knew; had met 2 didn't have; had bought 3 had already started; arrived 4 broke; had forgotten 5 met

page 72

1 1 to be 2 be 3 pass 4 to get 5 be 6 to speak

2 1 likes 2 may 3 must 4 works 5 should 6 seems 7 might 8 wants

3 1 Can he ski? 2 He can't play poker.
3 She mustn't sing. 4 He may not go this week. 5 Must she work on Sunday?

page 73

1 1 must write 2 must hurry/go 3 must stop 4 must pay 5 must study 6 must speak 7 must go

2 2 A; must phone 3 E; must go 4 C; must have 5 D; must see

3 1 Must I pay 2 Must I come 3 Must I sit 4 Must I answer 5 Must I stay

page 74

1 1 You mustn't wash 2 You mustn't make 3 You mustn't use 4 You mustn't smoke

2 2 D; needn't make 3 C; needn't make 4 A; needn't drive 5 B; needn't give

3 1 mustn't 2 needn't 3 mustn't 4 needn't 5 needn't 6 mustn't 7 mustn't 8 needn't 9 needn't 10 mustn't

page 75

1 1 has to have 2 has to wear 3 has to be 4 has to carry 5 has to be

2 2 A; do we have to 3 D; Do I/we have to 4 B; Do they have to 5 C; Do I/we have to

3 1 don't have to close 2 doesn't have to water 3 doesn't have to post 4 don't have to go 5 don't have to speak 6 doesn't have to arrive

page 76

1 1 He didn't have to learn Russian. 2 He had to learn maths. 3 He didn't have to learn music. 4 He had to play football. 5 He didn't have to write poems. 6 He had to write stories.

2 1 Did John have to pay for his lessons? 2 Did Mary have to take an exam last year? 3 Did Joe and Sue have to wait a long time for a train? 4 Did you have to show your passport at the airport? 5 Did the children have to walk home? 6 Did Peter have to cook supper?

3 1 'll have to get 2 won't have to go 3 Will ... have to speak 4 'll have to play 5 'll have to ask 6 won't have to work 7 Will ... have to get

page 77

1 1 shouldn't say; should say 2 should eat; shouldn't eat 3 should be; shouldn't leave 4 shouldn't drive; should stop 5 should drink; shouldn't wear

2 1 'What time should I arrive?' 2 Who should I phone 3 'What should I wear?' 4 'Where should I sit?' 5 Where should I put

3 1 must 2 should 3 should 4 must 5 must 6 must 7 should

In these answers, we usually give **either** contracted forms (for example *I'm, don't*) or full forms (for example *I am, do not*). Normally both are correct.

ANSWER KEY 293

pages 78–79

1 1 He can't play tennis, but he can play baseball.   2 He can play the piano, but he can't play the violin.   3 He can't remember names, but he can remember faces.   4 He can eat oranges, but he can't eat cherries.

2 1 'Can he cook?'   2 'Can she speak Spanish?'   3 'How much can they pay?'   4 'Can you drive a bus?'   5 'Can you wear red?'   6 'Can you see the sea?'   7 'Can you read music?'   8 'What can he do?'

5 1 could name   2 could count   3 could read   4 could not write   5 could tell   6 could remember   7 could not walk

6 1 to be able to   2 been able to   3 been able to   4 to be able to

7 1 will be able to eat   2 will be able to play   3 will be able to travel   4 will be able to remember   5 Will ... be able to do

pages 80–81

1 1 It may not rain.   2 We may buy a car.   3 Joe may not be at home.   4 Ann may need help.   5 The baby may be hungry.   6 I may not change my job.   7 She may be married.   8 He may not want to talk to you.

2 2 E; may not have   3 B; may stay   4 C; may not be   5 D; may snow.   6 F; may give

3 1 might find   2 might send   3 might fall   4 might make   5 might buy

4 1 might not finish   2 might miss   3 might give   4 might not believe   5 might not pass   6 might not know

5 1 be a pilot.   2 He might be a businessman.   3 She might be an opera singer.   4 He might be a lawyer or a politician.   5 She might be a lawyer or a politician.   6 He might be a chef.   7 She might be a gardener.

page 82

1 1 He must want something.   2 She must be French.   3 He must read a lot.   4 That must be interesting.   5 He must have very big feet.   6 You must know Paul Baker.

2 1 She must speak Italian or English.   2 She must have long/fair hair.   3 She must play golf.   4 She must have a lot of / lots of / plenty of money.   5 She must be interested in Russia / history / Russian history.   6 She must have a dog.

3 1 He can't be American.   2 He can't be a teacher.   3 She can't have many friends.   4 We can't need petrol.   5 He can't be hungry.   6 The film can't be very good.

page 83

1 1 pass   2 clean   3 hold   4 drive   5 lend

2 1 Can you open the door?   2 Could you give me an envelope?   3 Can you pass me the sugar?   4 Could you watch my children for a minute?   5 Could you tell me the time?   6 Could you possibly change some dollars for me?

3 Can you give me a receipt?   2 Can you bring me the menu?   3 Can you give me an estimate?   4 Can you give me your price list?   5 Can you bring me the bill?

pages 84–85

1 1 Can/Could I have a glass of water (, please)?   2 Can/Could I use your pencil (, please)?   3 Can/Could I have some more coffee (, please)?   4 Can/Could I put my coat here (, please)?

2 1 Could I use your calculator, please?   2 Could I leave early today, please?   3 Could I take your photo, please?   4 Could I borrow your newspaper, please?   5 Could I turn on the TV, please?

3 2 E; can play   3 B; can eat   4 D; can turn on   5 F; can watch   6 A; can park

4 1 You can't smoke here.   2 You can't take photos here.   3 You can't cycle here.   4 You can't use mobile phones here.

5 1 Can I make a cup of tea (OR one) for you?   2 Can I help you?   3 Can I drive you to the station?   4 Can I get some aspirins for you?

6 1 may not talk   2 may not leave   3 may use   4 may take   5 may leave   6 may use   7 may do

page 86

1 1 What shall I buy for Sandra's birthday?   2 When shall I phone you?   3 Shall I pay now?   4 Shall I clean the bathroom?   5 How many tickets shall I buy?   6 Where shall I leave the car?   7 What time shall I come this evening?   8 Shall I shut the windows?

2 1 Shall we go out this evening?   2 Shall we have a game of cards?   3 How shall we travel to London?   4 What shall we do at the weekend?   5 Where shall we go on holiday?   6 Shall we look for a hotel?   7 What time shall we meet Peter?   8 How much bread shall we buy?

3 1 Shall I post your letters?   2 Shall I do your shopping?   3 Shall I make your bed?   4 Shall I read to you?   5 Shall I drive you to the station?   6 Shall I make you a cup of tea?

page 87

1 2 A; 'd better not drink   3 F; 'd better not sit   4 C; 'd better call   5 E; 'd better go   6 D; 'd better stop

2 1 'd better   2 should   3 'd better   4 should   5 'd better   6 should

page 88

1 1 I'd like a black T-shirt, please.   2 Would you like an aspirin?   3 Would you like the newspaper?   4 I'd like an ice cream, please.   5 Would you like some more toast?   6 I'd like a receipt.

2 1 I'd like / I wouldn't like to be taller.   2 I'd like / I wouldn't like to be younger.   3 I'd like / I wouldn't like to be older.   4 I'd like / I wouldn't like to go to the moon.   5 I'd like / I wouldn't like to live in a different country.   6 I'd like / I wouldn't like to have a lot of dogs.   7 I'd like / I wouldn't like to write a book.

3 1 Would   2 like   3 Would   4 Yes, I do.   5 would like   6 don't   7 wouldn't

page 89

1 1 People used to travel on foot or on horses.   2 Most people didn't use to go to school.   3 Most people didn't use to learn to read.   4 People used to cook on wood fires.   5 Most people didn't use to live very long.   6 Most / A lot of people used to work very long hours.

2 1 Ann used to study German. Now she studies French.   2 Bill used to live in London. Now he lives in Glasgow.   3 Mary used to read a lot. Now she watches TV.   4 Joe used to be a driver. Now he's a hairdresser.   5 Alice used to drink coffee. Now she drinks tea.   6 Peter used to have lots of girlfriends. Now he's married.

3 1 Did you use to have dark hair?   2 Did you use to play football?   3 Where did you use to work?   4 Did you use to enjoy your work?   5 Did you use to go to a lot of parties?

pages 90–91

1 1 should have locked   2 should have been   3 should have put   4 should have brought   5 should have arrived   6 should have brought

2 1 shouldn't have eaten   2 shouldn't have spent   3 shouldn't have gone   4 shouldn't have played

3 1 could have married   2 could have lent   3 could have studied   4 could have won   5 could have been   6 could have gone

4 1 She may have broken her leg.   2 I may have lost my keys.   3 Alice may have gone back home.   4 My great-grandfather may have been a soldier.   5 I may have found a new job.   6 This house may have been a school once.

5 1 She must have gone home.   2 I must have left it on the bus.   3 She must have forgotten.   4 John must have taken it.

page 92

1 1 ✗ 2 ✗ 3 ✗ 4 ✓ 5 ✓ 6 ✗

2 1 must   2 shouldn't   3 must not   4 should   5 needn't   6 have to

3 1 I will be able to speak French soon.   2 Everybody had to fill in a big form last year.   3 Everybody will have to fill in a big form next year.

4 1 You must phone Martin.   2 Ann might be here this evening.   3 You needn't wait.   4 People shouldn't watch TV all the time.   5 Shall I open a window?

5 1 ✓ 2 ✗ 3 ✗ 4 ✗

6 1 must   2 can't   3 may have gone

7 1 Can/Could I have a cup of coffee (,please)?   2 Could I (possibly) take a photograph of you, please?   3 Can/Could you close the door, (please) John?

page 94

1 1 B   2 E   3 H   4 C   5 F   6 G   7 D

2 1 is spoken   2 studied   3 spent   4 was broken   5 are made   6 was written   7 will be opened   8 was driving; was stopped

In these answers, we usually give **either** contracted forms (for example *I'm, don't*) or full forms (for example *I am, do not*). Normally both are correct.

ANSWER KEY   295

page 95

1 1 is 2 am 3 is 4 Are 5 is 6 is 7 are 8 Are

2 1 is written 2 are watched 3 are sold 4 is known 5 is pronounced 6 is spoken 7 is played 8 are cleaned

3 1 is not spelt; is it spelt? 2 is not usually seen; is it seen? 3 is not pronounced; is it pronounced? 4 are not found; are they found? 5 is not paid; is she paid?

page 96

1 1 will be opened 2 will be spoken 3 will be finished 4 will be cleaned 5 will be sent

2 1 won't be taken; will they be taken? 2 won't be built; will it be built? 3 won't be spoken; will be spoken?

page 97

1 1 was 2 were 3 were 4 were 5 was 6 was

2 1 were taken 2 were left 3 was cleaned 4 were met 5 was told 6 was sent

3 1 was not educated; was he educated? 2 were not posted; were they posted? 3 was not cooked; was it cooked? 4 was not made; was it made? 5 was not paid; was it paid?

page 98

1 1 it's being cleaned. 2 she's being interviewed 3 my watch is being repaired. 4 I'm being sent 5 my hair is being cut.

2 (*Possible answers*:) Baggage is being checked/x-rayed. Boarding passes are being checked / printed. Business people are being met. Cars are being parked. Departures are being announced. Passports are being checked. Reservations are being made/checked. Tickets are being sold / checked.

page 99

1 1 has been arrested 2 has been bought 3 has been killed 4 have been found 5 has been chosen

2 1 It's never been ridden. 2 It's never been worn. 3 It's never been opened. 4 It's never been used. 5 It's never been played.

page 100

1 2 C 3 A 4 E 5 B

2 1 The younger children were given picture books. Picture books were given to the younger children. 2 Anna and Joe were lent a car by the Watsons. A car was lent to Anna and Joe by the Watsons. 3 Nathan was promised a new computer. A new computer was promised to Nathan. 4 Some people were sent two invitations by mistake. Two invitations were sent to some people by mistake. 5 Most of us were shown a film about Wales. A film about Wales was shown to most of us.

3 1 Cathy wasn't promised a place. Who was promised a place? Was anybody promised a place? 2 We weren't given enough time. Who was given enough time? Was anybody given enough time? 3 Jon was not shown the hall. Who was shown the hall? Were any of the musicians shown the hall? 4 I was not given an explanation. Who was given an explanation? Was anybody given an explanation?

page 101

1 1 by the government. 2 by loud music 3 by my granddaughter. 4 by a farmer 5 by a tree

2 1 'Who was it written by?' 2 'Who was it sung by?' 3 'Who was it painted by?' 4 'Who was it directed by?' 5 'Who was it built by?' 6 'Who was it chosen by?'

3 1 by Shakespeare 2 ~~by people who watch birds~~ 3 ~~by mountain climbers~~ 4 by Frank Lloyd Wright 5 ~~by translators~~ 6 ~~by sugar companies~~ 7 by an English person

pages 102–103

1 1 Ann's mother made this sweater. This sweater was made by Ann's mother. 2 Janet paid the electricity bill last week. The electricity bill was paid by Janet last week. 3 The first television was built by J. L. Baird in 1924. J. L. Baird built the first television in 1924.

2 1 B 2 B 3 A 4 B 5 A

3 1 are covered 2 are spent 3 has 4 walk 5 do not eat 6 are left 7 sleep 8 are made 9 is not known 10 live 11 are cut down

4 1 will be spoken 2 were sent 3 is used 4 'It's being repaired.' 5 has my name been

5 1 will be taught   2 was spoken   3 is being painted.   4 have been moved.   5 are pronounced

page 104

1 1 posted   2 weren't paid   3 speaks   4 isn't pronounced   5 will be built   6 is being cleaned   7 have been invited

2 1 is made   2 were killed   3 will be done 4 is spoken

3 1 A   2 B   3 B   4 A

4 1 are being followed.   2 has been stolen. 3 is being repaired.   4 have been moved. 5 have been sent   6 are … being interviewed.

5 1 Meal tickets were given to all the passengers. 2 Ellen has been shown the plans for the new building.   3 A week's holiday has been promised to all the office workers.   4 Laura was sent a bill for the repairs.

pages 106–107

1 1 Are you tired?   2 Is he at home? 3 Must you go now?   4 Can they speak Spanish?   5 Will you be here tomorrow? 6 Will she arrive by train?   7 Has she forgotten her keys?   8 Is your sister playing tennis?

2 1 Do you drink coffee?   2 Do you like jazz? 3 Did you know Andrew?   4 Did you go skiing last winter?   5 Do you work in London?

3 1 Does he speak Arabic?   2 Does he know Mr Peters?   3 Does he work at home?   4 Did he live in Birmingham?   5 Did he go home last week?

4 1 C   2 B   3 A   4 B   5 B   6 A   7 A

5 1 Is your sister Caroline talking to the police? 2 Do all the people here understand Spanish? 3 Did most of the football team play well? 4 Is everybody in the office working late today?   5 Is the man at the table in the corner asleep?   6 Does the 7.30 train for London leave from Platform 2?

pages 108–109

1 1 'Why are you here?'   2 'Where have you been today?'   3 'When are you going to Glasgow?'   4 'How do you like Scotland?' 5 'How did you come here?'   6 'Why did you come by car?'   7 'Where do you live?' 8 'When are you leaving?'   9 'When will we see you again?'

2 1 How far is   2 How tall is   3 How fast was 4 How often do you   5 How big is   6 How long did you   7 How well do you

3 2 C; What colour   3 D; What sort/kind of 4 B; What size   5 F; What colour   6 H; What sort/kind of   7 E; What time   8 G; What size

4 1 'What's your new girlfriend like?'   2 'What are your new neighbours like?'   3 'What's your new car like?'   4 'What's your new house like?'   5 'What's your new job like?' 6 'What's your new school like?'

pages 110–111

1 1 plays   2 made   3 did she marry?   4 does this word mean?   5 did you say?   6 told

2 1 came to her party?   2 did he catch? 3 goes to the station?   4 does he speak? 5 does she like?

3 1 Alice.   2 Who loves Ann? Pete.   3 Who does Ann love? Joe.   4 Who loves Alice? Fred.   5 Who does Joe love? Mary.   6 Who does Pete love? Ann.   7 Who loves Pete?

5 1 (a) What did Mary buy?   (b) Who bought a coat?   2 (a) What did the bus hit? (b) What hit that tree?   3 (a) Who lost the office keys?   (b) What did Ann lose? 4 (a) What is Fred studying?   (b) Who is studying Arabic?   5 (a) Who hates computers?   (b) What does Mike hate?

6 1 Who first reached the North Pole?   2 Who wrote *War and Peace*?   3 Who built the Great Wall of China?   4 Who painted *Sunflowers*?

pages 112–113

1 1 Milk isn't red. / Milk's not red.   2 The children aren't at home.   3 Joe hasn't been to Egypt.   4 You mustn't give this letter to her mother.   5 I won't be in the office tomorrow.   6 I couldn't swim when I was two years old.   7 We weren't in Birmingham yesterday.   8 I'm not English.

4 1 Shakespeare didn't live in New York. 2 Phone books don't tell you about words. 3 The earth doesn't go round the moon. 4 Most Algerians don't speak Russian. 5 Cookers don't keep food cold.   6 The Second World War didn't end in 1955. 7 John doesn't know my sister.

6 1 don't   2 wasn't   3 doesn't/can't   4 haven't 5 aren't   6 won't   7 didn't/couldn't 8 didn't/couldn't   9 hasn't   10 'm not

7 2 A   3 B   4 C

In these answers, we usually give **either** contracted forms (for example *I'm, don't*) or full forms (for example *I am, do not*). Normally both are correct.

ANSWER KEY 297

page 114

1 1 Nobody lives in that house.   2 I'll never understand my dog.   3 The children told me nothing.   4 I have no money.   5 I could hardly see the road.

2 1 I saw nobody.   2 We had no trouble.
3 My parents never go out.   4 I looked for the dog, but it was nowhere in the house.
5 I ate nothing yesterday.   6 It hardly rained for three months.   7 Nobody spoke.

3 1 My grandmother never drives fast.
2 Andrew doesn't play the guitar.   3 When she talked, I understood nothing.   4 I don't like Ann's new shoes.   5 Nothing happened this morning.   6 There's nowhere to sit down in the station.   7 I hardly watch TV.
8 Nobody wants to play tennis.

page 115

1 1 Can't you swim?   2 Don't you speak Spanish?   3 Weren't the shops open?
4 Hasn't Ann arrived?   5 Didn't she know him?   6 Why aren't you working?

2 1 Don't you speak Arabic?   2 Isn't that Bill over there?   3 Didn't you study at Oxford?
4 Isn't this your coat?   5 Isn't her mother a doctor?   6 Wasn't Joe at the party?

3 1 Aren't they late!   2 Doesn't she look tired!
3 Isn't that child dirty!   4 Isn't it hot!
5 Doesn't John work hard!

4 1 No   2 No   3 Yes   4 Yes   5 Yes   6 No

page 116

1 1 Has she been to America?   2 Does she like dancing?   3 Can she swim?   4 Will she be here tomorrow?   5 Did she watch TV yesterday?

2 1 Ann isn't at work. / Ann's not at work.
2 I haven't forgotten your face.   3 Peter doesn't drive taxis.   4 We didn't go to Portugal.   5 You mustn't use that one.

3 1 What colour   2 How tall   3 What sort/kind of

4 1 ✗   2 ✗   3 ✓   4 ✗   5 ✗   6 ✓   7 ✓

5 1 Who cooked dinner?   2 What did Julia cook?   3 What hit Joe?   4 Who did the ball hit?   5 What does Ann play?   6 Who plays the guitar?

6 1 No   2 Yes   3 Yes   4 No

7 1 ✗   2 ✓   3 ✗   4 ✓   5 ✗

page 118

1 1 –   2 to   3 –   4 –; to   5 –; to   6 to

2 1 to learn   2 help   3 to see   4 buy   5 to hear   6 to go

3 1 not to have   2 not to break   3 not to go to sleep   4 not to make   5 not to have
6 not to talk

page 119

1 1 to drive   2 to catch   3 to ask for
4 to wait for   5 to meet   6 to buy
7 to finish   8 to learn

2 1 I stood on a chair to clean the top of the fridge.   2 Roger's gone to town to buy a book.   3 We moved closer to the fire to get warm.   4 Use this key to open the front door.   5 I left a note to tell George about the meeting.   6 Jane got a part-time job to earn some pocket money.

3 1 to weigh   2 to bake   3 to fry   4 to boil
5 to mix   6 to cut

pages 120–121

1 1 refuse to   2 started to   3 promised to
4 expected to   5 ('ve) tried to   6 ('ve) decided to   7 want to   8 ('m) learning to
9 plan to   10 needed to   11 forgot to
12 seemed to   13 began to
14 ('ve) continued to   15 prefer to

2 1 needs to   2 agreed to   3 decided to
4 tried to   5 learnt/learned to
6 promised to   7 forgot to   8 refused to
9 want to   10 started to   11 prefers to
12 continued to   13 hopes to   14 seemed to
15 began to

pages 122–123

1 1 Sarah would like John to cook tonight.
2 The policeman wants the man to move his car.   3 Helen's mother wants her to wash her face.   4 Bill would like Andy to help him.   5 Roger would like Karen to lend him some money.   6 Jake wants Peter to be quiet for a minute.   7 David would like Alice to have dinner with him.   8 Mike would like the government to put more money into schools.

2 1 Her boss wants her to work harder.
2 Her little brother wants her to buy him a bicycle.   3 Her dog wants her to take him for a walk.   4 Her boyfriend wants her to go to America with him.   5 Her friend Martha wants her to lend her a blue dress.   6 Her guitar teacher wants her to buy a better guitar.   7 Her mother wants her to spend every weekend at home.   8 Her sister wants her to go to Russia with her.

3 1 I didn't tell Alan to go home.   2 I asked Fred to be quiet.   3 Do you expect her to phone?   4 I helped Joe to carry the books.
5 The policewoman told me to show her my driving licence   6 Ann helped me to finish the work.   7 I asked the shop assistant to help me.   8 I need you to stay with me.

5 1 They want me to buy a yacht.   2 They want me to buy a bike.   3 They want me to buy a motorboat.   4 They want me to buy a plane.
5 They want me to buy a motorbike.

pages 124–125

1 1 Eleanor is silly to listen to Mark.
2 Elizabeth was wrong to take the train without a ticket.   3 I was stupid to sit on my glasses.   4 I was wrong to wash a white shirt with a red one.   5 You're silly to believe Luke.   6 You're right to eat a good breakfast.
7 You were crazy to lend money to Chris.

2 1 sorry to say   2 unhappy to think   3 happy not to have   4 pleased to find   5 surprised to find   6 happy to be   7 pleased to see

3 2 C; to eat   3 E; to find   4 D; to read
5 B; to open

4 1 It's good to see you.   2 Grammar is sometimes difficult to understand.
3 That mountain is impossible to climb.
4 This shirt is nice to wear.   5 The word 'sixth' is hard to pronounce.   6 This furniture is easy to clean.

page 126

1 1 Alice is old enough to work part-time.
2 Alice isn't old enough to leave home.
3 Mark is old enough to leave school.
4 Cathy is old enough to leave home.
5 Cathy isn't old enough to vote.   6 John is old enough to change his name.   7 Liz is old enough to drive a bus.

2 1 Helen is too ill to work.   2 My grandfather is too old to travel.   3 I'm too bored to listen any longer.   4 Cara's too hot to play tennis.
5 I'm too hungry to work.

3 1 This box is too heavy to lift.   2 This soup is too salty to eat.   3 This book is too boring to finish.   4 That plate is too hot to touch.
5 Some animals are too small to see.
6 That sign is too dirty to read.

page 127

1 1 homework to do.   2 letters to post?
3 video to watch.   4 dress to wear
5 shopping to do   6 friend to see

2 1 anything to wear.   2 somewhere to work.
3 nothing to do   4 nobody/no one to teach.
5 something to finish.   6 nowhere to go.
7 somebody/someone to love.   8 anywhere to stay   9 anyone/anybody to help
10 something to carry.

page 128

1 1 It was nice to have   2 It was interesting to see   3 it was a bit hard to understand
4 It was very easy to make   5 It was expensive to eat   6 it was dangerous to swim.   7 it was impossible to be

2 1 It's important to practise grammar.
2 It's important not to translate everything.
3 It's important to read a lot.   4 It's important to read things that interest you.   5 It's not necessary to have perfect pronunciation.
6 It's important to have good enough pronunciation.   7 It's important not to make too many mistakes.   8 It's not necessary to speak without mistakes.   9 It's important to practise listening to English.   10 It's important to know 3,000 – 5,000 words.   11 It's not necessary to know 50,000 words.
12 It's important to have a good English-English dictionary.   13 It's important to have a good bilingual dictionary.

page 129

1 1 skiing; reading   2 flying; going by train
3 eating; washing   4 writing; speaking OR speaking; writing   5 understanding; listening
6 shopping; shaving

4 NO SMOKING 3   NO FISHING 5
NO CYCLING 4   NO CAMPING 2

In these answers, we usually give **either** contracted forms (for example *I'm, don't*) or full forms (for example *I am, do not*). Normally both are correct.

ANSWER KEY   299

pages 130–131

1 1 taking 2 eating 3 shopping. 4 driving
   5 stopping

2 1 They've just finished playing tennis.
   2 All that week, it kept raining. 3 It's just
   stopped snowing. 4 He's given up smoking.
   5 He can't help thinking of/about Annie.
   6 They're going shopping. 7 She's
   practising writing.

3 1 washing 2 watching 3 working
   4 playing 5 wearing 6 studying

pages 132–133

1 2 C 3 A 4 D 5 B

2 1 hearing 2 smoking 3 going 4 watching
   5 washing

3 1 Bob is quite good at running, but not very
   good at cycling. 2 Sue is not very good
   at drawing, but quite good at singing.
   3 Mark is quite good at swimming, and very
   good at running. 4 Bob is bad at swimming,
   but quite good at singing. 5 Jane is very
   good at running, and quite good at cycling.
   6 Mark is not very good at singing, but quite
   good at drawing.

5 1 Ellie stayed awake by drinking lots of
   coffee. 2 Eric drank three glasses of water
   without stopping. 3 Charles woke us up
   by turning the TV on. 4 You can find out
   the meaning of a word by using a dictionary.
   5 Mike paid for his new house without
   borrowing any money. 6 Sue lost her
   driving licence by driving too fast, too often.
   7 Carl did all his homework without asking
   for any help. 8 Teresa cooks all her food
   without using any salt.

6 1 after swimming 2 Since passing her exam
   3 before visiting her 4 after breaking her
   leg 5 Before crashing his car 6 since
   getting her new job

page 134

1 1 to see 2 help 3 to buy 4 to go 5 not to

2 1 to work 2 to see 3 smoking. 4 driving
   5 to buy 6 to talk 7 sending 8 talking.
   9 to come 10 speaking.

3 1 A 2 C 3 C 4 A 5 D

4 1 I was surprised to find a cat in my bed.
   2 I was sorry not to have time to phone you.
   3 My phone number is easy to remember.

5 1 A 2 A

6 1 It's too heavy to lift. 2 He's old enough to
   vote. 3 I'm too tired to drive.

7 1 The boss wants Mary to answer the phone.
   2 Ann would like Pat to look after the
   children.

page 136

1 2 A; laugh 3 C; wait 4 B; ask 5 E; belong
   6 J; listen 7 H; Look 8 G; think 9 F; talks
   10 I; happened

2 1 in 2 to 3 to 4 at 5 to 6 at 7 about
   8 about 9 for

3 1 for 2 at 3 to 4 after 5 for 6 for
   7 about 8 to 9 for 10 about 11 into
   12 on 13 to

page 137

1 1 to 2 from 3 about 4 with 5 for 6 to

2 1 What are you thinking about? 2 Who
   does she work for? 3 Who/What were you
   talking about? 4 What are you interested
   in? 5 What are you looking at? 6 Who did
   you stay with?

3 1 What 2 Who 3 What 4 to 5 for
   6 Where

4 1 What do you cut wood with? An axe or
   a saw. 2 What do you shave with? A razor.
   3 What do you make holes with? A drill.
   4 What do you cut hair with? Scissors.

pages 138–139

1 1 get 2 go 3 round. 4 on. 5 back
   6 up 7 lie 8 Go

2 1 up 2 down. 3 back

3 1 on 2 on 3 down 4 off 5 down
   6 back 7 up 8 look 9 pick 10 give
   11 let 12 fill 13 take 14 Break

4 1 Could you turn the TV down? Could you
   turn it down? 2 You can throw the
   potatoes away. You can throw them away.
   3 Why don't you take your glasses off?
   Why don't you take them off?
   4 Please put that knife down. Please put
   it down. 5 Shall I fill your glass up?
   Shall I fill it up? 6 I'll switch the heating on.
   I'll switch it on.

page 140

1 1 I lent my bicycle to Joe yesterday.
2 I often read Lucy stories.   3 Carol teaches
mathematics to small children.   4 Ruth
showed the others the photo.   5 Sue often
gives flowers to her mother.   6 Could you
buy me a newspaper?   7 I tried to find my
parents a hotel room.   8 Could you pass
Mr Andrews this paper?   9 Bob has written
Ann a ten-page letter.   10 I want to get
Peter a good watch for Christmas.

2 1 Sally gave Fred a book.   2 Fred gave Annie
flowers.   3 Annie gave Luke a picture.
4 Luke gave Mary a sweater.   5 Mary gave
Joe a camera.

3 1 find   2 Give; give   3 buy

page 141

1 1 has his tyres checked   2 has his oil
changed   3 has his car repaired   4 has his
shoes cleaned   5 has his/the gardening done

2 1 She should have it repaired.   2 He should
have them cleaned.   3 They should have it
repaired.   4 He should have it cut.   5 They
should have it serviced.

page 142

1 TURN LEFT B   DON'T TOUCH D
DO NOT PICK FLOWERS C

2 1 turn   2 go   3 Turn   4 take   5 turn

3 1 Hurry up!   2 Be careful!   3 Help!
4 Have a good holiday.   5 Sleep well.
6 Don't forget   7 Wait for me!   8 Have
some more   9 Follow me   10 Don't worry.
11 Come; sit; make yourself at home.

page 143

1 1 Let's not go for a walk.   2 Let's play tennis.
3 Let's play cards.   4 Let's go swimming.
5 Let's not go swimming.   6 Let's go skiing.
7 Let's watch TV.   8 Let's go to France/Paris.

2 1 Athens.   2 to Copenhagen.   3 go to
Vienna.   4 'Let's go to Prague.'   5 'Let's go to
Warsaw.'   6 'Let's go to Moscow.'   7 'Let's go
to Marrakesh.'   8 'Let's go to Istanbul.'
9 'Let's go to Bangkok.'   10 'Let's go to
Beijing.'   11 'Let's go to Mexico City.'
12 'Let's go to Rio.'

page 144

1 1 to   2 at   3 for   4 about   5 for   6 for
7 after   8 –   9 for   10 on

2 1 'Where are you from?'   2 'What are you
waiting for?'   3 'Who are you writing to?'
4 'What are you looking at?'   5 'What/Who
are you talking about?'

3 1 A, B, D   2 E   3 A, D   4 A, C   5 C   6 A

4 1 up   2 round   3 fill   4 turn   5 on   6 Put
7 up   8 back.   9 careful   10 Come
11 worry.   12 Have   13 out   14 Make

page 146

1 1 a   2 an   3 a   4 a   5 an   6 a   7 an   8 a

2 1 an old friend   2 a big apple   3 an unhappy
child   4 an early train   5 a rich uncle
6 an easy job   7 a hard exercise
8 a European language   9 a small book

4 1 an envelope   2 A calculator   3 a torch.
4 a hammer.   5 A knife

page 147

1

SING. COUNT.	PL. COUNT.	UNCOUNT.
nose	mountains	meat
piano	photos	music
river	songs	oil
table	windows	snow

2 1 –   2 an   3 –   4 –   5 –   6 a   7 –   8 an   9 –

3 1 a   2 one   3 a   4 one   5 a   6 One

pages 148–149

1 1 the   2 the   3 an   4 a; a   5 the   6 a; the
7 the   8 the   9 The   10 a   11 the   12 the;
the

2 2 F; a   3 E; the   4 B; the   5 C; the   6 A; a

3 1 a   2 a   3 An   4 The   5 the   6 The   7 the
8 a   9 the   10 the   11 the

4 1 This is a mouse. It's the smallest animal in
the group.   2 This is a monkey. It's the most
intelligent animal in the group.   3 This is an
eagle. It's the fastest bird in the group.
4 This is a parrot. It's the only blue and
yellow bird in the group.   5 This is a pigeon.
It's the smallest bird in the group.   6 This is
a spider. It's the only creature with eight legs
in the group.   7 This is an ant. It's the only
creature with six legs in the group.   8 This is
a snake. It's the only creature with no legs in
the group.   9 This is a frog. It's the only
green creature in the group.

page 150

1 1 He's a cook. 2 He's a builder.
3 She's a driver. 4 He's a teacher.
5 She's a photographer. 6 She's a dentist.
7 He's a hairdresser. 8 She's a musician.
9 He's a shop assistant.

3 1 A bag is a container. 2 A hammer is
a tool. 3 A piano is an instrument.
4 A bus is a vehicle. 5 A screwdriver is
a tool. 6 A guitar is an instrument.
7 A box is a container. 8 A hotel is
a building.

page 151

1 1 a long neck. 2 big ears. 3 a loud voice.
4 a big beard. 5 dark hair.

2 A: 1 a 2 – 3 a 4 –
B: 1 a 2 a 3 – 4 – 5 – 6 a 7 a

page 152

1 (*Possible answers*:) Artists paint pictures.
Builders build houses. Cats don't like dogs.
Horses eat grass. Photographers take
photos. Pianists play music. Shop
assistants sell things. Students learn
things. Teachers teach things.
(*Other answers are possible.*)

2 1 Books 2 the books 3 English people
4 The flowers 5 Life 6 the words
7 The food 8 Water; ice 9 the windows

3 1 drivers 2 money 3 understand;
understand 4 think 5 think
6 things; things

pages 154–155

1 1 Spanish; Peru 2 Uncle Eric.; Lake
Superior. 3 Oxford Street; London.
4 Napoleon 5 Kilimanjaro; Africa.
6 France/Switzerland; Switzerland./France.

2 1 Himalayas 2 Denmark 3 Japanese
4 People's Republic of China 5 Trafalgar
Square 6 Mediterranean 7 Ireland
8 United Kingdom 9 USA

3 1 the 2 the 3 the 4 – 5 the 6 the 7 –
8 –

4 1 – 2 – 3 the 4 the 5 – 6 the 7 –
8 the 9 the 10 – 11 – 12 the 13 –
14 – 15 the 16 – 17 – 18 the 19 the
20 the

pages 156–157

1 1 lunch; Tuesday. 2 Easter; September.
3 next

2 1 bed 2 university 3 church 4 hospital
5 work; car

3 1 by boat 2 to school OR at school
3 at work 4 in hospital

4 2 G; a 3 C; a 4 F; a 5 D; a 6 E; a 7 A; an

5 1 Pat and I work in the same office.
2 We're going to the theatre tonight.
3 My room is at the top of the house.
4 Would you like to live in the country?
5 We usually go to the mountains at
Christmas.

page 158

1 1 an 2 a 3 an 4 a 5 a 6 an 7 a 8 an
9 a

2 COUNTABLE: diamond; holiday; price;
photo; shop
UNCOUNTABLE: coffee; hair; snow;
information; music

3 1 a 2 the; the 3 a 4 – 5 – 6 The 7 the
8 a 9 the 10 The; the 11 –

4 1 – 2 – 3 – 4 a 5 a 6 the 7 the 8 the
9 a 10 – 11 a 12 a 13 the 14 the 15 the
16 a 17 The 18 the 19 the 20 the 21 a
22 the 23 the 24 The 25 the

5 1 a 2 the 3 a 4 the 5 a 6 the 7 a
8 the 9 an 10 the 11 a 12 the

pages 160–161

1 1 these 2 This 3 These 4 These 5 this

2 1 those 2 those 3 that 4 Those 5 that

3 (*Possible answers:*) This plate is blue. That
plate is white. These glasses are green. Those
glasses are red. These spoons are black. That
spoon is silver. This saucer is blue. Those
saucers are white. This bowl is green. That
bowl is red. (*Other answers are possible.*)

4 1 I'm enjoying 2 will be 3 Those 4 was

5 1 that 2 that 3 This 4 those 5 this
6 these 7 This 8 That 9 this 10 those

pages 162–163

1 1 any 2 any 3 some 4 some 5 any
6 some 7 any 8 any 9 any

2 1 any more to drink. 2 any foreign languages. 3 any games 4 any sleep 5 any English newspapers

3 1 Could I have some coffee? 2 Would you like some bread? 3 Would you like some rice? 4 Could I have some tomatoes? 5 Would you like some more potatoes? 6 Could I have some more milk?

4 2 E 3 D 4 B 5 A 6 C 7 F

5 1 buy any. 2 some tomorrow. 3 some; you. 4 want any. 5 any good 6 put some

page 164

1 1 wasn't 2 didn't do 3 didn't have 4 didn't ask 5 didn't find

2 1 She doesn't speak any German.
2 He hasn't written any letters to her.
3 We get no rain here. 4 There's no post on Sundays. 5 She's got no brothers or sisters.

3 1 Sorry, no milk. 2 Any phone calls for me? 3 No more money. Any problems today?

4 1 None. 2 no 3 none 4 None 5 no; none

page 165

1 1 Nothing 2 anywhere 3 no one 4 anything 5 everywhere. 6 No one 7 Nowhere 8 something 9 Everyone 10 anybody 11 Everything 12 somewhere

2 1 anybody/anyone 2 nowhere 3 anything. 4 No one / Nobody 5 nothing. 6 everything

page 166

1 2 D 3 E 4 C 5 F 6 B 7 H 8 L 9 K 10 J 11 I 12 G

2 1 He bought some mustard, because he likes mustard. 2 He bought some mushrooms, because he likes mushrooms.
3 He didn't buy any carrots, because he doesn't like carrots. 4 He didn't buy any vinegar, because he doesn't like vinegar.
5 He bought some rice, because he likes rice.
6 He didn't buy any pepper, because he doesn't like pepper. 7 He bought some cornflakes, because he likes cornflakes.
8 He didn't buy any oil, because he doesn't like oil.

page 167

1 1 any boy 2 Any colour 3 any supermarket. 4 any question 5 any problems 6 Any day 7 any bank. 8 Any bus

2 2 F; Anywhere 3 A; anything. 4 B; anybody./anyone. 5 C; anywhere 6 E; anything.

page 168

1 1 much 2 much 3 many 4 many 5 much 6 much 7 many 8 many 9 much 10 many 11 many

2 1 How many symphonies did Beethoven write? 2 How many cents are there in a dollar? 3 How many kilometres are there in a mile? 4 How many states are there in the USA? 5 How much blood is there in a person's body? 6 How much air do we breathe every minute?

page 169

1 1 have 2 are 3 has 4 work 5 is 6 need

2 1 a lot / lots of work 2 a lot / lots of ideas 3 a lot / lots of football 4 a lot / lots of languages 5 a lot / lots of houses 6 a lot / lots of sleep

page 170

1 1 a little 2 a few 3 a few 4 a little 5 a few 6 a little 7 a few 8 a little 9 a little 10 a few

2 1 a little 2 little 3 few 4 a few 5 a few 6 few

3 1 There was only a little room on the bus. OR There wasn't much room on the bus.
2 Only a few people learn foreign languages perfectly. OR Not many people learn foreign languages perfectly. 3 She has only (got) a few friends. OR She hasn't (got) many friends. 4 We only get a little rain here in summer. OR We don't get much rain here in summer. 5 This car only uses a little petrol. OR This car doesn't use much petrol.
6 There are only a few flowers in the garden. OR There aren't many flowers in the garden.

In these answers, we usually give **either** contracted forms (for example *I'm, don't*) or full forms (for example *I am, do not*). Normally both are correct.

ANSWER KEY 303

page 171

1 1 enough 2 not enough 3 not enough
4 not enough water

2 1 enough time 2 enough girls. 3 enough
chairs. 4 enough work. 5 enough money
6 enough salt

3 1 not loud enough 2 not comfortable
enough 3 not bright enough 4 not easy
enough 5 not clear enough 6 not fresh
enough 7 not deep enough

4 1 warm enough 2 enough beds 3 often
enough 4 quiet enough 5 enough milk
6 enough help 7 sweet enough

page 172

1 1 too 2 too much 3 too many 4 too
much 5 too 6 too much 7 too
8 too many 9 too many 10 too

2 1 too low 2 too short 3 too light 4 too
soft 5 not wide enough 6 not cheap
enough 7 not wet enough 8 not thin
enough

3 (*Possible answers*:) 1 too many (pairs of) socks
2 enough (pairs of) boots 3 too many
pocket torches 4 not enough (tubes of) sun-
cream 5 too many waterproof jackets 6 too
many pairs of sunglasses 7 too much bread
8 too much cheese 9 not enough water
10 not enough oranges 11 not enough
chocolate 12 enough soap 13 too many
toothbrushes (*Other answers are possible.*)

page 173

1 1 all (of) 2 all of 3 All 4 all (of) 5 all of
6 all 7 All of 8 All (of)

2 1 The buses all run on Sundays. 2 The films
all start at 7 o'clock. 3 Our secretaries all
speak Arabic. 4 These coats all cost the same.

3 1 These children can all swim. 2 Our
windows are all dirty. 3 Sorry, the tickets
have all gone. 4 The shops will all be open
tomorrow.

page 174

1 1 Every animal breathes air. 2 She's read
every book in the library. 3 I paid every
bill. 4 Every computer is working today.
5 Every language has verbs. 6 Every
London train stops at Reading.

2 1 all 2 every 3 every 4 all 5 Every
6 All 7 All 8 every 9 Every 10 All
11 All 12 every

page 175

1 1 Each 2 every 3 each 4 each 5 every/
each 6 Every 7 each 8 each

2 1 Every one 2 every 3 every one. 4 Every
one; every one 5 every 6 every one.

page 176

1 1 Both 2 both 3 either 4 Both; neither
5 either 6 both 7 Either 8 neither; either;
both

2 1 both sides 2 Both; parents 3 both
directions. 4 Both teams 5 both knees
6 both; ear-rings/socks 7 both ends
8 both; socks.

3 1 both these books 2 both doors 3 both of
you 4 both our jobs 5 both shops 6 both
my uncles

page 177

1 1 not much of the time 2 any of my
friends 3 enough of that meat 4 some of
the big plates 5 a few of her ideas 6 most
of these mistakes

2 1 – 2 of 3 of 4 of 5 – 6 – 7 of 8 of
9 – 10 of

3 1 Most 2 most of the 3 Most of the
4 Most 5 Most 6 most of the 7 Most
8 most 9 most of the 10 most

page 178

1 1 this. 2 that 3 those 4 This

2 1 I need 2 no letters 3 'Nothing.'
4 'Anywhere.' 5 beautiful eyes
6 much 7 many 8 lots of 9 think
10 is 11 many 12 too 13 big enough?
14 Is

3 1 every 2 each 3 every 4 each
5 everything. 6 all 7 everybody

4 1 Both 2 either 3 every one 4 Most
5 many of 6 A lot. 7 a little 8 few

5 1 She only has / She's only got a little
money. OR She hasn't got / She doesn't have
much money. 2 I have / I've got a lot of
friends in Edinburgh.

pages 180–181

1 1 her   2 us   3 him   4 they   5 him   6 them?
7 her; she

2 1 He   2 them   3 him   4 They   5 her   6 She

3 1 They   2 It   3 It   4 them   5 it   6 it
7 them.   8 they

5 1 'He has moved to London.'   2 'They are on
that chair.'   3 'I like them.'   4 'She is going
to study medicine.'   5. 'No, it is difficult.'

6 1 It's warm.   2 It's windy.   3 It's snowing.
4 It's hot.   5 It's raining.   6 It's sunny.
7 It's cloudy.   8 It's cold.

pages 182–183

1 1 his   2 our   3 Whose   4 its   5 my   6 their
7 his   8 her   9 your   10 his   11 its

2 1 John sold his bike to Peter.   2 Peter sold his
dog to Mary.   3 Mary sold her house to Pat
and Sam.   4 Pat and Sam sold their motorbike
to Bill.   5 Bill sold his piano to Alice.   6 Alice
sold her coat to Michael.   7 Michael sold his
camera to Helen.   8 Helen sold her guitar to
Marilyn.   9 Marilyn sold her hair-dryer to
Tom.   10 Tom sold his dictionary to Ann.

3 1 their son Joe   2 their daughter Emma
3 their camper van.   4 her brother Frank
5 her sister Lucy   6 his sister Mary
7 his brother Eric   8 their friend Pete

page 184

1 1 I prefer our house to theirs.   2 Her hair
looks better than yours.   3 Yours looks
terrible.   4 That dog looks like ours.

2 1 The towel is not theirs.   2 The razor is his.
3 The red toothbrush is his.   4 The green
toothbrush is hers.   5 The toothpaste is
theirs.   6 The make-up is hers.   7 The soap
is hers.   8 The green washcloth is hers.
9 The hair-dryer is hers.   10 The dressing-
gown is his.   11 The shampoo is theirs.

page 185

1 1 him   2 herself   3 themselves
4 yourselves   5 him

2 1 myself   2 'Himself.'   3 yourself.
4 ourselves   5 herself   6 yourselves
7 themselves.

3 1 yourself   2 themselves.   3 myself.
4 ourselves   5 herself.

4 1 each other   2 themselves.   3 each other
4 yourselves   5 each other

page 186

1

I	me	my	mine	myself
you	you	your	yours	yourself
he	him	his	his	himself
she	her	her	hers	herself
it	it	its	–	itself
we	us	our	ours	ourselves
you	you	your	yours	yourselves
they	them	their	theirs	themselves

2 1 his   2 her   3 my   4 mine   5 ours
6 Whose   7 its   8 theirs   9 me   10 I like it
11 her   12 It is   13 It is   14 got up
15 each other   16 meet   17 enjoyed myself
18 myself   19 his   20 It's

3 1 his   2 each other   3 they   4 her   5 she
6 they   7 They   8 it's   9 Hers   10 their
11 his   12 she's   13 him   14 her
15 herself.   16 them   17 they're
18 each other   19 I   20 they

page 188

1 + -*s*: cats, chairs, gardens, hotels, planes,
ships, tables, times, trees
+ -*es*: boxes, brushes, churches, classes,
dresses, gases, glasses, watches, wishes

2 + -*s*: guys, holidays, keys, ways
-*y* → -*ies*: copies, countries, families, parties

3 1 children   2 students   3 want   4 cities
5 wives   6 do   7 teeth   8 watches   9 babies
10 matches   11 guys   12 work   13 people

page 189

1 class ✓   club ✓   Communist Party ✓
company ✓   crowd ✓   idea ✗   lunch ✗
question ✗   room ✗   school ✓   train ✗

2 2 D; say   3 A; want   4 B; play   5 C; haven't

3 1 dark glasses.   2 shorts.   3 scissors   4 black
trousers   5 silk pyjamas.

In these answers, we usually give **either** contracted forms (for example *I'm*, *don't*)
or full forms (for example *I am*, *do not*). Normally both are correct.

ANSWER KEY   305

pages 190–191

1 love, meat, music, oil, salt, snow, sugar, wool

2 some baggage a fridge some furniture
a handbag a holiday some knowledge
some luck a newspaper a problem
a station some travel some work

3 1 baggage 2 travel. 3 spaghetti 4 news
5 advice 6 furniture 7 work

4 1 a job 2 a journey 3 a piece of advice
4 a piece of information 5 a piece of news

5 1 a glass 2 glass 3 chocolate 4 a chocolate
5 paper 6 a paper 7 an iron 8 iron
9 a chicken 10 chicken

6 1 bottle 2 jug 3 box 4 cup 5 mug
6 jar 7 can 8 bag 9 glass 10 packet

page 192

1 1 this one. 2 a new one. 3 another one.
4 last one. 5 small one. 6 blue ones.

page 193

1 1 Alice and John's house 2 artists' ideas
3 my dog's ears 4 those dogs' ears
5 those men's faces 6 his girlfriend's piano
7 their grandchild's birthday 8 their
grandchildren's school 9 ladies' hats
10 my aunt and uncle's shop 11 Patrick's
books 12 a photographer's job 13 our
postman's cat 14 postmen's uniforms
15 Joyce's pen 16 the thief's bag
17 the thieves' car 18 that woman's brother
19 most women's desks 20 your mum
and dad's bedroom

2 1 their grandparents' 2 children's
3 the other children's 4 and Cara's
5 The two girls' 6 a man's
7 the shopkeeper's 8 local people's

3 1 My sister's secretary's office 2 Jane's
children's bicycles 3 Rob's family's holiday
flat

pages 194–195

1 1 Ann's house 2 the doctor's house
3 Oliver's book 4 the teacher's car
5 the children's money 6 Susan's money

2 1 The builder's car is parked in front of
Anna's house. 2 Do you know the tall
woman's address? 3 The children's bedtime
is eight o'clock. 4 Alice and Pat's brothers
are both in the army.

3 1 What's your brother's name? What's the
name of that book? 2 Is there anything in
the children's pockets? Is there anything in
the pockets of that coat? 3 You can see the
church from Emma's window. You can see
the church from the window of the living
room. 4 Why are John's arms so dirty?
Why are the arms of your chair so dirty?

4 1 a year's course 2 a week's holiday
3 a day's journey 4 an hour's drive
5 a minute's wait

5 1 The grey pullover is Tamsin's. She bought
it at Fenwick's. 2 The black leather jacket is
Tamsin's. She bought it at Brown's. 3 The
blue shirt is Simon's. He bought it at Chell's.
4 The brown leather jacket is Simon's. He
bought it at Jimmy Choo's. 5 The navy
blue pullover is Simon's. He bought it at
Hunt's. 6 The red shirt is Tamsin's. She
bought it at Ben de Lisi's. 7 The yellow
scarf is Simon's. He bought it at Ungaro's.

pages 196–197

1 1 business address, e-mail address, home
address 2 aspirin bottle, milk bottle,
perfume bottle 3 jazz singer, opera singer,
pop singer 4 garden wall, kitchen wall,
prison wall 5 army uniform, police
uniform, prison uniform 6 garden chair,
kitchen chair

2 2 F; office building 3 D; dog food
4 A; computer engineer 5 B; language
school 6 E; baby clothes 7 G; knife drawer

3 1 a metal box 2 chocolate cakes 3 a plastic
fork 4 vegetable soup 5 a leather jacket
6 cotton shirts 7 a paper plate 8 tomato
salad 9 a stone wall

4 1 an office manager 2 a coffee machine
3 a coffee drinker 4 an animal lover 5 floor
cleaner 6 a tennis player 7 a letter opener
8 a cigar smoker 9 a mountain climber

5 1 telephone book 2 teacher's book
3 Elizabeth's journey 4 train journey
5 aunt's home 6 holiday home
7 brother's interview 8 job interview

page 198

1 foxes, journeys, countries, matches, books,
tables, feet, people/persons, knives, mice

2 1 ✗ 2 ✗ 3 ✗ 4 ✗ 5 ✗ 6 ✓

3 1 some 2 some 3 a 4 some 5 some 6 a

4 1 ✗ 2 ✗ 3 ideas 4 ✗ 5 ✗ 6 journeys 7 ✗
8 governments 9 classes 10 ✗

5 (*Possible answers:*) trousers, shorts, pyjamas,
jeans, tights, pants, glasses, scissors

6 1 ✓ 2 ✓ 3 ✓ 4 ✗ 5 ✗ 6 ✓ 7 ✓ 8 ✗
9 ✗ 10 ✗ 11 ✗ 12 ✓

7 1 a bus driver 2 a mountain climber
3 a tennis player

pages 200–201

1 1 a beautiful little girl 2 in a red coat 3 was
walking through a dark forest 4 with a big
bag 5 of wonderful red apples 6 to see her
old grandmother. 7 Under a tall green tree
8 she saw a big bad wolf 9 with long white
teeth

2 1 'Good morning, little girl', said
2 the big bad wolf. 3 'Where are you going
4 with that heavy bag 5 on this fine day?'
6 'I'm going to see my old grandmother'
7 said the little girl. 8 'She lives in a small
house 9 near the new supermarket.'

3 1 friendly 2 little 3 stupid. 4 big

4 1 beautiful and intelligent 2 cold, hungry
and tired

5 1 'That car looks expensive.' 2 'Jane seems
happy.' 3 'I feel ill.' 4 It gets dark very
early here in winter. 5 My parents are
getting old.

6 1 'The train is late.' 2 'He looks Australian.'
3 'Your hair looks beautiful.' 4 My memory
is getting very bad. 5 I want to become rich
and famous.

pages 202–203

1 1 slow 2 interestingly 3 beautifully.
4 easy 5 perfect 6 badly. 7 happy
8 angry. 9 strong 10 quietly

2 1 finally 2 sincerely 3 loudly 4 thirstily
5 probably 6 usually 7 nicely
8 wonderfully 9 coldly 10 unhappily
11 comfortably

3 1 I read the letter carefully/slowly. 2 I bought
a computer yesterday. 3 Write your name
carefully/clearly. 4 You must see the doctor
tomorrow. 5 He speaks four languages
correctly/perfectly. 6 You didn't write the
address clearly/correctly. 7 I don't like skiing
much.

5 1 sorry 2 empty. 3 written; interesting.
4 tired. 5 cooked 6 finished.

pages 204–205

1 1 Jake always eats fish. He even eats fish for
breakfast. 2 Ann often plays tennis, but she
only plays in the evenings. 3 Ed usually
puts tomato sauce on everything. He
probably puts it on ice cream. 4 Your sister
is certainly a good singer. She is also a very
interesting person. 5 My mother is still
asleep. I think she is probably ill.
6 I always get to the station on time, and the
train is always late.

2 1 Do you often play cards? 2 Have you ever
been to Tibet? 3 Are you always happy?
4 Does the boss ever take a holiday? 5 Do
you usually eat in restaurants? 6 Is Barbara
still ill?

3 (*Possible answers:*) Ann never plays football.
Bill plays football three times a week. Ann
plays tennis once a week. Bill hardly ever
plays tennis. Ann often goes skiing. Bill
never goes skiing. Ann goes to the theatre
every week. Bill goes to the theatre two or
three times a year. Ann goes to the cinema
three or four times a year. Bill goes to the
cinema twice a month. Ann never goes to
concerts. Bill goes to concerts every week.
(*Other answers are possible.*)

4 go climbing 1 go swimming 8
go sailing 4 go wind-surfing 12
go skiing 10 go skating 11 go fishing 3
go shopping 7 go to the opera 9
go to the theatre 2 go to concerts 5

page 206

1 1 boring 2 bored 3 interested 4 interesting

2 1 annoying. 2 frightened.; frightening.
3 exciting; excited. 4 surprising.; surprised.

page 207

1 1 well. 2 early 3 hard 4 weekly 5 hardly

2 1 Daily 2 lately 3 fast 4 hardly 5 early

3 1 fast 2 daily 3 hard 4 late 5 hardly
6 friendly 7 silly 8 lonely.

In these answers, we usually give **either** contracted forms (for example *I'm, don't*)
or full forms (for example *I am, do not*). Normally both are correct.

ANSWER KEY 307

page 208

1 1 greener; greenest 2 safer; safest 3 richer; richest 4 smaller; smallest 5 stranger; strangest 6 finer; finest 7 higher; highest 8 wider; widest 9 nearer; nearest 10 whiter; whitest

2 1 bigger; biggest 2 hotter; hottest 3 newer; newest 4 wetter; wettest 5 slimmer; slimmest

3 1 lazier; laziest 2 hungrier; hungriest 3 sleepier; sleepiest 4 angrier; angriest 5 dirtier; dirtiest

4 1 more careful; most careful 2 more beautiful; most beautiful 3 more intelligent; most intelligent 4 more dangerous; most dangerous 5 more important; most important 6 more boring; most boring 7 more interested; most interested

5 1 further/farther 2 better 3 worse.

page 209

1 1 the nicest 2 the best 3 more expensive 4 more dangerous 5 the most dangerous? 6 bigger

2 1 shorter 2 the most intelligent 3 quieter 4 the coldest 5 louder 6 the biggest

pages 210–211

1 1 Dogs are friendlier than cats. 2 Dogs are more intelligent than cats. 3 Train travel is cheaper than air travel. 4 Air travel is faster than train travel. 5 The Sahara is hotter than the Himalayas. 6 The Himalayas are colder than the Sahara.

2 1 The Amazon is longer than all the other rivers in South America. 2 Blue whales are heavier than all the other whales. 3 Mont Blanc is higher than all the other mountains in the Alps. 4 Cheetahs are faster than all the other big cats.

3 1 is more careful than him. / than he is. 2 hungrier than me. / than I am. 3 shorter than you. / than you are. 4 are more excited than us. / than we are. 5 is more beautiful than her. / than she is.

---

4 Mark is a bit / a little taller than Simon. Mark is a bit / a little younger than Simon. Simon is a bit / a little older than Mark. Mark is a lot / much richer than Simon. Mark's car is a lot / much faster than Simon's car. Simon's car is a lot / much slower than Mark's car. Mark's car is a bit / a little more comfortable than Simon's car. Mark's car is a lot / much noisier than Simon's car. Simon's car is a lot / much quieter than Mark's car.

5 1 More than a year and less than a century 2 More than a week/fortnight and less than a year 3 More than a week and less than a month 4 More than a day and less than a fortnight/month

page 212

1 2 F; n 3 E; q 4 A; r 5 C; m 6 B; p 7 J; s 8 G; u 9 I; t 10 H; v

2 1 In the 1970s, the Beatles were the richest musicians in the world. 2 Eric says that Eleanor is the best singer in the group. 3 When I was a child, my father was the tallest man in our town. 4 In this country, February is the coldest month of the year. 5 Who is the oldest of your three aunts? 6 Helen is very intelligent, but she is the quietest person in my class.

page 213

1 1 Lee talks to people more politely than Ben. 2 Liam works more carefully than John. 3 Simon goes swimming more often than Karen. 4 My car runs more quietly than my sister's car. 5 Annie talks more slowly than Rob.

2 1 earlier. 2 later. 3 more. 4 nearer 5 less. 6 faster.

pages 214–215

1 Picture A is Jean; Picture B is Cassie. 1 Cassie is not as slim as Jean. 2 Cassie is not as tall as Jean. 3 Jean's skirt is not as long as Cassie's. 4 Cassie's bag is not as big as Jean's. 5 Jean's coat is not as heavy as Cassie's. 6 Cassie's glass is not as big as Jean's.

2   1 The other doctor isn't as nice as you. / as
    you are.   2 His boss isn't as interesting as
    him. / as he is.   3 My mother isn't as slim as
    me. / as I am.   4 The Browns are not as
    careful as us. / as we are.

4   1 Eric has twice as many cousins as Tony.
    2 Ben eats three times as many sandwiches
    every day as Jo.   3 Helen has nearly
    as many computer games as Adrian.   4 Chris
    drinks twice as many cups of coffee a day
    as Liz. OR Liz drinks half as many cups of
    coffee a day as Chris.   5 Mike has just as
    many books as David. OR David has just as
    many books as Mike.   6 Nedjma doesn't
    have as much free time as Ali.

page 216

1   really, completely, possibly, happily

2   more interesting; most interesting   thinner;
    thinnest   cheaper; cheapest   easier; easiest
    worse; worst   farther/further;
    farthest/furthest   better; best

3   1 There are interesting films on TV tonight.
    2 There's a good cheap restaurant in Dover
    Street.   3 He's tall, dark and good-looking.
    4 She's the best pianist in the world.
    5 My sister is much taller than me.
    6 Anna is the most beautiful person here.
    7 I am very interested in the lessons.

4   1 He was wearing dirty black trousers.
    2 She speaks Chinese very well.   3 I lost my
    keys yesterday.

5   1 terrible   2 slowly   3 badly   4 unhappy

6   1 They've been happily married for 15 years.
    2 We often go to New York.   3 Ann and
    Simon are always late.   4 She's certainly
    an interesting person.

7   1 hard   2 friendly   3 terribly; late
    4 more slowly

8   1 A is not as fast as B.   2 C is more expensive
    than A.   3 A is not as expensive as B.
    4 B is the most expensive.   5 B is not as big
    as C.   6 C is (much) bigger than A.   7 C is
    the biggest.

page 218

1   1 so   2 although   3 but   4 and   5 while
    6 because

2   1 I'll be glad when this job is finished.
    2 I'll be very angry if you do that again.
    3 I'd like to talk to you before you go home.
    4 I watched TV until John came home.
    5 I'll see you again after we come back from
    holiday.

3   1 so   2 when   3 and   4 although
    5 because   6 and   7 because   8 and
    9 until   10 although   11 before

page 219

1   1 I put on two sweaters, because it was very
    cold. Because it was very cold, I put on two
    sweaters.   2 I'm going to work in Australia
    when I leave school. When I leave school,
    I'm going to work in Australia.   3 I go and see
    Felix if I want to talk to somebody. If I want
    to talk to somebody, I go and see Felix.
    4 Ann made coffee while Bill fried some eggs.
    While Bill fried some eggs, Ann made coffee.
    OR Bill fried some eggs while Ann made coffee.
    While Ann made coffee, Bill fried some eggs.
    5 I was interested in the conversation, although
    I didn't understand everything. Although
    I didn't understand everything, I was interested
    in the conversation. OR I didn't understand
    everything, although I was interested in the
    conversation. Although I was interested in
    the conversation, I didn't understand
    everything.   6 We went to a restaurant,
    because there was no food in the house.
    Because there was no food in the house,
    we went to a restaurant.   7 We'll have a big
    party when John comes home. When John
    comes home, we'll have a big party.   8 I stayed
    with friends while my parents were travelling.
    While my parents were travelling, I stayed with
    friends.   9 I go for long walks at the weekend
    if the weather's fine. If the weather's fine, I go
    for long walks at the weekend.   10 Come and
    see us as soon as you arrive in Scotland.
    As soon as you arrive in Scotland, come and
    see us.

1 1 There's always a lot of work after we get back from holiday.   After we get back from holiday, there's always a lot of work.
2 I usually clean the house before my mother comes to visit.   Before my mother comes to visit, I usually clean the house.   3 I listen to music for half an hour before I start work.   Before I start work, I listen to music for half an hour.   4 I got very ill after I left school.   After I left school, I got very ill.   5 I started playing hockey after I stopped playing football.   After I stopped playing football, I started playing hockey.   6 We moved to London before we got married.   Before we got married, we moved to London.

2 1 2, 1   2 1, 2   3 2, 1   4 2, 1   5 2, 1

1 1 hear   2 make   3 leaves   4 write
2 1 finds   2 travels   3 will help   4 starts.
3 1 get   2 your brother is in England.   3 my father goes into hospital.   4 the/our new car is ready.   5 he goes back to work.

1 1 Because the rooms were dirty, I changed my hotel. I changed my hotel because the rooms were dirty. The rooms were dirty, so I changed my hotel.   2 Because the taxi was late, we missed the train.   We missed the train because the taxi was late.   The taxi was late, so we missed the train.   3 Because I didn't like the film, I walked out of the cinema.   I walked out of the cinema because I didn't like the film.   I didn't like the film, so I walked out of the cinema.

2 1 Although I felt ill, I went on working. I went on working although I felt ill. I felt ill but I went on working.   2 Although she was very kind, I didn't like her. I didn't like her although she was very kind. She was very kind but I didn't like her.   3 Although he's a big man, he doesn't eat much. He doesn't eat much, although he's a big man. He's a big man, but he doesn't eat much.

3 2 C   3 A   4 D   5 B   6 H   7 F   8 I   9 G

4 1 Because of my unhappiness, I didn't want to see anybody.   2 In spite of her hunger, she didn't eat anything.   3 We had to drink a lot because of the heat.   4 We had to stop playing because of the rain.   5 She kept all the windows open in spite of the cold.
6 I couldn't go away last weekend because of (my/the) work.   7 In spite of his interest in the lesson, he went to sleep.   8 I couldn't understand her because of my tiredness.   9 In spite of my thirst, I didn't drink anything.

1 1 My company has offices in London, Tokyo, New York and Cairo.   2 I've invited Paul, Alexandra, Eric, Luke and Janet.   3 I'll be here on Tuesday, Thursday, Friday and Saturday.   4 She's got five cats, two dogs, a horse and a rabbit.   5 He plays golf, rugby, hockey and badminton.   6 She addressed, stamped and posted the letter.

2 1 She has painted the kitchen, the living room and the dining room.   2 Bob was wearing a pink shirt, blue jeans and white trainers.   3 Can you give me a knife, (a) fork and (a) spoon, please?   4 Many people speak English in India, Singapore and South Africa.   5 I've written and posted six letters this morning.

1 1 I think that she's either Scottish or Irish.   2 I'd like to work with either animals or children.   3 He did well in both mathematics and history.   4 This car is neither fast nor comfortable.   5 She neither looked at me nor said anything.   6 I've got problems both at home and in my job.

2 1 Karl plays both the trombone and the saxophone.   2 Melanie plays neither the cello nor the drums.   3 Both Steve and Karen play the violin.   4 Neither Joanna nor Charles plays the guitar.   5 Karen plays neither the piano nor the trumpet.
6 Sophie plays both the guitar and the trumpet.   7 Neither Charles nor Steve plays the saxophone.   8 Both Sophie and Steve play the trumpet.

1 1 will have; go   2 will wait; comes.   3 come; will be   4 will be; goes

2 1 Although   2 because   3 but   4 so
5 When

3 1 Because the teacher was ill, the children had a holiday. The children had a holiday because the teacher was ill.   2 When I was in China, I made a lot of friends. I made a lot of friends when I was in China.   3 Until they built the new road, it was difficult to get to our village. It was difficult to get to our village until they built the new road.

4 1 before   2 Before   3 although   4 although
5 In spite of   6 because of   7 because of

5 1 ✓   2 ✗   3 ✓   4 ✗   5 ✗   6 ✓

1 1 If I can't sleep, I get up and read. I get up and read if I can't sleep.   2 If you take books from my room, please tell me. Please tell me if you take books from my room.   3 If you're hungry, why don't you cook some soup? Why don't you cook some soup if you're hungry?   4 If she arrived this morning, she will probably phone us this evening. She will probably phone us this evening if she arrived this morning.   5 If we catch the first train, we can be in London by 9.00. We can be in London by 9.00 if we catch the first train.

2 1 You can't park here unless you live in this street.   2 Unless you're over 15, you can't see this film.   3 I don't drive fast unless I'm really late.   4 Unless I'm going fishing, I get up late on Sundays.   5 We usually go for a walk after supper unless there's a good film on TV.

1 1 If I lose my job, I won't find another job.
2 If I don't find another job, I'll lose my flat.
3 If I lose my flat, I'll move back to my parents' house.   4 If I move back to my parents' house, I'll get very bored.   5 If I get very bored, I'll go swimming every day.
6 If I go swimming every day, I'll look very good.   7 If I look very good, I'll meet interesting people.   8 If I meet interesting people, I'll go to lots of parties.   9 If I go to lots of parties, I'll have a wonderful time.

2 1 will be; pass   2 leave; will catch   3 will work; needs   4 am not; will see   5 will study; has
6 will drive; can   7 marries; will not have
8 Will … stop; tells   9 talk; will … listen

3 1 If she goes to Egypt, she will have to learn Arabic.   2 If she goes to Brazil, she will have to learn Portuguese.   3 If she goes to Holland, she will have to learn Dutch.   4 If she goes to Kenya, she will have to learn Swahili.
5 If she goes to Greece, she will have to learn Greek.   6 If she goes to Austria, she will have to learn German.

1 1 could; would eat   2 were; would know
3 knew; would tell   4 asked; would … do
5 could; would … do

2 1 would buy; had   2 asked; would … say
3 would finish; didn't talk   4 would study; had   5 were; would watch   6 would be; didn't rain   7 would like; didn't talk

3 1 We would play cards if Jane and Peter were here.   2 If we had enough money, we would buy a new car. We would buy a new car if we had enough money.   3 If Fred answered letters, I would write to him. I would write to Fred if he answered letters.   4 If I could find my camera, I would take your photo.
I would take your photo if I could find my camera.   5 If I could understand the words, I would enjoy opera. I would enjoy opera if I could understand the words.

4 (*Possible answers:*) 1 If I heard a strange noise in the night, I would phone the police.
2 If I found a lot of money in the street, I would try to find the person who had lost it.
3 If I saw a child stealing from a shop, I would tell the child to stop.   4 If a shop assistant gave me too much change, I would tell him/her.   5 If I found a dead mouse in my kitchen, I would throw it out.   6 If I found a suitcase on the pavement outside a bank, I would leave it.   7 If I found a friend's diary, I would give it to him/her without reading it.
(*Other answers are possible.*)

In these answers, we usually give **either** contracted forms (for example *I'm, don't*) or full forms (for example *I am, do not*). Normally both are correct.

ANSWER KEY   311

page 232

1 1 lived 2 could 3 go 4 started 5 gave
6 need 7 gave 8 thought 9 was 10 go

2 1 have; I'll 2 had; I'd 3 get; will 4 got;
would 5 did; would 6 do; will 7 go;
won't 8 went; wouldn't

page 233

1 1 'If I were you, I'd take a holiday.' 2 'If I
were you, I'd join a club.' 3 'I would fly if I
were you.' 4 'If I were you, I'd call the
police at once.' 5 'I wouldn't sell it if I
were you.'

2 1 If I were you, I'd start a business. 2 If I
were you, I'd put the money in the bank.
3 If I were you, I'd buy a sports car. 4 If I
were you, I'd have a big party. 5 If I were
you, I'd travel round the world. 6 If I were
you, I'd stop work. 7 If I were you, I'd give
the money away.

page 234

1 1 could go and see him. 2 could watch
a film. 3 we could go cycling. 4 could
get up late. 5 could have breakfast in the
garden. 6 I could write to Henry. 7 we
could go to the cinema more often.

2 1 If he could drive, he could get a job at
Calloway Ltd. 2 If he had a passport, he
could get a job at Patterson Travel. 3 If he
could cook, he could get a job at Fred's Café.
4 If he liked children, he could get a job at
Crowndale School. 5 If he liked animals, he
could get a job at the City Zoo. 6 If he could
swim, he could get a job at the Leisure Centre.

page 235

1 1 had been 2 had worked 3 had taken
4 had not played 5 would have studied
6 Would … have crashed 7 wouldn't have
slept 8 had come; would have had
9 hadn't broken down; would have been
10 Would … have studied; had liked
11 would not have got; had not wanted
12 Would … have helped; had asked

2 1 If I had caught the 8.15 train, I would
have sat by a beautiful foreign woman.
2 If I had sat by a beautiful foreign woman,
I would have fallen in love and married her.

3 If I had fallen in love and married her,
I would have gone to live in her country.
4 If I had gone to live in her country,
I would have worked in her father's
diamond business. 5 If I had worked in her
father's diamond business, I would have
become very rich. 6 If I had become very
rich, I would have gone into politics. 7 If I
had gone into politics, I would have died in
a revolution.

3 1 If she hadn't opened the door, the cat
wouldn't have eaten her supper. 2 If the cat
hadn't eaten her supper, she wouldn't have
gone to the shop. 3 If she hadn't gone to
the shop, she wouldn't have seen the
advertisement. 4 If she hadn't seen the
advertisement, she wouldn't have got a new
job. 5 If she hadn't got a new job, she
wouldn't have met my father.

page 236

1 1 If I need help, I ask my brother. I ask my
brother if I need help.

2 1 cleaned 2 will come 3 would
understand 4 leave 5 would sell

3 1 ✗ 2 ✓ 3 ✗ 4 ✗

4 1 bought; would 2 go; see; I'll 3 lived;
would 4 went; wouldn't

5 1 You can't go there unless you have a visa.
2 Unless you go now, I'll call the police.

6 1 ✓ 2 ✗ 3 ✗ 4 ✓ 5 ✓

7 1 hadn't drunk; would have slept 2 had
had; would have gone 3 would have gone;
hadn't met

pages 238–239

1 1 who 2 which 3 which 4 which 5 who
6 which 7 which 8 who 9 who

2 1 took 2 live 3 she is 4 lost 5 bought
6 is parked 7 it cuts 8 writes

3 1 The man and woman who live in flat 1
play loud music all night. 2 The woman
who lives in flat 2 broke her leg skiing.
3 The three men who live in flat 3 play golf
all day. 4 The students who live in flat 4
haven't got much money. 5 The doctor
who lives in flat 5 has three children. 6 The
man who lives in flat 6 drives a Rolls-Royce.
7 The two women who live in flat 7 are
hiding from the police. 8 The man and
woman who live in flat 8 are from Scotland.

4 1 The bus which goes to Oxford isn't running today.   2 Yesterday I met a man who works with your brother.   3 The child who didn't come to the party was ill.   4 Can you pick up the papers which are lying on the floor?
5 The eggs which I bought yesterday were bad.
6 Here's the book which you asked me to buy for you.   7 I don't like the man who is going out with my sister.

page 240

1 1 Joe's got a motorbike that can do 200 km an hour.   2 Is that the computer that doesn't work?   3 Those are the trousers that I use for gardening.   4 A man that lives in New York wants to marry my sister.   5 The doctors that looked at my leg all said different things.
6 The flowers that you gave to Aunt Sarah are beautiful.   7 The children that play football with Paul have gone on holiday.

2 1 an insect that doesn't make honey and can bite you.   2 a bird that can't fly   3 a bird that eats small animals and birds   4 an animal that flies at night and hears very well
5 a machine that can fly straight up
6 a plane that doesn't have an engine
7 a thing that can fly to the moon

page 241

1 1 O   2 S   3 O   4 O   5 S   6 O
2 1 the languages she spoke   2 a man I helped   3 the weather we have had   4 the car you bought
3 1 I'm working for a man I've known for twenty years.   2 They played a lot of music I didn't like.   3 The campsite we found was very dirty.   4 I'm going on holiday with some people I know.   5 That book you suggested to me is very good.   6 The ring she lost belonged to her grandmother.

page 242

1 1 the girl that I was talking about   2 the people that I work for   3 the house that I live in   4 the music that you're listening to   5 the bus that I go to work on
2 1 the girl I was talking about   2 the people I work for   3 the house I live in   4 the music you're listening to   5 the bus I go to work on

3 1 Eric is the man she works for.   2 Monica is the woman she plays tennis with.   3 Karen is the woman she reads to.   4 Ann and Joe are the people she baby-sits for.   5 Bill is the man she is in love with.
4 1 The man she works for gave her chocolates.
2 The woman she plays tennis with gave her a clock.   3 The 80-year-old woman she reads to gave her theatre tickets.   4 The people she baby-sits for gave her a picture.   5 The man she is in love with gave her flowers and ear-rings.

page 243

1 1 What he did made everybody angry.
2 Take what you want.   3 Soap – that's what I forgot to pack!   4 She gave me a watch. It was just what I wanted.   5 That child does what he likes.   6 What I need is some food.
3 1 that   2 What   3 what   4 that   5 what
6 that   7 that   8 what
4 1 Mary got what Barbara wanted.   2 Sally got what Helen wanted.   3 Jane got what Ann wanted.   4 Barbara got what Jane wanted.
5 Helen got what Sally wanted.

page 244

1 1 ✗   2 ✗   3 ✓   4 ✓   5 ✗   6 ✓   7 ✓   8 ✗   9 ✓
2 1 I know a man who writes film music.
2 Yesterday I saw a film which you would like.   3 The bus which I took got to London twenty minutes late.   4 The car which I bought last month isn't very good.
3 1 The tickets that I got were very expensive.
2 These are the scissors that I use for cutting paper.   3 The woman that gives me tennis lessons is from Brazil.   4 The man that works in the corner shop is always very friendly.
4 1 The clock I bought doesn't work.
2 I didn't like the film I saw last night.
3 can't change   4 can't change
5 1 a boy (that) I talked to   2 the people (that) I work for   3 the hotel (that) we stayed in
4 the place (that) I drove to

In these answers, we usually give **either** contracted forms (for example *I'm, don't*) or full forms (for example *I am, do not*). Normally both are correct.

ANSWER KEY 313

pages 246–247

1 1 he 2 she 3 her. 4 they; their

2 1 told 2 said 3 said 4 say 5 told 6 tell 7 told 8 said

3 2 C 3 E 4 B 5 D

4 1 She said (that) her sister needed a car.
2 He said (that) he had to phone Andrew.
3 She said (that) nobody wanted to help her.
4 She said (that) the radio didn't work,
5 He said (that) he would be in Paris in July.
6 He said (that) he liked the red sweater.
7 He said (that) he couldn't swim. 8 She said (that) her parents were travelling. 9 She said (that) the lessons were very good. 10 The said (that) they hadn't heard from Joe.

5 He thought (that) cats had nine lives. He thought (that) his father knew everything. He thought (that) spaghetti grew on trees. He thought (that) the teacher lived in the school. He thought (that) he would be rich one day. He thought (that) his mother had always been old.

page 248

1 1 She asked him where he lived. 2 She asked him where he worked. 3 She asked him where he was going. 4 She asked him where he had been. 5 She asked him what the number of his car was. 6 She asked him why he was driving on the right.

2 1 She asked him whether it was his car.
2 She asked him if/whether he had a driving licence. 3 She asked him if/whether he had it with him. 4 She asked him if/whether he always drove with the door open. 5 She asked him if/whether he was listening to her.

3 1 They asked her if/whether she was married. 2 They asked her if/whether she had children. 3 They asked her where she had worked before. 4 They asked her why she wanted to change her job. 5 They asked her if/whether she could speak any foreign languages. 6 They asked her what exams she had passed.

page 249

1 1 They say (that) they live in Greece.
2 She says (that) she went to Belfast yesterday. 3 He says (that) he's been ill.
4 She thinks (that) it's going to rain.
5 She says (that) she'll ask her sister.
6 They believe (that) they're going to be rich. 7 He wants to know if/whether lunch is ready. 8 I don't remember where I put my keys.

2 1 Can you tell me where I can buy tickets?
2 Do you know how much it costs? 3 Can you tell me if/whether John has phoned?
4 Can you tell me if/whether I must pay now? 5 Can you tell me if/whether Maria likes steak? 6 Do you know where I parked the car?

3 (*Possible answers*:) 1 I don't know what languages Irish people speak. 2 I know what elephants eat. 3 I don't care if/whether the British Museum opens on Christmas Day. 4 I don't want to know if/whether King William II was a tall man. 5 I'd like to know if/whether birds dream. (*Other answers are possible.*)

page 250

1 2 I 3 C 4 F 5 D 6 A 7 B 8 H 9 E

2 1 that place. 2 the week before.
3 the day before. 4 that day.
5 that night. 6 the next day.

3 1 He said (that) he loved that place.
2 He said (that) he had seen a great film the day before. 3 He said (that) he was going to another party that night. 4 He asked (me) if/whether I wanted to play tennis the next day. 5 He said (that) his girlfriend would be there the next week.

page 251

1 1 Eric asked Sue to give him her phone number. 2 The boss told Joe to work late.
3 Mary asked Sue not to tell Karen about Bill. 4 Mr Sanders asked Fred not to smoke in his car. 5 The general told Colonel Walker to take 100 men and cross the river.
6 Ann told Mary not to study so hard.

2 1 His girlfriend told him to write to her every day.   2 His mother told him to keep his room clean.   3 His father told him to work hard.   4 His sister told him not to go to too many parties.   5 His brother told him to get a lot of exercise.   6 His mother told him to change his shirt every day.   7 His father told him not to go to bed late.   8 His brother told him to be careful with money.   9 His sister told him not to play cards for money.   10 His grandmother told him to eat properly.

page 252

1   1 ✗   2 ✗   3 ✓   4 ✓   5 ✗
2   1 had been   2 told   3 was having   4 was doing   5 had had   6 the … before   7 would   8 said   9 had   10 had lost   11 to buy   12 if/whether   13 was   14 was   15 would   16 was living   17 had spent   18 to send   19 to give   20 told   21 hadn't heard   22 where   23 was living.   24 if/whether   25 wanted

pages 254–255

1   1 on   2 at   3 on   4 on   5 at; on   6 on   7 on   8 at; on
2   1 at   2 in   3 in   4 at   5 at   6 in   7 at; in   8 in   9 in   10 at; in; on   11 in   12 in
3   1 I'll see you next Wednesday.   2 It rained non-stop last week.   3 Business was bad last month.   4 Shall we go out this evening?   5 We're going to America next month.   6 Ann had a car crash last Wednesday.   7 I'm going to change my job next year.   8 My holiday is in August every year.   9 I've spent too much money already this month.   10 The new school will be open next March.
4   1 In five days   2 In a week   3 In two weeks / a fortnight   4 In a month   5 In a year   6 In 100 years
5   1 March the twenty-first / the twenty-first of March, nineteen ninety-nine   2 February the fourteenth / the fourteenth of February, nineteen sixty   3 July the twenty-eighth / the twenty-eighth of July, eighteen forty-six   4 May the sixth / the sixth of May, two thousand and three   5 May the ninth / the ninth of May, nineteen eighty-four

page 256

1   1 until/till lunchtime.   2 until/till Saturday.   3 until/till the age of 14.   4 until/till the end.   5 until/till July.
2   1 He washed the/his car from 8.00 to/until/till 9.00.   2 He talked to the woman next door from 9.00 to/until/till 9.15.   3 He played tennis from 10.00 to/until/till 11.00.   4 He talked to friends from 11.00 to/until/till 11.30.   5 He went for a walk from 11.30 to/until/till 12.45.
4   1 by   2 until   3 by   4 by   5 by   6 until

page 257

1   1 for   2 during   3 during   4 for; during   5 during   6 for   7 during   8 for
2   1 while they were playing   2 during the lesson   3 during the war   4 while she was teaching   5 while he was speaking   6 while they were talking   7 during her illness   8 while it was snowing
3   (*Possible answers:*) 1 for a long time   2 for ever.   3 for a minute or two   4 for a couple of hours   5 for a moment   6 for a few minutes   7 for an hour or so   8 for life.
(*Other answers are possible.*)

page 258

1   1 in   2 on   3 in   4 on   5 in   6 on   7 on   8 in   9 on   10 on
2   1 in my diary.   2 in the office   3 on her first finger.   4 'In the cupboard.'   5 on the roof of the car.   6 in your car   7 On his T-shirt   8 on the wall   9 in a little village   10 on a piece of paper; in my pocket.

page 259

1   1 at the cinema   2 at the station.   3 at the party   4 at a Chinese restaurant   5 at a theatre   6 at work.   7 at breakfast
2   1 at the bottom   2 at the end   3 at the top   4 at the top   5 at the beginning

In these answers, we usually give **either** contracted forms (for example *I'm, don't*) or full forms (for example *I am, do not*). Normally both are correct.

ANSWER KEY   315

page 261

1 1 above 2 by 3 above 4 by 5 behind
6 under 7 against

2 1 under 2 between; opposite 3 against
4 behind 5 near 6 in front of 7 near

3 1 by 2 between 3 opposite 4 near
5 behind 6 against 7 under 8 in front of
9 in front of

pages 262–263

1 1 up the steps 2 through the gate 3 over
the fence 4 past the café 5 round the
corner 6 out of the shop 7 across the river
8 along the yellow line 9 under the bridge
10 into the water 11 off the bike 12 down
the mountain

2 (*Correct words:*) 1 along the road 2 up the
mountain 3 down the stairs 4 over the
wall 5 into the bank 6 round the corner
7 through the door 8 off the table 9 out
of the church 10 under the bridge 11 past
the bank 12 across the river

3 1 out of; across 2 down; over 3 along;
through; into 4 up; into; off 5 past; under;
round

4 1 to 2 in 3 to 4 from; to OR to; from
5 in 6 to 7 at 8 at

page 264

1 1 on 2 at 3 in 4 on 5 at 6 – 7 on
8 at 9 at

2 1 in 2 at 3 at 4 on 5 on 6 on 7 in
8 at 9 on 10 to 11 at

3 1 until 2 from; until 3 by 4 in 5 by 6 in

4 1 for 2 during 3 while 4 for 5 during

5 1 between 2 above 3 in front of
4 opposite 5 against 6 through 7 along;
by/near 8 out of; round/across 9 past;
under; round

pages 266–267

1 1 won't you? 2 has he? 3 – 4 isn't it?
5 can he? 6 isn't it? 7 was it? 8 –

2 1 isn't it? 2 aren't we? 3 isn't she?
4 won't you? 5 can't he? 6 doesn't she?
7 doesn't it?

3 1 is he? 2 can you? 3 do they? 4 does
she? 5 do they?

4 1 They've lived in France, haven't they?
2 They all went home early, didn't they?
3 It rained all last week, didn't it? 4 Her
brother writes for the newspapers, doesn't
he? 5 I need a visa, don't I? 6 You'd like a
holiday, wouldn't you? 7 The train was late,
wasn't it? 8 Sarah forgot your birthday,
didn't she?

5 1 wasn't there? 2 aren't there? 3 isn't
there? 4 has there? 5 were there?

7 1 They're paper clips, aren't they? 2 It's a
diary, isn't it? 3 It's a hole-punch, isn't it?
4 It's an address book, isn't it? 5 They're
rulers, aren't they? 6 They're calculators,
aren't they?

page 268

1 1 it isn't / it's not. 2 he hasn't. 3 they do.
4 you can't. 5 he doesn't. 6 I do. 7 she
wouldn't. 8 it wasn't. 9 I'm not.

3 1 I'm not. 2 it is. 3 she does. 4 it doesn't.
5 he did.

page 269

1 2 C; Don't you? 3 B; Are they? 4 F; Is it?
5 D; Has he? 6 E; Can't you?

2 (*Possible answers:*) 1 'Congratulations.'
2 'Say 'hello' to her for me.' 3 'Good luck.'
4 'That's interesting.' 5 'What a pity.'
6 'What a nuisance.' 7 'I am sorry.'
8 'That's a surprise.' 9 'That's terrible.'
(*Other answers are possible.*)

page 270

1 1 'Are you?' 2 'Joe didn't phone yesterday.'
3 'I'm feeling ill.' 4 'John needs help.'
5 You don't remember David 6 'Have you?'
7 can't they?

2 1 don't you? 2 Yes, I do. 3 didn't he?
4 he didn't. 5 Is he? 6 does he?
7 Yes, it is. 8 Aren't you? 9 don't you?
10 Yes, I do. 11 haven't you?
12 Yes, I have. 13 Are you? 14 Yes, I would.
15 can I? 16 Yes, you can. 17 Will he?

page 271

1 1 ... but I do. 2 ... 'I have.' 3 ... but I
don't think she will. 4 ... I hope he has.
5 ... 'Of course I will.' 6 ... but I can
tomorrow.

2 1 'They hope to.'   2 she didn't want to.
3 I'd like to.   4 I used to. / I'd like to.
5 'Sorry, I forgot to.'   6 'It's starting to.'

3 1 I couldn't understand what he wanted
from me.   2 She doesn't know what she's
doing.   3 The bus is late again.   4 Do you
speak French?   5 I haven't seen them.
6 I don't think so.

pages 272–273

1 1 'So is Alice.'   2 'So does my father.'   3 'So
can I.'   4 'So does Mary.'   5 'So has Eric.'

2 1 neither/nor was the meat.   2 'Neither/Nor
has Annie.'   3 'Neither/Nor does this one.'
4 'Neither/Nor can I.'   5 neither/nor will his
friends.

3 1 'My car does.'   2 her sister hasn't.
3 our dog can't.   4 'The train doesn't.'
5 the back door was.   6 'Her second one did.'

4 1 Eric plays tennis, and so does Dan.
2 Julie isn't tall, but Denise is.   3 Denise
doesn't laugh a lot, and neither/nor does
Paul.   4 Dan can ski, but Rachel can't.
5 Julie has been to America, and so has
Denise.   6 Eric isn't tall, and neither/nor is
Paul.   7 Julie doesn't play tennis, but Dan
does.   8 Paul doesn't like dancing, but
Rachel does.

page 274

1 1 can't you?   2 won't she?   3 have you?
4 doesn't he?   5 was there?

2 1 They've gone home, haven't they?
2 We need tickets, don't we?   3 You'd like
some more coffee, wouldn't you?   4 Mike
was away yesterday, wasn't he?

3 1 she wasn't.   2 he doesn't.
3 she wouldn't.   4 it doesn't.

4 1 Is she?   2 Did they?   3 Can he?
4 Were you?   5 Won't you?

5 1 so can Susan   2 neither/nor has the
3.45.   3 'Neither/Nor was I.'   4 neither/nor
did Sally.   5 so does his brother.

6 1 … but I do.   2 … 'I have.'   3 … but I don't
think he will.   4 … 'I'm trying to.'

7 1 The car won't start. I don't know why.
2 'Have you seen my mother today?'   'I don't
think so.'   3 Sorry, you can't come in here.

In these answers, we usually give **either** contracted forms (for example *I'm, don't*)
or full forms (for example *I am, do not*). Normally both are correct.

ANSWER KEY   317

index

a/an 145–158
   a and *an*: the difference 146
   and *one* 147
   and *the*: the difference 148
   in descriptions 151
   not used before *my* etc 183
   with jobs 150
a bit with comparatives 211
(a) few
   and *(a) few of* 177
   and *(a) little* 170
a hundred/thousand etc 156
(a) little
   and *(a) few* 170
   with comparatives 211
a lot
   a lot of 169
   with comparatives 211
able 79
above 260
across 262–263
active or passive 94; 102–103
adjectives 199–201, 206–212,
   214–215
   + infinitives with *to* 124–126
   + prepositions 278–279
   after *become, get, seem, look,*
      feel 201
   and adverbs: the difference
      202
   comparatives and superlatives
      208–212
   position 200–201
   with *and* 200–201
adverb particles (*away, back, up*
   etc) 138–139
adverbs 202–205, 207, 213
   comparatives 213
   position 202–205
advice: uncountable 190
afraid
   be afraid 3
   afraid to ... 124
after 220, 280
   + present with future meaning
      221
   after ...*ing* 133
against 260
age with *be* 3
ago 46
   ago, since and *for* 280
agree
   agree to ... 120
   not used in progressive forms
      28
all
   all, everybody and *everything*
      173
   all (of) 173
   and *every* 174
   position 173

along 262–263
already
   already, yet and *still* 281
   position 204–205
   with present perfect 60
also: position 204–205
although 218
   and *but* 222
   and *in spite of* 223
always: position 204–205
am 2
am/are/is/was/were as passive
   auxiliary (*it is done* etc) 94
am/are/is ...*ing* (present
   progressive) 21–27
and 200–201, 218, 224
   with adjectives 200–201
annoyed and *annoying* 206
another 280
any
   and *any of* 177
   and *not any, no* and *none* 164
   and *some* 162–163, 166
   meaning '*one or another – it's*
      not important which' 167
anybody 165, 167
anyone 165
anything 165, 167
   anything to ... 127
anywhere 165, 167
are 2
aren't I? 115, 277
arrive at/in 136, 263
articles (*a/an* and *the*) 145–158
   see also *a/an*; see also *the*
as and *like* 280
as I/me 214
as, than and *that* 281
as ... *as* 214–215
   as much/many as 215
   as soon as + present with
      future meaning 221
ask
   ask for 136
   ask somebody to do something
      123, 251
at
   and *in* (place) 259
   and *to* 263
   at church/school etc without
      the 156
   at Christmas/Easter etc 254
   at, in and *on* (time) 254–255
auxiliary verbs: see *be, do,*
   have, tenses and modal
   auxiliary verbs

baggage: uncountable 190
be 2–7
   as passive auxiliary (*it is done*
      etc) 94

be cold/hungry etc 3
be in/out/away/back 138
be able to 79
been and *gone* 55
I've been etc (present perfect)
   61
because 218
   and *because of* 223
   and *so* 222
   and *why* 282
become with adjectives 201
been and *gone* 55
before 220
   + present with future meaning
      221
   before ...*ing* 133
begin
   begin ...*ing* 120
   begin to ... 120
behind 260
believe
   believe in 136
   not used in progressive forms
      28
belong to 136
better
   better, best 208, 213
   had better 87
between 260
boring and *bored* 206
born 280
borrow: not used with two
   objects 140
both
   and *both of* 176
   both ... *and* 225
   both, either and *neither* 176
   position 176
bread: uncountable 190
bring
   bring back 138
   with two objects 140
but 218
   and *although* 222
buy with two objects 140
by
   (place) 260
   (time) 256
   by car, bus etc 156, 279
   by ...*ing* 133
   by whom? and *who* ... *by?* 101
   with passives 101

can 72, 78–9, 82–85
   ability 78–79
   can see 281
   can hear 280
   can't be and *may not be* 80
   can't: certainty 82
   can't help ...*ing* 130
   permission 84–85

requests 83
see also *could*
certainly: position 204–205
chicken: countable or
    uncountable 191
chocolate: countable or
    uncountable 191
cinema: *the cinema* 157
clever to … 124
coffee: countable or uncountable
    191
cold: *be cold* 3
collective nouns 189
colour with *be* 3
come back 138
commas with *and* 224
comparative
    and superlative (*faster, fastest*
        etc) 208–213
    adjectives 208–212
    adverbs 213
conjunctions 217–226
    and 224
    both … and, either … or, neither
        … nor 225
    because, because of, so,
        although, but, in spite of
        222–223
    before and *after* 220
    place of conjunctions 219
    tenses with time conjunctions
        221
continue
    continue …ing 120
    continue to … 120
contractions (*I'm, don't* etc)
    277
    forms of *be* (*I'm, you're* etc)
        2–3
    negative forms of *be* (*he's not /*
        he isn't etc) 3
cook with two objects 140
could 79, 83–84, 90
    ability 79
    could have done 90
    meaning '*would be able to*' 234
    permission 84
    requests 83
countable and uncountable
    nouns 147, 190–191
country: *the country* 157
crazy to … 124

daily: adjective and adverb 207
decide to … 120
definitely: position 204–205
depend: not used in progressive
    forms 28
describe: not used with two
    objects 140
determiners (*this, some, all* etc)
    159–178
did: auxiliary in questions and
    negatives 42–44, 106
difficult to … 125
dislike …ing 130

do
    auxiliary in questions and
        negatives 16–19, 42–44, 46,
        106
    do …ing 280
    do and *make* 280
    in negative imperatives (*Do*
        not …) 142
    in question tags and short
        answers 266–268
    with *have* 8–9, 11
down 262–263
dropping words: see leaving out
    words
during, *for* and *while* 257

each
    and *every* 175
    each other 185
early: adjective and adverb 207,
    213
easy to … 125
either
    either, neither and *both* 176
    either … or 225
    I'm not either etc 273
else 280
enjoy …ing 130
enough 171
    and *enough of* 177
    enough to … after adjective
        126
    not enough 172
even: position 204–205
ever 280
    position 204–205
    with present perfect 58
every
    and *all* 174
    and *each* 175
everybody 165
    and *all* 173
everyone 165
    and *every one* 175
everything 165
    and *all* 173
everywhere 165
excited and *exciting* 206
expect
    expect somebody to do something
        123
    expect to … 120
experience: countable or
    uncountable 191
explain 280
    not used with two objects 140

family: singular or plural verb
    189
farther/further, farthest/furthest
    208, 213
fast: adjective and adverb 207,
    213
feel
    progressive and non-
        progressive forms 29

    with adjectives 201
fetch with two objects 140
few, a few, little and *a little* 170
fill in, fill up 138
find with two objects 140
finish …ing 130
first, second etc with *the* 148
for
    and *since* 61
    for, since and *ago* 280
    for, during and *while* 257
forget
    forget to … 120
    forget to … or *forget …ing* 281
friendly: adjective ending in *-ly*
    207
frightened and *frightening* 206
from … to 256, 263
furniture: uncountable 190
future 31–40
    future passive 96
    going to 32–33, 38
    present progressive 34, 38
    present with future meaning
        after *when*, etc 221
    present with future meaning
        after *if* 229
    simple present 39
    will 35–38

genitive: see possessive
get 280
    get into / out of / on / off 136
    get out 138
    get to 263
    get up 138
    have got 10
    in passives 94
    with adjectives 201
    with two objects 140
give
    give back 138
    give up 138
    give up …ing 130
    with two objects 140
    with two objects (passive) 100
glad to … 124
glass: countable or uncountable
    191
glasses 189
go
    go away 138
    go back 138
    go in/out 138
    go …ing 130
    go on 138
going to: future auxiliary 32–33,
    38
gone and *been* 55
good to … 125
got
    have got 10
    see also *get*
government: singular or plural
    verb 189
group nouns 189

had 8–11
    auxiliary in past perfect 68
    had better 87
    had to 76
hair: uncountable 190
half as … as 215
happen to … 136
happy to … 124
hard
    adjective and adverb 207, 213
    hard to … 125
hardly 114
    adjective and adverb 207
    hardly ever: position 204–205
    with *any* 163
hate
    hate …ing 130
    hate to … 131
    not used in progressive forms 28
have 8–11
    auxiliary in perfect tenses 52, 62, 68
    have got 10
    have lunch/a shower etc 11
    have something done 141
    have to 75–76
    have to and *must* 75
    present perfect (*I've had* etc) 61
    with *do* 8–9; 11
he 180–181
hear
    and *listen to* 280
    can hear 280
    see/hear + object + infinitive without *to* or *-ing* form 281
help somebody to do something 123
her
    personal pronoun 180–181
    possessive 182–183
here → *there* in indirect speech 250
hers 184
herself 185
him 180–181
himself 185
his 182–183, 184
home 280
hope
    hope so/not 281
    hope to … 120
hot: *be hot* 3
how 108
    how long have you …? 61–63
    how much/many … : subject in questions 110
hundred: *a hundred* 156
hungry: *be hungry* 3
hurry up 138

I 180–181
    I or *me* etc after *as* 214
    I or *me* etc after *than* 210

if 218, 227–236
    + present with future meaning 229
    if I go and *if I went*: the difference 232
    if and *when* 281
    if I were you … 233
    in indirect questions 248
    in sentences with *would* 230–1
    in sentences with *would have* 235
    position 228
imperatives 142
in
    and *at* (place) 259
    and *on* (place) 258
    in, *at* and *on* (time) 254–255
    in bed/prison etc without *the* 156
    in front of 260
    in or *of* after superlatives 212
    in spite of 223
indirect speech 245–252
    here and *now* words 250
    indirect questions 248
    infinitives 251
    present reporting verbs 249
    pronouns 247
    tenses 246–7
infinitives (*to go* etc) 117–128
    after adjectives 124–125
    after *it is/was* + adjective 128
    after *nothing* 127
    after *some* + noun 127
    after adjectives with *too/enough* 126
    after verbs 120–123
    after *would like* 88
    indirect speech 251
    infinitive of purpose 119
    negative infinitives 118
    not used after *think* 281
    to instead of complete infinitive 271
    with and without *to* 118
    without *to* after *do* 106, 113
    without *to* after modal verbs 72
information: uncountable 190
-ing forms
    after prepositions 132–133
    after verbs 130–131
    after *to* 133
    as subjects 129
interested
    and *interesting* 206
    be interested 3
    interesting to … 125
into 262–263
iron: countable or uncountable 191
irregular
    irregular plurals 188
    irregular verbs 275
is 2

isn't it? etc 266–267
it 180–181
    it is/was + adjective + infinitive 128
its 182–183
    and *it's* 183

jeans 189
just 281
    just as … as 215
    position 204–205
    with present perfect 60

keep (on) …ing 130
know
    not used in progressive forms 28
    present perfect (*I've known*) 61
knowledge: uncountable 190

late
    adjective and adverb 207
    and *lately* 207
laugh at 136
learn to … 120
leaving out
    leaving out *that* 240
    leaving out words in spoken English 271
lend
    with two objects 140
    with two objects (passive) 100
less than 211, 213
let
    and *make* 281
    let in 138
let's 143
lie down 138
light: countable or uncountable 191
like and *as* 280
like
    like …ing 130
    like to … 131
    not used in progressive forms 28
    would like 88
listen
    and *hear* 280
    listen to 136
little, *a little*, *few* and *a few* 170
lonely: adjective ending in *-ly* 207
look
    look after/for 136
    look at 136
    look out 138
    look round 138
    look, see and *watch* 281
    look up 138
    progressive and non-progressive forms 29
    with adjectives 201
lot: *a lot of / lots of* 169

love
 love ...ing 130
 love to ... 131
 not used in progressive forms 28
lovely: adjective ending in *-ly* 207
luck: uncountable 190
luggage: uncountable 190

make
 and *do* 280
 and *let* 281
 with two objects 140
many
 and *many of* 177
 and *much* 168
 too many 172
mass nouns: see **countable and uncountable nouns**
matter: not used in progressive forms 28
may
 and *might* 80–81, 85
 may have done 90
 may not be and *can't be* 80
 permission 85
 possibility 80–81
me
 and *I* 180–181
 me or *I* etc after *as* 214
 me or *I* after *than* 210
mean: not used in progressive forms 28
might and *may* 80–81
million: *a million* 156
mind
 mind ...ing 130
 not used in progressive forms 28
mine 184
modal auxiliary verbs (*can, must* etc) 71–92
monthly: adjective and adverb 207
more
 comparatives (*more interesting* etc) 208, 213
 more than 211, 213
most
 and *most of* 177
 superlatives (*most interesting* etc) 208
mountains: *the mountains* 157
much
 and *many* 168
 and *much of* 177
 too much 172
 with comparatives 211
must 72–74, 82
 and *have to* 75
 and *should* 77
 certainty 82
 must have done 90
 mustn't and *needn't* 74
 obligation 72–74

my 182–183
myself 185
names with or without *the* 154–155
near 260
 nearer 213
nearly as ... as 215
need
 need somebody to do something 123
 need to ... 120
 needn't and *mustn't* 74
 not used in progressive forms 28
negatives 112–115
 am/are/is/was/were not 3, 4–7
 contractions 277
 have not / do not have 8–11
 modal auxiliary verbs (*mustn't, can't* etc) 72
 negative infinitives 118
 negative questions 115
 not going to 33
 past perfect 68
 past progressive 48
 present perfect 52
 simple past 42–43
 simple present 18–19
 will not / won't 35
 with *nobody, never* etc 114
neither
 neither am I etc 273
 neither, either and *both* 176
 neither ... nor 225
never 114
 position 204–205
 with *any* 163
 with present perfect 58
news: uncountable 190
nice to ... 125
no
 determiner 164
 in negatives 114
 no ...ing 129
 no, not any and *none* 164
 no one 165
no and *yes* in answers to negative questions 115
nobody 114, 165
non-progressive verbs 28–29
none 164
nor am I etc 273
not
 after *hope* 281
 not any, no and *none* 164
 not as ... as 214
 not either 273
 not quite as ... as 215
 not to ... 118
nothing 114, 165
 nothing to ... 127
nouns 187–198
 countable and uncountable 147, 190–191
 group nouns 189
 noun + noun 196–197

 noun + preposition 278–279
 possessive *'s* and *s'* 193–195
 singular and plural 188–189
now → *then* in indirect speech 250
nowhere 114, 165
 nowhere to ... 127

of
 after *all* 173
 after *both* 176
 after determiners (*some, most* etc) 177
 of or *in* after superlatives 212
off 262–263
offer with two objects 140
often: position 204–205
on
 and *in* (place) 258
 on, at and *in* (time) 254–255
one and *a/an* 147
one(s) 192
only
 position 204–205
 with *the* 148
opposite 260
our 182–183
ours 184
ourselves 185
out of 262–263
over 262–263

pair 189
pants 189
paper: countable or uncountable 191
pass with two objects 140
passive (*it is done* etc) 93–104
 by 101
 future (*it will be done* etc) 96
 passive or active 102–103
 present perfect (*it has been done* etc) 99
 present progressive (*it is being done* etc) 98
 simple past (*it was done* etc) 97
 simple present (*it is done* etc) 96
 verbs with two objects 100
past: preposition 262–263
past continuous: see **past progressive**
past participles (*worked, broken, seen* etc)
 in perfect tenses 52–53, 62, 68
 in passives 94
past perfect (*I had done* etc) 68–69
 with *if* 235
past progressive (*I was ...ing*) 48–49
 past progressive or simple past 49
past simple: see **simple past**

past tenses 41–50
  past progressive 48
  past tense meaning '*not real*'
    or '*not probable*' 230–233
  simple past 42–47
  simple past and past
    progressive: the difference
    49
pay
  and *pay for* 136
  with two objects 140
people: *most people* or *most of the*
  people 177
perfect tenses 51–70
  present perfect 52–67
  past perfect 68–69
personal pronouns (*I, you* etc)
  180–181
phrasal verbs 138–139
pick up 138
place names with or without
  the 154–155
plan to … 120
pleased to … 124
plural and singular nouns
  188–189
police 189
possessive '*s* and *s*' 193–195,
  197
possessives
  mine, yours etc 184
  my, your etc 182–183
practise …*ing* 130
prefer
  not used in progressive forms
    28
  prefer …*ing* 120
  prefer to … 120
prepositions 253–264
  + -*ing* form 132–133
  after particular verbs,
    adjectives and nouns 136,
    278–279
  at (place) 259
  at, in and *on* (time) 254–255
  common expressions
    beginning with prepositions
    279
  for, during and *while* 257
  from … *to, until* and *by* 256
  in and *on* (place) 258
  movement 262–263
  place 258–261
  position in questions 137
  position with relative
    pronouns 242
present continuous: see present
  progressive
present perfect (*I have worked*
  etc) 52–67
  be, have and *know* 61
  forms 52–53
  news 56–57
  present perfect continuous:
    see **present perfect**
    progressive

present perfect or simple past
  54–55, 57, 65–67
present perfect passive (*It has*
  been done etc) 99
present perfect progressive (*I*
  have been …*ing*) 62–63
present perfect progressive or
  simple 64
up to now 58–59, 61–64
with *already, yet* and *just* 60
present progressive (*I am* …*ing*)
  21–27
forms 21
passive (*it is being done* etc) 98
present progressive or simple
  present 27
questions 24
use 22–23
verbs not used in progressive
  forms 28–29
with future meaning 34, 38
present simple: see **simple**
  present
present tenses 13–30
  present progressive 21–25
  simple present 14–20
  simple present and present
    progressive: the difference
    26–27
  verbs not used in progressive
    forms 28–29
  with future meaning after
    when 221
  with future meaning after *if*
    229
probably: position 204–205
promise
  promise to … 120
  with two objects 140
  with two objects: passive 100
pronouns: see **personal**
  pronouns, relative
  pronouns
progressive: see **present**
  progressive, past
  progressive, present
  perfect progressive, non-
  progressive verbs
put
  put down 138
  put on 138
pyjamas 189

question tags 266–267, 270
question words 108–109
questions: 105–111
  am/are/is/was/were 2, 4–7
  going to 32
  have 8–11
  indirect questions 248
  modal auxiliary verbs (*must,*
    can etc) 72
  negative questions 115
  past perfect 68
  past progressive 48
  present perfect 53

  present progressive 24
  simple past 44–45
  simple present 16–17
  will 35
  without *do* 45, 110–111
  word order with prepositions
    137
  yes/no questions 106–7

radio: *the radio* 157
read with two objects 140
recognise: not used in
  progressive forms 28
reflexive pronouns (*myself* etc)
  185
refuse to … 120
relative pronouns (*who, whom,*
  which, that, what) 237–244
  leaving out relative pronouns
    240
  that 240
  what 243
  who and *which* 238–9
  word order with prepositions
    242
remember
  not used in progressive forms
    28
  remember to … or *remember*
    …*ing* 281
reply questions 269–270
reported speech: see **indirect**
  speech
right
  be right 3
  right to … 124
round 262–263

'*s* and *s*' 193–195, 197
sad to … 124
same: *the same* 157, 281
say
  and *tell* 246
  not used with two objects
    140
scissors 189
sea: *the sea* 157
see
  can see 281
  progressive and non-
    progressive forms 29
  see + object + infinitive
    without *to* or -*ing* form 281
  see, look and *watch* 281
seem to … 120
  with adjectives 201
send
  with two objects 140
  with two objects (passive)
    100
shall
  future auxiliary 35
  shall I/we …? in offers and
    suggestions 86
she 180–181
short answers 268, 270

shorts 189
should 72, 77
  and *had better* 87
  and *must* 77
  meaning '*would*' in sentences
    with *if* 231
  should(n't) have done 90
show
  with two objects 140
  with two objects (passive) 100
silly
  adjective ending in *-ly* 207
  silly to ... 124
simple past (*I worked* etc)
    42–47, 49
  forms 42–43
  passive (*it was done* etc) 97
  past tense meaning '*not real*' or
    '*not probable*' 230–233
  negatives 42–43
  questions 44
  questions without *did* 45
  simple past or past progressive
    49
  simple past or present perfect
    54–55, 57, 65–67
  use 46
simple present (*I work* etc)
    14–20; 26–29
  forms 14
  negatives 18–19
  questions 16–17
  passive (*it is done* etc) 95
  simple present or present
    progressive 26–27
  use 15
  with future meaning 39, 221,
    229
since
  and *for* 61
  since, for and *ago* 280
  since ...ing 133
singular and plural nouns
    188–189
sit down 138
size with *be* 3
so
  adverb after *hope* 281
  and *such* 281
  so am I etc 272–273
so
  conjunction 218
  so and *because* 222
some
  + noun + infinitive 127
  and *any* 162–163
  and *some of* 177
  or no article 166
somebody 165
  somebody to ... 127
someone 165
something 165
  something to ... 127
sometimes: position 204–205
somewhere 165
  somewhere to ... 127

sooner 213
spaghetti: uncountable 190
spelling
  adverbs ending in *-ly* 202
  comparative and superlative
    adjectives 208
  noun plurals 188
  possessive *'s* and *s'* 193
  simple past 42
  simple present *-s/-es* 14
spoken grammar 265–274
  question tags 266–267, 270
  reply questions 269–270
  short answers 268, 270
stand up 138
start
  start ...ing 120
  start to ... 120
still
  position 204–205
  still, yet and *already* 281
stop ...ing 130
stupid to ... 124
such and *so* 281
suggest
  suggest ...ing 130
  not used with two objects 140
superlative adjectives (*oldest,
    most interesting* etc) 208–212
surprised
  and *surprising* 206
  surprised to ... 124
switch on/off 138

take
  take away 138
  take off 138
  with two objects 140
talk about 136
teach with two objects 140
team: singular or plural verb
    189
tell
  and *say* 246
  tell somebody to do something
    123, 251
  with two objects 140
tenses 13–70
  future 31–40
  in indirect speech 246–247,
    249
  past 41–50
  past tense meaning '*not real*' or
    '*not probable*' 230–233
  perfect 51–70
  present 13–30
  present with future meaning
    39, 221, 229
  with *if* 229–235
  with time conjunctions 221
than
  than, as and *that* 281
  than I/me 210
  than with comparatives 210
that and *this* 160–161

that
  leaving out *that* 241, 246
  relative pronoun 240
  that, than and *as* 281
the 145–158
  and *a/an*: the difference 148
  common expressions without
    the 156–157
  not used before *my* etc 183
  not used with general ideas
    152
  pronunciation 146
  the same 157, 281
  with names 154–155
theatre: *the theatre* 157
their 182–183
theirs 184
them 180–181
there is 6–7
  is there etc in question tags
    267
these 160–161
they 180–181
think
  not used with infinitive 281
  progressive and non-
    progressive forms 29
  think about 136
  think so 281
thirsty: *be thirsty* 3
this
  not used before *my* etc 183
  this → that in indirect speech
    250
  this, that, these and *those*
    160–161
thousand: *a thousand* 156
through 262–263
throw away 138
tights 189
till 256
time: countable or uncountable
    191
to
  infinitive with or without *to*
    118
  to instead of complete
    infinitive 271
to
  preposition + *...ing* 133
  and *at* 263
  to school/church etc without *the*
    156
too
  + adjective + infinitive with *to*
    126
  and *too much/many* 172
  and *very* 282
too meaning '*also*': *I am too* etc
    273
travel: uncountable 190
trousers 189
try
  try to ... 120
  try to ... or *try ...ing* 282

turn
  turn on/off 138
  turn round 138
  turn up/down 138
TV: without *the* 157
twice *as ... as* 215

uncountable nouns 147,
    190–191
under 260, 262–263
understand: not used in
    progressive forms 28
unhappy *to ...* 124
unless 228
until 218, 256
  + present with future meaning
    221
up 262–263
  meaning '*completely*' 138
us 180–181
used *to* 89
usually: position 204–205

verbs
  + adverb particle (*out, away*
    etc) 138–139
  + infinitive 120–121
  + *...ing* 130–131
  + object + infinitive 122–123
  + preposition 136, 278–279
  not used in progressive forms
    28–29
  with two objects 140
  with two objects: passive 100
very
  and *too* 282
  very much: position 203

wait
  wait for 136
  wait for something to happen
    282
wake *up* 138
want
  not used in progressive forms
    28
  want somebody to do something
    122
  want to ... 120
was 4
was/were *...ing* (past
    progressive) 48–49
wash *up* 138
watch, *look* and *see* 281
we 180–181
weekly: adjective and adverb
    207
well: adjective and adverb 207
were 4
  after *if* 233
what 109, 110
  and *which* 282
  subject in questions 45, 110
  what a ...! 156
  what ... about? etc 137

what colour? with *be* 3
  what ... like? 110
  what size? with *be* 3
what: relative pronoun 243
when
  + present with future meaning
    221
  and *if* 281
  in questions 108
  with past perfect 69
  with past tenses 49
where
  in questions 108
  where ... to / from? 137
whether in indirect questions
    248
which
  and *what* 282
  subject in questions 110
  and *who*: relative pronouns
    238–239
while 218
  + present with future meaning
    221
  while, during and *for* 257
who
  and *which*: relative pronouns
    238–239
  and *whom* 282
  subject in questions 45, 110
  who ... by? 101
  who ... for? etc 137
whom 239
  and *who* 282
  by whom? 101
whose? 182–183, 184
why
  and *because* 282
  in questions 108
will 35–38
  in passives (*it will be done* etc)
    96
without
  with *any* 163
  without ...ing 132–133
won't 35–38
word order
  adjectives 200–201
  adverbs 203–205
  ago 280
  all 173
  already 60
  both 176
  conjunctions (*when, because*
    etc) 219
  enough 171
  if 228
  indirect questions 248
  just 60
  phrasal verbs (*take away* etc)
    139
  position of *all* 173
  prepositions in questions 137
  prepositions with relative
    pronouns 242

questions 106–108, 110
  questions with long subjects
    17, 24, 35, 44, 53, 107
  questions with *who/what* as
    subject 110
  verbs with two objects (*give*
    etc) 140
  very much 203
  yet 60
work: uncountable 190
worse, *worst* 208, 213
would
  with *if* 230–233
  would have ... with *if* 235
  would like 88
  *would like somebody to do
    something* 122
write with two objects 140
wrong
  be wrong 3
  wrong to ... 124

yes
  and *no* in answers to negative
    questions 115
  yes/no questions 106–107
yet
  yet, still and *already* 281
  yet with present perfect 60
you 180–181
your 182–183
yours 184
yourself 185
yourselves 185